THE COMPACT READER

SHORT ESSAYS BY
METHOD AND THEME

ELEVENTH EDITION

THE COMPACT READER

SHORT ESSAYS BY METHOD AND THEME

Jane E. Aaron

Ellen Kuhl Repetto

bedford/st.martin's
Macmillan Learning

Boston | New York

For Bedford/St. Martin's

Vice President, Editorial, Macmillan Learning Humanities: Edwin Hill
Executive Program Director for English: Leasa Burton
Senior Program Manager: John E. Sullivan III
Executive Marketing Manager: Joy Fisher Williams
Director of Content Development, Humanities: Jane Knetzger
Developmental Editor: Alexandra DeConti
Content Project Manager: Lidia MacDonald-Carr
Senior Workflow Project Manager: Jennifer Wetzel
Production Coordinator: Brianna Lester
Media Project Manager: Rand Thomas
Media Editor: Daniel Johnson
Manager of Publishing Services: Andrea Cava
Project Management: Lumina Datamatics, Inc.
Composition: Lumina Datamatics, Inc.
Text Permissions Editor: Mark Schaefer, Lumina Datamatics, Inc.
Photo Researcher: Kerri Wilson, Lumina Datamatics, Inc.
Permissions Editor: Angela Boehler
Permissions Associate: Allison Ziebka
Permissions Manager: Kalina Ingham
Director of Design, Content Management: Diana Blume
Cover Design: William Boardman
Cover Image: MirageC/Getty Images
Printing and Binding: LSC Communications

Manufactured in the United States of America.

1 2 3 4 5 6   23 22 21 20 19 18

For information, write: Bedford/St. Martin's, 75 Arlington Street, Boston, MA 02116

ISBN 978-1-319-05635-3   (Student Edition)
ISBN 978-1-319-17116-2   (Instructor's Annotated Edition)

Acknowledgments

Text acknowledgments and copyrights appear at the back of the book on pages 437–439, which constitute an extension of the copyright page. Art acknowledgments and copyrights appear on the same page as the art selections they cover.

PREFACE

▶

Long a favorite for its flexibility, *The Compact Reader* seamlessly combines four texts—a short-essay reader, a rhetorical reader, a thematic reader, and a brief rhetoric—into one slim volume. Three dozen engaging, high-quality essays come with all the editorial support of a larger book, but at a much lower price.

The eleventh edition has been refreshed with the teachers and students who use it in mind and features exciting new readings, streamlined explanations, extra help with source-based writing, additional visual elements, and more. Although much is new, the most popular aspects of the book remain the same. The structure is simple and easy to use: four chapters in Part One guide students through the interrelated processes of critical reading and writing; ten chapters in Part Two focus on the rhetorical methods of development, with each chapter's selections centering on a common theme; and two chapters in a new Part Three offer just enough information to help students integrate and document source materials effectively. Updated, revitalized, and clarified throughout, *The Compact Reader* is more stimulating and helpful than ever.

Four Books in One

The core of *The Compact Reader* remains its selections. Thirty-six short essays and twenty annotated paragraphs (half of them new) provide interesting reading that will enliven class discussion and spark good writing. The selections represent both emerging voices—including a student writer in every chapter—and established favorites such as Langston Hughes, David Sedaris, and Joan Didion. The book's unique structure suits courses that call for brief essays, whether they take a rhetorical or a thematic approach.

A Short-Essay Reader

The essays in *The Compact Reader* average just two or three pages apiece so that students can read them quickly, analyze them thoroughly, and emulate them successfully. A few longer essays, such as David Brooks's classic "People Like Us," help students make the transition to more challenging material.

A Rhetorical Reader

Above all, the essays offer clear models for writing, but they also show the rhetorical methods—narration, example, comparison, and contrast so on—at work in varied styles for varied purposes. Three essays and two annotated paragraphs illustrate each method, and the final chapter of readings, on argument, expands on this format with a more detailed introduction to the method and double the number of essays. The introductions to the methods draw connections among purpose, subject, and method, helping students analyze and respond to any writing situation. Extensive "Writing with the Method" topics at the end of each chapter suggest avenues for students' own work.

A Thematic Reader

Each chapter of readings also has a unifying thematic focus that shows five writers developing ideas on the same general subject and provides diverse perspectives to stimulate students' critical thinking, discussion, and writing. Links among the readings in each chapter are highlighted with an overview of the theme at the start of the introduction, a "Connections" question after every essay, and a set of theme-based writing topics at the end.

A Brief Rhetoric

Concise and to the point, the four chapters in Part One guide students through the essential skills of reading, drafting, revising, and editing, illustrated by a student essay in progress. A detailed, practical introduction to each of the ten rhetorical methods in Part Two opens with a discussion of the concepts to look for when reading and suggests specific strategies for developing an essay, from choosing a subject through editing the final draft. Checklists and "Focus" boxes throughout the book emphasize the importance of rewriting and highlight the problems and opportunities most likely to merit attention when working in a specific method. And the two chapters of Part Three outline the basics of using readings and research to support academic writing.

A thoroughly integrated glossary helps students access the guidance they need when they need it. Key terms throughout *The Compact Reader* are printed in boldface, signaling to students that detailed explanations are provided in the back of the book. The entries themselves function as an informal index and reference, defining and illustrating more than a hundred terms with specific links to fuller discussions in the text.

Helpful Editorial Support

As always, the reading selections in *The Compact Reader* are accompanied by thorough yet unobtrusive instructional guidance that helps students develop and master the rigors of critical reading and writing.

- *Quotations and a journal prompt* precede every essay. These pre-reading materials get students thinking and writing about the essay's core topic, helping them to form and express their own ideas before they read the essay itself.

- *Headnotes introducing the author and the essay* place every selection in a context that helps focus students' reading.

- *Gloss notes* explain cultural allusions, historical references, and specialized vocabulary that students may not understand without help.

- *Detailed questions* after each essay guide students' analysis of meaning, purpose and audience, method and structure, and language. A question labeled "Other Methods" highlights the writer's interweaving of methods, showing students how the rhetorical modes might be fluidly combined.

- *Writing topics* after each selection give students specific direction for their own work. Among these, "Journal to Essay" topics help students build their journal writing into finished essays, "Cultural Considerations" topics lead students to consider similarities and differences among cultures, focused "Research" topics prompt students to expand their understanding of a subject by locating and synthesizing sources, and "Connections" topics encourage students to make thematic or rhetorical links to other selections in the book.

A Brisk New Edition

Developed with the input of teachers who use or have used *The Compact Reader* over three decades, the eleventh edition has been revised and updated to meet the interests and needs of contemporary students.

Engaging New Readings

Half the selections are new to this edition. Sixteen new essays and ten new paragraphs in Part Two touch on inviting themes that encourage students to laugh, to reflect, and to explore. Ranging in subject from media mass and entertainment to politics and culture, the new readings present a mix of real student writers, remarkable emerging voices, and recent works by well-known favorites. For instance:

- Student Kaitlyn Haskie, in "A Paradigm Shift: Indigenous Peoples in the New Millennium," draws on sources and her Navajo heritage to consider the ways in which modern technologies are both enhancing and eroding traditional cultures.

- In a paragraph from "The Meaning of 'Despacito' in the Age of Trump," Moises Velasquez-Manoff picks apart the elements of a popular song to celebrate diversity in America.

- *New York Times* columnist Nikolas Kristof takes issue with the debilitating effects of joblessness while asking, "Where's the Empathy?"

- With wit and precision, Amy Tan relays the exhilaration of a spelunking adventure in "The Darkest Moment of My Life."

Facilitating an up-to-date focus on science and technology, all of the selections modeling Cause-and-Effect Analysis (Chapter 13) are new. And every social justice–themed essay in Argument and Persuasion (Chapter 14) is new as well, with that chapter freshly organized into a solo student argument on police brutality, a paired debate over income inequality, and a three-essay casebook on the issue of Confederate memorials.

Stronger Visual Appeal

A highlight of the new batch of readings is a significant increase in visual elements throughout the book. Eleven of the essays (a third of the total) now include images—such as cartoons, graphics, and photographs—meant to capture students' interest and showcase the expanding uses of visual evidence in writing.

A Renewed Focus on the Themes

Beyond showing students *how* to write, the thematically related selections in each chapter of Part Two give students something interesting to talk and write *about*. To highlight this benefit, the chapter introductions have been reorganized to foreground the themes and give students an advance taste of how the readings are connected by subject as well as by method. Half of the themes are new to this edition, chosen for their contemporary relevance and for their capacity to appeal to students' imaginations: Facing Fear (Chapter 5), Distinguishing Ourselves from Others (Chapter 9), Feeling at Home (Chapter 11), Understanding Science and Technology (Chapter 13), and Seeking Social Justice (Chapter 14).

Improved Guides to Reading and Writing

At the request of instructors who use the book, *The Compact Reader* now does even more as a reference to guide students through the process of drafting, revising, and editing their writing on their own.

- *Streamlined explanations.* Wherever practical, parenthetical cross-references and comments have been stripped away, helping to make important discussions and concepts more self-contained and simpler to follow. Chapter 4 on Editing in particular is now significantly shorter and easier to navigate, with a tighter focus on catching and fixing the most common errors. And a handful of the method introductions — for Division or Analysis (Chapter 8), Process Analysis (Chapter 10), and Cause-and-Effect Analysis (Chapter 13) — have been simplified as well.

- *Enhanced coverage of key writing topics.* Chapters 2 and 3, on drafting and revising, now place more attention on a writer's purpose, as does an expanded discussion of evaluating sources in Chapter 15. In addition, the book makes a stronger distinction between drafting a working thesis and revising it, with a fresh emphasis in Chapter 2 on the common need to adjust one's main idea while writing, and renewed explanations, now in Chapter 3, of how to revise a thesis statement effectively.

- *Interactive media.* Throughout the book, new integrated callouts to Macmillan Learning's *LaunchPad Solo for Readers and Writers* direct students to online resources that provide additional help with key concepts (such as critical reading and supporting details) and offer practice with editing and revising.

An Emphasis on Academic Work

In recognition of the rising importance of academic writing in composition courses, the former Appendix, "Working with Sources," is now a new Part Three comprising two full chapters on research and documentation. Updated guidelines for finding and synthesizing sources put more emphasis on writing in response to reading, provide additional tips for assessing the credibility and bias of materials found online, and include a new checklist for evaluating sources. For ease of reference, extensive citation models following the most recent MLA style are now housed in a separate chapter that features new directories to the models, more — and more current — examples, and an updated sample of a student's research paper.

Additional examples of documented writing appear throughout *The Compact Reader*. Half of the student essays now illustrate varying degrees of source-based writing, from writing in response to a selection in the book (Nicole Lang and Olivia Melendez), to essays developed with evidence from research (Nicole Lang, Kaitlyn Haskie, and Zoe Krey), to full-scale research papers (Saanya Ojha and Jarrod Ballo). And for the first time, two of the professional selections (by James Kakalios and Derek Thompson) formally cite their sources as well.

Acknowledgments

Several instructors helped to shape this edition of *The Compact Reader*, offering insights from their experience and suggestions for improvement. Hearty thanks to Syble Davis, Houston Community College; Deanna Drew, Los Angeles Harbor College; Marie Eckstrom, Rio Hondo College; Dorothy Erickson, Anna Maria College; Lisa Fitzgerald, Long Beach City College; Rebecca Fleming, Columbus State Community College; Pamela Howell, Midland College; Marie Iglesias-Cardinale, Genesee Community College; Carla Kirchner, Southwest Baptist University; Jill Lahnstein, Cape Fear Community College; Jessica Lindberg, Georgia Highlands College; Carol Trunzo, Ashland University; and Lesley Yoder, Boston University. And special thanks to Kim Sanabria, Eugenia Maria de Hostos Community College, whose contributions to the seventh edition continue to influence the book's content and features.

The unfailingly supportive people at Bedford/St. Martin's once again contributed greatly to this project. Edwin Hill, Leasa Burton, Joy Fisher Williams, and John Sullivan provided encouraging leadership and good ideas. Lexi DeConti enthusiastically and expertly helped to conceive the book's new features, select readings and visuals, connect with the student writers, and solve problems. William Boardman created the striking new cover, and Lidia MacDonald-Carr deftly shepherded the manuscript through production on a demanding schedule. Deep and happy thanks to all.

Jane E. Aaron
Ellen Kuhl Repetto

We're All In. As Always.

▶

Bedford/St. Martin's is as passionately committed to the discipline of English as ever, working hard to provide support and services that make it easier for you to teach your course your way.

Discover **curriculum solutions** that offer flexible custom options, combining carefully developed print and digital textbook resources, acclaimed works from Macmillan's trade imprints, and your own course or program materials to create a customized project uniquely suited for your students' needs. Based on your enrollment size, you could also return money to your department with royalties and raise your institutional profile with a high-impact author visit through the Macmillan Author Program ("MAP").

Rely on **outstanding service** from your Bedford/St. Martin's sales representative and editorial team. Contact us or visit *macmillanlearning.com* to learn more about any of the options below.

Choose a Format

Bedford/St. Martin's offers a choice of formats. Pick what works best for you and your students:

- **Paperback.** To order the paperback edition of *The Compact Reader*, use ISBN 978-1-319-05635-3.

- **E-book.** *The Compact Reader* is now available in a digital edition using the popular EPUB format. For details and information on ordering from our e-book partners, visit *macmillanlearning.com/ebooks*.

Select Digital Resources

Add value to your course by packaging Macmillan Learning's *LaunchPad Solo for Readers and Writers* with *The Compact Reader* at a significant discount. Offering instruction tailored to individual students' unique needs, *LaunchPad Solo for Readers and Writers* features several innovative digital tools:

- **Multiple-choice comprehension quizzes** for every essay in *The Compact Reader* help to quickly gauge students' understanding of the assigned reading.

- **Twenty-five additional reading selections.** A range of classic and contemporary essays include labels indicating Lexile levels and comprehension quizzes to help scaffold instruction in critical reading.

- **Diagnostics that help establish a baseline for instruction.** Brief tests identify areas of strength and opportunities for improvement to help students plan a course of study. Visual reports track performance by topic, class, and student as well as their improvement over time.

- **Pre-built units that support a learning arc.** Each unit includes a pre-test, multimedia instruction and assessment, and a post-test that assesses what students have learned about critical reading, the writing process, using sources, grammar, style, and mechanics. Dedicated units also offer help for multilingual writers.

- **Video introductions** offer overviews of many unit topics and illustrate the concepts at hand.

- **Adaptive quizzing for targeted learning.** Most units include *Learning-Curve*, game-like quizzing that focuses on the areas in which each student needs the most help.

Order ISBN 978-1-319-24834-5 to package *LaunchPad Solo for Readers and Writers* with *The Compact Reader* at a significant discount. Students who rent or buy a used book can purchase access, and instructors may request free access, at *macmillanlearning.com/readwrite*. Contact your sales representative for more information.

Access Instructor Resources

You have a lot to do in your course. We want to make it easy for you to find the support you need—and to get it quickly.

- **Find community support** at the Bedford/St. Martin's *English Community* (*community.macmillan.com*), where you can follow the *Bits* blog for new teaching ideas, download titles from the *Macmillan Professional Resources* series, and review projects in the pipeline.

- **An extensive instructor's manual,** *Resources for Teaching* The Compact Reader, is available bound into an instructor's edition of the book or as a downloadable PDF on the instructor tab of the online catalog (*macmillanlearning.com/compactreader/catalog*). Aimed to help you integrate the text into your course and use it in class, the manual includes an overview of the book's organization and chapters, ideas for combining the reader with other course materials, sample syllabi, and varied resources for each selection: teaching tips, content and vocabulary quizzes, and detailed answers to all the critical-reading questions.

Council of Writing Program Administrators (WPA) Outcomes Statement for First-Year Composition

▶

The following chart provides detailed information on how *The Compact Reader* helps students build proficiency and achieve the learning outcomes that writing programs across the country use to assess their students' work: rhetorical knowledge; critical thinking, reading, and writing; writing processes; and knowledge of conventions.

WPA Outcomes	Relevant Features of *The Compact Reader*, 11e
RHETORICAL KNOWLEDGE	
Learn and use key rhetorical concepts through analyzing and composing a variety of texts	▪ The organization of *The Compact Reader* supports students' understanding of key rhetorical concepts. **Part One** explores in detail the reading and writing strategies most often required of college students. **Part Two** makes up a rhetorical reader, with ten comprehensive **chapter introductions** that explain how the strategies suit authors' purposes, and multiple readings that illustrate each method. ▪ In Chapter 1, **Reading**, students learn how to assess **context** and how to read critically, using annotation to analyze written and visual texts (pp. 1-16). ▪ Chapter 2, **Developing an Essay**, shows students how to identify their own **purpose, audience**, and **thesis** (pp. 17–31) through an understanding of the rhetorical situation. ▪ All essays in Part Two are followed by questions on **Meaning, Purpose and Audience**, and **Method and Structure**. A question labeled **Other Methods** highlights how writers use multiple rhetorical strategies to convey their messages. ▪ **Writing Topics** following each reading and **Writing with the Method** suggestions at the end of the chapter prompt students to write using the rhetorical method focused on in that chapter.
Gain experience reading and composing in several genres to understand how genre conventions shape and are shaped by readers' and writers' practices and purposes	▪ Chapters 5–14 are **organized by rhetorical method and by theme**, with at least five reading selections per chapter to give students experience and practice. ▪ **Twenty paragraphs** and **thirty-six essays** span a variety of topics, disciplines, and genres. ▪ Each reading selection features a **robust apparatus** that guides students through analyzing texts and writing for a variety of purposes and in a range of styles.
Develop facility in responding to a variety of situations and contexts calling for purposeful shifts in voice, tone, level of formality, design, medium, and/or structure	▪ Chapter introductions explain how each rhetorical method can be used to achieve an author's purpose. ▪ Students are introduced to the importance of structure in Chapter 2 and in the introductions to Chapters 5–14, in sections labeled **Organizing**, and critical reading questions following every essay highlight the writer's uses of method and language.

(continued)

WPA Outcomes	Relevant Features of *The Compact Reader*, 11e
RHETORICAL KNOWLEDGE *(continued)*	
	▪ A discussion of revising for tone in Chapter 3 (p. 39) and a boxed **Focus on Tone** feature in Chapter 14 (p. 343) provide guidance to help students adopt the appropriate voice and level of formality in their writing. ▪ Chapter 4 on **Editing** presents thorough advice, with examples, on how to achieve clear and effective language and sentence structure.
Understand and use a variety of technologies to address a range of audiences	▪ In-text callouts to **LaunchPad Solo for Readers and Writers** direct students to online tutorials on important writing concepts that help students learn through interaction, and adaptive **LearningCurve** quizzes allow students to practice reading and writing skills at their own pace.
Match the capacities of different environments (e.g., print and electronic) to varying rhetorical situations	▪ Research coverage in Part Three, **Brief Notes on Working with Sources**, gives instruction specific to research and project planning, from taking notes to finding and evaluating sources, in both print and online spaces.
CRITICAL THINKING, READING, AND COMPOSING	
Use composing and reading for inquiry, learning, critical thinking, and communicating in various rhetorical contexts	▪ Chapter 1, Reading, gives students tools to read critically and as writers, so they can understand the **rhetorical context** and the writer's choices, and then apply those tools to their own writing. ▪ Chapter 2, Developing an Essay, presents writing as **inquiry**, as a process of **gathering ideas and exploring topics**. ▪ A **Journal Response** prompt preceding each reading, and a set of critical reading questions and writing prompts after, encourage students to **write to learn** through informal writing and through composing full essays using any of the ten rhetorical methods.
Read a diverse range of texts, attending especially to relationships between assertion and evidence, to patterns of organization, to the interplay between verbal and nonverbal elements, and to how these features function for different audiences and situations	▪ A lively collection of **thirty-six classic and contemporary essays** from professional and student writers provides outstanding models carefully chosen to engage students and to clearly illustrate the rhetorical strategy at work in each chapter. ▪ Every chapter in Part Two features two **paragraphs annotated to show the rhetorical choices** writers make to achieve their purposes. ▪ This book's unique **dual organization** offers flexibility, grouping readings both by rhetorical method and by theme, giving students the option to analyze multiple sources of information on subjects of their choice. Themes include science and technology, social justice, and fear. Nearly a third of the essays include images to capture students' interest and encourage them to analyze the relationship between **visual and verbal elements**. ▪ Chapter 14, **Argument and Persuasion/Seeking Social Justice**, provides thorough coverage of making and **supporting claims**, and Chapter 15, **Writing with Source Material**, provides information on integrating sources responsibly.

WPA Outcomes	Relevant Features of *The Compact Reader*, 11e
Locate and evaluate (for credibility, sufficiency, accuracy, timeliness, bias, and so on) primary and secondary research materials, including journal articles and essays, books, scholarly and professionally established and maintained databases or archives, and informal electronic networks and Internet sources	■ Part Three, **Brief Notes on Working with Sources**, reviews the skills involved in research and synthesis, with dedicated sections on Asking Questions (p. 389), Finding Sources in print and online (p. 389), Evaluating Sources (p. 390), and Synthesizing Sources (p. 393) in Chapter 15. Chapter 16 includes models for MLA-style citations and a sample research paper. ■ Writing suggestions labeled **Research** following many of the essays direct students to locate and integrate appropriate source material on focused topics. ■ Helpful **checklists and directories** in Part Three make useful **reference tools**: Checklist for Evaluating Sources (p. 392), Directory to MLA In-Text Citation Models (p. 400), and Directory to MLA Works-Cited Models (p. 405).
Use strategies — such as interpretation, synthesis, response, critique, and design/redesign — to compose texts that integrate the writer's ideas with those from appropriate sources	■ The chapters in Part One offer clear advice on **Reading Critically** (p. 5), **Generating Ideas** (p. 19), and **Forming a Thesis** (p. 24), stressing the importance of marshalling sufficient **evidence** and **support** to develop an original idea. ■ The chapter introductions, reading questions, and writing prompts that accompany the essays in Part Two ask students to **interpret**, **respond to**, and **critique** the readings and the writers' choices, engaging in academic **conversation**. ■ Chapter 15, **Writing with Source Material**, models strategies for taking effective notes; using signal phrases to **integrate** quotations, summaries, and paraphrases smoothly; synthesizing sources; and avoiding plagiarism. ■ See also the previous section, "Locate and evaluate..."

PROCESSES

Develop a writing project through multiple drafts	■ Part One, A Compact Guide to Reading and Writing, leads students through the process of writing an essay in four chapters on **Reading, Developing an Essay, Revising**, and **Editing** while following the development of a student essay in multiple stages: Nicole Lang's First Draft (p. 30), Nicole Lang's Revised Draft (p. 41), and Nicole Lang's Editing and Final Draft (p. 54). ■ Helpful **checklists** — for Critical Reading (p. 8), Effective Thesis (p. 26), Revision (p. 41), and Editing (p. 53) — serve as reference tools during the writing process.
Develop flexible strategies for reading, drafting, reviewing, collaborating, revising, rewriting, rereading, and editing	■ The chapter introductions in Part Two take students through the steps of **Forming a Thesis, Organizing, Drafting**, and **Revising and Editing** an essay using particular rhetorical methods (e.g., "Developing a Descriptive Essay," p. 92).
Use composing processes and tools as a means to discover and reconsider ideas	■ A detailed section on **Generating Ideas** in Chapter 2 (p. 19) covers talking with others, journal writing, freewriting, brainstorming, and using the methods of development. ■ The reading apparatus includes questions for journaling, discussion, and homework, to guide students to **use writing to discover new ideas and writing topics**.

(continued)

WPA Outcomes	Relevant Features of *The Compact Reader*, 11e
PROCESSES *(continued)*	
Experience the collaborative and social aspects of writing processes	■ A section on **Talking and Listening** in Chapter 2 (p. 20) offers guidelines for productive class participation. ■ The journal response, critical reading questions, and writing topics that accompany each reading can be used for **group discussion and writing**.
Learn to give and to act on productive feedback to works in progress	■ A general **Checklist for Revision** in Chapter 1 and method-specific revision checklists in Chapters 5–15 provide useful benchmarks for **peer review** workshops. ■ A **sample essay in progress** by Nicole Lang is shown in stages through Chapters 2, 3, and 4, illustrating a student's process during drafting, revising, and editing—and presenting a low-stakes opportunity for students to practice critiquing another student's drafts.
Adapt composing processes for a variety of technologies and modalities	■ The book assumes that most students compose in digital spaces, and instructions in a number of Writing Topics and other prompts reflect and encourage this use of the digital space. ■ Instructions for research and collecting notes on sources in Part Three assume that students are working mostly with technology, so the advice offers strategies and a checklist for **evaluating sources** found online.
Reflect on the development of composing practices and how those practices influence their work	■ **Journal Response** prompts before each reading ask students to discover and apply their prior knowledge to the reading selection.
KNOWLEDGE OF CONVENTIONS	
Develop knowledge of linguistic structures, including grammar, punctuation, and spelling, through practice in composing and revising	■ Chapter 4, **Editing**, covers common grammar and mechanics errors and presents clear examples of corrections. Coverage includes sentence fragments, run-ons and comma splices, subject-verb agreement, pronouns, misplaced and dangling modifiers, parallelism, and more. ■ **Focus** boxes in Chapters 5–14 guide students as they survey their drafts for editing opportunities especially relevant to each method, such as verbs in narration and shifts in process analysis.
Understand why genre conventions for structure, paragraphing, tone, and mechanics vary	■ Chapter introductions for the rhetorical strategies in Part Two explain how each strategy serves a writer's **purpose**. ■ An emphasis on combining strategies throughout, especially in reading questions labeled **Other Methods**, further emphasizes distinct rhetorical strategies and variation.
Gain experience negotiating variations in genre conventions	■ In addition to the support in chapter introductions mentioned above, **Writing Topics** after every essay and **Writing with the Method** and **Writing about the Theme** prompts at the end of each chapter in Part Two encourage students to apply the rhetorical strategies to real-world genres and situations and use them in their writing.

WPA Outcomes	Relevant Features of *The Compact Reader*, 11e
Learn common formats and/or design features for different kinds of texts	▪ Model student essays in the book are presented in **MLA style**. Chapter 16 features a fully formatted example of a student research paper, with annotations highlighting **formatting conventions**.
Explore the concepts of intellectual property (such as fair use and copyright) that motivate documentation conventions	▪ Chapter 15, **Writing with Source Material**, explains why outside sources can help writers articulate their position in a conversation and extend their own ideas, and how doing so requires **thoughtful documentation** when **integrating** quotations, paraphrases, or summaries. ▪ A dedicated section, **Avoiding Plagiarism** (p. 397) further explores these concepts.
Practice applying citation conventions systematically in their own work	▪ Part Three, **Brief Notes On working with Sources**, offers detailed guidance on taking notes to avoid plagiarism as well as **model citations in MLA style**.

CONTENTS

▶

PART TWO
SHORT ESSAYS BY METHOD AND THEME 57

11 ▶ COMPARISON AND CONTRAST
FEELING AT HOME   235

14 ▶ **ARGUMENT AND PERSUASION**
SEEKING SOCIAL JUSTICE   329

THE COMPACT READER

SHORT ESSAYS BY
METHOD AND THEME

PART ONE

A COMPACT GUIDE TO READING AND WRITING

1

READING

This collection of essays has one purpose: to help you become a better reader and writer. It combines examples of good writing with explanations of the writers' methods, questions to guide your reading, and ideas for your own writing. In doing so, it shows how you can adapt the processes and techniques used by others as you learn to communicate clearly and effectively.

Writing well is not an inborn skill but an acquired one: you become proficient by writing and rewriting, experimenting with different strategies, and listening to the responses of readers. How, then, can it help to read the work of other writers?

- *Reading introduces you to new information and ideas.* People routinely share facts, observations, discoveries, and ways of thinking in writing. Reading what others have to say lets you learn about subjects and perspectives that would otherwise remain unknown to you, gives you knowledge worth exploring further, and can spark ideas.

- *Reading gives you insights on your own experience.* As many of the essays collected here demonstrate, personal experience can be a rich and powerful source of material for writing. But the knowledge gained from reading can help pinpoint just what is remarkable in your own experience. Such insight not only reveals subjects for writing but also improves your ability to communicate with others whose experiences naturally differ from your own.

- *Reading exposes you to a broad range of strategies and styles.* Just seeing how widely these vary—as much as the writers themselves—should assure you that there is no fixed standard of writing. It should also encourage you to find your own strategies and style. At the same time, you will see that writers do make choices to suit their subjects, their purposes, and especially their readers. Writing is rarely easy, even for the pros, but the more models you have to choose from, the more likely you are to succeed at it.

■ *Reading makes you sensitive to the role of audience in writing.* As you become skilled at reading the work of other writers critically, discovering intentions and analyzing choices, you will see how a writer's decisions affect you as audience. Training yourself to read attentively and critically is the first step to becoming a more objective reader of your own writing.

Reading Attentively

This chapter offers strategies for making the most of your reading—in this book and elsewhere. These strategies are reinforced in Chapters 5–14, each of which introduces a method of developing a piece of writing:

narration	process analysis
description	comparison and contrast
example	definition
division or analysis	cause-and-effect analysis
classification	argument and persuasion

These methods correspond to basic and familiar patterns of thought and expression, common in our daily musings and conversations as well as in writing for all sorts of purposes and audiences: social-networking sites, blogs, and online discussion boards; college papers, lab reports, and examinations; business memos and reports; letters to the editors of newspapers; and articles in popular magazines.

As writers we draw on the methods, often without realizing it, to give order to our ideas and even to find ideas. For instance, a writer narrates, or tells, a story of her experiences to understand and convey the feeling of living her life. As readers, in turn, we have expectations for these familiar methods. When we read a narrative of someone's experiences, for example, we expect enough details to understand what happened, we anticipate that events will be told primarily in the order they occurred, and we want the story to have a point—a reason for its being told and for our bothering to read it. Building an awareness of such expectations can sharpen your skills as a critical reader and as a writer.

In Part Two of this book, a full chapter on each method explains how it works, shows it in action in two annotated paragraphs, and gives advice for using it to develop your own essays. Three essays in each chapter provide clear examples that you can analyze and learn from (with the help of specific reading questions) and that you can refer to while writing (with the help of specific writing suggestions).

To make your reading more interesting and also to stimulate your writing, the sample paragraphs and essays in each chapter all focus on a common subject, such as travel, popular culture, or diversity. You'll see how flexible the methods are as they help five writers produce five unique pieces on the same theme. You'll also find a springboard for producing your own unique pieces, whether you take up some of the book's writing suggestions or jump off with your own topics.

Reading Critically

Much of the reading we do every day is superficial: we skim a newsfeed, magazine, or Web site, noting headings and scanning visuals to get the gist of the content before settling on what catches our interest. But such skimming is not really reading, for it allows neither a deep understanding of the subject nor an appreciation of the writer's unique ideas and craftwork.

To get the most out of reading, we must invest ourselves in the process, applying our own ideas and emotions and paying attention not just to the subject matter but also to the writer's interpretation of it. This kind of reading is **critical** because it looks beneath the surface of a piece of writing. (The common meaning of *critical* as "negative" doesn't apply here: critical reading may result in positive, negative, or even neutral reactions.)

Critical reading can be enormously rewarding, but it takes care and time. A good method for developing your own skill in critical reading is to prepare yourself beforehand and then read a work at least twice to uncover what it has to offer.

▶ Previewing

Preparing to read need involve no more than a few minutes as you form some ideas about the author, the work, and your likely response:

■ *What is the author's background, what qualifications does he or she bring to the subject, and what approach is he or she likely to take?* The biographical information provided before each paragraph and essay in this book should help answer these questions; many periodicals, Web sites, and books offer similar information on their authors.

- *What does the title convey about the subject and the author's attitude toward it?* Note, for instance, the quite different attitudes conveyed by these three titles on the same subject: "Safe Hunting," "In Touch with Ancient Spirits," and "Killing Animals for Fun and Profit."

- *What can you predict about your own response to the work?* What might you already know about its subject? Based on the title and other clues (such as headings or visuals), are you likely to agree or disagree with the author's views? *The Compact Reader* helps ready you for reading by providing a two-part feature before each essay. First, quotations from varied writers comment on the selection's general subject to give you a range of views. And second, a journal prompt encourages you to write about your thoughts on the subject before you see what the author has to say. By giving you a head start in considering the author's ideas and approach, writing *before* reading encourages you to read more actively and critically.

▶ Annotating

After developing some expectations about a piece of writing, read it through carefully to acquaint yourself with the subject, the author's reason for writing about it, and the way the author presents it. Try not to read passively, letting the words wash over you, but instead interact directly with the work to discover its meaning, the author's intentions, and your own responses.

One of the best aids to **active reading** is making notes to yourself, a practice often called **annotation**. Ideally, if you own the book, you can make notes right on the pages themselves, but you might also use sticky notes, a separate piece of paper, or a digital file to record your thoughts. As you practice making notes, you will probably develop a personal code meaningful only to you. As a start, however, try this system:

- *Underline, bracket, or check passages* that you find particularly effective or that seem especially important to the author's purpose.

- *Circle words or phrases* you don't understand so that you can look them up when you finish.

- *Put question marks in the margins* next to unclear passages.

- *Jot down associations* that occur to you, such as examples from your own experience, disagreements with the author's assumptions, or connections to other works you've read.

When you have finished such an active reading, your annotations might look like those below. (The paragraph is from the end of the essay reprinted on pp. 9–11.)

I learned, once the world became larger than Sandra Walker and me and Worcester, Massachusetts, that we are born with few tools with which to build our little shacks of life, and we are born with even less knowledge of how to use those tools. I don't know what I would have done if I hadn't had it in me to write those letters, those stories, to Sandra. I was able to crawl into December, and I woke up one day and knew, without a letter from Sandra, without anyone telling me so, that wherever in the universe Sandra Walker would end up I would not be there with her. I made peace with that, and I think I had a sense that I wasn't really eighteen anymore, but fast going on twenty.

True?

? (shacks of life)

✔

Like a toddler

Why?

So he grew ← up, but just a little bit?

To answer questions like those in the annotations above, count on reading an essay at least twice. Multiple readings increase your mastery of the material; more important, once you have a basic understanding of a writer's subject, second and third readings will reveal details and raise questions that you might not have noticed on the first pass. Reading an essay several times also helps you uncover how the many parts of the work—for instance, the organization, the tone, and the evidence—contribute to the author's purpose.

▶ Using a Reading Checklist

When first rereading an essay, start by writing a one- or two-sentence **summary** of each paragraph and image—in your own words—to increase your mastery of the material. Then let the essay rest in your mind for at least an hour or two before approaching it again. On later readings, dig beneath the essay's surface by asking questions such as those

CHECKLIST FOR CRITICAL READING

- *Why did the author choose this subject?*
- *Who is the intended audience?* What impression does the author wish to make on readers?
- *What is the author's point?* Can you find a direct statement of the thesis, or main idea, or is the thesis implied?
- *What details does the author provide to support the thesis?* Is the supporting evidence reliable? complete? convincing?
- *How does the author organize ideas?* What effect does that arrangement have on the overall impact of the work?
- *What do language and tone reveal about the author's meaning, purpose, and attitude?*
- *How successful is the work as a whole, and why?*

in this checklist above. Note that the questions provided after each essay in this book offer more targeted versions of the ones presented here. Answering both the questions in the checklist and the questions for individual readings will ensure a thorough analysis of what you read.

Analyzing a Sample Essay

Critical reading—and the insights to be gained from it—can best be illustrated by examining an actual essay. The annotated passage on the previous page comes from "Shacks" by Edward P. Jones. The entire essay is reprinted here in the same format as other selections in this book, with quotations from other writers to get you thinking about the essay's subject, a suggestion for exploring your attitudes further in your journal, a biographical note on the author, and an introductory note on the essay.

We tell ourselves stories in order to live.　　　　　　　　—Joan Didion

Almost all good writing begins with terrible first efforts. You need to start somewhere.　　　　　　　　—Anne Lamott

As you become proficient . . . your style will emerge, because you yourself will emerge, and when this happens you will find it increasingly easy to break through the barriers that separate you from other minds, other hearts—which is, of course, the purpose of writing, as well as its principal reward.　　　　　　　　—William Strunk Jr, and E. B. White

JOURNAL RESPONSE　Reflect on your experiences with writing—whether for school, for friends, or for your own purposes. Does writing come naturally to you, or do you struggle to express your thoughts? How so? What do you expect to gain from taking a writing class in college?

Edward P. Jones

Born in 1950, Edward P. Jones has been hailed as a major voice of Southern literature. Although his childhood in Washington, DC, was marked by poverty and instability, Jones showed an early love for reading and won a scholarship to the College of the Holy Cross in Worcester, Massachusetts. He completed his BA in 1972 and went through a brief period of homelessness before obtaining a clerical job with *Science* magazine and publishing his first short story in *Essence*—both in the same week. Jones went on to earn an MFA from the University of Virginia, and for eighteen years he edited tax newsletters during the day while writing fiction in his spare time. His tales of urban life—collected in *Lost in the City* (1992) and *All Aunt Hagar's Children* (2006)—have won popular and critical acclaim, and his novel *The Known World* (2003), about black slaveholders, was awarded the Pulitzer Prize and the National Book Critics Circle Award. Now a professor of English at George Washington University, Jones has also taught at Princeton, the University of Maryland, and the University of Virginia. He lives in Arlington, Virginia.

Shacks

In this essay written for a special "Starting Out" issue of *The New Yorker* in 2011, Jones reflects on a life lesson he stumbled across in his first semester of college. By engaging in an eager yet futile effort to build a romance, Jones discovered a talent he hadn't known he had.

In my first months as a college freshman, I cared more than anything   1
about a young woman with whom I'd gone to high school—Sandra
Walker, a thin, brown-skinned woman who might not have been pretty
enough for the rest of the universe but was more than pretty enough for
me. She was at college in Atlanta and I was in Worcester, Massachusetts.
I had never kissed her, for she was true to someone else. I don't think I'd
even so much as touched the back of her hand, but I cared for her, and the
only way I knew how to express what I felt at that point in my life was to
write letters, and write letters I did. Three and four and five a week I wrote.
All of them were more than five pages long and many went to fifteen
pages—so thick once they had been folded that I had to reinforce the
envelopes with tape. I had always written legibly, but the fear was so great
that Sandra Walker might not be able to decipher even one syllable I had
written that I began printing everything, and to this day the only cursive
writing I do is my signature.

Things like that get in the blood, and they become who you are.   2
I never received a strongly positive response from Sandra, but the crumbs,
the letters sharing with me only the minutiae of her life, were enough to
keep me writing—September and October and November. There wasn't
much beyond the crumbs. Imagining as best I could what a young woman
at the front door of the rest of her life might want to hear from a young
man, I put all the hope I had into each letter, using the limited language of
an eighteen-year-old who knew books of mathematics but not much else.
It is amazing the little shacks of life we can build when it seems that so
much is at stake. Before it was all over, the letters—from what I can remember, for I have not seen any of them since the day I sent them off—became
grand and fanciful creations about some marvelous future that Sandra
Walker and I could have. It was a world of fiction, of course, a place conjured up in my imagination, because, as my mother could have told Sandra,
I could barely take care of myself and would not have known what to do
with, first, a girlfriend, and then a wife and all the children we were supposed to have.

But I was alone in the wilderness in Worcester, away from Washington,   3
DC, my home, for the first time, and I needed some shack of life.
I know now that had I been someone who knew only how to paint pic-
tures, I would have done that. I would have made my case with painting
after painting, wrapping them with care and sending them off to Atlanta.
Or if I had known how to carve little figures in wood I would have carved
Sandra and me and our happy future in oak or maple or whatever wood
I could salvage in Worcester. Or I would have weighed poor Sandra down
with volumes of poetry or tapes of songs with her name in every title.

I learned, once the world became larger than Sandra Walker and me   4
and Worcester, Massachusetts, that we are born with few tools with which
to build our little shacks of life, and we are born with even less knowledge
of how to use those tools. I don't know what I would have done if I hadn't
had it in me to write those letters, those stories, to Sandra. I was able to
crawl into December, and I woke up one day and knew, without a letter
from Sandra, without anyone telling me so, that wherever in the universe
Sandra Walker would end up I would not be there with her. I made peace
with that, and I think I had a sense that I wasn't really eighteen anymore,
but fast going on twenty.

Even read quickly, Jones's essay would not be difficult to comprehend: the author draws on a story from his time as a college student to
make a point about talent. In fact, a quick reading might give the impression that Jones produced the essay effortlessly, artlessly. But close, critical
reading reveals a carefully conceived piece whose parts work both independently and together to achieve the author's purpose.

One way to uncover the underlying intentions and relations in a
piece of writing is to answer a series of questions about the work. The
following questions proceed from the general to the specific—from overall meaning through purpose and method to word choices—and they
parallel the more specific questions provided after the essays in this book.
Here the questions come with possible answers for Jones's essay. (The
paragraph numbers can help you locate the appropriate passages in
"Shacks" as you follow the analysis.)

▶ Meaning

*What is the main idea of the essay—the chief point the writer makes about the
subject, to which all other ideas and details relate? What are the subordinate
ideas that contribute to the main idea?*

Jones states his main idea (or **thesis**) near the end of his essay: "[W]e
born with few tools with which to build our little shacks of life, and we are
born with even less knowledge of how to use those tools" (paragraph 4).
As we mature, he is saying, we discover our talents and desires and learn
what to do with them. Jones leads up to and supports his idea by narrating an episode from his own life—his compulsive writing of letters to a
woman he longed for during his first semester of college (1–2)—and by
contemplating other ways he might have approached her (3), to reach a

larger truth. The story is developed with specific details from Jones's memory, such as the bulk of the envelopes (1); with descriptions of the raw talents he had, such as written expression, persistence, and imagination (1–2); and with examples of the talents he lacked, such as taking care of a family (2) or painting and carving (3).

▶ Purpose and Audience

Why did the author write the essay? What did the author hope readers would gain from it? What did the author assume about the knowledge and interests of readers, and how are these assumptions reflected in the essay?

Jones seems to have written his essay for two interlocking reasons: to show, and thus explain, that we all feel an inherent need to do something constructive with our lives—to find our "shacks"— and to argue gently that individual talents must be identified and developed before they can be used to full advantage.

Jones assumes that his readers, like him, are people who have gone to college, people to whom the emotional turmoil of the first semester will feel familiar. He comments, for instance, on the reality that he "could barely take care of [him]self" (2) and on the loneliness of being "away from . . . home, for the first time" (3). But he also expresses hopes of being "at the front door of the rest of . . . life" (2) and reveals an imagination full of "grand and fanciful creations about some marvelous future" (2), taking pains to show (with some hint of embarrassment) the lengths to which he practiced his only skill—letter writing—to try to secure his desires.

At the same time, Jones seems to expect that readers of *The New Yorker*—with that magazine's emphasis on culture and the arts—will be aware that he is now an established fiction writer and therefore will grasp that his youthful letters, the "stories" (4) he conjured and sent out, built the foundation for his future life. However, readers who do not recognize this point are still likely to understand and appreciate his main idea.

▶ Method and Structure

What method or methods does the author use to develop the main idea, and how do those methods serve the author's subject and purpose? How does the organization serve the author's subject and purpose?

As writers often do, Jones develops his main idea with a combination of the methods discussed in this book. His primary support for his idea consists of **narration** — a story about letter writing as a means of romance. The narrative is developed with **description**, especially of the letters Jones wrote (as in paragraphs 1–2), and with **classification** and **examples** of the forms of expression he might have tried if he had the talent (3). Jones relies on **division or analysis** to tease apart the elements of his messages to Sandra Walker, and he uses **comparison and contrast** to show the differences between his letters and her responses (2). In addition, he draws on **definition** to give meaning to the "shacks" metaphor that shapes the essay (title, 2–4).

While using many methods to develop his idea, Jones keeps his organization fairly simple. He does not begin with a formal introduction or a statement of his idea but instead starts right off with his story, the inspiration for his idea. In the first paragraph he narrates and describes his efforts to connect with a former classmate by writing letters to her. Then, in paragraph 2, he explains why he persisted despite her unresponsiveness and suggests that those letters may have served an as-yet undiscovered purpose in his life. Still delaying a statement of his main idea, Jones contrasts his writing with other forms of communication, which he sees as talents different from his own (3). Finally, he relates his awakening to the truth of his situation and zeroes in on his main idea (4). Although he has withheld this idea until the end, we see that everything in the essay has been controlled by it and directed toward it.

▶ Language

How are the author's main idea and purpose revealed at the level of sentences and words? How does the author use language to convey his or her attitudes toward the subject and to make meaning clear and vivid?

Perhaps Jones's most striking use of language to express and support his idea is in his **figures of speech**, creative expressions that imply meanings beyond or different from their literal meanings. As is often the case, you may need to puzzle over some of his words before you can fully understand their meaning. This is particularly true of Jones's central metaphor, "shacks of life" (title and paragraphs 2–4). A **metaphor** is a figure of speech that compares two unlike things by saying one is the other: in this case, Jones equates physical shelters and the goals that people create to shape their existence. The **connotations** of "shack" add more layers of meaning: shacks are simple structures, often temporary or unstable, and they tend to be associated with people of limited means. Jones's idea, it seems, is that a person doesn't need much to build a life, just enough "tools" (4)—another metaphor, for skills or talents—to give it purpose.

The essay includes several additional inventive figures of speech. In paragraph 2 alone Jones uses metaphors such as the behaviors "that get in the blood," the "crumbs" offered by his female correspondent, and "the front door of the rest of her life"—separate from, but cleverly echoing, the "shacks" metaphor. Calling the small city of Worcester, Massachusetts, a "wilderness" (3) is **hyperbole**, or deliberate exaggeration, suggesting the author's emotional isolation more than the physical reality of place. And finally, the last paragraph depends on contrasting **images** of infancy (captured in "born" and "crawl") and adulthood (not "eighteen anymore, but fast going on twenty") to reinforce Jones's admission that his maturation and understanding were incomplete.

Jones's ideas gain additional impact with **parallelism**, the use of similar grammatical form for ideas of equal importance. For instance, every sentence of paragraph 3 except the first uses the phrase "I would have," building rhythm and stressing the young man's desperate need to communicate. The balanced phrase "those letters, those stories" (4) clarifies that his missives were an early form of fiction writing. Similarly, the **repetition** of "we are born with" (4) emphasizes both the author's lingering immaturity and his point that raw talents in their infancy must be nurtured in order to thrive.

These notes on Jones's essay show how a reader can arrive at a deeper, more personal understanding of a piece of writing by attentive, thoughtful analysis. Guided by the questions at the end of each essay and by your own sense of what works and why, you'll find similar lessons and pleasures in all of this book's readings.

Reading Visuals

Much of what you read will have a visual component—a photograph, perhaps, or a drawing, chart, table, or graph. In many cases such images stand alone, and sometimes their function is merely decorative, but often they contribute to the overall meaning and effect of a written work. Many essays in this book, in fact, are accompanied by images related to their subjects, and several incorporate visuals for a purpose: Scott Adams's "Funny Business" (p. 156) reprints one of the author's classic *Dilbert* comic

strips; David Brooks's "People Like Us" (p. 189) includes a political cartoon to illustrate a point; Jessica Sayuri Boissy's "One Cup at a Time"
(p. 281) showcases Japanese calligraphy; Derek Thompson's "The Making
of Hits" (p. 312) presents two graphs as evidence; and in "Where's the
Empathy?" (p. 357), Nicholas Kristof offers personal photographs to support his argument.

Like written texts, visual texts are composed. That is, the people who
create them do with images what writers do with words: they come to the
task with a purpose, an audience, and a message to convey. You can and
should, therefore, "read" visuals actively. Don't simply glance over images
or take them at face value. Instead, examine them closely and with a critical eye.

Reading visuals critically draws on the same skills you use for closely
reading written works. The checklist for critical reading on page 8 can get
you started. Determining who created an image, why, and for whom, for
instance, will help you tease out details that you might have missed at
first look.

Examining each element of a visual composition—such as the place-
ment and arrangement of objects; the focus; and the uses of color, light,
and shadow—will give you a greater appreciation of its intent and overall
effect. Notice what first captures your attention, where your eye is drawn,
and how different parts of the image interact to create a dominant impression. Finally, if the visual accompanies written text, such as an essay or
advertisement, ask yourself what it contributes to the writer's meaning
and purpose.

Consider, for example, one student's annotations on a photograph
of a college classroom. The picture on the next page was taken by pho-
tographer Damon Winter and was included in "The Women of West
Point," a 2014 *New York Times Magazine* photo essay about female
students at the elite military academy. The woman facing the camera is
Brigade Commander Lindsey Danilack, the top cadet of her graduating
class.

Wall splits image in half— gender divide?

Teacher is in military uniform.

Window highlights her—but also keeps her isolated.

Male students have their backs to the camera.

Staring right at us. She looks bored, or maybe annoyed.

Is that caution tape? Why?

Damon Winter/*The New York Times*/Redux

As Winter's photograph demonstrates, visual images can pack many layers of meaning into a condensed space. Learning to unpack those layers is a skill worth cultivating.

2

DEVELOPING AN ESSAY

Analyzing a text as shown in the preceding chapter is valuable in itself: it can be fun, and the process helps you better understand and appreciate whatever you read. But it can make you a better writer, too, by showing you how to read your own work critically, broadening the range of strategies available to you, and suggesting subjects for you to write about.

The reading selections collected in this book are accompanied by a range of material designed to help you use your reading to write effectively. Each sample paragraph is annotated to help you see how the writer used a particular method to express an idea, and every essay is followed by several detailed questions that will help you read it critically and examine the writing strategies that make it successful. Accompanying the questions are writing topics—ideas for you to adapt and develop into essays of your own. Some of these call for your analysis of the essay; others lead you to examine your own experiences or outside sources in light of the essay's ideas. Chapters 5–14 each conclude with two additional sets of writing topics: one provides a range of subjects for using the chapter's method of development; the other encourages you to focus on thematic connections.

To help you develop your writing, *The Compact Reader* also offers several tools that guide you through composing effective essays. This chapter and the next two (on revising and editing) offer specific ways to strengthen and clarify your work as you move through the writing process, presented as a sequence of stages: analyzing the writing situation, generating ideas, focusing, shaping, revising, and editing. As you'll discover, these stages are actually somewhat arbitrary because writers rarely move in straight lines through fixed steps. Instead, just as they do when thinking or talking, writers continually circle back over covered territory, each time picking up more information or seeing new relationships, until their meaning is clear to themselves and can be made clear to readers. No two writers work in exactly the same way, either. Still, viewing the process in stages helps sort out its many activities so you can develop the process or processes that work best for you. Complementing the general overview of the writing process in Part One of this book are the more specific introductions to the methods of development—narration, comparison and contrast, definition, and so on—in Part Two. These method introductions follow the pattern set here by also moving through stages, but they take up the particular concerns of each method, such as organizing a comparison or clarifying a definition.

Getting Started

Every writing situation involves several elements: you communicate a *thesis* (central idea) about a subject to an *audience* of readers for a particular *purpose*. At first you may not be sure of your idea or your purpose. You may not know how you want to approach your readers, even when you know who they are. Your job in getting started, then, is to explore options and make choices.

▶ Considering Your Subject and Purpose

A **subject** for writing may arise from any source, including your observations or reading, a suggestion in this book, or an assignment from your instructor. In the previous chapter, Edward P. Jones's essay on his first months of college demonstrates how an excellent subject can be found by examining one's own experience. Whatever its source, the subject should be something you care enough about to probe deeply and to stamp with your own perspective.

This personal stamp comes from your **purpose**, your reason for writing. The purpose may be one of the following:

- *To entertain* readers with a humorous, exciting, or moving story.
- *To reflect on* the thoughts and emotions triggered by an observation or experience.
- *To explain* a subject so that readers understand it or see it in a new light.
- *To persuade* readers to accept an idea or opinion or to take a certain action.

A single essay may sometimes have more than one purpose: for instance, a writer might both explain what it's like to have a disability and try to persuade readers to respect special parking zones for people with disabilities. Your reasons for writing may be clear to you early on, arising out of the subject and its significance for you. But you may need to explore your subject for a while—even to the point of writing a draft—before you know what you want to do with it.

▶ Considering Your Audience

Either very early, when you first begin exploring your subject, or later, as a check on what you have generated, you may want to make a few notes on your anticipated **audience**. The notes are optional, but thinking about audience definitely is not. Your topic and purpose, as well as your thesis, supporting ideas, details and examples, organization, style, tone, and language—all should reflect your answers to the following questions:

- *Who will read your writing?*
- *What impression do you want to make on readers?*
- *What do readers already know about your subject? What do they need to know?*
- *What are your readers' likely expectations and assumptions about your subject?*
- *How can you build on your readers' previous knowledge, expectations, and assumptions to bring them around to your view?*

These considerations are crucial to achieving the fundamental purpose of all public writing: communication. Accordingly, they come up again and again in the chapter introductions and the questions after each essay.

▶ Generating Ideas

Ideas for your writing—whether your subject itself or the many smaller ideas and details that shape what you have to say about it—may come to you in a rush, or you may need to hunt for them. (You may also need to do some research to learn more about your subject or to gather support for your ideas. See Part Three of this book.) Writers use a variety of discovery techniques, from jotting down thoughts while they pursue other activities to writing with total concentration for a set period. Here are a few techniques you might try.

Talking with Others

When you write, you essentially join a conversation on a subject: you add to what other writers have said with your own thoughts. So it makes sense that one of the best ways to generate ideas for writing is to talk with other people. Speaking and listening will give you new insights into a subject and reveal connections that you may not have found on your own. That is why much of your time in class will be spent discussing what you read. To get the most out of those conversations, follow these guidelines:

- *Be prepared.* Do the assigned reading, and jot down your thoughts and questions before class. If you will be discussing one of the essays in this book, you can use the questions that accompany the essay to help prepare your notes.

- *Pay attention.* When others speak, listen. Even if you disagree with people or detect flaws in their reasoning, respect their points of view. Ask questions, and try to express their thoughts in your own words to better understand them.

- *Build on each other's ideas.* The purpose of discussion is to discover new perspectives and to find common ground, so feel free to add your own thoughts to what others have to say.

As you discuss readings and exchange ideas with others, you'll almost certainly discover new ways of thinking about a subject. Write those ideas down. Later, you can explore them further using the other techniques described in this section.

Journal Writing

Many writers keep a **journal**, a record of thoughts and observations. Whether on paper or on screen, journal entries give you an opportunity to explore ideas just for yourself, free of concerns about readers who will judge what you say or how you say it. Regular journaling can also make you more comfortable with the act of writing and build your confidence. Indeed, writing teachers often require their students to keep journals or blogs for these reasons.

In a journal you can write about whatever interests, puzzles, or disturbs you. Here are just a few possible uses:

- *Prepare* for a class by taking notes on the assigned reading.
- *Record* summaries of classroom discussions.

- *Analyze* a situation that's causing you problems.
- *Imitate* a writer you admire, such as a poet or songwriter.
- *Explore* your reactions to a movie or television program.
- *Confide* your dreams and fears.

Any of this material could provide a seed for writing, but you can also use a journal deliberately to develop ideas for assignments. One approach is built into this book: before every essay you will find several quotations and a suggestion for journal writing—all centering on the topic of the essay. In responding to the quotations and journal prompt preceding Edward P. Jones's "Shacks" (p. 9), for example, you might examine your attitudes toward writing, recount a particular episode from your own first months of school, or consider your reasons for taking a writing class. One student, Nicole Lang, wrote this journal entry in response to the material preceding Jones's essay:

> Does writing come easily to me? No! I mean, I have no trouble commenting on somebody's Facebook post or sending out a tweet to my friends, but papers for school? Nightmare! Writing is HARD. I don't feel like I have anything to say and then if I do think of something I just get stuck. Who cares what I think? I guess that's the point of this class. To learn, right? But I wouldn't be here if it wasn't required, that's for sure.

Writing for herself, Lang felt free to explore what was on her mind, without worrying about correctness and without trying to make it clear to external readers what she meant by words such as *nightmare* and *stuck*. By articulating her mixed feelings about writing, Lang established a personal context in which to read Jones's essay, and that context made her a more engaged, more critical reader.

Lang used journal writing for another purpose as well: to respond to Jones's essay *after* she read it.

> Interesting that writing letters (who writes letters anymore?) helped Jones get through a difficult time in college. And I like the idea of "little shacks of life," that we don't need all that much to be happy—but aren't most of us in college because we want something better than a shack? Sure, Jones's shack apparently led him to a career as a writer, and it's nice that his infatuation with Sandra turned into a defining moment of his college experience, but not everyone is so lucky.

As this entry makes clear, Lang didn't come to any conclusions about writing or about Jones's essay. She did, however, begin to work out ideas that would serve as the start of a more considered critical response later on. (Further stages of Lang's writing process appear throughout the rest of this chapter and in the two chapters that follow.)

Freewriting

To discover ideas for a particular assignment, you may find it useful to try **freewriting**, or writing without stopping for a set amount of time, usually ten to fifteen minutes. In freewriting you push yourself to keep writing, following ideas wherever they lead, paying no attention to completeness or correctness or even sense. When she began composing an essay response to "Shacks," Nicole Lang produced this freewriting:

> In the context of Jones's essay, it seems like college is an extension of high school. If that's true, then why go to college at all? College is expensive. Really expensive. But it's practically required for a good job so you have to come up with the money somehow. Loans! Jones was lucky he got to spend three months daydreaming. Who can afford that now? Not everyone can waste an entire semester building "shacks"—postponing reality. For a lot of us being an adult is not something that can be put off.

Notice that this freewriting is rough: the tone is informal, as if Lang were speaking to herself; some thoughts are left dangling; some sentences are shapeless or incomplete; some ideas are repeated. But none of this matters because the freewriting is just exploratory. Writing rapidly, without pausing to rethink or edit, actually pulled insights out of Lang. She moved from being vaguely uneasy with Jones's essay to developing an argument inspired by it. Then, with a more definite focus, she could begin drafting in earnest.

Brainstorming

Another technique that helps to pull ideas from you is **brainstorming**, listing ideas without stopping to judge or change them. As in freewriting, write without stopping for ten or fifteen minutes, jotting down everything that seems even remotely related to your subject. Don't stop to reread and rethink what you have written; just keep pulling and recording ideas, no matter how silly or dull or irrelevant they seem. When your time is up, look over the list to identify the promising ideas, and discard the rest. Depending on how promising the remaining ideas are, you can resume brainstorming, try freewriting about them, or begin a draft.

Using the Methods of Development

The ten methods of development addressed in Part Two of this book can also help you expand your thinking. Try asking the following questions to spark ideas about your subject:

- **Narration:** What is the story in the subject? How did it happen?
- **Description:** How does the subject look, sound, smell, taste, and feel?
- **Example:** How can the subject be illustrated? What are some instances of it?
- **Division or Analysis:** What are the subject's parts, and how are they related or significant?
- **Classification:** What groups or categories can the subject be sorted into?
- **Process Analysis:** How does the subject work, or how does someone do it?
- **Comparison and Contrast:** How is the subject similar to or different from something else?
- **Definition:** What are the subject's meanings, characteristics, and boundaries?
- **Cause-and-Effect Analysis:** Why did the subject happen? What were or may be its consequences?
- **Argument and Persuasion:** Why do you believe as you do about the subject? Why do others have different opinions? How can you convince others to accept your opinion or believe as you do?

The kinds of questions suggested by these methods can open up perspectives you may not have considered; they can also help you begin to focus and shape your thoughts. As you explore your subject and begin to draft, you might use the methods singly, with one dominating in an essay, or in combination, with different methods supporting varied aspects of your subject. Whether taken individually or together, each method provides a direction that can help you achieve your particular purpose for writing.

LearningCurve For more practice, visit *LaunchPad Solo for Readers and Writers*: LearningCurve > Patterns of Organization

Forming a Thesis

Have you ever read a news item or magazine article and wondered, "What's the point?" Whether consciously or not, we expect a writer to *have* a point, a central idea that he or she wants readers to take away from the work. We also expect that idea to determine the content of the work—so that everything relates to it—and we expect the content in turn to demonstrate or prove the idea.

Arriving at a main idea, or **thesis**, is thus an essential part of the writing process. Sometimes it will occur to you the moment you hit on your subject—for instance, if you think of writing about the new course registration system because you want to make a point about its unfairness. More often, you will need to explore your thoughts for a while—even to the point of writing a draft or more—before you pin down just what you have to say. Even if your thesis will evolve over time, however, it's a good idea to draft it early because it can help keep you focused as you generate more ideas, seek evidence, and organize your thoughts.

▶ Identifying Your Main Point

A thesis is distinct from the subject of an essay. The subject is what an essay is about; the thesis captures a writer's unique understanding of one aspect of that subject. In the case of "Shacks," for example, the subject is college, but Jones's thesis—that struggling with self-expression can help young adults discover their talents and ambitions—makes a strong point that readers may not have contemplated on their own. In the essay draft that appears at the end of this chapter, student writer Nicole Lang takes the same subject—college—but she makes a completely different point: that contemporary students cannot afford to take their education for granted.

The distinction between a subject and a thesis is evident throughout this book. Each chapter of readings focuses on a single subject—such as travel, the environment, or happiness—yet the individual paragraphs and essays demonstrate the writers' unique perspectives on particular aspects of those general topics. The readings in Chapter 5, for instance, all center on the subject of fear, but no two writers take the same approach. Sherman Alexie recalls mustering the courage to step in a creek despite his inability to swim; Michael Ondaatje captures the mystery of a deadly snake that seemed immortal; Langston Hughes writes about a tense church revival to make a point about innocence and faith; Jennifer Finney Boylan uses a memorable incident to examine the anxieties raised by transgender identity; and student writer Lauren Fulmore reflects on the consequences of a runaway imagination.

To move from a general subject to a workable thesis for your own writing, keep narrowing your focus until you have something to say about the subject. For example, one student writer wanted to write about family but quickly discovered that the topic is too broad to work with. He then narrowed the subject to adoptive families, but even that covered too much territory. As he continued to tighten his focus, he first thought to discuss adopted children who try to contact their birth parents, then considered explaining how adoptees can locate the necessary information, and finally decided to discuss how legal and other barriers can impede adoptees' efforts to find their birth parents. In a few steps, the writer turned a broad subject into a manageable idea worth pursuing. The process isn't always simple, but it is a necessary first step in finding a working thesis.

▶ Drafting a Working Thesis

Once you've narrowed your subject and have something to say about it, the best way to focus on your thesis is to write it out in a **thesis sentence** (or sentences): an assertion that makes your point about the subject. Edward P. Jones states his thesis near the end of his essay "Shacks" (p. 9):

> [W]e are born with few tools with which to build our little shacks of life, and we are born with even less knowledge of how to use those tools.

Jones's thesis statement, while poetic, nonetheless ties together all the other ideas and details in his essay; it also reflects his purpose in writing the essay and focuses his readers on a single point.

All effective thesis sentences do the same: they go beyond generalities or mere statements of fact to express the writer's unique perspective on the subject. Notice the differences in the following sentences that Nicole Lang considered for her response to "Shacks":

ANNOUNCEMENT OF TOPIC   In this essay, I will discuss the purpose of going to college.

STATEMENT OF FACT   Many college students take out loans to finance their education.

GENERAL STATEMENT   Not everyone has the time or resources to dedicate an entire semester to building "shacks" and postponing reality.

EFFECTIVE THESIS   For those who struggle just to pay for the opportunity, a college education has to serve the more concrete purpose of preparing for employment.

CHECKLIST FOR AN EFFECTIVE THESIS

- *Have you narrowed your subject to a focused topic?* Can that topic be managed in the space and time available for your writing project?

- *What main point do you want to make about your topic?* Can you express that point as a debatable assertion or a unique perspective? Be sure that your thesis does more than announce your topic, repeat a fact, or make a broad generalization. Instead, use the opportunity to explicitly state your opinion or articulate your fresh idea.

- *What is your purpose for writing?* Your thesis should make it clear to readers whether you intend to entertain them, express your thoughts and feelings, explain a point or concept, or persuade them of an idea.

- *Does your thesis control the content of your essay?* Every subpoint and supporting detail in your draft should support your main idea.

- *Where, if at all, will you state your thesis?* It may help readers to know the point of your essay from the start, or they may be more receptive to your main idea if you withhold it until the end. If you choose not to state your thesis outright, readers should nonetheless be able to recognize your controlling idea without difficulty.

The first sentence identifies the topic of the paper, but it gives no indication of the writer's purpose or perspective. The second sentence merely expresses a fact, not a main idea worth developing in an essay. The third sentence offers an opinion, but because it's a very broad assertion that few would dispute, it fails to capture readers' interest or make a significant point. The final sentence, however, makes a strong assertion about a narrow subject and gives readers an idea of what to expect from the rest of the essay.

In academic writing, the thesis sentence usually comes near the beginning of an essay, typically at the end of the first paragraph, where it serves as a promise to examine a particular subject from a particular perspective. But as Edward P. Jones demonstrates by stating his thesis at the end of "Shacks," the thesis sentence may come elsewhere as long as it controls the whole essay. The thesis may even go unstated, as some essays

---

in this book illustrate, but it still must govern every element of the work as if it were announced.

Be aware, also, that because the main point of an essay may (and often does) change over the course of the writing process, the thesis may also change, sometimes considerably. Maintaining a willingness to adjust your thesis sentence as you draft and revise your work will help to keep you from writing yourself into a corner.

Organizing

Writers vary in the extent to which they arrange their material before they begin drafting, but most do establish some plan. A good time to do so is after you've explored your subject and come up with a good stock of ideas about it. Before you begin drafting, you can look over what you've got and consider the best ways to organize it.

▶ Creating a Plan

A writing plan may consist of a simple list of key points, a fuller list that also includes specifics, or even a detailed formal outline—whatever gives order to your ideas and provides some direction for your writing.

As you'll see in later chapters, many of the methods of development suggest specific structures, most notably narration, description, classification, process analysis, and comparison and contrast. But even when the organization is almost built into the method, you'll find that some subjects demand more thoughtful plans than others. You may be able to draft a straightforward narrative of a personal experience with very little advance planning. But a nonpersonal narrative, or even a personal one involving complex events and time shifts, may require more thought about arrangement.

Though some sort of plan is almost always useful when drafting, resist any temptation at this stage to pin down every detail in its proper place. A huge investment in planning can hamper you during drafting, making it difficult to respond to new ideas and even new directions that may prove fruitful.

▶ Developing Paragraphs

Most essays consist of three parts: the introduction and the conclusion (discussed in the next section) and the **body**, the most substantial and longest part, which develops the main idea or thesis.

As you explore your subject, you will generate ideas that directly support your thesis as well as more specific examples, details, and other evidence to support these ideas. In the following informal outline for Nicole Lang's first draft (pp. 30–31), you can see how each supporting idea, or subpoint, helps to build her working thesis:

> WORKING THESIS   Not everyone has the time or resources to dedicate an entire semester to building "shacks" and postponing reality.
>
> SUBPOINT   Many students are already adults.
>
> SUBPOINT   Other students are in school specifically for job training.
>
> SUBPOINT   A lot of students take on significant debt and will need jobs with good incomes to pay it off.

Lang uses specific evidence to develop each subpoint into a **paragraph**, each one essentially a mini-essay with its own main idea and supporting evidence.

When you seek a plan for your ideas, look first for your subpoints, the main supports for your thesis. Use these as your starting points to work out your essay one chunk (or paragraph) at a time. You can sketch the supporting details and examples into your organizational plan, or you can wait until you begin drafting to get into the specifics.

▶ Considering the Introduction and Conclusion

You may not know for sure how you want to begin and end your essay until you're drafting or revising. Still, it can be helpful to consider the introduction and conclusion early on, so you have a sense of how you might approach readers and what you might leave them with.

The basic opening and closing serve readers by demonstrating your interest in their needs and expectations:

- The **introduction** draws readers into the essay and focuses their attention on the main idea and purpose, often stated in a thesis sentence.

- The **conclusion** ties together the elements of the essay and provides a final impression for readers to take away with them.

These basic forms allow considerable room for variation. One essay may need two paragraphs of introduction but only a one-sentence conclusion,

 **LearningCurve**   For more practice, visit *LaunchPad Solo for Readers and Writers*: LearningCurve > Topic Sentences and Supporting Details

whereas another essay may require no formal introduction but a lengthy conclusion. How you begin and end depends on your subject and purpose, the kind of essay you are writing, and the likely responses of your readers.

Specific strategies for opening and closing essays are suggested in each chapter introduction of Part Two and in the Glossary under *introductions* and *conclusions*.

Drafting

However detailed your organizational plan is, try not to view it as a rigid taskmaster while you are writing your essay. **Drafting** is your chance to give expression to your ideas, filling them out, finding relationships, drawing conclusions. If you are like most writers, you will discover much of what you have to say while in the process of putting your thoughts into words. In fact, if your subject is complex or difficult for you to write about, you may need several drafts just to work out your ideas and their relationships.

▶ Writing, Not Revising

Some writers draft rapidly, rarely looking up from the keyboard. Others draft in fits and starts, gazing out the window or doodling as much as writing. Any method that works is fine, but one method rarely works: collapsing drafting and revising into one stage, trying to do everything at once.

Write first; then revise. Concentrate on *what* you are saying, not on *how* you are saying it. You pressure yourself needlessly if you try to produce a well-developed, coherent, interesting, and grammatically correct paper all at once. You may have trouble getting words down because you're afraid to make mistakes, and worrying about mistakes may distract you from exploring your ideas fully. Awkwardness, repetition, wrong words, grammatical errors, misspellings — these and other more superficial concerns can be attended to in a later draft. The same goes for considering your readers' needs: like many writers, you may find that attention to readers during the first draft inhibits the flow of ideas. If so, postpone that attention until the second or third draft.

If you experience writer's block or just don't know how to begin, start writing the part you're most comfortable with. Writing in paragraph chunks will also make drafting more manageable. You can start with your thesis sentence — or at least keep it in view as a reminder of your purpose and main idea. But if you find yourself pulled away from the thesis by a new idea, let go and follow, at least for a while. If your purpose and main idea change as a result of such exploration, you can always revise your thesis accordingly.

▶ Nicole Lang's First Draft

Some exploratory work by student Nicole Lang appears throughout this chapter. What follows is the first draft she subsequently wrote on the purpose of college. The draft is very rough, with frequent repetitions, wandering paragraphs, unsupported ideas, and many other flaws. But such weaknesses are not important at this early stage. The draft gave Lang the opportunity to discover what she had to say, to explore her ideas, and to link them in rough sequence.

> In Edward P. Jones's essay "Shacks," he writes about his first semester of college. He recalls writing three to five letters each week to his high school crush, Sandra Walker, in the hopes that she would come to love him. Unfortunately, his attempts to win Sandra's affection were met with little enthusiasm. This experience gave him something important that helped him get through a difficult time of adjustment for students entering college, but when he says, "It is amazing the little shacks of life we can build when it seems that so much is at stake," I can't help but wonder what was really at stake for Jones. Not everyone has the luxury to indulge in three months of emotional growth, to look for talents they may not even know they have. Not everyone has the time or resources to dedicate an entire semester to building "shacks" and postponing reality.
>
> Jones seems to think of college as an extension of high school. A place to grow up, if just a little. That may be true for some people. But adulthood cannot be put off for many students.
>
> A growing number of college students are adults over the age of 25. Getting a degree will give them the skills they need for a better job and prove to employers that they can work hard. Jones's understanding that his infatuation with Sandra turned into a defining moment of his college experience is nice, but he doesn't represent the financially burdened students of today.

Writing doesn't come as easily to me as it did for Jones. While I struggle, I understand the importance of the education I am receiving. Its important to find a career path that feels meaningful and fulfilling. But it is also important to find a job that can give you economic stability that will outweigh the significant cost of the degree. Although it would be nice to discover ourselves while we're here, it all comes down to time and money.

Jones's "shack" in college led him to a successful career as a writer, but not everyone is as lucky. Our shacks are different, and some are built later than others. For students who struggle just to pay for the opportunity, college serves the more concrete purpose of preparing us for employment—and that's OK.

3
REVISING

▶

The previous chapter took you through the first-draft stage of the writing process, when you have a chance to work out your ideas without regard for what others may think. This chapter describes the crucial next stage, when you actively consider your readers: revising to focus and shape your meaning.

Revision means "re-seeing." Looking at your draft as your reader would, you cut, add, and reorganize until the ideas make sense on their own. Revision is not the same as editing. In revising, you make fundamental changes in content and structure. **Editing** comes later: once you're satisfied with the revised draft, you work on the sentences and words, attending to grammar, punctuation, and the like (addressed in the next chapter). The separation of these two stages is important because attention to little changes distracts from a view of the whole. If you try to edit while you revise, you'll be more likely to miss the big picture. You may also waste effort perfecting sentences you'll later decide to cut.

Reading Your Own Work Critically

Perhaps the biggest challenge of revision is reading your own work objectively, as a reader would. To gain something like a reader's critical distance from your draft, try one or more of the following techniques:

- *Put your first draft aside for at least a few hours—and preferably overnight—before attempting to revise it.* You may have further thoughts in the interval, and you will be able to see your work more objectively when you return to it.

- *Ask others to read and comment on your draft.* Your teacher may ask you and your classmates to exchange drafts so that you can help each other revise. But even without such a procedure, you can benefit from another person's responses. Keep an open mind to comments, and ask questions when you need more information.

■ *Make an outline of your draft* by listing what you cover in each paragraph. Such an outline can show gaps, overlaps, and problems in organization.

■ *Read the draft out loud.* Speaking the words and hearing them can help to create distance from them.

■ *Imagine you are someone else*—a friend, perhaps, or a particular person in your intended audience—and read the draft through that person's eyes, as if for the first time.

■ *Print a double-spaced copy of your draft.* It's much easier to read text on paper than on a screen, and you can spread out printed pages to see the whole paper at once. Once you've finished revising, transferring changes to the computer or tablet requires little effort.

Looking at the Whole Draft

Revision starts with seeing your draft as a whole, focusing mainly on your purpose and thesis, the support for your thesis, and the movement among ideas. You want to determine what will work and what won't for readers—where the draft strays from your purpose, leaves a hole in the development of your thesis, does not flow logically or smoothly, digresses, or needs more details. Besides rewriting, you may need to cut entire paragraphs, condense paragraphs into sentences, add passages of explanation, rearrange sections, or try a different approach.

▶ Purpose

In the press of drafting, you may lose sight of why you are writing. Your **purpose** may change as you work out your meaning, so that you start in one place and end somewhere else or even lose track of where you are. You might have intended to write a persuasive argument, for instance, but ended up explaining your subject. Or if assigned to analyze another writer's work, you might have stopped at summarizing it. Your first goal in revising, then, is to see that your essay is well focused. Readers should grasp a clear purpose right away, and they should find that you have achieved it at the end. They should see your main idea, your thesis, very early, usually by the end of the introduction, and they should think that you have proved or demonstrated your point when they reach the last paragraph.

You may find that you need to upend your essay, plucking your thesis out of the conclusion and starting over with it, providing the subpoints and details to develop it (such was the case for student writer Nicole Lang, whose revised response to Edward P. Jones's "Shacks" appears at the end of this chapter). Or you may determine that your draft needs more (or different) details and evidence to support your points, perhaps less. You'll probably find the second draft much easier to write because you'll know better what you want to accomplish, and the next round of revision after that will go even more smoothly.

▶ Thesis

Like many writers, you might sometimes start with one **thesis** and finish with another, essentially discovering what you think about a subject by writing about it. In many cases you'll need to revise your thesis to reflect what you actually wrote in your draft. In other cases you might want to rewrite your thesis statement simply to improve its impact on readers.

An effective thesis statement makes a strong assertion about a narrow aspect of a subject and gives a sense of the writer's purpose. The following examples show how a student writing about adoption moved from an explanatory to a persuasive purpose between the early stages of the writing process and the final draft of his essay.

> WORKING THESIS   Adopted children can contact their birth parents, although sometimes the process is difficult.

> REVISED THESIS   Adopted children often need persistence to locate information about their birth parents.

> FINAL THESIS   Laws and traditions unfairly hamper adopted children from seeking information about their birth parents.

The first two sentences identify the subject of the essay, but they are broad and bland, and neither clearly focuses on the writer's interest: the impediments to obtaining information. In contrast, the final sentence

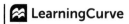 **LearningCurve**   For more practice, visit *LaunchPad Solo for Readers and Writers*: LearningCurve > Topics and Main Ideas

makes a definitive assertion and clearly conveys the writer's persuasive purpose. Thus the sentence lets readers know what to expect: an argument that adopted children should be treated more fairly when they seek information about their birth parents, along with some discussion of the "laws and traditions" that hamper adoptees' searches, what is "unfair" and "fair" in this situation, and what changes the writer proposes.

▶ Development

Part of establishing that your draft fulfills your purpose is making sure that your thesis is fully developed. When you **develop** an idea, you provide concrete and specific details, examples, facts, opinions, and other evidence to make the idea vivid and true in readers' minds. Readers will know only as much as you tell them about your thesis and its support. Gaps, vague statements, and unsupported conclusions will undermine your efforts to win their interest and agreement.

Consider, for example, the following paragraph from Nicole Lang's first draft of her essay responding to Edward P. Jones's "Shacks":

> Jones seems to think of college as an extension of high school. A place to grow up, if just a little. That may be true for some people. But adulthood cannot be put off for many students.

Lang felt she had a good point about adult students, but on reviewing her draft she realized she hadn't backed up her **generalization** with any evidence. So in revision she added an example from her personal experience:

> Jones seems to think of college as an extension of high school. A place to grow up, if just a little. That may be true for some people. But adulthood cannot be put off for many students. For example, my cousin Robert is 29 years old and he has a young child and a job that barely pays the bills. He takes nite classes at a community college so he can qualify for a better position, he does not have time at this stage in his life to dream about "some marvelous future." His shack is his son, and so he spends his time making a better life for himself and his family.

Notice that Lang's revised paragraph, while better developed and more convincing, contains several errors of grammar, punctuation, and spelling. That's fine; she'll attend to those details when she edits.

Development begins in **sentences,** when you use the most **concrete** and **specific words,** you can muster to explain your meaning. At the level of the **paragraph,** these sentences develop the paragraph's topic. Then, at the level of the whole essay, these paragraphs develop the governing thesis. The key to adequate development is a good sense of your readers' needs for information and evidence. The list of questions for considering your audience in the previous chapter (p. 19) can help you estimate these needs as you start to write; reconsidering the questions when you revise can help you see where your draft may fail to address, say, readers' unfamiliarity with your subject or possible resistance to your thesis.

The introduction to each method of development in Chapters 5–14 includes specific advice for meeting readers' needs when using the method to develop paragraphs and essays. When you sense that a paragraph or section of your essay is thin but you don't know how to improve it, you can also try the techniques for generating ideas discussed in Chapter 2 (pp. 19–23).

▶ Unity

When a piece of writing has **unity,** all its parts are related: the paragraphs build the central idea of the whole essay, and the sentences build the central idea of each paragraph. Readers do not have to wonder what the essay is about or what a particular passage has to do with the rest of the piece. Revising for unity strengthens your thesis by ensuring that every paragraph centers on your essay's main idea.

Consider Nicole Lang's revised draft that appears at the end of this chapter. Her thesis sentence states, "For those of us who struggle just to pay for the opportunity, a college education has to serve the more concrete purpose of preparing for employment," and each paragraph clearly develops this idea, highlighting who those struggling students are, why they're in college, and how they expect to pay for it. This unity is true of Lang's revised draft but not of her first draft, where she opened with a lengthy discussion of Jones's "Shacks." Some summary is helpful, of course, but the details blurred Lang's focus on today's college students and their goals. Recognizing as much, Lang condensed her summary of "Shacks" to a single sentence when she revised. Deleting the distracting details also helped Lang clarify her introduction and her own purpose in writing.

Following the introduction, the paragraphs in the **body** of an essay are almost like mini-essays themselves, each developing an idea, or subpoint, that supports the thesis. In fact, each body paragraph should have its own thesis, called its *topic*, usually expressed in a **topic sentence** or sentences. The rest of the paragraph develops the topic with specifics. In this paragraph from the final draft of Nicole Lang's "Foundations," for example, the topic sentence is underlined:

> <u>Students in more traditional schools need to keep their eyes on the real world, too.</u> The typical college graduate will start out owing nearly $40,000 in loans (Taibbi). While it is important to find a career path that feels meaningful and fulfilling, it is just as important to earn an income that will outweigh the cost of higher education. We therefore need to focus on academic programs that will directly benefit our job prospects and help us repay our debts. With limited resources, most of us cannot afford shacks into which we can retreat—at least not yet.

Notice that every sentence of this paragraph relates to the topic sentence. Lang achieved this unity in revision. In her first draft, she focused the opening sentences of this paragraph on herself:

> Writing doesn't come as easily to me as it did for Jones. While I struggle, I understand the importance of the education I am receiving.

If you look back at the full paragraph above, you'll see that Lang deleted these sentences and substituted a final one that focuses on the paragraph's topic: the need for students to plan for life after college.

Your topic sentences will not always fall at the very beginning of your paragraphs. Sometimes you'll need to create a transition from the preceding paragraph before stating the new paragraph's topic, or you'll build the paragraph to a topic sentence at the end. Sometimes, too, you'll write a paragraph with a topic but without a topic sentence. In all these cases, you'll need to have an idea for the paragraph and to unify the paragraph around that idea, so that all the specifics support and develop it.

▶ Coherence

Writing has **coherence** when readers can follow it easily and can see how the parts relate to each other. The ideas develop in a clear sequence, the sentences and paragraphs connect logically, and the connections are clear and smooth. The writing flows.

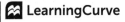 **LearningCurve** For more practice, visit *LaunchPad Solo for Readers and Writers*: LearningCurve > Topic Sentences and Supporting Details

Coherence starts as sentences build paragraphs. Writers can draw on several devices to achieve coherence, including **repetition and restatement** of key words and phrases, **pronouns** such as *they* and *them* to substitute for nouns, and **parallelism**, the use of similar grammatical structures for related ideas. Every paragraph you write will require some devices to tie the sentences together.

One of the most useful devices for achieving paragraph coherence is a liberal use of **transitions**, words and expressions that clearly link the parts of sentences and whole sentences. Transitions may indicate time (*later, soon*), place (*nearby, farther away*), similarity (*also, likewise*), difference (*in contrast, instead*), and many other relationships. Check all your paragraphs to be sure that each sentence connects with the one before and that readers will see the connection without having to stop and reread.

Transitions work to link ideas between paragraphs as well as within them. When the ideas in two paragraphs are closely related, a simple word or phrase at the start of the second one may be all that's needed to show the relation. In each example below, the underlined transition opens the topic sentence of the paragraph:

> Moreover, the rising costs of health care have long outpaced inflation.
>
> However, some kinds of health-care plans have proved much more expensive than others.

When a paragraph is starting a new part of the essay or otherwise changing direction, a sentence or more at the beginning will help explain the shift. In the next example, the first sentence summarizes the preceding paragraph, the second introduces the topic of the new paragraph, and the third gives the paragraph's topic sentence:

> Traditional health-care plans have thus become an unaffordable luxury for most individuals and businesses. The majority of those with health insurance now find themselves in so-called managed plans. Though they do vary, managed plans share at least two features: they pay full benefits only when the insured person consults an approved doctor, and they require prior approval for certain procedures.

Notice that underlined transitions provide further cues about the relationship of ideas.

▶ Organization

Although transitions help alert readers to movement from one idea to another, they can't achieve coherence by themselves. Just as important is an overall **organization** that develops ideas in a clear sequence and directs readers in a familiar pattern:

- A **spatial organization** arranges information to parallel the way we scan people, objects, or places: top to bottom, left to right, front to back, near to far, or vice versa. This scheme is especially useful for description.

- A **chronological** organization arranges events or steps as they occurred in time, first to last. Such an arrangement usually organizes a narrative or a process analysis and may also help with cause-and-effect analysis.

- A **climactic** organization proceeds in order of climax, usually from least to most important, building to the most interesting example, the most telling point of comparison, the most significant argument. A climactic organization is most useful for example, division or analysis, classification, comparison and contrast, definition, and argument and persuasion, and it can also work for cause-and-effect analysis.

The introduction to each method of development in Part Two gives detailed advice on organizing with these arrangements and variations on them.

When revising your draft for organization, try outlining it by jotting down the topic sentence of each paragraph and the key support for each topic. The exercise will give you some distance from your ideas and words, allowing you to see the structure like a skeleton. Will your readers grasp the logic of your arrangement? Will they see why you move from each idea to the next one? After checking the overall structure, be sure you've built in enough transitions between sentences and paragraphs to guide readers through your ideas.

▶ Tone

The **tone** of writing is like the tone of voice in speech: it expresses the writer's attitude toward his or her subject and audience. In writing we express tone with word choice and sentence structure. Notice the marked differences in these two passages discussing the same information on the same subject:

> Voice mail can be convenient, sure, but for callers it's usually more trouble than it's worth. We waste time "listening to the following menu choices," when we just want the live person at the end. All too often, there isn't even such a person!

For callers the occasional convenience of voice mail generally does not compensate for its inconveniences. Most callers would prefer to speak to a live operator but must wait through a series of choices to reach that person. Increasingly, companies with voice-mail systems do not offer live operators at all.

The first passage is informal, expresses clear annoyance, and with *we* includes the reader in that attitude. The second passage is more formal and more objective, reporting the situation without involving readers directly.

Tone can range from casual to urgent, humorous to serious, sad to elated, pleased to angry, personal to distant. The particular tone you choose for a piece of writing depends on your purpose and your audience. For most academic and business writing, you will be trying to explain or argue a point. Your readers will be interested more in the substance of your writing than in a startling tone, and indeed an approach that is too personal, casual, or hostile could put them off.

Tone is something you want to evaluate in revision, along with whether you've achieved your purpose and whether you've developed your thesis adequately for your audience. But adjusting tone is largely a matter of replacing words and restructuring sentences, work that could distract you from an overall view of your essay. If you think your tone is off base, you may want to devote a separate phase of revision to it, after addressing unity, coherence, and the other matters discussed in this chapter.

Using a Revision Checklist

The following checklist summarizes the advice on revision given in this chapter. Use the checklist to remind yourself what to look for in your first draft. But don't try to answer all the questions in a single reading of the draft. Instead, take the questions one by one, rereading the whole draft for each. That way you'll be able to concentrate on each element with minimal distraction from the others.

Note that the introductions to the methods of development in Chapters 5–14 also have their own revision checklists. Combining this list with the one for the method you're using will produce a more targeted set of questions.

CHECKLIST FOR REVISION

- *What is your purpose in writing?* Will it be clear to readers? Do you achieve it?

- *What is your thesis?* Where is it made clear to readers? Could your thesis statement be more effective?

- *How well developed is your essay?* Where might readers need more information and evidence to understand your ideas and find them convincing?

- *How unified is your essay?* How does each body paragraph support your thesis? (Look especially at your topic sentences.) How does each sentence in the body paragraphs support the topic sentence of the paragraph?

- *How coherent is your essay?* Do repetition and restatement, pronouns, parallelism, and transitions link the sentences in paragraphs?

- *Does the overall organization clarify the flow of ideas?* How does your introduction work to draw readers in and preview your purpose and thesis? How does your conclusion work to pull the essay together and give readers a sense of completion?

- *What is the tone of your essay?* Is it appropriate for your purpose and your audience?

Nicole Lang's Revised Draft

Considering questions like those in the revision checklist led student writer Nicole Lang to revise the rough draft we saw at the end of the previous chapter. Lang's revision follows. Notice that she changed her thesis statement to reflect what she had written and added supporting details for several points. She also came up with a title that helped her focus her main idea, revamped the introduction, tightened many passages, improved the coherence of her essay, and wrote a wholly new conclusion to sharpen her point. She did not try to improve her style or fix errors at this stage, leaving those activities for later editing.

Foundations

In Edward P. Jones's essay "Shacks," he ~~writes about his first semester~~

~~of college.~~ He recalls writing ~~three to five~~ letters ~~each~~ week to his high

school crush~~/ Sandra Walker, in the hopes that she would come to love him.~~

~~Unfortunately, his attempts to win Sandra's affection were met with little~~

and discovering a sense of purpose
~~enthusiasm.~~ This experience gave him something important‸that helped

him get through a difficult time of adjustment for students entering

.   But when Jones mentions our ability to find structure when
college~~/ but when he says,~~ "It is amazing the little shacks of life we can

"   think about what
build when it seems that‸so much is at stake," I can't help but‸wonder

is at stake for college students today.
~~what was really at stake for Jones.~~ Not everyone has the luxury to indulge

in three months of emotional growth, to look for talents they may not even

know they have. ~~Not everyone has the time or resources to dedicate an~~

~~entire semester to building "shacks" and postponing reality.~~ For those of us

who struggle just to pay for the opportunity, a college education has to serve the more

concrete purpose of preparing for employment.

Jones seems to think of college as an extension of high school. A

place to grow up, if just a little. That may be true for some people. But

adulthood cannot be put off for many students. For example, my cousin Robert

is 29 years old and he has a young child and a job that barely pays the bills. He takes nite

classes at a community college so he can qualify for a better position, he does not have

time at this stage in his life to dream about "some marvelous future." His shack is his

son, and so he spends his time making a better life for himself and his family.

A growing number of college students are adults over the age of 25.

They come from a wide variety of backgrounds and enroll for a number of reasons

and they all understand the demands of a tough job market in a down economy.

particular
Getting a degree will give them the skills they need for a ‸better job and

prove to employers that they can work hard. ~~Jones's understanding~~

~~that his infatuation with Sandra turned into a defining moment of his~~

~~college experience is nice, but he doesn't represent the financially burdened~~

~~students of today.~~ Such vocational training is important and deserves respect.
Those in more traditional schools need to keep there eye on the real world, too.
~~Writing doesn't come as easily to me as it did for Jones. While I~~
The average student will graduate owing nearly $40,000 in student loans (source).
~~struggle, I understand the importance of the education I am receiving.~~

Its important to find a career path that feels meaningful and fulfilling. But

                              necessary to earn an income
it is also ~~important to find a job that can give you economic stability~~ that

will outweigh the ~~significant~~ cost of ~~the degree. Although it would be nice~~

~~to discover ourselves while we're here, it all comes down to time and~~

~~money.~~ higher education. This means we need to focus our time and effort on

academic programs that will directly benefit our job prospects and put us in a position

to repay our debts. With limited resources, not everyone can afford shacks they can

retreat into. At least not yet.

~~Jones's "shack" in college led him to a successful career as a writer,~~

~~but not everyone is as lucky. Our shacks are different, and some are built~~

~~later than others. For students who struggle just to pay for the opportunity,~~

~~college serves the more concrete purpose of preparing us for employment—~~

~~and that's OK.~~

Jones makes a good point that a successful life depends on some kind of structure.
To be truly sturdy, however, any structure requires a solid foundation. That's what college
provides. We should certainly hope to discover ourselves and our hidden talents while
we're here. But for financially burdened students the realities of higher education all come
down to time and money. We have to be practical even as we dream.

4
EDITING

The final stage of the writing process is **editing** to clarify and clean up your work. In editing you turn from global issues of purpose, thesis, development, unity, coherence, organization, and tone to more particular issues of grammar, punctuation, and clarity. The primary goals of editing are to fix common errors and to tighten and polish sentences so that your words can shine.

Like revision, editing requires that you gain some distance from your work so that you can see it objectively. Try these techniques:

- *Work on a clean copy of your revised draft.* Edit on a printout if you can: it's easier to spot problems on paper than on a screen.

- *Read your revised draft aloud* so that you can hear the words. But be sure to read what you have actually written, not what you may have intended to write but didn't.

- *Try reading your draft backward sentence by sentence.* You'll be less likely to get caught up in the flow of your ideas and thus more likely to catch errors.

- *Keep a list of problems that others have pointed out in your previous writing.* Add this personal list to the editing checklist on page 53.

Checking for Common Errors

The first goal of editing is to express your ideas as clearly as possible, without sentence errors that might distract, confuse, or annoy readers. The guidelines here can help you catch some of the most common mistakes.

▶ Sentence Fragments

A **sentence fragment** is a word group that is punctuated like a sentence but lacks a subject, is missing a verb, or expresses just part of a thought.

Experienced writers sometimes use fragments deliberately, but it's safest to make sure each sentence is complete by adding the necessary verb or subject or by attaching the word group to a nearby sentence:

FRAGMENT   The price of oil unpredictable and rising.

COMPLETE   The price of oil is unpredictable and rising.

FRAGMENT   Consumers are warming up to alternative heating systems. Such as heat pumps and solar panels.

COMPLETE   Consumers are warming up to alternative heating systems, such as heat pumps and solar panels.

▶ Run-on Sentences and Comma Splices

Two complete sentences in a row need to be clearly separated. If they run together with nothing between them, they create a **run-on sentence**. If they run together with only a comma between them, they create a **comma splice.**

RUN-ON   Pellet stoves are especially popular suppliers can't keep up with demand.

COMMA SPLICE   Pellet stoves are especially popular, suppliers can't keep up with demand.

You can correct run-on sentences and comma splices by ending each sentence with a period; by inserting a semicolon (and maybe a conjunctive adverb such as *however* or *therefore*); or by separating the clauses with a comma along with *and, but, or, nor, for, so,* or *yet*:

EDITED   Pellet stoves are especially popular. Suppliers can't keep up with demand.

EDITED   Pellet stoves are especially popular; suppliers can't keep up with demand.

EDITED   Pellet stoves are especially popular; therefore, suppliers can't keep up with demand.

EDITED   Pellet stoves are especially popular, and suppliers can't keep up with demand.

LearningCurve   For more practice, visit *LaunchPad Solo for Readers and Writers*: LearningCurve > Sentences

▶ Subject-Verb Agreement

The subject and verb in a sentence should match in grammatical form. That is, you should use singular verbs with singular subjects and plural verbs with plural subjects. Watch especially for the following situations.

■ *When a group of words comes between the subject and the verb*, be careful not to mistake a noun in that word group (such as *pellets* below) for the subject of the sentence:

MISMATCHED   The use of construction waste to make wood pellets contribute to their appeal.

MATCHED   The use of construction waste to make wood pellets contributes to their appeal.

■ *With compound subjects* (joined by *and*), use a plural verb:

MISMATCHED   Low carbon emissions and the renewability of sawdust adds to the belief that pellets are environmentally friendly.

MATCHED   Low carbon emissions and the renewability of sawdust add to the belief that pellets are environmentally friendly.

▶ Pronouns

A **pronoun**—*I, you, he, she, they, it*, and so forth—refers to or replaces a noun in a sentence. Imprecise and mismatched pronouns are common in casual speech, but they can be distracting in writing. When you edit, aim for formal usage.

■ *Check that pronouns have clearly stated antecedents.* An **antecedent** is the noun to which a pronoun refers. Rewrite sentences in which the reference is vague or only implied:

VAGUE   Text messaging while driving is dangerous, but it doesn't deter everyone.

CLEAR   Text messaging while driving is dangerous, but the risk doesn't deter everyone.

IMPLIED   Despite numerous studies showing that distracted driving causes accidents, they keep typing.

CLEAR   Despite numerous studies showing that distracted drivers cause accidents, they keep typing.

■ *Match pronouns and the words they refer to.* Singular nouns and pronouns take singular pronouns; plural nouns and pronouns take plural pronouns. The most common error occurs with singular indefinite pronouns such as *anybody, anyone, everyone, nobody,* and *somebody.* We often use these words to mean "many" or "all" and then mistakenly refer to them with plural pronouns:

MISMATCHED   Everyone must check in before they can vote.

MATCHED   Everyone must check in before he or she can vote.

MATCHED   All students must check in before they can vote.

▶ Misplaced and Dangling Modifiers

A **modifier** is a word, phrase, or clause that describes another word (or words) in a sentence. Make sure that modifiers clearly modify the intended words. Misplaced and dangling modifiers can be awkward or even unintentionally amusing:

MISPLACED   We watched as the falling snow swirled around our feet in amazement.

CLEAR   We watched in amazement as the falling snow swirled around our feet.

DANGLING   Enjoying the quiet of the forest, the crack of a hunter's rifle startled me out of my reverie.

CLEAR   Enjoying the quiet of the forest, I was startled out of my reverie by the crack of a hunter's rifle.

▶ Shifts

As you edit, check that your use of pronouns and verbs is consistent. Straighten out any unnecessary **shifts**, or inconsistencies, in person, tense, or voice.

■ *Person.* Don't shift needlessly among the first person (*I, we*), second person (*you*), and third person (*he, she, they*):

INCONSISTENT   We were frightened, but you had to stay calm.

CONSISTENT   We were frightened, but we had to stay calm.

■ *Tense.* Don't shift needlessly between the present tense and the past tense of verbs:

INCONSISTENT   The tornado siren howls so loudly it rattled the walls.

CONSISTENT   The tornado siren howled so loudly it rattled the walls.

■ *Voice.* Don't shift needlessly between the active voice and the passive voice of verbs (see below for an explanation of voice):

> INCONSISTENT   The <u>police</u> <u>told</u> us to leave our belongings behind, and <u>we</u> <u>were advised</u> to notify family members.

> CONSISTENT   The police told us to leave our belongings behind, and <u>they</u> <u>advised</u> us to notify family members.

For more help avoiding shifts, see "Focus on Verbs" on page 66 and "Focus on Consistency" on page 212.

Making Sentences Clear and Effective

Clear and effective sentences convey your meaning concisely and precisely. In editing you want to ensure that readers will understand you easily, follow your ideas without difficulty, and stay interested in what you have to say.

▶ Conciseness

In drafting, we often circle around our ideas, making various attempts to express them. As a result, sentences may use more words than necessary to make their points. To edit for conciseness, focus on the following changes.

■ *Put the main meaning of the sentence in its subject and verb.* Generally, the subject should name the actor, and the verb should describe what the actor did or was. Notice the difference in these two sentences (the subjects and verbs are underlined):

> WORDY   The <u>use</u> of calculators by students <u>is</u> sometimes why they fail to develop math skills.

> CONCISE   <u>Students</u> who use calculators sometimes <u>fail</u> to develop math skills.

■ *Prefer the active voice.* In the active voice, a verb describes the action done *by* the subject (*We grilled vegetables*), whereas in the passive voice, a verb describes the action done *to* the subject (*Vegetables were grilled,* or, adding who did the action, *Vegetables were grilled by us*). The active voice is usually more concise and more direct than the passive:

WORDY PASSIVE   Calculators were withheld from some classrooms by school administrators, and the math performance of students with and without the machines was compared.

CONCISE ACTIVE   School administrators withheld calculators from some classrooms and compared the math performance of students with and without the machines.

■ *Delete unneeded repetition and empty phrases.* Words that don't add meaning will interfere with readers' understanding and interest:

WORDY   The nature of calculators is such that they remove the drudgery from math but can also for all intents and purposes interfere with the development of cognitive mental skills.

CONCISE   Calculators remove the drudgery from math but can also interfere with the development of cognitive skills.

For additional advice on reducing wordiness, see "Focus on Conciseness" on page 304.

▶ Emphasis

You can emphasize important ideas by combining sentences or altering their structure. Following are the most common techniques.

■ *Use subordination to de-emphasize what's less important.* Subordination places minor information in words or word groups that modify the sentence's subject and verb:

UNEMPHATIC   Computers can manipulate film and photographs. We cannot trust these media to represent reality.

EMPHATIC   Because computers can manipulate film and photographs, we cannot trust these media to represent reality.

■ *Use coordination to balance equally important ideas.* Coordination emphasizes the equality of ideas by joining them with a comma and a coordinating conjunction (*and, but, or, nor, for, so,* or *yet*):

UNEMPHATIC   Two people may be complete strangers. A photograph can show them embracing.

EMPHATIC   Two people may be complete strangers, but a photograph can show them embracing.

■ *Use the ends and beginnings of sentences to highlight ideas.* The end of a sentence is its most emphatic position, and the beginning is next most emphatic. Placing the sentence's subject and verb in one of these positions draws readers' attention to them. In these sentences the core idea is underlined:

> UNEMPHATIC   With digital images, <u>filmmakers can entertain us</u>, placing historical figures alongside today's actors.

> EMPHATIC   <u>Filmmakers can entertain us</u> with digital images that place historical figures alongside today's actors.

> MORE EMPHATIC   With digital images that place historical figures alongside today's actors, <u>filmmakers can entertain us</u>.

▶ Parallelism

Parallelism is the use of similar grammatical structures for elements of similar importance, either within or among sentences. The technique can relate ideas to improve coherence:

> PARALLELISM WITHIN A SENTENCE   Smoking can <u>worsen heart disease</u> and <u>cause lung cancer</u>.

> PARALLELISM AMONG SENTENCES   Smoking has less well-known effects, too. <u>It can cause</u> gum disease. <u>It can impair</u> blood circulation. And <u>it can reduce</u> the body's supply of vitamins and minerals.

To make the elements of a sentence parallel, repeat the forms of related words, phrases, and sentences:

> NONPARALLEL   Harris expects dieters to give up <u>bread</u>, <u>dairy</u>, and <u>eating meat</u>.

> PARALLEL   Harris expects dieters to give up bread, dairy, and <u>meat</u>.

> NONPARALLEL   <u>Harris emphasizes</u> denial, but <u>with Marconi's plan</u> you can eat whatever you want in moderation.

> PARALLEL   Harris emphasizes denial, but <u>Marconi emphasizes</u> moderation.

For more examples of editing for parallel structure, see "Focus on Parallelism" on page 243.

▶ Variety

Variety in the structure and length of sentences helps keep readers alert and interested, but it also makes your writing clearer and easier to follow. You can use several techniques to achieve variety:

- *Vary the lengths of sentences.* A very short sentence amid longer sentences can focus readers' attention on a key point.

- *Vary the beginnings of sentences.* Rather than begin every sentence with its subject, for instance, try inserting **transitions** or using subordination to start some sentences with modifiers.

- *Vary the structure of sentences.* Strings of sentences similar in structure march like soldiers down the page and make it difficult for readers to pick out important points. Emphasize important points by making them the subjects and verbs of sentences, and de-emphasize less important elements by turning them into modifying phrases and clauses.

For examples and more strategies, see "Focus on Sentence Variety" on page 123.

Choosing the Best Words

The words you choose can have a dramatic effect on how readers understand your meaning, perceive your attitude, and respond to your thesis.

▶ Denotations and Connotations

The **denotation** of a word is its dictionary meaning, the literal sense without emotional overtones. A **connotation** is an emotional association the word produces in readers. Using incorrect or inappropriate words will confuse or annoy readers.

Using a word with the wrong denotation muddies understanding. Be especially careful to distinguish words with similar sounds but different meanings, such as *to/too/two*, *their/there/they're*, *it's/its*, and *lose/loose*, and words with related but distinct meanings, such as *reward/award* and *famous/infamous*. Spell checkers and autocorrect functions can't catch words that are spelled correctly but used incorrectly. Consult a dictionary whenever you are unsure of a word's spelling or definition.

Using words with strong connotations can shape readers' responses to your ideas, for good or for ill. For example, describing a group's *enthusiasm* for its cause is quite different from describing its *mania*: the latter connotes much more intensity, even irrationality. Words can backfire if they spark inappropriate associations.

▶ Concrete and Specific Language

Clear, exact writing balances **abstract** and **general** words, which provide outlines of ideas and things, with **concrete** and **specific** words, which limit and sharpen. You need abstract and general words for broad statements that set the course for your writing, expressing concepts or referring to entire groups. But you also need concrete and specific words to make your meaning precise and vivid by appealing to readers' senses and experiences:

> VAGUE   The pollution was apparent in the odor and color of the small stream.

> EXACT   The stagnant stream smelled like rotten eggs and ran the greenish color of coffee with nonfat milk.

Concrete and specific language is crucial in any kind of writing. Readers can't be expected to understand or agree with general statements unless they know what evidence the statements are based on. The evidence is in the details, and the details are in concrete and specific words. (See also "Focus on Concrete and Specific Language" on p. 95.)

▶ Figures of Speech

You can make your writing concrete and specific, even lively and forceful, with **figures of speech**, expressions that imply meanings beyond or different from their literal meanings. Here are some of the most common figures.

- A **simile** compares two unlike things with the use of *like* or *as*: *The car spun around like a top. Coins as bright as sunshine lay glinting in the chest.*

- A **metaphor** also compares two unlike things, but more subtly, equating them without *like* or *as*: *The words shattered my fragile self-esteem. The laboratory was her prison, the beakers and test tubes her guards.*

- **Personification** is a simile or metaphor that attributes human qualities or powers to things or abstractions: *The breeze sighed and whispered in the grasses. The city squeezed me tightly at first but then relaxed its grip.*

- **Hyperbole** is a deliberate overstatement or exaggeration: *The dentist filled the tooth with a bracelet's worth of silver. The children's noise shook the rafters.*

By briefly translating experiences and qualities into vividly concrete images, figures of speech can be economical and powerful when used sparingly. Be careful not to combine them into confusing or absurd images, such as *Soccer players danced around the field like bulls ready for a fight.* Be careful, also, not to resort to **clichés**, worn phrases that have lost their power: *ripe old age, thin as a rail, goes on forever.* Be suspicious of any expression you have heard or read before. If you do find a cliché in your writing, cure it by substituting plain language (for instance, *seems endless* for *goes on forever*) or by substituting a fresh figure of speech (*thin as a sapling* for *thin as a rail*).

Using an Editing Checklist

The checklist below summarizes the editing advice given in this chapter and adds a few other technical concerns. Some of the items will be more relevant for your writing than others: you may have little difficulty with variety in sentences, but you may worry that your language is too general. Concentrate your editing efforts where they're needed most, and then survey your draft to check for other problems.

CHECKLIST FOR EDITING

- *Where do sentences need editing for grammar and punctuation* — so that, for instance, sentences are complete; subjects and verbs agree; pronouns are used effectively; modifiers make sense; commas and semicolons are used appropriately; and tense is consistent?

- *Is each sentence as concise as it can be?*

- *How well have you used sentence structure, variety, parallelism, and other techniques to emphasize ideas and hold readers' interest?*

- *Have you used the right words?* Where can you clarify meaning with concrete and specific words or with figures of speech?

- *Where might spelling be a problem?* Look up any word you're not absolutely sure of. (You'll still have to proofread a spell-checked paper; spell checkers don't catch everything.)

Nicole Lang's Editing and Final Draft

The following paragraph comes from the edited draft of Nicole Lang's "Foundations." On the opposite page, Lang's full final draft appears with notes in the margins highlighting its thesis, structure, and uses of the methods of development. If you compare the final version with the first draft on pages 30–31, you'll see clearly how Lang's revising and editing transformed the essay from a rough exploration of ideas to a refined, and convincing, essay.

EDITED PARAGRAPH

~~Those~~ *Students* in more traditional schools need to keep ~~there~~ *their* eye*s* on the real world, too. The ~~average student will graduate~~ *typical college graduate will start out* owing nearly $40,000 in ~~student~~ loans (~~source~~ *Taibbi*). ~~Its~~ *While it is* important to find a career path that feels meaningful and fulfilling/ ~~But~~ it is ~~also necessary~~ *just as important* to earn an income that will outweigh the cost of higher education. ~~This means we~~ *We therefore* need to focus ~~our time and effort~~ on academic programs that will directly benefit our job prospects and ~~put us in a position to~~ *help us* repay our debts. With limited resources, ~~not everyone can~~ *most of us cannot* afford shacks ~~they~~ *into which we* can retreat ~~into. At~~ *—at* least not yet.

FINAL DRAFT

Nicole Lang

Professor Binari

English 100A

19 January 2018

Foundations

    Edward P. Jones, in "Shacks," reflects on his first semester of college. He recalls writing letters to his high school crush and in doing so discovering a sense of purpose, a "shack," that helped him get through a difficult time of adjustment. But when Jones wonders at our ability to find structure when "so much is at stake" (10), I can't help but think about what is at stake for

Brief summary of Jones's essay

Author's name in text and page number in parentheses refer to "Works Cited" at end of paper college students today. Unlike Jones, not everyone has the luxury to indulge in three months of emotional growth, or to look for talents they may not even know they have. For those who struggle just to pay for the opportunity, a college education has to serve the more concrete purpose of preparing for employment.

Introduction establishes point of contention with Jones

Thesis statement

Jones seems to think of college as an extension of high school—a place to grow up, if just a little (11). That may be true for some people. But for many students, adulthood is not something that can be put off. For example, my cousin Robert is twenty-nine years old and has a young child and a job that barely pays the bills. His shack is his son. He takes night classes at a community college so he can qualify for a better position, and he does not have time to dream about "some marvelous future" (10). Instead, he spends his time actively constructing a better life for himself and his family.

Classification: types of college students

Example of adult student

My cousin is not unusual. A growing number of college students are adults over twenty-five. They come from a wide variety of backgrounds and enroll for a number of reasons, but they all understand the demands of a tough job market in a down economy. They also understand that getting a certificate or a degree will give them the skills they need for particular jobs and prove to employers that they can work independently. Such vocational training is important and deserves respect.

Classification: types of college students

Cause-and-effect analysis: why adult students go to college

Students in more traditional schools need to keep their eyes on the real world, too. The typical college graduate will start out owing nearly $40,000 in loans (Taibbi). While it is important to find a career path that feels meaningful and fulfilling, it is just as important to earn an income that will outweigh the cost of higher education. We therefore need to focus on academic programs that will directly benefit our job prospects and help us repay our debts. With limited resources, most of us cannot afford shacks into which we can retreat—at least not yet.

Classification: types of college students

Name in parentheses identifies source of supporting point

Cause-and-effect analysis: why students need to consider future income

Jones makes a good point that a successful life depends on some kind of structure. To be truly sturdy, however, any structure requires a solid foundation. That's what college provides.

Conclusion extends Jones's metaphor and restates Lang's thesis

Although we should certainly hope to discover ourselves and our hidden talents while we're here, for financially burdened students the realities of higher education all come down to time and money. We have to be practical as we build on our dreams.

Works Cited

Jones, Edward P. "Shacks." *The Compact Reader: Short Essays by Method and Theme*, edited by Jane E. Aaron and Ellen Kuhl Repetto, 11th ed., Bedford/St. Martin's, 2019, pp. 9–11.

Taibbi, Matt. "The Great College Loan Swindle." *Rolling Stone*, 3 Nov. 2017, www.rollingstone.com/politics/features/taibbi-the-great-college-loan-swindle-w510880.

"Works Cited" begins on a new page and gives publication information for Lang's sources (see Chapter 16)

PART TWO

SHORT ESSAYS BY METHOD AND THEME

5

NARRATION

▶

FACING FEAR

You narrate every time you tell a story about something that happened. **Narration** helps us make sense of events and share our experiences with others; consequently, it is one of the longest-standing and most essential methods of communicating. You can use narration to entertain friends by retelling an amusing or scary experience, to summarize a salesclerk's actions in a letter complaining about bad customer service, to relate what went wrong in a ball game, or to persuade skeptics by means of several stories that the logging industry is sincere about restoring clear-cut forests. Storytelling is instinctive to the ways we think and speak; it's no surprise, then, that narration should figure into so much of what we read and write.

All the authors in this chapter, for instance, saw reasons to share frightening moments from their lives, and for that purpose narration is the obvious choice. Sherman Alexie, in a paragraph, remembers the emotional hurt of being bullied. Michael Ondaatje, in another paragraph, recalls his stepmother's inability to kill a cobra, perhaps because it embodied his dead father. In essays, Langston Hughes pinpoints the moment during a church revival when he lost his faith, while Jennifer Finney Boylan recounts a period of despair and self-loathing. And Lauren Fulmore's narrative explores the ways children's stories spurred her to risk adventure.

Reading Narration

Narration relates a sequence of events that are linked in time. By arranging events in an orderly progression, a narrative illuminates the stages leading to a result. Sometimes the emphasis is on the story itself, as in fiction, biography, autobiography, some history, and much journalism. But often a narrative serves some larger point, as when a paragraph or a brief story about an innocent person's death helps to strengthen an argument for stricter punishments for drunk drivers. When used as a primary means of developing an essay, such pointed narration usually relates a sequence of events that led to new knowledge or had a notable outcome. The point of the narrative—the idea the reader is to take away—then determines the selection of events, the amount of detail devoted to them, and their arrangement.

Though narration arranges events in time, narrative time is not real time. An important event may fill whole pages, even though it took only minutes to unfold; a less important event may be dispensed within a sentence, even though it lasted for hours. Suppose, for instance, that a writer wants to narrate the experience of being mugged to show how courage came unexpectedly to his aid. He might provide a slow-motion account of the few minutes' encounter with the muggers, including vivid details of the setting and of the attackers' appearance, a moment-by-moment replay of his emotions, and exact dialogue. At the same time, he might compress events that merely fill in background or link main events, such as how he got to the scene of the mugging or the follow-up questioning by a police detective. And he might entirely omit many events, such as a conversation overheard at the police station, that have no significance for his point.

The point of a narrative influences not only which events are covered and how fully but also how the events are arranged. There are several possibilities:

- A straight **chronological order** *is most common* because it relates events in the sequence of their actual occurrence. It is particularly useful for short narratives, for those in which the last event is the most dramatic, and for those in which the events preceding and following the climax contribute to the point being made.

- *The final event, such as a self-revelation, may come first*, followed by an explanation of the events leading up to it.

- *The entire story may be summarized first* and then examined in detail.

- **Flashbacks**—*shifts backward rather than forward in time*—*may recall events* whose significance would not have been apparent earlier. Flashbacks are common in movies and fiction: a character in the midst of one scene mentally replays another.

In addition to providing a clear organization, writers also strive to adopt a consistent **point of view**, a position relative to the events, conveyed in two main ways:

- *Pronouns* indicate the storyteller's place in the story: the first-person *I* if the narrator is a direct participant; the third-person *he, she, it,* or *they* if the writer is observing or reporting.
- *Verb tense* indicates the narrator's relation in time to the sequence of events: present (*is, run*) or past (*was, ran*).

Combining the first-person pronoun with the present tense can create great immediacy ("I feel the point of the knife in my back"). At the other extreme, combining third-person pronouns with the past tense creates more distance ("He felt the point of the knife in his back"). In between these extremes are combinations of first person with past tense ("I felt . . .") or third person with present tense ("He feels . . ."). The choice depends on how involved the writer is in the events and on his or her purpose.

Analyzing Narration in Paragraphs

Sherman Alexie (born 1966) is a celebrated poet, fiction writer, and filmmaker who, as a member of the Spokane/Coeur d'Alene tribe, explores American Indian issues and experiences, especially as they apply to reservation life. The following story comes from *You Don't Have to Say You Love Me* (2017), Alexie's memoir of his mother's life and death.

In my memory, the Arlee powwow grounds were bordered on one side by a creek. . . . I ran with those Indian kids to that creek, which was maybe two feet deep and flowing fast. The creek was perhaps five feet wide. And I remember running back and forth across a pedestrian bridge. A bridge across a creek? If my memory is true, then that creek must have been a popular destination. I remember those other Indian kids kicking off their sneakers and socks and splashing into the creek. It was only two feet deep. But I didn't know how to swim. And so I was afraid. But then, bravely and irrationally, I pulled off my new

Past tense

Transitions (underlined)

Chronological order

Point of view: direct participant

moccasins, set them on that little bridge, and stepped into the water. . . . And then I heard a commotion behind me. A different kind of laughter. And I turned around to see an older Indian kid pick up my new moccasins from the bridge and drop them into the creek.

Purpose: to express the pain of being bullied

Michael Ondaatje (born 1943) is a poet, fiction writer, essayist, and filmmaker. The following paragraph is from *Running in the Family* (1982), Ondaatje's memoir of his childhood in Ceylon, now called Sri Lanka, off the southern tip of India.

After my father died, a grey cobra came into the house. My stepmother loaded the gun and fired at point blank range. The gun jammed. She stepped back and reloaded but by then the snake had slid out into the garden. For the next month this snake would often come into the house and each time the gun would misfire or jam, or my stepmother would miss at absurdly short range. The snake attacked no one and had a tendency to follow my younger sister Susan around. Other snakes entering the house were killed by the shotgun, lifted with a long stick and flicked into the bushes, but the old grey cobra led a charmed life. Finally one of the old workers at Rock Hill told my stepmother what had become obvious, that it was my father who had come to protect his family. And in fact, whether it was because the chicken farm closed down or because of my father's presence in the form of a snake, very few other snakes came into the house again.

Chronological order

Past tense

Transitions (underlined)

Point of view: participant observer

Purpose: to relate a colorful, mysterious story

Developing a Narrative Essay

▶ Getting Started

You'll find narration useful whenever relating a sequence of events can help you make a point, sometimes to support the thesis of a larger paper, sometimes *as* the thesis of a paper. If you're assigned a narrative essay, probe your own experiences for a significant or interesting situation, such as an encounter involving strong emotion, a humorous or embarrassing incident, a dramatic scene you witnessed, or a learning experience. If you have the opportunity to do research, you might choose a topic dealing with the natural world (such as the Big Bang theory for the origin of the universe) or an event in history or politics (such as how a local activist worked to close down an animal research lab).

Explore your subject by listing all the events in sequence as they happened. You may find the traditional journalist's questions helpful:

- *Who* was involved?
- *What* happened?
- *When* did it happen?
- *Where* did it happen?
- *Why* did it happen?
- *How* did it happen?

These questions will lead you to examine your subject from all angles. Then you need to decide which events should be developed in great detail because they are central to your story, which merit compression because they merely contribute background or tie the main events together, and which should be omitted altogether because they are irrelevant to the story or might clutter your narrative.

While you are weighing the relative importance of events, consider also what your readers need to know in order to understand and appreciate your narrative:

- *What information will help locate readers in the narrative?*
- *How will you expand and compress events to keep readers' attention?*
- *What details about people, places, and feelings will make events vivid?*
- *What is your attitude toward the subject*—lighthearted, sarcastic, bitter, serious?—and how will you convey it in your choice of details?
- *What should your point of view be?* Do you want to involve readers intimately by using the first person and the present tense? Or does that seem overdramatic, less appropriate than the more detached, objective view that would be conveyed by the third person or the past tense or both?

▶ Forming a Thesis

Whatever your subject, you should have some point to make about it:
Why was the incident or experience significant? What does it teach or
illustrate? If you can, phrase this point in a sentence before you start to
draft. For instance:

> I used to think small-town life was boring, but one taste of the city made
> me appreciate the leisurely pace of home.

> A recent small earthquake demonstrated the hazards of inadequate civil
> defense measures.

Sometimes you may need to draft your story before the point of it becomes
clear to you, especially if the experience had a personal impact or if the
event was so recent that writing a rough draft will allow you to gain some
perspective.

Whether to state your main point outright in your essay, as a thesis
sentence, depends on the effect you want to have on readers. You might
use your introduction to lead to a statement of your thesis so that readers
will know from the start why you are telling them your story. Then again, to
intensify the drama of your story, you might decide to withhold your
thesis sentence for the conclusion or omit it altogether. Remember,
though, that the thesis must be evident to readers even if you don't state
it explicitly: the narrative needs a point.

▶ Organizing

Narrative essays often begin without formal **introductions**, instead drawing the reader in with one of the more dramatic events in the sequence.
But you may find an introduction useful to set the scene for your narrative, to summarize the events leading up to it, to establish the context for
it, or to lead in to a thesis statement if you want readers to know the point
of your story before they start reading it.

The arrangement of events in the **body** of your essay depends on both
the order in which they occurred and the point you want to make. To narrate a trip during which one thing after another went wrong, you might
find a strict chronological order most effective. To narrate your experience
of city life, you might interweave events in the city with contrasting flashbacks to your life in a small town, or you might start by relating one especially memorable experience in the city, drop back to explain how you
ended up in that situation, and then go on to tell what happened afterward. To narrate an earthquake that began and ended in an instant, you

might sort simultaneous events into groups—perhaps what happened to buildings and what happened to people—or you might arrange a few people's experiences in order of increasing drama. Narrative time can be manipulated in any number of ways, but your scheme should have a purpose that your readers can see, and you should stick to it.

Let the ending of your essay be determined by the effect you want to leave with readers. You can end with the last event in your sequence, or the one you have saved for last, if it conveys your point and provides a strong finish. Or you can summarize the aftermath of the story if it contributes to the point. You can also end with a formal **conclusion** that states your point—your thesis—explicitly. Such a conclusion is especially useful if your point unfolds gradually throughout the narrative and you want to emphasize it at the finish.

▶ Drafting

Drafting a narrative can be less of a struggle than drafting other kinds of papers, especially if you're close to the events and you use a straight chronological order. But the relative ease of storytelling can be misleading if it causes you to describe events too quickly or to write without making a point. While drafting, be as specific as possible. Tell what the people in your narrative were wearing, what expressions their faces held, how they gestured, what they said. Specify the time of day, and describe the weather and the surroundings (buildings, vegetation, and the like). All these details may be familiar to you, but they won't be to your readers.

At the same time, try to remain open to what the story means to you, so that you can convey that meaning in your selection and description of events. If you know before you begin what your thesis is, let it guide you. But the first draft may turn out to be a search for your thesis, so that you'll need another draft to make it evident in the way you relate events.

You may want to experiment with **dialogue**—quotations of what participants said, in their words. Dialogue can add immediacy and realism as long as it advances the narrative and doesn't ramble beyond its usefulness. In reconstructing dialogue from memory, try to recall not only the actual words but also the sounds of speakers' voices and the expressions on their faces—information that will help you represent each speaker distinctly. And keep the dialogue natural sounding by using constructions typical of speech. For instance, most speakers prefer contractions such as *don't* and *shouldn't* to the longer forms *do not* and *should not*; and few speakers begin sentences with *although*, as in the overly formal "Although we could hear our mother's voice, we refused to answer."

Whether you are relating events in strict chronological order or manipulating them for some effect, try to make their sequence in real time and the distance between them clear to readers. Instead of signaling sequence with the monotonous *and then . . . and then . . . and then* or *next . . . next . . . next*, use informative **transitions** that signal the order of events (*afterward, earlier*), the duration of events (*for an hour, in that time*), or the amount of time between events (*the next morning, a week later*).

▶ Revising and Editing

When your draft is complete, revise and edit it by answering the following questions and considering the information in the Focus box below.

FOCUS ON VERBS

Narration depends heavily on verbs to clarify and enliven events. Weak verbs, such as forms of *make* and *be*, can sap the life from a story. Strong verbs sharpen meaning and engage readers:

WEAK   The wind made an awful noise.

STRONG   The wind roared around the house and rattled the trees.

WEAK   The pounding rain was alarming to us.

STRONG   The pounding rain alarmed us.

Verbs in the active voice (the subject does the action) usually pack more power than verbs in the passive voice (the subject is acted upon):

WEAK PASSIVE   Shelter was sought in the basement.

STRONG ACTIVE   We sought shelter in the basement.

While strengthening your verbs, also ensure that they're consistent in tense. The tense you choose, present or past, should not shift:

INCONSISTENT   As the water slowly rose, we held a conference to consider our options. It takes only a minute to decide to evacuate.

CONSISTENT   As the water slowly rose, we held a conference to consider our options. It took only a minute to decide to evacuate.

See pages 48–49 for a discussion of passive versus active voice and pages 47–48 for advice on avoiding shifts.

- *Is the point of your narrative clear, and does every event you relate contribute to it?* Whether or not you state your thesis, it should be obvious to readers. They should be able to see why you have lingered over some events and compressed others, and they should not be distracted by insignificant events and details.

- *Is your organization clear?* Be sure that your readers will understand any shifts backward or forward in time.

- *Have you used transitions to help readers follow the sequence of events?* Transitions such as *meanwhile* or *soon afterward* serve a dual purpose: they keep the reader on track, and they link sentences and paragraphs so that they flow smoothly.

- *If you have used dialogue, is it purposeful and natural?* Be sure all quoted speech moves the action forward. And read all dialogue aloud to check that it sounds like something someone would actually say.

LearningCurve To practice editing for weak and passive verbs, visit
LaunchPad Solo for Readers and Writers > LearningCurve >
Active and Passive Voice

Nothing is more restful than conformity.   —Elizabeth Bowen

We all try to be alike in our youth.   —Ethel Alec-Tweedie

This above all: to thine own self be true, / And it must follow, as the night the day, / Thou canst not then be false to any man.   —William Shakespeare

JOURNAL RESPONSE   When have you experienced a powerful desire to think, look, or act like others, especially your peers? Write a journal entry about your experience.

Langston Hughes

A poet, fiction writer, playwright, critic, and humorist, Langston Hughes described his writing as "largely concerned with depicting Negro life in America." He was born in 1902 in Joplin, Missouri, and grew up in Illinois, Kansas, and Ohio. After dropping out of Columbia University in the early 1920s, Hughes worked at odd jobs while struggling to gain recognition as a writer. His first book of poems, *The Weary Blues* (1925), helped seed the Harlem Renaissance, a flowering of African American music and literature centered in the Harlem district of New York City during the 1920s. The book also generated a scholarship that enabled Hughes to finish college at Lincoln University. In all of his work — including *The Negro Mother* (1931), *The Ways of White Folks* (1934), *Shakespeare in Harlem* (1942), *Montage of a Dream Deferred* (1951), and *Ask Your Mama* (1961) — Hughes captured and projected the rhythms of jazz and the distinctive speech, subtle humor, and deep traditions of African American people. He died in New York City in 1967.

Salvation

A chapter in Hughes's autobiography, *The Big Sea* (1940), "Salvation" is a simple yet compelling narrative about a frightful moment of deceit and disillusionment. As you read Hughes's account, notice how the opening two sentences set up every twist of the story.

I was saved from sin when I was going on thirteen. But not really saved. 1
It happened like this. There was a big revival at my Auntie Reed's church. Every night for weeks there had been much preaching, singing, praying, and shouting, and some very hardened sinners had been brought to

Christ, and the membership of the church had grown by leaps and bounds. Then just before the revival ended, they held a special meeting for children, "to bring the young lambs to the fold." My aunt spoke of it for days ahead. That night, I was escorted to the front row and placed on the mourner's bench with all the other young sinners, who had not yet been brought to Jesus.

My aunt told me that when you were saved you saw a light, and 2 something happened to you inside! And Jesus came into your life! And God was with you from then on! She said you could see and hear and feel Jesus in your soul. I believed her. I have heard a great many old people say the same thing and it seemed to me they ought to know. So I sat there calmly in the hot, crowded church, waiting for Jesus to come to me.

The preacher preached a wonderful rhythmical sermon, all moans 3 and shouts and lonely cries and dire pictures of hell, and then he sang a song about the ninety and nine safe in the fold, but one little lamb was left out in the cold. Then he said: "Won't you come? Won't you come to Jesus? Young lambs, won't you come?" And he held out his arms to all us young sinners there on the mourner's bench. And the little girls cried. And some of them jumped up and went to Jesus right away. But most of us just sat there.

A great many old people came and knelt around us and prayed, old 4 women with jet-black faces and braided hair, old men with work-gnarled hands. And the church sang a song about the lower lights are burning, some poor sinners to be saved. And the whole building rocked with prayer and song.

Still I kept waiting to *see* Jesus. 5

Finally all the young people had gone to the altar and were saved, but 6 one boy and me. He was a rounder's son named Westley. Westley and I were surrounded by sisters and deacons praying. It was very hot in the church, and getting late now. Finally Westley said to me in a whisper: "God damn! I'm tired o' sitting here. Let's get up and be saved." So he got up and was saved.

Then I was left all alone on the mourner's bench. My aunt came and 7 knelt at my knees and cried, while prayers and songs swirled all around me in the little church. The whole congregation prayed for me alone, in a mighty wail of moans and voices. And I kept waiting serenely for Jesus, waiting, waiting—but he didn't come. I wanted to see him, but nothing happened to me. Nothing! I wanted something to happen to me, but nothing happened.

I heard the songs and the minister saying: "Why don't you come? My   8
dear child, why don't you come to Jesus? Jesus is waiting for you. He wants
you. Why don't you come? Sister Reed, what is this child's name?"

"Langston," my aunt sobbed.   9

"Langston, why don't you come? Why don't you come and be saved?   10
Oh, Lamb of God! Why don't you come?"

Now it was really getting late. I began to be ashamed of myself,   11
holding everything up so long. I began to wonder what God thought
about Westley, who certainly hadn't seen Jesus either, but who was now
sitting proudly on the platform, swinging his knickerbockered legs and
grinning down at me, surrounded by deacons and old women on their
knees praying. God had not struck Westley dead for taking his name in
vain or for lying in the temple. So I decided that maybe to save further
trouble, I'd better lie, too, and say that Jesus had come, and get up and
be saved.

So I got up.   12

Suddenly the whole room broke into a sea of shouting, as they saw   13
me rise. Waves of rejoicing swept the place. Women leaped in the air. My
aunt threw her arms around me. The minister took me by the hand and
led me to the platform.

When things quieted down, in a hushed silence, punctuated by a few   14
ecstatic "Amens," all the new young lambs were blessed in the name of
God. Then joyous singing filled the room.

That night, for the last time in my life but one—for I was a big boy   15
twelve years old—I cried. I cried, in bed alone, and couldn't stop. I buried
my head under the quilts, but my aunt heard me. She woke up and told
my uncle I was crying because the Holy Ghost had come into my life, and
because I had seen Jesus. But I was really crying because I couldn't bear to
tell her that I had lied, that I had deceived everybody in the church, that
I hadn't seen Jesus, and that now I didn't believe there was a Jesus anymore, since he didn't come to help me.

Meaning

1. What is the main point of Hughes's narrative? What change occurs in
   him as a result of his experience?

2. What finally makes Hughes decide to get up and be saved? How does this
   decision affect him afterward?

3. What do you make of the connection between the title and the first two
   sentences? What is Hughes saying here about "salvation"?

4. If you are uncertain of the meanings of any of the words listed below, try to guess them from the context of the essay. Then look them up to see how close your definitions were to those in the dictionary. Test out the new words by using each of them in a sentence or two of your own.

dire (3)   rounder (6)   deacons (6)

Purpose and Audience

1. Why do you think Hughes wrote "Salvation" as part of his autobiography more than two decades after the experience? Was his purpose simply to express feelings prompted by a significant event in his life? Did he want to criticize his aunt and the other adults in the congregation? Did he want to explain something about childhood or about the distance between generations? What passages support your answer?

2. What does Hughes seem to assume about his readers' familiarity with the kind of service he describes? What details help make the procedure clear?

3. How do dialogue, lines from hymns, and details of other sounds (paragraphs 3–10) help re-create the increasing pressure Hughes feels? What other details contribute to this sense of pressure?

Method and Structure

1. Why do you think Hughes chose narration to explore the themes of this essay? Can you imagine an **argument** essay that would deal with the same themes? What might its title be?

2. Where in his narrative does Hughes insert explanations, compress time by summarizing events, or jump ahead in time by omitting events? Where does he expand time by drawing moments out? How do each of these insertions and manipulations of time relate to Hughes's main point?

3. In paragraph 1 Hughes uses several transitions to signal the sequence of events and the passage of time: "for weeks," "Then just before," "for days ahead," "That night." Where does he use similar signals in the rest of the essay?

4. OTHER METHODS   Hughes's narrative also explains a process: we learn how a revival meeting works. Why is this **process analysis** essential to the essay?

Language

1. What does Hughes's language reveal about his adult attitudes toward his experience? Does he feel anger? bitterness? sorrow? guilt? shame? amusement? What words and passages support your answer?

2. Hughes relates his experience in an almost childlike **style**, using many short sentences and beginning many sentences with *And*. What effect do you think he is trying to achieve with this style?

3. Hughes expects to "see" Jesus when he is saved (paragraphs 2, 5, 7), and afterward his aunt thinks that he has "seen" Jesus (15). What does each of them mean by *see*? What is the significance of the difference in Hughes's story?

Writing Topics

1. JOURNAL TO ESSAY   Continuing from your journal response (p. 68), write a narrative essay about a time when others significantly influenced the way you thought, looked, or acted—perhaps against your own true beliefs or values. What was the appeal of the others' attitudes, appearance, or behavior? What did you gain by conforming? What did you lose? Use specific details to explain how and why the experience affected you.

2. Hughes says, "I have heard a great many old people say the same thing and it seemed to me they ought to know" (paragraph 2). Think of a piece of information or advice that you heard over and over again from adults when you were a child. Write a narrative essay about an experience in which you were helped or misled by that information or advice.

3. CULTURAL CONSIDERATIONS   It seems that Hughes wants to be saved largely because of the influence of his family and his community. Westley (paragraphs 6 and 11) represents another kind of influence, peer pressure, that often works against family and community. Think of an incident in your own life when you felt pressured by peers to go against your parents, religion, school, or another authority. Write a narrative essay telling what happened and making it clear why the situation was important to you. What were the results?

4. CONNECTIONS   When Hughes doesn't see Jesus and then lies to satisfy everyone around him, he feels betrayed and pained. How does Hughes's experience differ from the one cheerfully reported by Michael Ondaatje (p. 62), in which a potentially deadly snake is said to be Ondaatje's deceased father, "who had come to protect his family"? Write an essay analyzing what elements these narratives have in common and any significant differences between them.

The only thing we have to fear is fear itself.　　—Franklin Delano Roosevelt

There is a crack in everything; that's how the light gets in.　　—Leonard Cohen

The bravest thing I ever did was continuing my life when I wanted to die.

—Juliette Lewis

JOURNAL RESPONSE　Have you ever had a moment when you feared there was no hope for the future? What brought on the crisis? Why did you despair? How did things turn out? In a short journal entry, reflect on a difficult time that had a lasting influence on the course of your life.

Jennifer Finney Boylan

Jennifer Finney Boylan is a prolific writer whose work is filled with wry observations about the human condition. Born James Boylan in Valley Forge, Pennsylvania, in 1958, her youth was marked by confusion — as a boy and a young man Boylan felt the tug of female identity, yet married Deirdre "Grace" Finney in 1988 and settled down to a more or less conventional life. Though she has written more than a dozen novels, collections of short stories, memoirs, and (under a pseudonym) books for young adults, Boylan is perhaps best known for *She's Not There* (2003), a poignant and personal examination of transgender issues, her decision to undergo sex-change surgery in her early forties, and the response of those around her (especially Finney, to whom she remains happily married with two children). Boylan is also an op-ed columnist for the *New York Times*, has served as a consultant for the documentary series *I Am Cait* and the Amazon series *Transparent*, and is a civil rights advocate who appears regularly on television and radio. A graduate of Wesleyan University, she has taught creative writing and American literature at Johns Hopkins University, University College Cork in Ireland, Ursinus College, Colby College, and Barnard College of Columbia University, where she is a writer in residence. She lives in New York City and in Belgrade Lakes, Maine.

In the Early Morning Rain

A spate of suicides by lesbian, gay, bisexual, and transgendered teenagers in the first decade of the twenty-first century inspired a group of openly gay adults to launch the *It Gets Better* project, a collection of *YouTube* videos, personal essays, and social media advocacy meant to assure LGBTQ youth that the bullying and self-loathing they might endure through high school and college will not torment them forever. "In the Early Morning Rain," a passage originally from *She's Not There* and revised in 2012, is Boylan's contribution to the project.

When I was young there was a time when I figured, the hell with it. I'd never even said the word *transgender* out loud. I couldn't imagine saying it, ever. I mean, please.

So instead, one day a few years after I got out of college, I loaded all my things into the Volkswagen and started driving. I wasn't sure where I was going, but I knew I wanted to get away from the Maryland spring, with its cherry blossoms and its bursting tulips and all its bullshit. I figured I'd keep driving farther and farther north until there weren't any people. I wasn't sure what I was going to do then, but I was certain something would occur to me that would end this transgender business once and for all.

I set my sights on Nova Scotia. I drove to Maine and took a ferry out of Bar Harbor. I drove onto the *SS Bluenose* and stood on the deck and watched America drift away behind me, which as far as I was concerned was just fine.

There was someone walking around in a rabbit costume on the ship. He'd pose with you and they'd snap your picture and an hour or so later you could purchase the photo of yourself with the rabbit as a memento of your trip to Nova Scotia. I purchased mine. It showed a sad-looking boy — *I think that's a boy* — with long hair reading a book of poetry as a moth-eaten rabbit bends over him.

In Nova Scotia I drove the car east and north for a few days. When dusk came, I'd eat in a diner, and then I'd sleep either in the car or in a small tent that I had in the back. There were scattered patches of snow up there, even in May. I kept going north until I got to Cape Breton, which is about as far away as you can get from Baltimore and still be on dry land.

In Cape Breton I hiked around the cliffs, looked at the ocean. At night I lay in my sleeping bag by the sea as breezes shook the tent. I wrote in my journal, or read the poetry of Robert Frost, or grazed around in the Modern Library's *Great Tales of Terror and the Supernatural*. I read one up there called "Oh, Whistle, and I'll Come to You, My Lad."[1]

In the car I listened to the Warlocks sing "In the Early Morning Rain"[2] on the tape deck. I thought about this girl I knew, Grace Finney. I thought about my parents. I thought about the clear, inescapable fact that I was

---

[1] A short story by English writer M. R. James (1862–1936). In the tale, a lonely professor on a seaside vacation inadvertently summons a ghost that manifests itself as a strong wind. [Editors' note.]

[2] The Warlocks were an early incarnation of the Grateful Dead. The song, written by Gordon Lightfoot, is about a traveler who misses a loved one but lacks the means to make the trip home. [Editors' note.]

female in spirit and how, in order to be whole, I would have to give up on every dream I'd had, save one.

I stayed in a motel one night that was officially closed for the season, 8 but which the operator let me stay in for half price. I opened my suitcase and put on my bra and some jeans and a blue knit top. I combed my hair out and looked in the mirror and saw a perfectly normal-looking young woman. *This is so wrong?* I said to myself in the mirror. *This is the cause of all the trouble?*

I thought about settling in one of the little villages around here, just 9 starting life over as a woman. I'd tell everyone I was Canadian.

Then I lay on my back and sobbed. Nobody would ever believe I was 10 Canadian.

Cape Breton Island, Nova Scotia.

Cindy Creighton/Shutterstock.com

The next morning I climbed a mountain at the far northern edge of 11 Cape Breton Island. I climbed up to the top, trying to clear my head, but it wouldn't clear. I kept going up and up, past the tree line, past the shrub line, until at last there was just moss.

There I stood, looking out at the cold ocean, a thousand miles below 12 me, totally cut off from the world.

A fierce wind blew in from the Atlantic. I leaned into it. I saw the 13 waves crashing against the cliff below. I stood right at the edge. My heart pounded.

I leaned over the edge of the precipice, but the gale blowing into my   14
body kept me from falling. When the wind died down, I'd start to fall,
then it would blow me back up again. I played a little game with the
wind, leaning a little farther over the edge each time.

Then I leaned off the edge of the cliff at a sharp angle, my arms held   15
outward like wings, my body sustained only by the fierce wind, and I
thought, *Well all right. Is this what you came here to do?*

Let's do it then.   16

Then a huge blast of wind blew me backward and I landed on the   17
moss. It was soft. I stared straight up at the blue sky, and I felt a
presence.

Are you all right, son? said the voice. *You're going to be all right. You're*   18
going to be all right.

Looking back now, I am still not sure whose voice that was. My guard-   19
ian angel? The ghost of my father? I don't know. Does it really change things
all that much, to give a name to the spirits that are watching out for us?

Still, from this vantage point—over twenty-five years later—my heart   20
tells me that was the voice of my future self, the woman that I eventually
became, a woman who, all these years later, looks more or less like the one
I saw in the mirror in the motel. Looking back on the sad, desperate young
man I was, I am trying to tell him something. *It will get better. It will not*
always hurt the way it hurts now. The thing that right now you feel is your great-
est curse will someday, against all odds, turn out to be your greatest gift.

It's hard to be gay, or lesbian. To be trans can be even harder. There   21
have been plenty of times when I've lost hope.

But in the years since I heard that voice—*Are you all right, son? You're*   22
going to be all right—I've found, to my surprise, that most people have
treated me with love. Some of the people I most expected to lose, when
I came out as trans, turned out to be loving, and compassionate, and kind.

I can't tell you how to get here from there. You have to figure that out   23
for yourself. But I do know that instead of going off that cliff, I walked
back down the mountain that morning and instead began the long, long
journey toward home.

Meaning

1. What main idea does Boylan hope readers will take from this very
   personal story?

2. What does the author mean by "in order to be whole, I would have to
   give up on every dream I'd had, save one" (paragraph 7)? What one
   dream could the young Boylan keep? Why would keeping it require
   giving up everything else?

3. If you are uncertain of the meanings of any of the words listed below, try to guess them from the context of the essay. Then look them up to see how close your definitions were to those in the dictionary. Test out the new words by using each of them in a sentence or two of your own.

memento (4)	tree line (11)	sustained (15)
grazed (6)	precipice (14)	

Purpose and Audience

1. Notice the shift in point of view from *I* throughout the essay to *you* in the last paragraph. What does this switch reveal about Boylan's imagined audience and her reasons for writing?

2. How do you think Boylan expects her audience to react to her story? Does she seem to assume readers will find her experience and feelings strange, or does she assume some other response? What in the essay makes you think as you do?

Method and Structure

1. Boylan offers more concrete and vivid details in paragraphs 11–17 than she does elsewhere. What is she describing here, and why does she focus on this particular episode? What function does this passage serve in the narrative?

2. What effect does the author's use of internal dialogue (in *italics*) have on her narrative?

3. OTHER METHODS Besides narration, Boylan also uses **definition** to explore the meaning of *transgender*. How does she define the term as it applies to her? What do *you* understand it to mean?

Language

1. Comment on the **irony** in paragraphs 9 and 10. How does Boylan use humor to lighten the mood of her story?

2. To what extent are the statements in paragraphs 18 and 19 to be taken literally? Does Boylan really believe that a spiritual presence spoke out loud? How can you tell?

Writing Topics

1. JOURNAL TO ESSAY Building on your journal response (p. 73), write a narrative based on some transformative experience of your own, still vivid in your memory. Use the first-person *I*, strong verbs, and plenty of descriptive detail to render vividly the crisis you felt and its effects on you.

2. In an essay, explain what *man* or *woman* means to you. Does your definition correspond to traditional assumptions about gender or is it more fluid, like Boylan's? What characteristics does your definition *not* include?

3. RESEARCH   Locate Gordon Lightfoot's lyrics to the song "Early Morning Rain" and a copy of M. R. James's story "Oh, Whistle, and I'll Come to You, My Lad." Read both closely, then write an analysis that explores the parallels between them and Boylan's narrative. Why do you suppose Boylan references these obscure works in her story? How does knowing their content affect your understanding of her experience?

4. CONNECTIONS   Like Boylan, Lauren Fulmore, in "Chasing Fairy Tales" (next page), also writes about running away and being rescued after hearing voices in the wind. In an essay of your own, compare these two writers' conceptions of the supernatural. How do they distinguish between what's real and what's imaginary? How are both influenced by fantasy and gothic literature? How are those influences reflected in the ways they tell their tales?

I didn't think much about the future when I was a child . . . but to the extent that I did imagine a future, it held an ever-widening range for my explorations—more hills and valleys, shorelines and dunes.

—Barbara Ehrenreich

You can't put a limit on anything. The more you dream, the farther you get.

—Michael Phelps

Adults are always asking children what they want to be when they grow up because they're looking for ideas.

—Paula Poundstone

JOURNAL RESPONSE When you were a child, adults probably asked you, "What do you want to be when you grow up?" What did you reply? Write a journal entry in which you recall your childhood fantasies.

Lauren Fulmore

Lauren Fulmore was born in 1993 and grew up in woodsy Hampstead, New Hampshire, an hour or so north of Boston. As a student at the University of New Hampshire, she studied nursing, played club lacrosse, and volunteered with people with developmental disabilities—while also supporting herself with a full-time job. Fulmore graduated in 2017 and is now a registered nurse at a university hospital in Nashville, Tennessee.

Chasing Fairy Tales
(Student Essay)

Fulmore wrote "Chasing Fairy Tales" for her required first-year writing course, in response to a prompt asking for a story about a "moment of realization" in her life. The essay was subsequently selected for *Transitions*, the University of New Hampshire's annual collection of exceptional student writing. In an imaginative personal narrative, Fulmore recounts a series of misadventures leading to injury to re-create the accidental discovery of a "magical" truth.

I grew up in a fairly stereotypical suburban household. My father was a   1
contractor and my mother a registered nurse. As the offspring of two working parents, my elder sister and I were called upon to do the chores that my full-time employed parents' busy schedules did not allow for. It was no more responsibility than that of any other child my age: I was responsible for my own laundry, cleaning the dishes, and other fairly

common tasks. However, to my overactive imagination and inclination toward drama, I felt as though I were a slave to my household. Often while "nursing bleeding hands" over the dishes or "laboring" over laundry I would picture myself as a character such as Cinderella, forced by her evil family to do all of the chores while they relaxed in leisure. In my fantasies I was always the victim of some type of switched-at-birth scenario in which my current "family" was holding me back from my true potential. It was this train of thinking that led to the phase in my life that my mother likes to call "the sneaky sevens."

It began one day after a particularly heavy load of chores. I had set-   2
tled into my favorite comfy laundry basket to do some daydreaming. Somewhere between fantasizing about my mystery parents and thinking about dinner, my seven-year-old logic realized that there was no reason for me to stay where I was. I was getting nothing done by feeling sorry for myself. If I was truly to fulfill my role as the heroine in the stories I had read, then sitting around doing laundry was not going to bring me any closer to my destiny. No, the time had come. I had talked myself into rebellion. So I devised my first escape.

The first step was preparation. With a handkerchief tied around an   3
old stick, I crafted my first bindle, just like I had seen in the old movies. I wrapped up a chunk of bread, a few slices of cheese, and an apple — just the essentials. I was sure this would last me the weeks I needed it to until I stumbled upon my real family. *Dear former family*, I began my attempt at a cordial last goodbye. I remember the combination of my chicken-scratch writing and the Hello Kitty notebook looking so juvenile. *I have left to find my true family. They will not make me do chores and I will be famous. Do not look for me, I'm not coming back*. Satisfied with my handiwork, I smudged my Lip Smacker glossed lips together and planted a child's attempt at a grown-up's kiss on the bottom of the note. It was perfect, like something out of *Gone with the Wind*. I then donned my hiking boots, embodying my inner Scarlett O'Hara, and crept out the back door into the woods, leaving my past life behind.

I spent the first few hours of my high-stakes runaway tramping   4
through the woods behind my house, vigorously putting distance between myself and the home of my enslavers. I knew it was only a matter of time before they would be after me. *As soon as the laundry is piled high and there are no more clean dishes, that's when they'll notice I'm gone*, I told myself bitterly. With a renewed sense of determination I continued my journey.

Sweat began to trickle down my spine as I stopped for a break on a   5
fallen tree, momentarily consumed by the image of the loving embrace

my beautiful mother would wrap me in upon my arrival. I smiled to myself, thinking of the magnificent ball my father would hold in honor of my glorious return home. My daydreaming continued as I trekked through the undergrowth, and the bright ambiance of the forest began to fade into another hazy, orange, summer afternoon. It wasn't long after when my subconscious awoke me from my thoughts. I took a second glance to my left and wondered aloud to myself, *Was that the same tree I had rested on not long ago?* I reevaluated my surroundings. I had been traveling in circles. Exasperated, I contemplated heading back to my captors; that's when I heard the voices.

They were quiet at first—hardly audible. They sounded more like the   6 high-pitched whine that wind tends to make when making its way through a crowded forest. However, I could swear the wind was calling my name. *This is it! My real family has finally found me!* I rushed toward the voices like a magnet to metal, heart beating out of my chest. Envisioning my mother's rosy pink cheeks and flowing blonde hair, I could practically already smell her sweet perfume as she wrapped me in a loving embrace. The voices were clearer now; I could see my regal father beaming at the sight of his long-lost daughter. "Lauren! Lauren!" the voices cried. "Where are you, Lauren!?"

"I'm here!" I cried. "I'm here!" Soon I would be united with my true   7 family.

I rushed into the clearing, bewildered with excitement and joy. I took   8 a look at the faces surrounding me; tired and exasperated faces gazed back at me. I stumbled back. Rubbing my eyes, I tried to make the faces reappear as the faces I desired. However, when I reopened my eyes I only found the concerned faces of my *former* family. *This can't be,* I thought to myself. *I can't go back to my old life. Not after I finally made it out.* Against my wishes and surrounded by a cloud of heartbreak and doom, I was begrudgingly led back to my cell.

Needless to say, I was watched with a careful eye. Long gone were the   9 days of solitude and quiet. A babysitter was hired on the nights my parents worked late; I was even banned from reading my fairy tales. My parents acted out of concern for my ability to distinguish fact from fiction; however, I looked at it as an unforgivable punishment. The sole source of comfort I found in that household had been stripped away from me. Without my books to lose myself in, it became less of a "want" to escape this dungeon; it became a dire need.

The drama of my plight faded as my parents realized that I had a   10 tendency to return after each of my "wild escapades." After a few more attempts at escaping my captors, they stopped searching for me. It was commonly known that I would be back in a few hours when I became hungry or when it began to get dark outside. My efforts became something like a joke to the family, but they were not a joke to me. I was determined.

My time away from home was nothing special. I would wander   11 around the woods that circled my backyard. I would overturn rocks and practice my balancing skills on fallen trees. Sometimes I would play pretend, fencing stone walls and bushes with my stick-turned-sword. Every second was an adventure, but my parents were always right. When my knapsack was devoid of my regular apple, bread, and cheese, or when the shadows from the trees began to take on the persona of monsters and murderers, I would begin my shameful and begrudging trudge back home, determined to return next time and succeed in my task of beginning a new life.

It was one day such as this; I was at the top of my favorite tree scout- 12 ing for incoming pirates. As my twisted-leaf-telescope reported no results, I began my descent to the ground. I tentatively placed my weight upon a branch; it groaned under my seventy-five pounds of skin and bone, yet stayed true. Assured in its strength, I placed my full weight upon the tree, and in one swift movement the limb broke and sent me cascading toward the ground as it gave way to nothing. My feet, finding nothing beneath them, shot out in front of me; my desperate hands grappled for something, anything, to hold on to. Shocked and confused by the branch's betrayal, I hardly had time to scream as I received a cruel beating from the ground.

Often in times of extreme trauma or stress, people describe the events   13 occurring around them as though they happened in slow motion, as though their brains, motivated by survival, kicked into turbo mode. As I lay there, under that backstabbing tree, time did just that. For what seemed like hours, my crippled seven-year-old body writhed in agony, as I was unable to control my movement. I lay there, watching the shadows from the trees grow darker and angrier as the sun began to set. The forest began to change from the peaceful, safe haven of my daytime frolicking to a mysterious, unknown lair, home to demons and monsters my own imagination could hardly fathom.

Heart beating out of my chest, I kept hoping and wishing that my   14 "real" family would come and find me, that my beautiful fairy godmother or king father would recognize my distress and choose this time to rescue me from both my current dire situation and my lifetime of finitude and animosity. However, as the shadows grew deeper and the painful shooting from my leg intensified, I began to realize, for the first time, that perhaps they were never coming.

As the cold from the ground began to seep through my skin, the stark reality of the situation began to creep into my heart. I didn't have a magical, enchanted family. I was average. The pain of the realization outshone the physical pain I was enduring. My worst fear had come true; I was nothing but a normal kid. Worse than that, I was a foolish normal child stuck in a very dangerous situation. For the very first time I realized that no amount of imagination or wishing was going to save me. I was all alone. 15

The wind began to whine in that pitiful way it did, serving only to add to my misery. I listened to it whine as I began to accept my fate. My short seven years were going to end, right here, under this tree. I would never take the bus to school again. I would never see my friends. Even the thought of doing the dishes one more time made my heart ache with longing. 16

Slowly a realization dawned upon me: *that can't be the wind howling.* I listened closer. *It almost sounds like voices.* It was distant at first, hardly audible over my pulsating heartbeat. I chalked it up to delusion from a loss of blood. But then I heard it again. Yes, it was definitely voices, and I might have been going crazy, but I could have sworn they were calling my name. 17

A sense of deranged, desperate hope washed over my entire being. I mustered up every spare bit of energy I had left. "I'm over here!" I croaked, my throat raw and exhausted. I flashed back to the last time I had heard voices in the forest: I had so entirely hoped that those voices belonged to my fictitious family. This time all I could hope to see was the worn, familiar face of my *real* mother, or even the imperfect, often-infuriating countenance of my *real* older sister. "I'm here," I screamed desperately. "Help me! I'm here!" 18

The harsh beam of a flashlight glared against my dirty, tear-stained face. I looked up to see the relieved faces of my *real* family. Not the family of my daydreams, but the family who worked full-time jobs to support me, the family who cared about me enough to worry when I was gone for too long. It was in that very moment I realized that no fantasy family, no matter how fantastic and alluring, would ever compare to my real family. I was giving up on the dream of being coated in jewels and whisked away on adventures on a daily basis, but in that moment it didn't matter. I had a family who loved me, and for an average seven-year-old girl, that is about as magical as it gets. 19

Meaning

1. Why did the seven-year-old Fulmore consider herself so mistreated that she felt compelled to run away on a regular basis?

2. Explain the **irony** of Fulmore's dream of finding her "real family" (paragraphs 3, 6, 14, 19).

3. Where in the essay does Fulmore state her thesis? Why do you suppose she chose to place it where she does?

4. If you are uncertain of the meanings of any of the words listed below, try to guess them from the context of the essay. Then look them up to see how close your definitions were to those in the dictionary. Test out the new words by using each of them in a sentence or two of your own.

bindle (3)	regal (6)	finitude (14)
cordial (3)	devoid (11)	animosity (14)
ambiance (5)	persona (11)	mustered (18)
subconscious (5)	betrayal (12)	countenance (18)
exasperated (5, 8)	lair (13)	alluring (19)

Purpose and Audience

1. What do you believe is Fulmore's purpose in recording these episodes from her childhood: to understand her experience? to tell her peers about her childhood? to do something else?

2. What assumptions does Fulmore make about her readers and their familiarity with children's literature? Why are the stories and characters she **alludes** to significant to her experience? Can readers not acquainted with fairy tales understand Fulmore's narrative?

3. How does dialogue help re-create the fear and relief Fulmore felt in the woods?

Method and Structure

1. What features of narration make it an ideal method for describing childhood experiences like the ones documented by Fulmore?

2. Examine Fulmore's organization of events. What major sections does the essay consist of, and what happens in each? Why does she jump between time periods? How does the manipulation of narrative time serve the overall purpose of the essay?

3. How does Fulmore build suspense in the second half of her story?

4. OTHER METHODS Fulmore makes extensive use of **description** in her essay, especially in portraying the woods surrounding her home. What do the descriptions contribute to her narrative? What **dominant impression** does Fulmore create?

Language

1. "Chasing Fairy Tales" is notable for the author's consistent use of strong verbs such as "smudged" (paragraph 3), "trekked" (5), "stumbled" (8), and "groaned" (12). Reread the essay, and pick out five or six additional examples. What weak verbs might Fulmore have used in their place? Why are the verbs she chose more effective?

2. Fulmore uses many figures of speech to enrich her prose, particularly when she recounts her emotional response to being injured and alone. List a few of the **metaphors, similes,** and **personifications** that you find especially effective. How do they contribute to the overall meaning of her essay?

3. Although she writes from the point of view of a seven-year-old girl, Fulmore uses relatively sophisticated vocabulary and sentence structures through most of her essay. How does the rhythm of her sentences reinforce her purpose?

Writing Topics

1. JOURNAL TO ESSAY In your journal response (p. 79), you described your childhood dreams for the future. Have your goals changed since then? Write an essay in which you describe your current ambitions. If they have changed, pinpoint the people or experiences that have caused you to modify your expectations. Do you believe that your plans will evolve in the future? Do you think that they could ever change completely?

2. "Chasing Fairy Tales" relies on narrative to recount an emotionally significant learning experience. Using the same method, write an essay in which you recapture one of the happiest or most exciting discoveries of your childhood: for example, finding a favorite hiding place, learning a skill such as skating or playing a musical instrument, making an unexpected friend, or receiving something you deeply desired. Use straightforward chronological time if that works best, or, like Fulmore, compress narrative time to emphasize the most significant moments.

3. In exploring the effects of children's books on Fulmore's imagination and her actions, "Chasing Fairy Tales" can be considered a literacy narrative,

a story about how a writer has learned (or is continuing to learn) to communicate through reading and writing. Try writing a literacy narrative of your own. You might consider how reading has influenced you, as a child or now. You might examine one or more of your experiences as a writer. Or you might reflect on some aspect of language that has challenged or inspired you. Whatever focus you choose, try to draw some conclusions about what written expression contributes to your life.

4. **CULTURAL CONSIDERATIONS**   In North America children are often tasked with household chores such as dusting, vacuuming, washing dishes, or doing laundry. Write about some task (or tasks) you have been responsible for. Was it something you did just because your parents forced you to, or did you enjoy any aspect of the experience? What lessons did you learn from your responsibility? Do you think it is a good idea for young people to help with housekeeping chores?

5. **CONNECTIONS**   Just as Fulmore explores how fairy tales made her unhappy as a child, Augusten Burroughs, in "Unhappily Ever After" (p. 275), suggests that wanting to be happy is itself a kind of fairy tale. In an essay, examine the function of fairy tales and folklore. Where do the stories come from? How do they influence children and adults alike? What purpose do they serve in modern cultures? How do they compare to other forms of mythology? Draw on the insights offered by Fulmore and Burroughs as you like, but feel free also to make your own observations and associations.

WRITING WITH THE METHOD

NARRATION

Select one of the following topics, or any other topic they suggest, for an essay developed by narration. Be sure to choose a topic you care about so that narration is a means of communicating an idea, not an end in itself.

Friends and Relations

1. An early infatuation
2. Another person's generosity or sacrifice
3. A wedding or funeral
4. An incident from family legend

The World around You

5. An interaction you witnessed on the street
6. A storm, a flood, an earthquake, or another natural event
7. The history of your neighborhood
8. A community event, such as a meeting, demonstration, or celebration
9. A time when a poem, story, film, song, or other work changed you

Lessons of Daily Life

10. An act of rebellion
11. A time when you had to deliver bad news
12. A moment of disappointment
13. Your biggest social blunder

Firsts

14. Your first day of school, as a child or more recently
15. The first time you met someone who became important to you
16. The first performance you gave
17. Your first job

Adventures

18. An especially satisfying sports experience, such as a run, tennis match, or bike ride
19. A surprising encounter with a wild animal
20. An episode of extrasensory perception
21. Solving a mystery
22. A trip to an unfamiliar place

WRITING ABOUT THE THEME

FACING FEAR

1. Vulnerability is a recurring theme in the essays and paragraphs in this chapter. Sherman Alexie (p. 61), Michael Ondaatje (p. 62), Langston Hughes (p. 68), Jennifer Finney Boylan (p. 73), and Lauren Fulmore (p. 79) all write in some way about psychological pain. After considering each writer's situation individually, write an essay analyzing the differences among these situations. Based on these narratives, which writers seem to have the most in common? Which of their responses seem most relatable to you?

2. While growing up inevitably involves fear and disappointment, most people experience security and happiness as well. Sherman Alexie was enjoying himself before his peers dropped his shoes in the water, Michael Ondaatje clearly finds comfort in his dead father's reappearance as a cobra, Jennifer Finney Boylan relishes her transition to womanhood, and Lauren Fulmore believes that breaking her leg strengthened her relationship with her family. Write a narrative essay about similarly mixed emotions from your experience, making sure to describe your feelings vividly so that your readers share them with you.

3. Life is full of epiphanies, or sudden moments of realization, insight, or understanding. Langston Hughes, Jennifer Finney Boylan, and Lauren Fulmore all report such moments at the ends of their essays: Hughes loses faith in a Jesus who would not help him in church, Boylan recognizes that what she thought was her "greatest curse" was in fact her "greatest gift," and Fulmore discovers that her normal childhood is in fact "magical." Write a narrative essay in which you tell of events leading to an epiphany of your own. Make sure both the events themselves and the nature of the epiphany are vividly clear.

6

DESCRIPTION

▶
EXPERIENCING NEW PLACES

Whenever you use words to depict or re-create a scene, an object, a person, or a feeling, you use **description**. A mainstay of conversation between people, description is likely to figure in almost any writing situation: an Instagram post may praise a friend's new spiky purple hair, a laboratory report may examine the colors and odors of chemicals, a business memo may distinguish the tastes of two competitors' gluten-free frozen pizzas, an insurance claim may explain the condition of an apartment after a kitchen fire. Because the method builds detail and brings immediacy to a subject, description is an important part of most essay writing as well.

The writers represented in this chapter all set out to explore their reactions to places they encountered in their travels. They probably didn't decide consciously to write descriptions but turned to the method intuitively as they chose to record the perceptions of their senses. Joan Didion evokes the sensory overload of New Orleans in the summertime, and Ian Frazier captures the haunting aspects of an abandoned prison camp in Siberia. Marta K. Taylor's experience of a family trip through the American desert climaxes in the glory of a lightning storm. Amy Tan's adventures in an Easter Island cave lead her to ponder the meaning of darkness. And Ken Chen's essay about a visit to Hong Kong attempts to express what it is about that city that makes tourists feel dizzy.

Reading Description

Description draws on perceptions of the five senses—sight, sound, smell, taste, and touch—to understand and communicate a particular experience of the world. The writer's purpose and involvement with the subject will largely determine how **objective** or **subjective** a description is.

■ *Objective description* strives for precision, trying to convey the subject impersonally, without emotion. This is the kind of description required in scientific writing—for instance, a medical diagnosis or a report on an experiment in psychology—where cold facts and absence of feeling are essential for readers to judge the accuracy of procedures and results. It is also the method of news reports and of reference works such as encyclopedias.

■ *Subjective description*, in contrast, draws explicitly on emotions, giving an impression of the subject filtered through firsthand experience. Instead of withdrawing to the background, the writer invests feelings in the subject and lets those feelings determine which details to describe and how best to describe them. State of mind—perhaps loneliness, anger, or joy—can be re-created by reference to sensory details such as numbness, heat, or sweetness.

In general, writers favor objective description when their purpose is explanation and subjective description when their purpose is self-expression or persuasion. But the categories are not exclusive, and most descriptive writing mixes the two. A news report on a tropical storm, for instance, might objectively describe bent and broken trees, fallen wires, and lashing rain, but the reporter's selection of details gives a subjective impression of the storm's fearsomeness.

Whether objective or subjective or a mixture of the two, effective description requires a **dominant impression**—a central theme or idea about the subject to which all the details relate. The dominant impression may be something a writer sees in the subject, such as the purposefulness of city pedestrians or the expressiveness of an actor. Or it may derive from an emotional response, perhaps pleasure (or dismay) at the purposefulness of the pedestrians, or admiration (or disdain) for the actor's technique. Whatever its source, the dominant impression serves as a unifying principle that guides both the writer's selection of details and the reader's understanding of the subject.

One aid in creating a dominant impression is a consistent **point of view**, the position from which a writer approaches a subject. Point of view in description has two main elements:

■ A *physical* relation to the subject, real or imagined. A writer could view a mountain, for instance, from the bottom looking up, from miles away across a valley, or from an airplane passing overhead. The first two points of view are *fixed* because the writer remains in one position and scans the scene from there; the third is *moving* because the writer changes position.

- A *psychological* relation to the subject, conveyed partly by pronouns. In subjective description, where feelings are part of the message, writers might use *I* and *you* freely to narrow the distance between themselves and the subject and between themselves and the reader. But in the most objective, impersonal description, writers will use *one* ("One can see the summit") or avoid self-reference altogether in order to appear distant from and unbiased toward the subject.

Once a physical and psychological point of view has been established, readers come to depend on it. Thus a **shift** from one view to another— zooming in from fifteen miles away to the foot of a mountain, abandoning *I* for the more removed *one*—can disorient readers and distract them from the dominant impression the writer intended to create.

Analyzing Description in Paragraphs

Joan Didion (born 1934), one of the country's foremost writers, consistently applies a journalist's eye for detail and a terse, understated style to examining American culture. The following description comes from *South and West* (2017), a collection of highlights from her notebooks.

In New Orleans in June the air is heavy with sex and death, not violent death but death by decay, overripeness, rotting, death by drowning, suffocation, fever of unknown etiology. The place is physically dark, dark like the negative of a photograph, dark like an X-ray: the atmosphere absorbs its own light, never reflects light but sucks it in until random objects glow with a morbid luminescence. The crypts above ground dominate certain vistas. In the hypnotic liquidity of the atmosphere all motion slows into choreography, all people on the street move as if suspended in a precarious emulsion, and there seems only a technical distinction between the quick and the dead.

Specific, concrete details (underlined once)

Figures of speech (underlined twice)

Point of view: moving, psychologically close

Dominant impression: living death

Ian Frazier (born 1951) is a staff writer for the *New Yorker*, an essayist, and the author of investigative travel books. This paragraph, from *Travels in Siberia* (2010), describes his first impressions of a World War II *lager*, or prison camp, deep in the wilds of Russia.

The *lager* lay in a narrow valley between sparsely wooded hills. The gray, scraggly trees, which did not make it to the hills' higher slopes, grew more thickly near the lager and partly surrounded it; a few small birches had sprung up inside what had been the camp's perimeter. Their bare branches contrasted with the white of the snow on the roof of the barracks, whose wall, set back under the eaves, was dark. In the whiteness of an open field, a guard tower tilted sideways like someone putting all of his weight on one leg. A ladder-like set of steps still led up to it, and two eye-like window openings added to the anthropomorphic effect. In the endless and pristine snow cover I saw no tire tracks, road ruts, abandoned oil drums, or other sign that any human had been here since the camp was left to the elements, half a century before.

> Specific, concrete details (underlined once)
>
> Point of view: fixed, psychologically distant
>
> Figures of speech (underlined twice)
>
> Dominant impression: anthropomorphism, or the attribution of human qualities to nonhuman objects

Developing a Descriptive Essay

▶ Getting Started

The subject for a descriptive essay may be any place, object, person, animal, or state of mind that you have observed closely enough or experienced sharply enough to invest with special significance. A room, a new casino, a chair, a tree, a passerby on the street, an armadillo, a feeling of fear, a sense of achievement—anything you have a strong impression of can prompt effective description.

Observe your subject directly, if possible, or recall it as completely as you can. Jot down the details that seem to contribute most to the impression you're trying to convey. You needn't write the description of those details yet—that can wait for drafting—but you do want to capture the possibilities in your subject.

You should start to consider the needs and expectations of your readers early on. If the subject is something readers have never seen or felt before, you will need enough objective details to create a complete picture in their minds. A description of a friend, for example, might focus on his distinctive voice and laugh, but readers will also want to know something about his appearance. If the subject is essentially abstract, like an emotion, you will need plenty of details to make it concrete for readers. And if the subject is familiar, as a local business or an old spruce tree on campus might be, you will want to skip obvious objective information in favor of fresh observations that will make readers see the subject anew.

▶ Forming a Thesis

When you have your subject, express in a sentence the dominant impression that you want to create for readers. The sentence will help keep you on track while you search for the sensory details that will make your description concrete and vivid. It should evoke a quality or an atmosphere or an effect, as these examples do:

> His fierce anger at the world shows in every word and gesture.
>
> The gleaming new casino is a thoroughly unnatural place, like a space station in a science-fiction movie.

Such a sentence can serve as the thesis of your essay. You don't necessarily need to state it outright in your draft; sometimes you may prefer to let the details build to a conclusion. But the thesis should hover over the essay nonetheless, governing the selection of every detail and making itself as clear to readers as if it were stated.

▶ Organizing

Though the details of a subject may not occur to you in any particular order, you will need to arrange them so that readers are not confused by rapid shifts in focus. You can give readers a sense of the whole subject in the **introduction** to your essay: objective details of location or size or shape, the incident leading to a state of mind, or the reasons for describing a familiar object. In the introduction you may also want to state your thesis—the dominant impression you will create.

The organization of the **body** of the essay depends partly on point of view and partly on dominant impression. If you take a moving point of view—say, strolling down a city street—the details will probably arrange themselves naturally. But a fixed point of view, scanning a subject from one position, requires your intervention. When the subject is a landscape, a person, or an object, you'll probably want to use a **spatial organization**: near to far, top to bottom, front to back, left to right, or vice versa. Other subjects, such as a suburban casino, might be better treated in groups of features: gamblers, gaming halls, bars and restaurants, insides of stores. Or a description of an emotional state might follow the **chronological order** of the event that aroused it. The specific order itself is not important, as long as there *is* an order that effectively channels readers' attention.

▶ Drafting

The challenge of drafting your description will be bringing the subject to life. Whether it is in front of you or in your mind, you may find it helpful to consider the subject one sense at a time—what you can see, hear, smell, touch, taste. Of course, not all senses are applicable to all subjects; a chair, for instance, may not have a noticeable odor, and you're unlikely to know its taste. But proceeding sense by sense can help you uncover details, such as the smell of a tree or the sound of a person's voice, that you might otherwise overlook.

Examining a subject one sense at a time is also one of the best ways to think of concrete words and figures of speech to represent sensations and feelings. For instance, does *acid* describe the taste of fear? Does an actor's appearance suggest the smell of soap? Does a casino sound like clattering coins? In creating distinct physical sensations for readers, such representations make meaning inescapably clear.

▶ Revising and Editing

When you are ready to revise and edit, use the questions and the Focus box below as a guide.

■ *Have you created the dominant impression you intended to create?* Check that you have plenty of specific details and that each one helps to pin down one crucial feature of your subject. Cut any irrelevant details that may have crept in. What counts is not the number of details but their quality and the strength of the impression they make.

■ *Are your point of view and organization clear and consistent?* Watch for confusing moves from one vantage point or organizational scheme to

another. Watch also for confusing and unnecessary **shifts** in pronouns, such as from *I* to *one* or vice versa. Any changes in point of
view or organization should be clearly essential for your purpose and
for the impression you want to create.

FOCUS ON CONCRETE AND SPECIFIC LANGUAGE

For readers to imagine your subject, you'll need to use **concrete**, **specific**
language that appeals to their experiences and senses. When editing
your description, keep a sharp eye out for vague words — such as *delicious*,
handsome, *loud*, and *short* — that force readers to create their own impressions or, worse, leave them with no impression at all. Using details that call
on readers' sensory experiences, say why delicious or why handsome,
how loud or how short. When stuck for a word, conjure up your subject
and see it, hear it, touch it, smell it, taste it.

The first sentence below shows a writer's initial attempt to describe
something she saw. The edited version that follows it is much more vivid.

VAGUE   Beautiful, scented wildflowers were in the field.

CONCRETE AND SPECIFIC   Backlit by the sun and smelling faintly
sweet, an acre of tiny lavender flowers spread away from me.

The writer might also have used **figures of speech** to show what she
saw: for instance, describing the field as "a giant's bed covered in a quilt
of lavender dots" (a metaphor) or describing the backlit flowers as "glow-
ing like tiny lavender lamps" (a simile).

Note that *concrete* and *specific* do not mean "fancy": good description
does not demand five-dollar words when nickel equivalents are just as
informative. The writer who uses *rubiginous* instead of *rusty red* actually
says less because fewer readers will understand the less common word,
and all readers will sense a writer showing off.

For more on concrete, specific language and figures of speech, see
pages 52–53.

LearningCurve   To practice editing for word choice, visit *LaunchPad Solo for Readers and Writers* > LearningCurve > Appropriate Language

Memory is the diary that we all carry about with us.   —Oscar Wilde

I might have seen more of America when I was a child if I hadn't had to spend so much of my time protecting my half of the back seat from incursions by my sister.   —Calvin Trillin

Memory is a complicated thing, a relative to truth but not its twin.
       —Barbara Kingsolver

JOURNAL RESPONSE   Recall a childhood event such as a family outing, a long car ride, a visit to an unfamiliar place, or an incident in your neighborhood. Imagine yourself back in that earlier time and write down details of what you experienced and how you felt.

Marta K. Taylor

Marta K. Taylor was born in 1970 and raised in Los Angeles. She attended a "huge" public high school there before being accepted into Harvard University. She graduated in 1992 with a degree in chemistry and is now a physician in Philadelphia, where she specializes in ear, nose, and throat surgery.

Desert Dance
(Student Essay)

Taylor wrote this description of a nighttime ride when she was a freshman in college taking the required writing course. The essay was published in the 1988–89 edition of *Exposé*, a collection of student writing published by Harvard.

We didn't know there was a rodeo in Flagstaff. All the hotels were   1 filled, except the really expensive ones, so we decided to push on to Winslow that night. Dad must have thought we were all asleep, and so we should have been, too, as it was after one a.m. and we had been driving all day through the wicked California and Arizona desert on the first day of our August Family Trip. The back seat of our old station wagon was down, allowing two eleven-year-old kids to lie almost fully extended and still leaving room for the rusty green Coleman ice-chest which held the packages of pressed turkey breast, the white bread, and the pudding snack-pacs that Mom had cleverly packed to save on lunch expenses and quiet the inevitable "Are we there yet?" and "How much farther?"

Jon was sprawled out on his back, one arm up and one arm down,   2
reminding me of Gumby[1] or an outline chalked on the sidewalk in a murder mystery. His mouth was wide open and his regular breath rattled
deeply in the back of his throat somewhere between his mouth and his
nose. Beside the vibration of the wheels and the steady hum of the engine,
no other sound disturbed the sacred silence of the desert night.

From where I lay, behind the driver's seat, next to my twin brother   3
on the old green patchwork quilt that smelled like beaches and picnics—
salty and a little mildewed—I could see my mother's curly brown head
slumped against the side window, her neck bent awkwardly against the seat
belt, which seemed the only thing holding her in her seat. Dad, of course,
drove—a motionless, soundless, protective paragon of security and
strength, making me feel totally safe. The back of his head had never
seemed more perfectly framed than by the reflection of the dashboard
lights on the windshield; the short, raven-colored wiry hairs that I loved so
much caught and played with, like tinsel would, the greenish glow with red
and orange accents. The desert sky was starless, clouded.

Every couple of minutes, a big rig would pass us going west. The   4
lights would illuminate my mother's profile for a moment and then the
roar of the truck would come and the sudden, the violent sucking rush of
air and we would be plunged into darkness again. Time passed so slowly,
unnoticeably, as if the whole concept of time were meaningless.

I was careful to make no sound, content to watch the rising and falling   5
of my twin's chest in the dim light and to feel on my cheek the gentle heat
of the engine rising up through the floorboards. I lay motionless for a long
time before the low rumbling, a larger sound than any eighteen-wheeler,
rolled across the open plain. I lifted my head, excited to catch a glimpse
of the rain that I, as a child from Los Angeles, seldom saw. A few seconds
later, the lightning sliced the night sky all the way across the northern
horizon. Like a rapidly growing twig, at least three or four branches, it
illuminated the twisted forms of Joshua trees and low-growing cacti. All
in silhouette—and only for a flash, though the image stayed many
moments before my mind's eye in the following black.

The lightning came again, this time only a formless flash, as if God   6
were taking a photograph of the magnificent desert, and the long, straight
road before us—empty and lonely—shone like a dagger. The trees looked
like old men to me now, made motionless by the natural strobe, perhaps
to resume their feeble hobble across the sands once the shield of night

---

[1] An animated clay character that inspired a series of bendable toys in the 1980s.
[Editors' note.]

returned. The light show continued on the horizon though the expected rain never came. The fleeting, gnarled fingers grasped out and were gone; the fireworks flashed and frolicked and faded over and over—danced and jumped, acting out a drama in the quick, jerky movements of a marionette. Still in silence, still in darkness.

I watched the violent, gaudy display over the uninhabited, endless   7 expanse, knowing I was in a state of grace and not knowing if I was dreaming but pretty sure I was awake because of the cramp in my neck and the pain in my elbow from placing too much weight on it for too long.

Meaning

1. What does Taylor mean by "state of grace" in paragraph 7? What associations does this phrase have? To what extent does it capture the dominant impression of this essay?

2. If you are uncertain of the meanings of any of the words listed below, try to guess them from the context of the essay. Then look them up to see how close your definitions were to those in the dictionary. Test out the new words by using each of them in a sentence or two of your own.

paragon (3)	gnarled (6)	marionette (6)
silhouette (5)	frolicked (6)	gaudy (7)
strobe (6)		

Purpose and Audience

1. Why does Taylor open with the sentence "We didn't know there was a rodeo in Flagstaff"? What purposes does the sentence serve?

2. Even readers familiar with the desert may not have had Taylor's experience of it in a nighttime lightning storm. Where does she seem especially careful about describing what she saw? What details surprised you?

Method and Structure

1. What impression or mood is Taylor trying to capture in this essay? How does the precise detail of the description help to convey that mood?

2. Taylor begins her description inside the car (paragraphs 1–5) and then moves out into the landscape (5–7), bringing us back into the car in her final thought. Why does she use such a sequence? Why do you think she devotes roughly equal space to each area?

3. Taylor's description is mainly subjective, invested with her emotions. Point to elements of the description that reveal emotion.

4. **OTHER METHODS** Taylor's description relies in part on **narration**. How does the narrative strengthen the essay's dominant impression?

Language

1. How does Taylor's **tone** help convey the "state of grace" she feels inside the car? Point out three or four examples of language that establish that mood.

2. Why do you think Taylor titles her essay "Desert Dance"?

3. Notice the words Taylor uses to describe Joshua trees (paragraphs 5–6). If you're already familiar with the plant, how accurate do you find Taylor's description? If you've never seen a Joshua tree, what do you think it looks like, based on Taylor's description? (Look up the plant online or in a dictionary or encyclopedia to test your impression.)

4. Taylor uses **similes** to make her description vivid and immediate. Find several examples, and comment on their effectiveness.

5. Taylor's last paragraph is one long sentence. Does this long sentence work with or against the content and mood of the paragraph? Why and how?

Writing Topics

1. JOURNAL TO ESSAY   Using subjective description, expand your journal response about a childhood event (p. 96) into an essay. Recalling details of sight, sound, touch, smell, and even taste, build a dominant impression for readers of what the experience was like for you.

2. Taylor's essay illustrates her feelings not only about the desert but also about her father, mother, and twin brother. Think of a situation when you were intensely aware of your feelings about another person (relative or friend). Describe the situation and the person in a way that conveys those feelings.

3. CULTURAL CONSIDERATIONS   Though she had evidently seen the desert before, Taylor had not seen it the way she describes it in "Desert Dance." Write an essay in which you describe your first encounter with something new—for instance, a visit to the home of a friend from a different social or economic background, a visit to a big city or a farm, an unexpected view of your own backyard. Describe what you saw and your responses. How, if at all, did the experience change you?

4. CONNECTIONS   Both Taylor and Amy Tan, in "The Darkest Moment of My Life" (next page), express awe at natural wonders. In a brief essay, analyze how these writers convey their sense of awe so that it is concrete, not vague. Focus on their words and especially on their figures of speech.

It is better to light a candle than to curse the darkness.   —Proverb

In order for the light to shine so brightly, the darkness must be present.
                                                                    —Francis Bacon

Deep into that darkness peering, long I stood there, wondering, fearing, /
Doubting, dreaming dreams no mortal ever dared to dream before.
                                                                    —Edgar Allan Poe

JOURNAL RESPONSE   What associations does darkness hold for you? Do you
think of the dark as something foreboding or frightening, for instance, or
do you find it soothing, even beautiful? In your journal, jot down your
thoughts on what it feels like to be in the dark.

Amy Tan

Amy Tan was born in 1952 in Oakland, California, the daughter of Chinese immigrants. She grew up in Northern California and majored in English and linguistics at
San Jose State University, where she received a BA and then an MA. Tan's first career
was as a business writer, crafting corporate reports and executives' speeches. Dis-
satisfied with her work, she began writing fiction. Her first book, *The Joy Luck Club*
(1989), a critical and popular success, is a series of interrelated stories about the
bonds between immigrant Chinese mothers and their American-born daughters.
Since *The Joy Luck Club* Tan has written five more novels: *The Kitchen God's Wife*
(1991), *The Hundred Secret Senses* (1995), *The Bonesetter's Daughter* (2001), *Saving
Fish from Drowning* (2005), and *The Valley of Amazement* (2013). She has also published two books for children, a collection of essays, *The Opposite of Fate* (2003), and
a memoir, *Where the Past Begins* (2017).

The Darkest Moment of My Life

Where the Past Begins is, as Tan describes it, a "writer's memoir," in which the author
looks back on her life and experiences through a novelist's lens. This essay, a slightly
shortened version of a chapter in the book, explores a moment of revelation in the
depths of a cave — and showcases Tan's wry sense of humor.

I recently went caving on Easter Island. Caving is a caver's term for going   1
into a cave, and true cavers require special equipment because the caves
they go into can be a little tricky to get into and out of. I was with people
who had that kind of equipment—helmets and headlamps, guano-proof

jumpsuits, knee pads, elbow guards, and gloves. I had on regular clothes and nitrile gloves, the kind that nurses use to give you a flu shot. Caving is fun for cavers who have no fear of becoming stuck in a hole or being buried alive. I had a little bit of fear, but I went along because the sun was blazing hot and it was like being baked in a toaster oven. There was no shade other than what was under the van. I figured I would be a lot cooler in a cave, and that's because I read somewhere that on average caves run about fifty-five degrees year-round. This cave was not average. It felt like I was in a sauna. When you factor in dragging yourself forward using your fingertips, you're soon hotter than you were outside and this might make you feel you are running out of cave oxygen. The cavers in jump-suits were really sweating. The next time someone tells you that a cave maintains an even temperature of fifty-five degrees, tell them I said that is a big fat lie.

The caves that cavers go into are not like those you see in movies — you know the ones, they're hidden behind fake bushes and open into a cavernous great room, with stalactites that resemble chandeliers, a stove made of rocks, a small pool for bathing children under a skylight, and sleeping chambers on other levels. That is a Hollywood set. I read that a caver's dream cave has an "advanced" rating, meaning, the passages might twist and turn or lead downward into something similar to a drain-pipe, and that your weight and gravity might push you downward into a U-bend that requires Houdini-like[1] flexibility. You wouldn't be able to back up vertically because you're constricted like a rabbit being swallowed by a giant anaconda. You know those stories about curious kittens that go into a drainpipe and wind up with just their piteously freaked faces stick-ing out? The kitten always gets rescued by passersby who cut open the pipe with an electric chain saw they happen to have in the trunk of the car. On Easter Island, no one will open a cave from the outside with a chain saw. For one thing, Easter Island is a World Heritage Site.[2] You can't even pick up a rock and take it home. A friend tried.

This is the reason you should always have a caving expert with you when caving — or even two experts, one leading you and one following you, so that you can be either pulled forward or pulled backward, as the better case may be. Our caving expert was named Seth. There were five

2

3

---

[1] Harry Houdini (1874–1926) was a magician and contortionist famous for tricks involving escape from tight spaces. [Editors' note.]

[2] The United Nations Educational, Scientific and Cultural Organization (UNESCO) has designated more than a thousand culturally significant landmarks as World Her-itage Sites to encourage international protections and preservation. [Editors' note.]

other people, including myself. Someone who had already come out of the caves earlier in the day let me borrow his helmet with headlamp. When we entered the cave, I was fooled by how spacious it was. It was like the Hollywood set, but without stalactites, because this cave was not limestone. Seth explained that the caves were lava tubes that formed when a volcano erupted and the lava, running down from volcano to ocean, slowed every now and then and developed crusts that eventually became tubes. When more lava flowed it squeezed through the tubes, which is similar to how bowels work, an unfortunate metaphor. The result is a cave that squeezed in and out, with some sections resembling a spelunking version of diverticulitis. This is important to remember because when you are moving ahead in a dark cave and looking down at water flowing and wondering if it will get deeper, you can easily bash your forehead when the ceiling suddenly drops a foot without any warning whatsoever. Never go fearlessly forward into the dark. I went from walking erect, to shuffling forward hunched over, then waddling in a crouched position, and then crawling on my stomach. It was like going backward on some evolutionary scale, *Homo erectus* to worm.

When you are in a cave, you cannot help but think who lived in this   4
place thousands of years ago. They had to move around inside the cave in all these postures. I would guess that a hunched position was the most used. Maybe the survival of the fittest meant genetic selection of the shortest or those with early osteoporosis. But that can't be true. As a race, the Rapa Nui[3] are particularly beautiful and have excellent posture. When I was crawling in a viscous substance, I tried to imagine it was brownie mix and not another kind of oozy substance befitting lava caves being called "the bowels of the Earth."

Finally, after what seemed like miles of cave crawling, we reached a   5
dead end with a waist-deep pool. The caving expert was not alarmed. Having consulted maps ahead of time, he had expected this. He suggested we take turns getting into the pool to cool off. We did not have to worry about creatures in the water since this was not an environment that would sustain life, not even plants. But then I got to thinking that it was possible that some species of bacteria could live in such a place. Bacteria always defy expectations. After all, the earliest strains came out of thermal vents and then became the start of life on Earth. Before we *Homo sapiens* were Neanderthals, we were bacteria. These are the kinds of things I think about when I am in a strange place. I imagine things.

---

[3] The Polynesian Rapa Nui people are indigenous to Easter Island and make up more than half the population. [Editors' note.]

The cave expert suggested we turn off our headlamps. In a few sec- 6
onds we were plunged into a lightless state. I had never considered what
pitch-black meant, but this was it. This was a deeper darker black than
what you would experience going into a darkroom. There was no electric hum, no pulse of the human race. When anyone spoke it felt like
the words departed the lips and immediately fell unconscious to the
floor, overcome by the heaviness of silence. I felt disoriented. Although
my feet were firmly on the floor of the cave, the space we occupied had
become formless. My body—not just my eyes—was aware of the total
lack of light. I sensed that the body has receptors for light. For one thing,
the melanin in our skin cells recognizes UV light. People who are tor-
tured and kept underground in solitary confinement without light often
become insane. The body and not just the eyes need light. I was in that
lightless part of the cave for only a minute before I realized this was the
darkest moment of my life. As far as the body was concerned, there was
nothing there. Only the mind could compensate for lack of stimuli. . . .

I thought the cave would be the perfect atmosphere for me as 7
writer—no stimuli, no distractions, nothing to capture the attention of
the eye. Imagination would be everything. I could simulate a state of
darkness by wearing a blindfold before the start of writing each day. I
could capture the state of nothingness. It would be like dreaming. Darkness and dreaming were good, expansive, without boundaries. I bet there
is a seminar on inner awareness that has capitalized on this idea. Perhaps
they even go into caves to experience the freedom of nothingness. "Out
of darkness comes enlightenment," that sort of thing.

I don't know how long my fellow spelunkers and I were in total dark- 8
ness. Time runs differently in the pitch-black. The diurnal body rhythm
starts switching to a nocturnal one, and some alteration of the brain
begins. Deep darkness condenses time and I suspect that an hour of this
could be the equivalent of an entire night. Seth instructed us to turn on
our lights and when we did, we saw a cockroach. We should have known
better. Like bacteria, cockroaches can live in any conditions.

All too soon it was time to return to our starting point: the outdoor 9
oven. What had seemed like a mile going in was now much shorter. Fear
of the unknown elongates time. We did not know what we were getting
into. Now we knew what we were getting out of.

The caving experience left me thinking about other moments people 10
typically refer to as "dark"—those involving tragedy. Why do we refer to
them as dark? Is being in darkness really such a negative experience? If
not, is there another metaphor that is closer to how I feel when I am overcome with despair? Is it a sensation that I am lost or falling? What I feel

most acutely is a vacuum, of being sucked out alive. I do not picture darkness where my mind is free to imagine all kinds of things. I picture only the one who I have just lost. I picture my mother. I picture my dog. I picture my friend Bill.

Darkness is no longer the word I would use for despair, not since   11
going into that cave. I now think that the metaphor of pitch-blackness is a good one for starting afresh, for thinking before writing. In darkness, the old forms and assumptions vanish. Time is suspended. Noise is blocked. In darkness, I have only imagination.

Meaning

1. Explain what Tan means when she says, "I realized this was the darkest moment of my life" (paragraph 6). Does she intend for readers to take this statement literally?

2. What is the dominant impression Tan creates of the cave she explored? Why, according to the author, was turning off the headlamps so revelatory for her?

3. Does Tan describe purely for the sake of describing, or does she have a thesis she wants to convey? If so, where does she most explicitly state this thesis?

4. If you are uncertain of the meanings of any of the words listed below, try to guess them from the context of the essay. Then look them up to see how close your definitions were to those in the dictionary. Test out the new words by using each of them in a sentence or two of your own.

guano (1)	diverticulitis (3)	*Homo sapiens* (5)
nitrile (1)	*Homo erectus* (3)	melanin (6)
stalactites (2)	osteoporosis (4)	stimuli (6)
spelunking (3)	viscous (4)	diurnal (8)

Purpose and Audience

1. Why do you think Tan felt compelled to write about the cave? Consider whether she might have had a dual purpose.

2. What kind of audience is Tan writing for: cavers? naturalists? tourists? writers? people from Easter Island? someone else? How do you know?

Method and Structure

1. Why does Tan refer to Hollywood depictions of caves in paragraphs 2 and 3? How do caves in the movies differ from and resemble the cave in her description?

2. How does the author organize her description? What is the effect of this organization?

3. What is the effect of the vivid **images** in paragraph 2? In what way does this imagery explain Tan's fear of the cave?

4. **OTHER METHODS** Paragraphs 3 and 4 explain the geological developments through which the cave was formed. How does this **process analysis** help Tan enhance the humor of her description?

Language

1. Notice that Tan's essay includes several **shifts** in person, from *I* to *you*. Is Tan writing carelessly, or does she shift to the second person for a purpose? What do Tan's shifts contribute to, or take away from, her essay? Explain your answer.

2. How many of the five senses does Tan appeal to in her description? Find words or phrases that seem especially precise in conveying sensory impressions.

3. Tan uses several **figures of speech**, such as "the sun was blazing hot and it was like being baked in a toaster oven" (paragraph 1) a **simile**. Find two or three other figures of speech, and analyze how **hyperbole** and **understatement** in particular contribute to the humor of her description.

Writing Topics

1. **JOURNAL TO ESSAY** In your journal response (p. 100) you listed some of your impressions of darkness. Were you surprised by Tan's conclusion that the sensation is a positive one? Or were you in agreement with her from the start? Write a descriptive essay of your own about something that you consider pleasing but others do not (or, conversely, something that others enjoy but you find unpleasant). Your subject could be a sensation or an activity, such as darkness or heat, caving or writing, or something else: a person, an animal, a natural phenomenon, an object you hold dear. Following Tan's essay as a model, focus on a specific instance involving your subject so that your details render the experience immediate and vivid in readers' minds.

2. Reread Tan's essay, paying particular attention to her use of concrete words and figures of speech that appeal to readers' fancy. Choose the details and language that you find most powerful or suggestive, and write a brief essay explaining how they contribute to Tan's dominant impression of the cave.

3. RESEARCH   In a travel magazine or the travel section of a newspaper, read a description of an exotic location you are unfamiliar with. Then write a comparison of that piece and Tan's essay, explaining which you find more interesting, and why. To what extent do the authors' purposes and audiences account for the differences you perceive in the descriptions?

4. CONNECTIONS   In her essay "In the Early Morning Rain" (p. 73), Jennifer Finney Boylan recalls feeling the kind of despair Tan imagines most people would describe as the "darkest moment" of their lives. Write a brief essay in which you compare and contrast Tan's and Boylan's attitudes toward hopelessness, as well as their assumptions about how dark feelings can be processed, even overcome. Be sure to support your analysis by citing details from each selection.

Travel in all the four quarters of the earth, yet you will find nothing anywhere. Whatever there is, is only here.   —Ramakrishna

Perhaps travel cannot prevent bigotry, but by demonstrating that all peoples cry, laugh, eat, worry, and die, it can introduce the idea that if we try and understand each other, we may even become friends.

—Maya Angelou

One's destination is never a place but rather a new way of looking at things.

—Henry Miller

JOURNAL RESPONSE   You've probably ventured beyond your hometown at least once in your life, perhaps on a family vacation, on a road trip with friends, or to the town or city where your current school is located. Think of one such trip and how the place you visited seemed strange to you. Were you surprised by people's behavior or unfamiliar with local customs? Could you understand the language or local dialect? Was the landscape different? In your journal, describe any discomfort you felt. (If you've never traveled, think of a place you'd like to go and imagine what it might be like to be there.)

Ken Chen

A writer and a lawyer, Ken Chen has expressed a desire to "engage with people who, whether they realize it or not, don't consider Asian Americans (or what they write) as important." He was born in 1979 in San Diego, California, and grew up in a blended family after his immigrant parents divorced. After graduating from the University of California at Berkeley in 2001 and Yale University Law School in 2005, Chen moved to New York City to begin a career in law. He is executive director for the Asian American Writers' Workshop, a nonprofit literary organization, and a cofounder of CultureStrike, an advocacy group that supports immigration and the arts. He is a regular contributor of articles and essays to a variety of publications, including *Palimpsest*, *Boston Review of Books*, and *Kyoto Journal*, and in 2009 he won the Yale Series of Younger Poets competition with his poetry collection *Juvenilia*.

City Out of Breath

In the following essay first published in the literary journal *Mānoa* in 2005 and later selected for *Best American Essays*, Chen relates his dizzying impressions of the distinctly unusual island city of Hong Kong. A colonial outpost under British rule for a century and a half, the region reverted to Chinese control in 1997, three years before Chen visited. Hong Kong was then, and is now, governed by communist China under a principle known as "one country, two systems," which grants the city and its environs some autonomy but holds them to mainland standards overall. The quasi-democratic system has in recent years spurred civic unrest and public protests, particularly by university students seeking a more representative electoral process.

So all night, we walk in one direction: up.   1

This is really the only direction you can go in Hong Kong, a direction   2 hinted at by skyscrapers and aspired to by the Hong Kong Stock Exchange. By "we," I mean my father, myself, and our guide—my stepgrandmother-to-be—who somehow possesses both our combined age and our combined speed. Trudging up the stairs behind her, my father and I are already panting. We stop and laugh—really only an excuse to catch our breath—but by the top of the stairs we're bent and sagging, our hands on our knees. And there, at the end of the street, she's waving at us to hurry up, almost as if to fan away whatever remains of our quaint Californian version of walking. When we catch up with her, she says, in what seems like an especially Chinese blend of ridicule and public affection, that we walk too slowly.

If an American city at night is film noir,[1] then Hong Kong is just a   3 camera blur. The residents of Kowloon[2] speed around with the same look on their faces, as if they're irked at their bodies for not being cars. You feel that if you stood still, the city would just rotate past you, as if you have no other choice but motion. Hong Kong accelerates as though located on another, faster-spinning earth. Anyone who has been there knows that time and space can flick off their objectivity and instead pulse and jump, symphonic rather than metronomic. In Hong Kong the world stretches time until time—along with space and language—goes elastic. It's like a Chinese painting in which conflicting perspectives soak through the landscape like radiation. A McDonald's sits next to a vegetable cart tended by a woman who looks about five hundred years old. The all-Chinese police band plays bagpipes and marches in kilts for the St. Patrick's Day parade. Street markets are the opposite of flowers: opening up at night and closing at day. In Hong Kong, all times are contiguous. All times are

---

[1] A style of detective movie characterized by dark shadows (*noir* is French for "black"), moodiness, and intrigue. [Editors' note.]

[2] A densely populated urban center across the harbor from Hong Kong center. [Editors' note.]

simultaneous. This essay is an attempt to describe a city that is itself already a description—Hong Kong is a description of time. This essay is also an experiment in time travel—an artifact of memory from July 2000. Hong Kong is now the same city but a different place. Prosperity—once the city's one-word gloss—is slowly becoming synonymous with Shanghai.[3] "I hear everyone's real depressed over there," I say at dinner to the mother of a friend of mine from Hong Kong. "That they're jealous, with all the jobs heading over to the mainland and all." She chews on a piece of lettuce and says, "Yes, they are jealous. But they have a right to be."

Five years later, we spend the next half-hour taking elevators that lead to stairs that lead to elevators. I don't have any idea where we're going and just follow my father, an immigrant from Taiwan whose Mandarin,[4] I realize, makes him only a third less lost than I am. He's following our guide, who, like Hong Kong itself, is all energy and no conversation. "We're headed for Victoria Peak today," my dad announced this morning. The touristy lookout could be the only spot where Hong Kong can be made comprehensible.   4

Suddenly our guide stops. Are we lost? This possibility is not surprising. It feels like we've been going in spirals, victims of some kind of geographic hoax. Our guide decides to ask for directions in Cantonese.[5] She stops a man with a dark complexion who reminds me of the vendors at the Taipei night market. He has short, wiry hair that resembles a scouring pad and is wearing a security guard's uniform. Chinese—I think—obviously. Probably a migrant from the mainland. "Where is Victoria Peak?" she asks him in Cantonese. The security guard looks at her and says, "Do you speak English?"   5

Dad and I look at each other. He says, "This is a strange city," and I start laughing, relieved that I'm not the only one who thinks so. We seem to be fumbling through different languages, shifting, testing, trying to find one we can all stand in. A bus rocking through the northern hills speaks to its passengers in Miltonic English: *Do not board or alight whilst bus is in motion.* (Lucifer alights. Buses throttle.[6]) And a week ago in   6

---

[3] The largest city in mainland China. [Editors' note.]

[4] A dialect of Chinese, spoken in the northern and southwestern districts of China and the official language for government, education, and media. [Editors' note.]

[5] A dialect of Chinese, spoken in southern China and the official language (along with English) of Hong Kong. [Editors' note.]

[6] John Milton (1608–74) was an English poet. With "Lucifer," or Satan, Chen alludes to *Paradise Lost*, Milton's epic poem about the biblical Garden of Eden and humanity's fall from grace. [Editors' note.]

Taiwan, my father had shed the most mundanely engrossing fear of any Chinese immigrant to America: his accent. He became a master of languages, all traces of self-consciousness suddenly gone from his voice. He chatted with taxi drivers and strangers about the drenching humidity or about which restaurants were good, casually code-switching to Taiwanese for jokes, Mandarin for information, and English for translation and one-word exclamations. When we showed up at the desk of the Taipei Hilton, the girls on staff spotted my dad and approached him in nervous English. He paused, got an odd look on his face—the fuzzy expression that Looney Tunes characters have when they're suspended in midair and about to fall—and said in Mandarin: "I'm Chinese!"

Back to searching for Victoria Peak, my father starts to ask the question in English, but someone interrupts. A Hong Kong yuppie standing thirty feet away muffles his cell phone in his blazer lapel and tells us the answer in rushed Cantonese. Some men in black blazers walk by, and some teens with blond spiky hair walk by, and some middle-aged men with grimy white aprons walk by—mostly Chinese, but otherwise unidentifiable. Indian? Polynesian? British? Hong Kong is an intensely international city. Every street in Kowloon is an intersection, not only of wet-walled alleys and futuristic buildings of glass, but also of the more transparent rays of cultures. 7

Somehow you are supposed to teach yourself how to comprehend Hong Kong's energy and flashy contradictions: Asian and Western; the encroaching Chinese mainland and the remnants of England; the greasy night markets of sticky-rice tamales and knockoff leather boots that slouch right across from Tiffany, Chanel, and Prada. The only things common to these are the offices sending air-conditioned blasts into the street, a kind of longing for money, and, most important, the sense of storytelling that the city seems to require as a visitor's pass. Hong Kong has a way of turning on your internal monologue. Walking becomes an act of silent storytelling, figuring people out. You feel like you are lost in some prelapsarian novel in which the plot has begun but the characters wait for you to name them. In some time, at some place, we step into an underground Cantonese restaurant and I see a gray-suited, red-tied man act like a parody of the States. American, I say, with an American accent: good-natured smiles, occasionally the slow English dispatched on foreigners and children, and a slightly uncomfortable look, as though he's worried he's outnumbered. 8

Finally we find Victoria Peak, by which I mean that we find the gondola to get us there. We buy tickets and step in, waiting to be hoisted up 9

fotoVoyager/Getty Images

Hong Kong as viewed from Victoria Peak.

into the humid nighttime atmosphere. The cab starts moving. At first, nothing in the windows but the ads on the sides of the tunnel, and then suddenly the city. Our gondola windows have become postcards. Hong Kong poses before us, bright, earnestly capitalist, electric, multiplying. A concrete wall blocks the view, and then the city is back again. Under us, a small red house sits on the cuff of the panorama. Light drops out of a pair of shutters, a door or window is open; someone is home. More stone, more wall. We hit the crest, reach our destination: Victoria Peak, the highest spot in Hong Kong and, for a tourist, the best. We have a God's-eye view of the skyline. The buildings shine yellow, white, orange, blue, all reflected in the dark bay waters; giant corporate logos shrink, skyscrapers huddle, and the city glows with a brilliant coolness. My eye seems too small to hold it all in.

We take the bus back. I sit on the top of a double-decker bus, on the 10 left side, in a city where they drive on the left side of the road. As we shake downhill, making acute turns, I begin to regret my seating preference: the wobbly tourists' corner. The bus hits a few branches, careens over double yellow lines, winds downhill. Whipped by full-motion vertigo, I grope for the metal railing, squeezing it as if for juice, and then laugh at my own cowardice. I gasp, then yawn in a slow, measured sort of panic, a civilized form of suffocation. Hong Kong—a city out of breath.

After we've been back from Victoria Peak for a few hours, I go to the 11 front desk of the hotel. A Hong Kong–Chinese woman in her mid-twenties looks up the Internet rates for me. She reads the per-minute charges off a small white card, and her voice compresses Mandarin, English, and Cantonese into a linguistic diamond: the Chinese-British accent. There's the Merchant-Ivory[7] sound, the lilt that movies tell us is cultured but that also seems austere and imperial, the way Chinese period films do. Yet the sound is also familiar, humble, and awkward: a Chinese voice wandering inside the English language. The sound of it reminds me of my parents. I can't get enough of it.

A few days later, we are ready to leave. Samuel Johnson[8] wrote that when one has tired of London, one has tired of life. But Hong Kong seems denser than any dream an American could have about London. We are suddenly sick of it. Everywhere is crowded: the restaurants at two on a Wednesday afternoon, the train platform every few minutes, the side-walks wet with people. This is the opposite of loneliness. It is the abundance of people that alienates us. 12

My father and I step into an underground Cantonese restaurant, the one with the red-tied American, and the other diners fly by us, blurred, the abstract expressionist's[9] version of people. A man sits across from us, the only person at his big round table. I'm guessing he's Indian. He has a sharp lawn mustache and a black satchel. A business-man from Britain? An engineer out for dinner? The other diners speed by us in streaks. I turn around and see the waiters coming by our table — or maybe just one waiter over and over — to set teacups upright, rip open chopsticks from their packaging, bring dishes, bring towels, even bring blankets when we say we are cold, bring the check. I hear another noise drift over the wheel of our table: the TV at the bar. The news is on: a fire yesterday in Tai O burns down homes in one of the few remaining fishing villages in Hong Kong, leaving seven hundred homeless. No, I'm getting it wrong. I'd read about it on the front page. There was no TV in that restaurant, not even a bar. Hong Kong quivers, not out of fear or sadness, but the way something quivers when our idea of it has changed. The waiters push out of the kitchen as if it's on fire, as if they're scrambling to escape it. 13

But the fire is Hong Kong. 14

---

[7] A film studio known for producing lavish movies on themes related to the English aristocracy. [Editors' note.]

[8] English poet, essayist, and linguist, 1709–84. [Editors' note.]

[9] Abstract expressionism is a school of art characterized by bright colors, hurried brushstrokes, and a deliberate lack of recognizable forms. [Editors' note.]

Meaning

1. "City Out of Breath" does not include a thesis statement. Does the essay have a main point, and if so, what is it? How can you tell?

2. What is "code-switching" (paragraph 6)? What does the term — and the practice — have to do with Chen's main idea?

3. Identify the sources of Chen's **allusions** to literature, art, and popular culture. What do these references contribute to his meaning?

4. How might Chen's last sentence have multiple meanings?

5. If you are uncertain of the meanings of any of the words listed below, try to guess them from the context of the essay. Then look them up to see how close your definitions were to those in the dictionary. Test out the new words by using each of them in a sentence or two of your own.

symphonic (3)	prelapsarian (8)	linguistic (11)
metronomic (3)	parody (8)	austere (11)
contiguous (3)	panorama (9)	imperial (11)
prosperity (3)	acute (10)	alienates (12)
encroaching (8)	vertigo (10)	

Purpose and Audience

1. In paragraph 3, Chen writes, "This essay is an attempt to describe a city that is itself already a description — Hong Kong is a description of time." What does he mean?

2. How does Chen make his experience vivid and clear for readers who have never been to Hong Kong?

Method and Structure

1. What dominant impression of the city does Chen create?

2. What point of view does the author take toward his subject?

3. How many of the five senses does Chen appeal to in his description? Find words or phrases that seem especially precise in conveying sensory impressions.

4. OTHER METHODS "City Out of Breath" uses **narration** almost as much as it uses description. While Chen relies on chronological order for most of the essay, in paragraphs 3 and 6 he flashes back to discussions and experiences in other places. What do these previous episodes contribute to his meaning and purpose?

Language

1. Note Chen's frequent use of the first person (*I* and *we*) and of the present tense. What does he achieve with this point of view?

2. A poet, Chen uses figures of speech to add depth to his descriptions. Locate two or three examples that you find especially striking, and explain their effect.

Writing Topics

1. **JOURNAL TO ESSAY**   Expanding on your journal response (p. 107), write a descriptive essay about the discomfort you felt when you first visited a new place. Consider not only what made you uncomfortable but also why you reacted the way you did. You may, if you wish, use your essay as an opportunity to contemplate the broader significance of your experience.

2. Think of a place to which you feel a special connection. The place can be urban or suburban or rural, and it need not be far away. In an essay, describe the place for readers who are completely unfamiliar with it and who may be skeptical about your enthusiasm for it. Use concrete, specific details and, if appropriate, figures of speech to show clearly why you value the place.

3. **CULTURAL CONSIDERATIONS**   Through most of his essay, Chen sees the other people in Hong Kong as foreign, so different and strange that interacting with them makes him laugh nervously. But as an American visiting the Chinese city, Chen is the foreigner in this situation. Imagine any of the scenarios he describes from the point of view of one of the Hong Kong residents, businesspeople, or workers he encounters. How might they have perceived him?

4. **CONNECTIONS**   Like Chen, David Sedaris, in "Me Talk Pretty One Day" (p. 131), relates an experience of discomfort with communicating in a different language. But while Chen emphasizes the awkwardness of listening to his father speak Chinese, Sedaris focuses on his own trouble understanding French. Write an essay analyzing what these two writers' examples have in common as well as any significant differences between them. How do their competing perspectives inform each other's experiences?

WRITING WITH THE METHOD

▶
DESCRIPTION

Select one of the following topics, or any other topic they suggest, for an essay developed by description. Be sure to choose a topic you care about so that description is a means of communicating an idea, not an end in itself.

People

1. An exceptionally neat or messy person
2. A person whose appearance and mannerisms are at odds with his or her real self
3. An annoying neighbor
4. A person you admire or respect
5. A person who intimidates you (teacher, salesperson, doctor, police officer, fellow student)

Places and Scenes

6. A department store, yard sale, or flea market
7. A frightening place
8. A prison cell, police station, or courtroom
9. Your home or workplace
10. A neighborhood devastated by foreclosures
11. A site of environmental destruction
12. The scene at a concert

Animals and Objects

13. Birds at a feeder
14. A work of art
15. An animal in a zoo, wildlife sanctuary, or rescue shelter
16. A prized possession

Sensations

17. The look and taste of a favorite or detested food
18. Waiting for important news
19. Being freed of some restraint
20. Sneezing
21. Skating, running, bodysurfing, skydiving, or some other activity
22. Extreme hunger, thirst, cold, heat, or fatigue

WRITING ABOUT THE THEME

▶

EXPERIENCING NEW PLACES

1. Although we tend to think of travel as a form of entertainment or relaxation, some of the writers in this chapter recognize that unfamiliar places can be difficult to come to terms with. Joan Didion's depiction of New Orleans in summertime (p. 91) and Ken Chen's portrayal of Hong Kong (p. 107) are most notable in this respect, but even Ian Frazier's look at an abandoned Siberian prison camp (p. 92) emphasizes the unsettling effects of its emptiness, and Amy Tan's experience of the Easter Island cave (p. 100) is initially unpleasant. Write a descriptive essay about a place that is special to you, emphasizing its strangeness rather than its beauty.

2. All of the writers in this chapter demonstrate strong feelings for the place, thing, or phenomenon they describe, but the writers vary considerably in the ways they express their feelings. For example, Ken Chen's own discomfort in Hong Kong colors all of his perceptions, whereas Marta Taylor's description of an electrical storm (p. 96) mixes serenity and awe. Write an essay analyzing the tone of these and the three other selections in this chapter: Joan Didion's and Ian Frazier's paragraphs on their travels and Amy Tan's essay about caving. Discuss which pieces you find most effective and why.

3. Each essay writer in this chapter vividly describes a specific place or thing that represents some larger, abstract concept: Marta Taylor's desert lightning represents the awesomeness of nature, the darkness of Amy Tan's cave represents the freedom of imagination, and Ken Chen's Hong Kong represents cultural dislocation. Think of a specific, tangible place or thing in your life that represents some larger, abstract idea and write a descriptive essay exploring this relationship.

7

EXAMPLE

▶

USING LANGUAGE

An **example** represents a general group or an abstract concept or quality. Steve McQueen is an example from the group of movie directors. A friend's texting at two in the morning is an example of her inconsiderateness—or desperation. We habitually use examples to bring broad ideas down to specifics so that others will take an interest in them and understand them. You might use examples to entertain friends with the idea that you're accident prone, to persuade family members that a sibling is showing self-destructive behavior that requires intervention, to demonstrate to voters that your local fire department deserves a budget increase, or to convince your employer that competing companies' benefits packages are more generous. Examples are so central to human communication, in fact, that you will use them in nearly everything you write and find them in nearly everything you read.

The authors of the readings in this chapter all have something to say about language—how we use it, abuse it, or change as a result of it. Their ideas likely came to them through encountering examples as they read, talked, and listened, so naturally they use examples to demonstrate those ideas. In one paragraph, Deborah Tannen draws on a single example to show the layers of meaning a simple phrase can convey. In the other, William Lutz uses two examples to illustrate how evasive doublespeak can be. Perri Klass's essay grapples with why doctors use peculiar and often cruel jargon and contemplates how it affects them. In another essay, David Sedaris uses humor to explore the difficulties of learning a second language. And student writer Olivia Melendez, inspired by Sedaris's example, considers her own experience speaking a foreign tongue in the country of its origin.

Reading Examples

The chief purpose of examples is to make the general specific and the abstract concrete. Since these operations are among the most basic in writing, it is easy to see why illustration or exemplification (the use of example) is among the most common methods of writing. Examples appear frequently in essays developed by other methods. In fact, as diverse as they are, all the essays in this book employ examples for clarity, support, and liveliness. If the writers had not used examples, we might have only a vague sense of their meaning, or worse, we might supply mistaken meanings from our own experiences.

While nearly indispensable in any kind of writing, exemplification may also serve as the dominant method of developing an essay. When a writer's primary goal is to convince readers of the truth of a general statement—whether a personal observation or a controversial assertion—using examples is a natural choice. Any of the following **generalizations**, for instance, might form the central assertion of an essay developed by example:

- *Generalizations about trends*: "E-books are now forcing the publishing industry to rethink the way it does business."
- *Generalizations about events*: "Some fans at the championship game were more competitive than the players."
- *Generalizations about institutions*: "A mental hospital is no place for the mentally ill."
- *Generalizations about behaviors*: "The personalities of parents are sometimes picked up by their children."
- *Generalizations about rituals*: "A funeral benefits the deceased person's family and friends."

How many examples are necessary to support a generalization? That depends on a writer's subject, purpose, and intended audience. Two basic patterns are possible:

- *A single extended example* of several paragraphs or several pages fills in needed background and gives the reader a complete view of the subject from one angle. For instance, the purpose of a funeral might be made clear with a narrative and descriptive account of a particular funeral, the family and friends who attended it, and the benefits they derived from it.
- *Multiple examples*, from a few to dozens, illustrate the range covered by the generalization. The competitiveness of a team's fans might be captured with three or four examples. But supporting the generalization

about mental hospitals might demand many examples of patients whose illnesses worsened in the hospital or (from a different angle) many examples of hospital practices that actually harmed patients.

Sometimes a generalization will merit support from both an extended example and several briefer examples, a combination that provides depth along with range. For instance, half the essay on mental hospitals might be devoted to one patient's experiences, and the other half to brief summaries of other patients' experiences.

When you read essays developed by illustration and exemplification, pay attention to how writers use examples to develop a point. Rarely will a simple list do an idea justice. Effective writers, as you will see, not only provide examples but also explain how those examples support their ideas.

Analyzing Examples in Paragraphs

Deborah Tannen (born 1945), a respected scholar with a knack for popular writing, is widely known for her prolific work on how people communicate. The following paragraph is from the book *Talking from 9 to 5* (1994), Tannen's best-selling exploration of gender differences in workplace communication.

Women are often told they apologize too much. The reason they're told to stop doing it is that, to many men, apologizing seems synonymous with putting oneself down. But there are many times when "I'm sorry" isn't self-deprecating, or even an apology; it's an automatic way of keeping both speakers on an equal footing.

> Generalization and topic sentence (underlined)

For example, a well-known columnist once interviewed me and gave me her phone number in case I needed to call her back. I misplaced the number and had to go through the newspaper's main switchboard. When our conversation was winding down and we'd both made ending-type remarks, I added, "Oh, I almost forgot—I lost your direct number, can I get it again?" "Oh, I'm sorry," she came back instantly, even though she had done nothing wrong and *I* was the one who'd lost the number. But I understood she wasn't really apologizing; she was just automatically reassuring me she had no intention of denying me her number.

> Single detailed example

William Lutz (born 1940) is an expert on doublespeak, which he defines as "language that conceals or manipulates thought. It makes the bad seem good, the negative appear positive, the unpleasant appear attractive or at least tolerable." In this paragraph from his book *Doublespeak* (1989), Lutz illustrates one use of this deceptive language.

Because it avoids or shifts responsibility, doublespeak is particularly effective in explaining or at least glossing over accidents. An air force colonel in charge of safety wrote in a letter that rocket boosters weighing more than 300,000 pounds "have an explosive force upon surface impact that is sufficient to exceed the accepted overpressure threshold of physiological damage for exposed personnel." In English: if a 300,000-pound booster rocket falls on you, you probably won't survive. In 1985 three American soldiers were killed and sixteen were injured when the first stage of a Pershing II missile they were unloading suddenly ignited. There was no explosion, said Major Michael Griffen, but rather "an unplanned rapid ignition of solid fuel."

Generalization and topic sentence (underlined)

Two examples

Developing an Essay by Example

▶ Getting Started

You need examples whenever your experiences, observations, or reading lead you to make a general statement: the examples give readers evidence for the statement so that they see its truth. An appropriate subject for an example paper is likely to be a general idea you have formed about people, things, the media, or any other feature of your life. Say, for instance, that you have noticed while watching television that many scripted programs aimed at teenagers deal with sensitive topics such as drug abuse, domestic violence, or chronic illness. There is your subject: teen dramas that address controversial social issues.

After choosing a subject, you should make a list of all the pertinent examples that occur to you. This stage may take some thought and even some further reading or observation. When you're making this list, focus on identifying as many examples as you can, but keep your intended readers at the front of your mind: what do they already know about your subject, and what more do they need to know in order to accept your view of it?

▶ Forming a Thesis

Having several examples of a subject is a good starting place, but you will also need a thesis that ties the examples together and gives them a point. A clear thesis is crucial for an example paper, because without it readers can only guess what your illustrations are intended to show.

To move from a general subject toward a workable thesis, try making a generalization based on what you know of individual examples:

> Some teen dramas do a surprisingly good job of explaining difficult social issues.

> Some teen dramas trivialize difficult social issues in their quest for ratings.

Either of these statements could serve as the thesis of an essay, the point you want readers to take away from your examples.

Avoid the temptation to start with a broad statement and then try to drum up a few examples to prove it. A thesis such as "Teenagers do poorly in school because they watch too much television" would require factual support gained from research. If your brother performs poorly in school and you blame his television habits, narrow your thesis so that it accurately reflects your evidence—perhaps "For my brother, the more time spent watching television the poorer the grades."

After arriving at your thesis, you should narrow your list of examples down to those that are most pertinent, adding new examples as necessary to persuade readers of your point. For instance, in illustrating the social value of teen dramas for readers who believe television is worthless or even harmful, you might concentrate on the programs or individual episodes that are most relevant to readers' lives, providing enough detail about each to make readers see the relevance.

▶ Organizing

Most example essays open with an **introduction** that engages readers' attention and gives them some context to relate to. You might begin the paper on teen dramas, for instance, by briefly narrating the plot of one episode. The opening should lead into your thesis sentence so that readers know what to expect from the rest of the essay.

Organizing the **body** of the essay may not be difficult if you use a single example, for the example itself may suggest a distinct method of development (such as narration) and thus a built-in arrangement. But an essay using multiple examples usually requires close attention to arrangement so that readers experience not a list but a pattern. Consider these guidelines:

- *With a limited number of examples*—say, four or five—use a **climactic** organization, arranging the examples in order of increasing importance, interest, or complexity. Then the strongest and most detailed example provides a dramatic finish.

- *With many examples*—ten or more—find some likenesses among them that will allow you to treat them in groups. For instance, instead of covering fourteen teen dramas in a shapeless list, you might group them by subject into shows dealing with family relations, those dealing with illness, and the like. Covering each group in a separate paragraph or two avoids the awkward string of choppy paragraphs that might result from covering each example independently. And arranging the groups themselves in order of increasing interest or importance further structures your presentation.

To conclude your essay, you may want to summarize by elaborating on the generalization of your thesis now that you have supported it. But the essay may not require a **conclusion** at all if you believe your final example emphasizes your point and provides a strong finish.

▶ Drafting

While you draft your essay, remember that your examples must be plentiful and specific enough to support your generalization. If you use fifteen different examples, their range should allow you to treat each one briefly, in one or two sentences. But if you use only three examples, say, you will have to describe each one in sufficient detail to make up for their small number. And if you use only a single example, you must be as specific as possible so that readers see clearly how it illustrates your generalization.

▶ Revising and Editing

To be sure you've met the expectations that most readers hold for examples, revise and edit your draft by considering the following questions and the information in the Focus box on the next page.

FOCUS ON SENTENCE VARIETY

While accumulating examples and detailing them during drafting — both essential tasks for a successful essay — you may find yourself writing strings of similar sentences:

> UNVARIED   One example of a teen drama that deals with chronic illness is *Rockingham Place*. Another example is *The Beating Heart*. Another is *Tree of Life*. These three shows treat misunderstood or little-known diseases in a way that increases the viewer's sympathy and understanding. The characters in *Rockingham Place* include a little boy who suffers from cystic fibrosis. *The Beating Heart* features a mother of four who is weakening from multiple sclerosis. *Tree of Life* deals with brothers who are both struggling with muscular dystrophy. All these dramas show complex, struggling human beings caught blamelessly in desperate circumstances.

The writer of this paragraph was clearly pushing to add examples and to expand them, but the passage needs editing so that the writer's labor isn't so obvious and the sentences are more varied and interesting:

> VARIED   Three teen dramas dealing with chronic illness are *Rockingham Place*, *The Beating Heart*, and *Tree of Life*. In these shows people with little-known or misunderstood diseases become subjects for the viewer's sympathy and understanding. A little boy suffering from cystic fibrosis, a mother weakening from multiple sclerosis, a pair of brothers coping with muscular dystrophy — these complex, struggling human beings are caught blamelessly in desperate circumstances.

As you review your draft, be alert to repetitive sentence structures and look for opportunities to change them: try coordinating and subordinating, varying the beginnings and endings of sentences, shortening some and lengthening others. For more on sentence variety, turn to pages 50–51.

■ *Is your generalization fully supported by your examples?* If not, you may need to narrow your thesis statement or add more evidence.

LaunchPad Solo macmillan learning   To practice revising for sentence variety, visit *LaunchPad Solo for Readers and Writers* > Style and Mechanics > Sentence Variety

- *Are all examples, or parts of a single example, obviously relevant to your generalization?* Be careful not to get sidetracked by interesting but unrelated information.

- *Are the examples specific?* Examples bring a generalization down to earth only if they are well detailed. For an essay on the social value of teen dramas, for instance, simply naming programs and their subjects would not demonstrate their value. Each drama would need a plot or character summary that shows how the program illustrates the generalization.

- *Do the examples, or the parts of a single example, cover all the territory mapped out by your generalization?* To support your generalization, you need to present a range of instances that fairly represents the whole. An essay would be misleading if it failed to acknowledge that not *all* teen dramas have social value. It would also be misleading if it presented several shows as representative examples of socially valuable teen programming when in fact they were the *only* instances.

A passage is not plain English—still less is it good English—if we are obliged to read it twice to find out what it means.
—Dorothy Sayers

I'm bilingual. I speak English and I speak educationese.
—Shirley Hufstedler

You and I come by road or rail, but economists travel on infrastructure.
—Margaret Thatcher

JOURNAL RESPONSE   What words or expressions have you encountered in your college courses or in your college's rules and regulations that have confused, delighted, or irritated you? Write a brief journal entry describing the language and its effects on you.

Perri Klass

Perri Klass is a pediatrician, a writer, and a knitter. She was born in 1958 in Trinidad and grew up in New York City and New Jersey. Klass obtained a BA from Harvard University in 1979, finished Harvard Medical School in 1986, and teaches journalism and pediatrics at New York University. Her publications are extensive: short stories and articles in *Mademoiselle*, the *New York Times*, the *New England Journal of Medicine*, and other periodicals; several novels, including *The Mystery of Breathing* (2004) and *The Mercy Rule* (2009); five essay collections; a memoir, *Every Mother Is a Daughter* (2005); and the parenting guide *Quirky Kids* (2003). Klass is the president and medical director of Reach Out and Read, a nonprofit group that works with pediatricians to distribute books to disadvantaged children.

She's Your Basic LOL in NAD

Most of us have felt excluded, confused, or even frightened by the jargon of the medical profession—that is, by the special terminology and abbreviations for diseases and procedures. In this essay Klass uses examples of such language, some of it heartless, to illustrate the pluses and minuses of becoming a doctor. The essay first appeared in 1984 as a "Hers" column in the *New York Times*.

"Mrs. Tolstoy is your basic LOL in NAD, admitted for a soft rule-out MI," the intern announces. I scribble that on my patient list. In other words Mrs. Tolstoy is a Little Old Lady in No Apparent Distress who is in the hospital to make sure she hasn't had a heart attack (rule out a myocardial   1 infarction). And we think it's unlikely that she has had a heart attack (a *soft* rule-out).

If I learned nothing else during my first three months of working in the hospital as a medical student, I learned endless jargon and abbreviations. I started out in a state of primeval innocence, in which I didn't even know that "s̄ CP, SOB, N/V" meant "without chest pain, shortness of breath, or nausea and vomiting." By the end I took the abbreviations so for granted that I would complain to my mother the English professor, "And can you believe I had to put down *three* NG tubes last night?"   2

"You'll have to tell me what an NG tube is if you want me to sympathize properly," my mother said. NG, nasogastric—isn't it obvious?   3

I picked up not only the specific expressions but also the patterns of speech and the grammatical conventions; for example, you never say that a patient's blood pressure fell or that his cardiac enzymes rose. Instead, the patient is always the subject of the verb: "He dropped his pressure." "He bumped his enzymes." This sort of construction probably reflects that profound irritation of the intern when the nurses come in the middle of the night to say that Mr. Dickinson has disturbingly low blood pressure. "Oh, he's gonna hurt me bad tonight," the intern may say, inevitably angry at Mr. Dickinson for dropping his pressure and creating a problem.   4

When chemotherapy fails to cure Mrs. Bacon's cancer, what we say is, "Mrs. Bacon failed chemotherapy."   5

"Well, we've already had one hit today, and we're up next, but at least we've got mostly stable players on our team." This means that our team (group of doctors and medical students) has already gotten one new admission today, and it is our turn again, so we'll get whoever is next admitted in emergency, but at least most of the patients we already have are fairly stable, that is, unlikely to drop their pressures or in any other way get suddenly sicker and hurt us bad. Baseball metaphor is pervasive: a no-hitter is a night without any new admissions. A player is always a patient—a nitrate player is a patient on nitrates, a unit player is a patient in the intensive-care unit, and so on, until you reach the terminal player.   6

It is interesting to consider what it means to be winning, or doing well, in this perennial baseball game. When the intern hangs up the phone and announces, "I got a hit," that is not cause for congratulations. The team is not scoring points; rather, it is getting hit, being bombarded with new patients. The object of the game from the point of view of the doctors, considering the players for whom they are already responsible, is to get as few new hits as possible.   7

These special languages contribute to a sense of closeness and professional spirit among people who are under a great deal of stress. As a   8 medical student, it was exciting for me to discover that I'd finally cracked the code, that I could understand what doctors said and wrote and could use the same formulations myself. Some people seem to become enamored of the jargon for its own sake, perhaps because they are so deeply thrilled with the idea of medicine, with the idea of themselves as doctors.

I knew a medical student who was referred to by the interns on the team as Mr. Eponym because he was so infatuated with eponymous terminology,[1] the more obscure the better. He never said "capillary pulsation" if he could say "Quincke's pulses." He would lovingly tell over the multinamed syndromes—Wolff-Parkinson-White, Lown-Ganong-Levine, Henoch-Schonlein—until the temptation to suggest Schleswig-Holstein or Stevenson-Kefauver or Baskin-Robbins became irresistible to his less reverent colleagues. 9

And there is the jargon that you don't ever want to hear yourself using. You know that your training is changing you, but there are certain changes you think would be going a little too far. 10

The resident was describing a man with devastating terminal pancreatic cancer. "Basically he's CTD," the resident concluded. I reminded myself that I had resolved not to be shy about asking when I didn't understand things. "CTD?" I asked timidly. 11

The resident smirked at me. "Circling The Drain." 12

The images are vivid and terrible. "What happened to Mrs. Melville?" 13

"Oh, she boxed last night." To box is to die, of course. 14

Then there are the more pompous locutions that can make the beginning medical student nervous about the effects of medical training. A friend of mine was told by his resident, "A pregnant woman with sickle-cell represents a failure of genetic counseling." 15

Mr. Eponym, who tried hard to talk like the doctors, once explained to me, "An infant is basically a brainstem preparation." A brainstem preparation, as used in neurological research, is an animal whose higher brain functions have been destroyed so that only the most primitive reflexes remain, like the sucking reflex, the startle reflex, and the rooting reflex. 16

The more extreme forms aside, one most important function of medical jargon is to help doctors maintain some distance from their patients. By reformulating a patient's pain and problems into a language that the patient doesn't even speak, I suppose we are in some sense taking those 17

---

[1] *Eponymous* means "named after"—in this case, medical terminology is named after researchers. [Editors' note.]

pains and problems under our jurisdiction and also reducing their emotional impact. This linguistic separation between doctors and patients allows conversations to go on at the bedside that are unintelligible to the patient. "Naturally, we're worried about adreno-CA," the intern can say to the medical student, and lung cancer need never be mentioned.

I learned a new language this past summer. At times it thrills me to hear myself using it. It enables me to understand my colleagues, to communicate effectively in the hospital. Yet I am uncomfortably aware that I will never again notice the peculiarities and even atrocities of medical language as keenly as I did this summer. There may be specific expressions I manage to avoid, but even as I remark them, promising myself I will never use them, I find that this language is becoming my professional speech. It no longer sounds strange in my ears—or coming from my mouth. And I am afraid that as with any new language, to use it properly you must absorb not only the vocabulary but also the structure, the logic, the attitudes. At first you may notice these new alien assumptions every time you put together a sentence, but with time and increased fluency you stop being aware of them at all. And as you lose that awareness, for better or for worse, you move closer and closer to being a doctor instead of just talking like one. 18

Meaning

1. What point does Klass make about medical jargon in this essay? Where does she reveal her main point explicitly?

2. What useful purposes does medical jargon serve, according to Klass? Do the examples in paragraphs 9–16 serve these purposes? Why, or why not?

3. If you are uncertain of the meanings of any of the words listed below, try to guess them from the context of the essay. Then look them up to see how close your definitions were to those in the dictionary. Test out the new words by using each of them in a sentence or two of your own.

primeval (2)	syndromes (9)	locutions (15)
terminal (6)	reverent (9)	jurisdiction (17)
perennial (7)	pompous (15)	

Purpose and Audience

1. What does Klass imply when she states that she began her work in the hospital "in a state of primeval innocence" (paragraph 2)? What does this phrase suggest about her purpose in writing the essay?

2. From what perspective does Klass write this essay: that of a medical professional? someone outside the profession? a patient? someone else?

To what extent does she expect her readers to share her perspective? What evidence in the essay supports your answer?

3. Given that she is writing for a general audience, does Klass take adequate care to define medical terms? Support your answer with examples from the essay.

Method and Structure

1. Why does Klass begin the essay with an example rather than a statement of her main idea? What effect does this example produce? How does this effect support her purpose in writing the essay?

2. Although Klass uses many examples of medical jargon, she avoids the dull effect of a list by periodically stepping back to make a general statement about her experience or the jargon—for instance, "I picked up not only the specific expressions but also the patterns of speech and the grammatical conventions" (paragraph 4). Locate other places—not necessarily at the beginnings of paragraphs—where Klass breaks up her examples with more general statements.

3. OTHER METHODS Klass uses several other methods besides example, among them **classification, definition**, and **cause-and-effect analysis**. What effects—positive and negative—does medical jargon have on Klass, other students, and doctors who use it?

Language

1. What is the **tone** of this essay? Is Klass trying to be humorous or tongue-in-cheek about the jargon of the profession, or is she serious? Where in the essay is the author's attitude toward her subject the most obvious?

2. Klass refers to the users of medical jargon as both *we/us* (paragraphs 1, 5, 6, 17) and *they* (7), and sometimes she shifts from *I* to *you* within a paragraph (4, 18). Do you think these **shifts** are effective or distracting? Why? Do the shifts serve any function?

3. Klass obviously experienced both positive and negative feelings about mastering medical jargon. Which words and phrases in the last paragraph reflect positive feelings, and which negative?

Writing Topics

1. JOURNAL TO ESSAY When she attended medical school, Perri Klass discovered a novel language to learn and with it some new attitudes. Working from your journal response (p. 125), write an essay about the new ways

of speaking and attitudes you have encountered in college. Have you been confronted with different kinds of people (professors, other students) from the ones you knew before? Have you had difficulty understanding some words people use? Have you found yourself embracing ideas you never thought you would or speaking differently? Have others noticed a change in you that you may not have been aware of? Have you noticed changes in the friends you had before college? Focus on a particular kind of obstacle or change, using specific examples to convey this experience to readers.

2. Klass's essay explores the "separation between doctors and patients" (paragraph 17). Has this separation affected you as a patient or as a relative or friend of a patient? If so, write an essay about your experiences. Did the medical professionals rely heavily on jargon? Was their language comforting, frightening, irritating? Based on your experience and on Klass's essay, do you believe that the separation between doctors and patients is desirable? Why, or why not?

3. **CULTURAL CONSIDERATIONS** Most groups focused on a common interest have their own jargon. If you belong to such a group—for example, runners, football fans, food servers, engineering students—spend a few days listening to yourself and others use this language and thinking about the purposes it serves. Which aspects of this language seem intended to make users feel like insiders? Which seem to serve some other purpose, and what is it? In an essay, explain what this jargon reveals about the group and its common interest, using as many specific examples as you can.

4. **CONNECTIONS** Perri Klass writes that medical jargon "contribute[s] to a sense of closeness and professional spirit among people who are under a great deal of stress" (paragraph 8) and that it helps doctors "maintain some distance from their patients" (17). Write an essay in which you analyze the function of "doublespeak," as presented by William Lutz (p. 120). Who, if anyone, is such language designed to help: accident victims? their families? someone else? Can a positive case be made for this language?

I always thought the saddest feeling in life is when you're dancing in a really joyful way, and then you hit your head on something.　—Lena Dunham

It is impossible to live without failing at something, unless you live so cautiously that you might as well not have lived at all.　—J. K. Rowling

That which does not kill us makes us stronger.　—Friedrich Nietzsche

JOURNAL RESPONSE　We've all suffered embarrassing moments. Think of a time when you felt humiliated or certain to fail. What happened? Is the embarrassment still as painful for you as it felt at the time? Reflect on the situation in your journal.

David Sedaris

David Sedaris's hilarious yet often touching autobiographical essays have earned him both popular and critical acclaim; he has received the Thurber Prize for American Humor and been named Humorist of the Year by *Time* magazine. Born in 1957, Sedaris grew up in North Carolina and attended the School of the Art Institute of Chicago, where he taught writing for several years before moving to New York City. Working odd jobs during the day and writing about them at night, Sedaris catapulted to near-overnight success in 1993 after reading on National Public Radio a piece about working as a department-store Christmas elf. Since then, he has been a frequent contributor to the *New Yorker*, *Esquire*, and public radio's *Morning Edition* and *This American Life*. Sedaris has published several best-selling collections of essays, including *Naked* (1996), *Me Talk Pretty One Day* (2000), *When You Are Engulfed in Flames* (2008), and *Let's Explore Diabetes with Owls* (2013). His most recent book is *Theft By Finding* (2017), a selection of the author's diary entries from his first twenty-five years as a writer. Currently living in the English countryside, Sedaris has also resided in Paris and rural France.

Me Talk Pretty One Day

In this title essay from *Me Talk Pretty One Day*, Sedaris launches his trademark wit at a favorite target: the French language. Learning to speak a new language, he shows, involves a mixture of humiliations and triumphs.

At the age of forty-one, I am returning to school and have to think of 1 myself as what my French textbook calls "a true debutant." After paying my tuition, I was issued a student ID, which allows me a discounted entry fee at movie theaters, puppet shows, and Festyland, a far-flung amusement park that advertises with billboards picturing a cartoon stegosaurus sitting in a canoe and eating what appears to be a ham sandwich.

I've moved to Paris with hopes of learning the language. My school is an easy ten-minute walk from my apartment, and on the first day of class I arrived early, watching as the returning students greeted one another in the school lobby. Vacations were recounted, and questions were raised concerning mutual friends with names like Kang and Vlatnya. Regardless of their nationalities, everyone spoke in what sounded to me like excellent French. Some accents were better than others, but the students exhibited an ease and confidence I found intimidating. As an added discomfort, they were all young, attractive, and well dressed, causing me to feel not unlike Pa Kettle[1] trapped backstage after a fashion show.

The first day of class was nerve-racking because I knew I'd be expected to perform. That's the way they do it here—it's everybody into the language pool, sink or swim. The teacher marched in, deeply tanned from a recent vacation, and proceeded to rattle off a series of administrative announcements. I've spent quite a few summers in Normandy, and I took a month-long French class before leaving New York. I'm not completely in the dark, yet I understood only half of what this woman was saying.

"If you have not *meimslsxp* or *lgpdmurct* by this time, then you should not be in this room. Has everyone *apzkiubjxow*? Everyone? Good, we shall begin." She spread out her lesson plan and sighed, saying, "All right, then, who knows the alphabet?"

It was startling because (a) I hadn't been asked that question in a while and (b) I realized, while laughing, that I myself did *not* know the alphabet. They're the same letters, but in France they're pronounced differently. I knew the shape of the alphabet but had no idea what it actually sounded like.

"Ahh." The teacher went to the board and sketched the letter *a*. "Do we have anyone in the room whose first name commences with an *ahh*?"

Two Polish Annas raised their hands, and the teacher instructed them to present themselves by stating their names, nationalities, occupations, and a brief list of things they liked and disliked in this world. The first Anna hailed from an industrial town outside of Warsaw and had front teeth the size of tombstones. She worked as a seamstress, enjoyed quiet times with friends, and hated the mosquito.

---

[1]A fictional hillbilly character featured in a series of books and movies in the 1940s and '50s. [Editors' note.]

"Oh, really," the teacher said. "How very interesting. I thought that everyone loved the mosquito, but here, in front of all the world, you claim to detest him. How is it that we've been blessed with someone as unique and original as you? Tell us, please." 8

The seamstress did not understand what was being said but knew that this was an occasion for shame. Her rabbity mouth huffed for breath, and she stared down at her lap as though the appropriate comeback were stitched somewhere alongside the zipper of her slacks. 9

The second Anna learned from the first and claimed to love sunshine and detest lies. It sounded like a translation of one of those Playmate of the Month data sheets, the answers always written in the same loopy handwriting: "Turn-ons: Mom's famous five-alarm chili! Turnoffs: insecurity and guys who come on too strong!!!!" 10

The two Polish Annas surely had clear notions of what they loved and hated, but like the rest of us, they were limited in terms of vocabulary, and this made them appear less than sophisticated. The teacher forged on, and we learned that Carlos, the Argentine bandonion[2] player, loved wine, music, and, in his words, "making sex with the womens of the world." Next came a beautiful young Yugoslav[3] who identified herself as an optimist, saying that she loved everything that life had to offer. 11

The teacher licked her lips, revealing a hint of the saucebox we would later come to know. She crouched low for her attack, placed her hands on the young woman's desk, and leaned close, saying, "Oh yeah? And do you love your little war?" 12

While the optimist struggled to defend herself, I scrambled to think of an answer to what had obviously become a trick question. How often is one asked what he loves in this world? More to the point, how often is one asked and then publicly ridiculed for his answer? I recalled my mother, flushed with wine, pounding the tabletop late one night, saying, "Love? I love a good steak cooked rare. I love my cat, and I love . . ." My sisters and I leaned forward, waiting to hear our names. "Tums," our mother said. "I love Tums." 13

The teacher killed some time accusing the Yugoslavian girl of masterminding a program of genocide, and I jotted frantic notes in the margins of my pad. While I can honestly say that I love leafing through medical 14

---

[2] A South American musical instrument, similar to a small accordion. [Editors' note.]

[3] A native of Yugoslavia, a former communist country in Eastern Europe divided after several wars into Bosnia and Herzegovina, Croatia, Kosovo, Macedonia, Montenegro, Serbia, and Slovenia. [Editors' note.]

textbooks devoted to severe dermatological conditions, the hobby is beyond the reach of my French vocabulary, and acting it out would only have invited controversy.

When called upon, I delivered an effortless list of things that I detest: 15 blood sausage, intestinal pâtés, brain pudding. I'd learned these words the hard way. Having given it some thought, I then declared my love for IBM typewriters, the French word for *bruise*, and my electric floor waxer. It was a short list, but still I managed to mispronounce *IBM* and assign the wrong gender to both the floor waxer and the typewriter.[4] The teacher's reaction led me to believe that these mistakes were capital crimes in the country of France.

"Were you always this *palicmkrexis*?" she asked. "Even a *fiuscrzsa tici-*   16 *welmun* knows that a typewriter is feminine."

I absorbed as much of her abuse as I could understand, thinking—but   17 not saying—that I find it ridiculous to assign a gender to an inanimate object incapable of disrobing and making an occasional fool of itself. Why refer to Lady Crack Pipe or Good Sir Dishrag when these things could never live up to all that their sex implied?

The teacher proceeded to belittle everyone from German Eva, who   18 hated laziness, to Japanese Yukari, who loved paintbrushes and soap. Italian, Thai, Dutch, Korean, and Chinese—we all left class foolishly believing that the worst was over. She'd shaken us up a little, but surely that was just an act designed to weed out the deadweight. We didn't know it then, but the coming months would teach us what it was like to spend time in the presence of a wild animal, something completely unpredictable. Her temperament was not based on a series of good and bad days but, rather, good and bad moments. We soon learned to dodge chalk and protect our heads and stomachs whenever she approached us with a question. She hadn't yet punched anyone, but it seemed wise to protect ourselves against the inevitable.

Though we were forbidden to speak anything but French, the teacher   19 would occasionally use us to practice any of her five fluent languages.

"I hate you," she said to me one afternoon. Her English was flawless.   20 "I really, really hate you." Call me sensitive, but I couldn't help but take it personally.

---

[4]In French, nouns are considered either male or female. Masculine nouns are preceded by the article *le*; feminine nouns are preceded by *la*. As is the case with English pronouns and antecedents, French nouns must agree in gender with the pronouns and adjectives used to describe them. [Editors' note.]

After being singled out as a lazy *kfdtinvfm*, I took to spending four 21
hours a night on my homework, putting in even more time whenever we
were assigned an essay. I suppose I could have gotten by with less, but
I was determined to create some sort of identity for myself: David the
hard worker, David the cut-up. We'd have one of those "complete this
sentence" exercises, and I'd fool with the thing for hours, invariably settling on something like "A quick run around the lake? I'd love to! Just give
me a moment while I strap on my wooden leg." The teacher, through
word and action, conveyed the message that if this was my idea of an
identity, she wanted nothing to do with it.

My fear and discomfort crept beyond the borders of the classroom 22
and accompanied me out onto the wide boulevards. Stopping for a coffee,
asking directions, depositing money in my bank account: these things
were out of the question, as they involved having to speak. Before beginning school, there'd been no shutting me up, but now I was convinced
that everything I said was wrong. When the phone rang, I ignored it. If
someone asked me a question, I pretended to be deaf. I knew my fear was
getting the best of me when I started wondering why they don't sell cuts
of meat in vending machines.

My only comfort was the knowledge that I was not alone. Huddled in 23
the hallways and making the most of our pathetic French, my fellow students and I engaged in the sort of conversation commonly overheard in
refugee camps.

"Sometime me cry alone at night." 24

"That be common for I, also, but be more strong, you. Much work 25
and someday you talk pretty. People start love you soon. Maybe tomorrow, okay."

Unlike the French class I had taken in New York, here there was no 26
sense of competition. When the teacher poked a shy Korean in the eyelid
with a freshly sharpened pencil, we took no comfort in the fact that,
unlike Hyeyoon Cho, we all knew the irregular past tense of the verb *to
defeat*. In all fairness, the teacher hadn't meant to stab the girl, but neither
did she spend much time apologizing, saying only, "Well, you should
have been *vkkdyo* more *kdeynfulh*."

Over time it became impossible to believe that any of us would ever 27
improve. Fall arrived and it rained every day, meaning we would now be
scolded for the water dripping from our coats and umbrellas. It was mid-
October when the teacher singled me out, saying, "Every day spent with
you is like having a cesarean section." And it struck me that, for the first
time since arriving in France, I could understand every word that someone was saying.

Understanding doesn't mean that you can suddenly speak the lan- 28
guage. Far from it. It's a small step, nothing more, yet its rewards are
intoxicating and deceptive. The teacher continued her diatribe and I settled back, bathing in the subtle beauty of each new curse and insult.

"You exhaust me with your foolishness and reward my efforts with 29
nothing but pain, do you understand me?"

The world opened up, and it was with great joy that I responded, 30
"I know the thing that you speak exact now. Talk me more, you, plus,
please, plus."

Meaning

1. Why do Sedaris and the other students have difficulty expressing their
   likes and dislikes in class?

2. Sedaris devotes the majority of his essay to enumerating the humiliations
   and frustrations he experienced as a student, but his feelings change
   markedly toward the end. What causes his shift in attitude?

3. In your own words, explain Sedaris's thesis. Where does he state it
   explicitly?

4. If you are uncertain of the meanings of any of the words listed below, try
   to guess them from the context of Sedaris's essay. Then look them up to
   see how close your definitions were to those in the dictionary. Test out
   the new words by using each of them in a sentence or two of your own.

   debutant (1)   dermatological (14)   temperament (18)
   saucebox (12)   inanimate (17)   diatribe (28)
   genocide (14)

Purpose and Audience

1. It can be painful to recall an embarrassing experience, yet Sedaris chooses
   to do so. What do you believe is his purpose in recording these episodes
   from his French class: to understand his experience? to mock his classmates? to express his frustrations? to argue a point about learning? to do
   something else?

2. What assumptions does Sedaris seem to make about his readers: their age,
   their nationality, their attitudes toward the French language, their experiences as students, and so on?

3. How does Sedaris characterize his classmates? his teacher? Does he mean
   for readers to take his examples literally? How can you tell?

4. What impression of himself does Sedaris create? How seriously does he
   expect readers to take him? What words and passages support your answer?

Method and Structure

1. How does Sedaris use examples for comic effect?

2. What generalizations do the examples in paragraphs 2–3 and 22 support?

3. What do Sedaris's examples reveal about his attitude toward his teacher and her methods? Does he feel anger? bitterness? shame? appreciation? amusement? Why do you think so?

4. OTHER METHODS "Me Talk Pretty One Day" relies on **narration** as much as it does example. How does Sedaris use **dialogue** to move his story forward?

Language

1. Analyze the structures and lengths of sentences in paragraph 2. What strategies does Sedaris use to achieve variety?

2. What is the effect of the many nonsense words, such as *meimslsxp* and *lgpd-murct* (paragraph 4), that Sedaris sprinkles throughout his essay? Why doesn't he simply repeat the French words or their English translations instead?

Writing Topics

1. JOURNAL TO ESSAY Reread your journal response and the quotations that precede Sedaris's essay (p. 131). Using specific examples, write an essay about the life lessons to be learned from failure.

2. If you are studying or have learned a second language, write an essay in which you explain the difficulty involved. Draw your examples not just from the new language's grammar and vocabulary but also from its underlying logic and attitudes. For instance, does one speak to older people differently in the new language? make requests differently? describe love or art differently? What do you expect to gain—or lose—from acquiring a new language? If you like, try to achieve humor in your essay by imitating Sedaris's style. (For a sample of another student's writing on this topic, see the next essay, Olivia Melendez's "The Chinese Kindergartener.")

3. CULTURAL CONSIDERATIONS As Sedaris points out, the French language assigns a gender to every noun, a convention that he finds bizarre and distracting but seems perfectly natural to native French speakers. Focusing on a single example, write an essay in which you contemplate the influence of language on culture, and vice versa. How might male and female forms for nouns, for instance, reflect social hierarchies? Why did feminists fight to eliminate the generic male pronoun from American English (until the late twentieth century, it was standard practice to use

he, his, and *man* to refer to both men and women)? Why does France have a government commission charged with banning English words like *weekend, volleyball,* and *surfer* from the French language? Other examples may come to mind; write about what interests you most.

4. **CONNECTIONS**   Both Sedaris and Kaitlyn Haskie, in "A Paradigm Shift: Indigenous Peoples in the New Millennium" (p. 320), suggest that the ways we communicate can create closeness to or distance from other people. Write an essay in which you examine how members of a group—say, students, faculty members, relatives, or people from a particular region— use language to establish the nature of their relationships.

Education is a progressive discovery of our own ignorance. —Will Durant

Curiosity is the gateway to everything you know you want, and comfort is like a beautiful prison. —Sarah Jessica Parker

All I really need to know I learned in kindergarten. —Robert Fulghum

JOURNAL RESPONSE Think of a time when you accomplished something after struggling with it over time: learning a skill such as skating or playing a musical instrument, communicating in a second (or third) language, winning over a new friend, achieving a health or fitness goal. What happened? What difficulties did you encounter, and how did it feel to finally succeed? Recall the events in your journal.

Olivia Melendez

Olivia Melendez was born in 1997 in Bridgeport, Connecticut, where she grew up in a culturally diverse neighborhood and household (her mother is Polish and her father is Puerto Rican). From a young age she was fascinated by different languages and cultures, so she enrolled with the Center for Global Studies at Brien McMahon High School in nearby Norwalk, Connecticut, with a focus on China. Now a student at Fairfield University, she is majoring in art history and reports that she enjoys visiting museums in New York City, watching movies, and spending time with her two rescue dogs. She expects to graduate in 2019 and hopes to pursue a graduate degree in art history and then start a career in the field, ideally as a curator of modern and contemporary art.

The Chinese Kindergartener
(Student Essay)

Melendez wrote this essay for her first-year college writing class and then published it in *Eloquentia Perfecta*, an annual anthology of Fairfield University students' writing, in 2016. With ample examples and careful thought, Melendez responds to David Sedaris's "Me Talk Pretty One Day" (p. 131) by recounting a similar learning experience of her own.

Learning a second language can be one of the most rewarding, painful, 1 thrilling, traumatic, beautiful, embarrassing human experiences. Like the

French class in Paris David Sedaris recounts in "Me Talk Pretty One Day," my journey of studying a foreign language in its native country was equal parts mortifying and eye-opening. If I were to put a single word to the experience, I don't think I could say the feeling is anything other than humbling.

At just fifteen years old, I had the opportunity to travel to China for fourteen days. Being a sophomore in high school, I had only been learning Chinese for a year and a half prior to my trip. It was the opportunity of a lifetime for me to develop my language skills in the country of its origin. The first week of the trip involved touring all over eastern China. This meant a new train, plane, or bus to a new city and a new hotel every day, and this was all shared by about sixteen of my classmates, our three teachers, and myself. Our days were filled with markets and malls and museums, and at the end of it all we returned to our hotel and laughed off our language blunders of the day together. The best parts of our first week were communicating with locals, and also being able to have your friend right behind you laughing at your inability to get across what you're saying. Not because you lack the vocabulary, but because the locals can't understand you past your American accent. During this week, I realized that when you're lost in a Chinese market, most of the vocabulary you learn in a textbook is of no use. In fact, during your average day, probably nothing from a textbook would be of use.

In the second week of the trip, my classmates and I were separated and sent to live with different host families in Shanghai. It was in this week I came to realize that my diligent study of classroom objects, articles of clothing, fruits, and vegetables would not aid me in asking my host mother to shut the windows at night because I hadn't packed for the freak midsummer cold front Shanghai was experiencing, and after sleeping on the floor underneath open windows for a week I was one night away from hypothermia. It was also in this week that I let my hunger override my fear of the concurrent avian influenza outbreak. I had no choice but to decide that eating chicken would probably be fine, as long as I was immediately following it with Tamiflu, seeing as chicken and egg dishes were all my host mother served.

The first night of my stay at my host family's house, my host sister, her mother, and I were sitting at the table, doing homework and watching a documentary about horses. Trying to spark up a conversation—and by *conversation* I mean "game of charades"—my host mother gestured for me to give her my Chinese language textbook, which I proudly did. She leafed through the pages, stopped to look at some of the pictures, and let out a giggle every few flips. Finally, she landed on the page that taught direction, the most complex grammar I had mastered to date. "Grandma is in the house." "I am in front of the house." "The cell phone is under the dog." This page really gave her a good laugh. In the first English words I had heard her speak, she said, "You're learning this? Here, we teach this in kindergarten."

Suddenly, my ability to tell you where my second-cousin-twice-removed was relative to the air conditioning felt like nothing. Before I had time to feel ashamed my host mother grabbed her daughter's English textbook off the table, handed it to me and said, "Would this be kindergarten level in America, too?" Not wanting to say no, thus giving her the power to put me down, and not wanting to say yes, and thus make my host sister feel the way I did in that moment, I simply said "我 不 知 道" ("I don't know"). Truth be told, her grammatical skills were impeccable, but her vocabulary was at a basic level.

In his essay, Sedaris tells the story of learning a foreign language through unsolicited embarrassment. When directed by his teacher to say what he loves and hates in French only to be mocked for his response, Sedaris asks himself, "how often is one . . . publicly ridiculed" for attempting a new language (133)? I asked this same question when my host mother put me down for my own language ability. In the moment the embarrassment seems defeating, especially when you are placed in a situation where "it's everybody into the language pool, sink or swim" (Sedaris 132). Yes, it's easy to retreat into not using the language at all in fear of further ridicule, especially if the feelings of "discomfort crept beyond the borders of the classroom and accompanied [you] out onto the wide boulevards" of the city you're in (Sedaris 135). However, silence is the easy way out. You have to risk sounding like a kindergartener.

While Sedaris's fears followed him outside of the classroom, mine were contained to the home I would be living in for another week and the family I would be sharing a one-room apartment with. Sedaris's fear of using French went as far as ignoring the phone when it rang and pretending to be deaf. My fear didn't go this far; however, like Sedaris I was "convinced that everything I said was wrong" (135). When you're confident in your language ability, it can feel like the world is in your hands. You feel capable, independent, and free. But when your faith in this ability is shattered, the simple, everyday things you take for granted in your own language—like being able to ask where the nearest bathroom is, or how to get to the entrance of the temple to find your group because your cell phone doesn't work overseas and your passport is in someone else's backpack—become tasks that require thought. The trust is broken between you and the language and you retreat into thinking not about how you can say what you want to say, but rather about how you can communicate in any way other than speech.

Sedaris and I also had moments of clarity after avoiding our respec- 8 tive languages. Sedaris's revelation came when his teacher compared the pain of teaching him to that of a cesarean section. It was the first moment where he grasped the meaning of an entire sentence. Not just the grammar. Not just key words. He understood the statement in its entirety (135). My moment was when we were clearing off the table after dinner, and my host father was attempting, through various gestures and *Google Translate* entries, to tell me that the chicken wings had been made with beer. As he walked into the kitchen snapping open another can, my host sister said to him, "I think you've had enough to drink," thinking that I wouldn't know what she was saying. But I sat on the couch with the biggest smile I'd had the whole trip. I finally felt like I was really learning, not through a textbook, but through listening and immersion, and that was the best feeling. Although, like Sedaris, I couldn't coherently respond, at least not without admitting to eavesdropping on what might have been a confrontation about my host father's relationship with alcohol. After this, all I wanted to hear was more Chinese.

I can't speak for Sedaris, but I did not come home fluent in a new 9 language. However, I did return with something of more value. In the moment, being told that my Chinese would be compared to that of a kindergartener was not the most encouraging learning experience I had ever had, but it forced me to abandon relying on traditional methods of learning. Textbooks are not going to allow you to understand when your host father may have a drinking problem, or when your teacher insults you, but listening, gesturing, and eavesdropping will. When I had that moment of clarity, my world, like Sedaris's, opened up and I was no longer ashamed of being elementary, because I wasn't stopping there.

Work Cited

Sedaris, David. "Me Talk Pretty One Day." *The Compact Reader: Short Essays by Method and Theme*, edited by Jane E. Aaron and Ellen Kuhl Repetto, 11th ed., Bedford/St. Martin's, 2019, pp. 134–35.

Meaning

1. Of attempting everyday interactions in China, Melendez observes that "probably nothing from a textbook would be of use" to a language learner (paragraph 2). Why, then, was she so bothered by her host mother's assessment of her textbook (4)? What effect did being compared to a kindergartener have on her?

2. What are the "traditional methods of learning" referred to in paragraph 9? What does Melendez mean by saying she was "forced . . . to abandon relying on [them]"? Does this sentence state her main idea? Why, or why not?

3. If you are uncertain of the meanings of any of the words listed below, try to guess them from the context of the essay. Then look them up to see how close your definitions were to those in the dictionary. Test out the new words by using each of them in a sentence or two of your own.

mortifying (1)	concurrent (3)	respective (8)
diligent (3)	impeccable (5)	immersion (8)
hypothermia (3)		

Purpose and Audience

1. What seems to be Melendez's purpose in this essay: to compose an academic response to an assigned class reading? to entertain readers with examples from her own experience? to do something else? How do you know?

2. Whom did Melendez assume as her audience? (Look back at the note on the essay, p. 139, if you're not sure.) How do her subject, evidence, and tone reflect her assumptions?

Method and Structure

1. Why do you think Melendez chose to examine her learning experience through examples? How do examples help her achieve her purpose in a way that another method might not? (Hint: What is lost when you skip from paragraph 7 to 9?)

2. What generalizations do the examples in paragraphs 3 and 8 support?

3. How does Melendez organize her examples? Which paragraphs fall into the introduction, body, and conclusion of her essay? What function does each part serve?

4. OTHER METHODS "The Chinese Kindergartener" uses **narration** to share the author's learning experience. How does Melendez manipulate narrative time to emphasize important details and hold readers' interest?

Language

1. How would you characterize Melendez's **tone**: serious? light? a mix of both? How does this tone reflect her intended audience and her attitude toward her subject?

2. Point out some instances of **irony** in the essay.

3. What does Melendez achieve by addressing the reader as *you* throughout the essay?

Writing Topics

1. JOURNAL TO ESSAY   Olivia Melendez relies on examples and narration to recount an awkward but exhilarating learning experience. Starting with your journal response (p. 139), write an essay in which you use the same methods to recapture one of the happiest or most exciting discoveries of your lifetime. Use straightforward chronological time if that works best, or like Melendez, compress narrative time to emphasize the most significant moments.

2. Like Melendez, you may recall the first time you felt that your "world . . . opened up" (paragraph 9) to its full potential. Write an essay in which you describe an experience that made you feel you were on your own, independent and in charge of your own life. This could be, for example, the first time you traveled abroad, drove a car alone, or left home for college. How did it feel to be so capable? Was it intimidating or liberating?

3. CULTURAL CONSIDERATIONS   As Melendez reports, the experience of studying abroad taught her more than new language skills. She developed an appreciation for Chinese family dynamics, for instance, and gained experience navigating markets and religious sites. Have you had, or will you have, an opportunity to study in a foreign country, whether for a few weeks of practicing a language, as was the case for Melendez, or perhaps with a semester abroad program offered by your school? What country would you want to spend time in, and why? What do you expect to gain from the experience? In an essay, consider the educational and personal benefits that come from spending time immersed in another culture.

4. RESEARCH   Pick an essay in this book, or in any source of your choosing, and using Melendez's essay as a model, respond to it. You might wish to write in agreement with the author, examining how his or her experience or opinion reflects or reinforces your own, or you might take issue with the author's thesis and supporting evidence, arguing against the essay's main idea. Perhaps you'll use the author's idea as a springboard to develop a new idea of your own. Whatever direction you take, be sure to integrate quotations and paraphrases from the source into your essay as Melendez does, following the guidelines provided on pages 139–145 of this book. And be sure that your response goes beyond mere summary of the source to reflect your own thoughts and opinions about it and its subject.

5. CONNECTIONS   "The Chinese Kindergartener" is a student writer's response to David Sedaris's "Me Talk Pretty One Day" (p. 131). Write an essay expressing your assessment of Melendez's piece. For instance, how well do you think her essay works as a response to a reading? Does she integrate evidence and ideas from her source effectively? In what ways were Melendez's learning experience similar to David Sedaris's? How were they different? How successful is Melendez in her attempts to approximate David Sedaris's style and brand of humor? Support your **analysis** with evidence from Melendez's text and the essay that prompted it.

WRITING WITH THE METHOD

EXAMPLE

Select one of the following statements, or any other statement they suggest, and agree *or* disagree with it in an essay developed by example. The statement you choose should concern a topic you care about so that the example or examples are a means of communicating an idea, not an end in themselves.

Family

1. In happy families, talk is the main activity.
2. Sooner or later, children take on the personalities of their parents.
3. "Traditional" families are anything but traditional.

Behavior and Personality

4. Rudeness is on the rise. ← social media & politics, racism
5. Facial expressions often communicate what words cannot say.
6. New technologies are making us stupid and lazy.

Education

7. The best college courses are the difficult ones.
8. College is not for everybody.
9. Students at schools with enforced dress codes behave better than students at schools without such codes.
10. Social activities are essential to a well-rounded education.

Politics and Social Issues

11. Social media can influence government actions.
12. Drug or alcohol addiction is not restricted just to "bad" people.
13. Unemployment is hardest on those over fifty years old.
14. The best musicians treat social and political issues in their songs.

Rules for Living

15. Murphy's Law: If anything can go wrong, it will go wrong, and at the worst possible moment.
16. A good friend offers help and support without being asked.
17. Lying may be justified by the circumstances.

2 ways to write
either expand
on one example
or one idea
w/ many examples

WRITING ABOUT THE THEME

USING LANGUAGE

1. Deborah Tannen (p. 119), William Lutz (p. 120), and Perri Klass (p. 125) discuss the power of language with a good deal of respect. Tannen refers to its social uses, Lutz to its effectiveness "in explaining . . . accidents," and Klass to its support as she became a doctor. Think of a time when you were in some way profoundly affected by language, and write an essay about this experience. Provide as many examples as necessary to illustrate both the language that affected you and how it made you feel.

2. Perri Klass, David Sedaris (p. 131), and Olivia Melendez (p. 139) all write about the difficulties of picking up a new language. Klass, in particular, expresses a concern that the new language is changing her, and not necessarily for the better. But even Sedaris and Melendez reveal some ambivalence about their efforts. As you see it, what are the advantages and disadvantages of learning a second or third (or fourth) language? How might understanding new grammars, alphabets, and concepts affect a person's worldview, for instance? How effectively can a person use a foreign language to communicate with those native to the tongue? As more and more countries instruct their young students in English, why should Americans bother to learn their languages at all? Write an essay that answers these questions, or any additional questions they raise for you, using examples from the selections and your own experience.

3. Deborah Tannen, William Lutz, Perri Klass, and David Sedaris discuss language use among people in a particular group. Tannen shows how women support each other by apologizing. Lutz shows how carefully chosen terminology used by the military can obscure meaning for civilians. Klass explains how medical students adopt jargon to initiate themselves into doctorhood. Sedaris considers how refugees and expatriates form bonds by learning a common language. Write an essay in which you examine how groups of people can use language to fit into or exclude others from such groups. Consider, for instance, a form of doublespeak, jargon, or slang among teachers, journalists, business leaders, or politicians, or perhaps why employees (or customers) might communicate in a language other than English in an American retail or work space. Does the language used embrace or reject membership in a group? How so?

8

DIVISION OR ANALYSIS

▶
LOOKING AT POPULAR CULTURE

Division and **analysis** are interchangeable terms for the same method. *Division* comes from a Latin word meaning "to force asunder or separate." *Analysis* comes from a Greek word meaning "to undo." Using this method, we separate a whole into its elements, examine the relations of the elements to one another and to the whole, and reassemble the elements into a new whole informed by the examination.

Analysis (as we will call it) is the foundation of **critical thinking**—the ability to see beneath the surface of things, images, events, and ideas; to uncover and test assumptions; to see the importance of context; and to draw and support independent conclusions. The method, then, is essential to college learning, whether in discussing literature, solving a math problem, or interpreting a historical event. It is also fundamental in the workplace, from choosing a career to making sense of market research. Analysis even informs and enriches life outside of school or work, whether we ponder our relationships with others, determine whether a new gaming system is worth buying, decide whether a movie was worthwhile, or evaluate an advertiser's messages.

Because popular culture is everywhere, and everywhere taken for granted, it is an especially tempting and rewarding target for writers. Having chosen to write critically about a cheering, disturbing, or intriguing aspect of popular culture, all the authors in this chapter naturally pursued the method of division or analysis. One paragraph, by Moises Velasquez-Manoff, dissects the surprisingly diverse elements of a hit song. The other paragraph, by Luci Tapahonso, analyzes a pizza commercial that especially appealed to American Indians. In the first essay, *Dilbert* cartoonist Scott Adams considers what makes newspaper readers laugh. Leslie Jamison then examines the television show *Intervention* to determine what makes it so addictive to viewers like herself. And student writer Saanya Ojha exposes the feminist messages lurking behind the Barbie doll franchise.

Reading Division or Analysis

At its most helpful, division or analysis peers inside an object, institution, work of art, policy, or any other whole. It identifies the parts, examines how the parts relate, and leads to a conclusion about the meaning, significance, or value of the whole. The subject of any analysis is usually singular—a freestanding, coherent unit, such as a bicycle or a poem, with its own unique constitution of elements. (In contrast, classification, the subject of the next chapter, usually starts with a plural subject, such as bicycles or the poems of the Civil War, and groups them according to their shared features.) A writer chooses the subject and with it a **principle of analysis**, a framework that determines how the subject will be divided and thus what elements are relevant to the discussion.

Sometimes the principle of analysis is self-evident, especially when the subject is an object, such as a bicycle or a camera, that can be "undone" in only a limited number of ways. Most of the time, however, the principle depends on the writer's view of the whole. In academic disciplines, distinctive principles are part of what each field is about and are often the subject of debate within the field. In art, for instance, some critics see a painting primarily as a visual object and concentrate on its composition, color, line, and other formal qualities; other critics see a painting primarily as a social object and concentrate on its content and context (cultural, economic, political, and so on). Both groups use a principle of analysis that is a well-established way of looking at a painting, yet each group finds different elements and thus meaning in a work.

Writers have a great deal of flexibility in choosing a principle of analysis, but the principle also must meet certain requirements: it should be appropriate for the subject and the field or discipline, it should be significant, and it should be applied thoroughly and consistently. Analysis is done not for its own sake but for a larger goal of illuminating the subject, perhaps concluding something about it. But even when the method leads to evaluation—the writer's judgment of the subject's value—the analysis should represent the subject as it actually is, in all its fullness and complexity.

Analyzing Division or Analysis in Paragraphs

Moises Velasquez-Manoff (born 1974) is a science writer and a regular opinion contributor for the *New York Times*. The following paragraph is condensed and adapted from "The Meaning of 'Despacito' in the Age of Trump," an essay-length analysis of the chart-topping song by Daddy Yankee and Luis Fonsi.

The song's success highlights a side of humanity that's curious, that doesn't cringe from difference so much as find inspiration in it. A transcendent side that takes joy in bringing together disparate parts, in creation, in play. Take "Despacito" itself. It begins with a steel-stringed Puerto Rican guitar called the cuatro, which most likely descended from an instrument brought to Spain from North Africa by Moors. The rolling reggaeton beat came out of Jamaica and, long before that, probably originated in West Africa. In rapping, Daddy Yankee employs an art form developed by urban African Americans, infusing it with the unique feel of Puerto Rican Spanish and slang. Mr. Fonsi's deliciously suggestive lyrics arguably belong to a tradition that stretches back to the lovelorn troubadours of medieval Spain, and beyond. The song is a fusion, an amalgam.

Principle of analysis (topic sentence underlined): elements of global influence

1. Puerto Rican guitar from North Africa

2. Jamaican reggaeton beat from West Africa

3. African American rapping with Puerto Rican language

4. Traditional Spanish lyrics

Luci Tapahonso (born 1953) is a poet and teacher. The paragraph below is from her essay "The Way It Is," which appears in *Sign Language*, a book of photographs (by Skeet McAuley) of life on the reservation for some Navajo and Apache Indians.

It is rare and, indeed, very exciting to see an Indian person in a commercial advertisement. Word travels fast when that happens. Nunzio's Pizza in Albuquerque, New Mexico, ran commercials featuring Jose Rey Toledo of Jemez Pueblo talking about his "native land—Italy" while wearing typical Pueblo attire—jewelry, moccasins, and hair tied in a chongo. Because of the ironic humor,

Principle of analysis: elements of the commercial that appealed to Indians

1. Rarity of an Indian in a commercial

2. Indian dress

because Indian grandfathers specialize in playing tricks   3. Indian humor
and jokes on their grandchildren, and because Jose Rey   4. Indian tradition
Toledo is a respected and well-known elder in the Indian   5. Respected Indian spokesperson
communities, word of this commercial spread fast
among Indians in New Mexico. It was the cause of recognition and celebration of sorts on the reservations and
in the pueblos. His portrayal was not in the categories   6. Realism
which the media usually associate with Indians but as a
typical sight in the Southwest. <u>It showed</u> Indians as we   Topic sentence
<u>live today—enjoying pizza as one of our</u> favorite foods,   (underlined) summarizes
<u>including humor and fun as part of our</u> daily lives, and   elements
<u>recognizing the importance of preserving</u> traditional
knowledge.

Developing an Essay by Division or Analysis

▶ Getting Started

Analysis is one of the readiest methods of development: almost anything
whole can be separated into its elements, from a lemon to a play by
Shakespeare to an economic theory. In college and at work, many writing assignments will call for analysis with a verb such as *analyze,
criticize, discuss, evaluate, interpret,* or *review.* If you need to develop your
own subject for analysis, think of something whose meaning or significance puzzles or intrigues you and whose parts you can distinguish and
relate to the whole—for instance, an object such as a machine, an art-
work such as a poem, a media product such as a news broadcast, an institution such as a hospital, a relationship such as stepparenting, or a social
issue such as homelessness.

Dissect your subject, looking at the actual physical thing if possible,
imagining it in your mind if necessary. Make detailed notes of all the elements you see, their distinguishing features, and how those features work
together. In analyzing someone's creation, tease out the creator's influences, assumptions, intentions, conclusions, and evidence. You may have
to go outside the work for some of this information—researching an
author's background, for instance, to uncover the biases that may under-
lie his or her opinions. Even if you do not use all this information in your

final draft, it will help you see the elements and help keep your analysis true to the subject.

If you begin by seeking meaning or significance in a subject, you will be more likely to find a workable principle of analysis and less likely to waste time on a hollow exercise. Each question below suggests a distinct approach to the subject's elements—a distinct principle of analysis—that makes it easier to isolate the elements and see their connections:

> To what extent is an enormously complex hospital a community in itself?
>
> What is the function of the front-page headlines in the local tabloid newspaper?
>
> Why did a certain movie have such a powerful effect on you and your friends?

▶ Forming a Thesis

A clear, informative thesis is crucial in division or analysis because readers need to know the purpose and structure of your analysis in order to follow your points. If your exploratory question proves helpful as you gather ideas, you can also use it to draft a thesis sentence: answer it in such a way that you state your opinion about your subject and reveal your principle of analysis.

> QUESTION To what extent is an enormously complex hospital a community in itself?
>
> THESIS SENTENCE The hospital encompasses such a wide range of personnel and services that it resembles a good-sized town.

> QUESTION What is the function of the front-page headlines in the local tabloid newspaper?
>
> THESIS SENTENCE The newspaper's front page routinely appeals to readers' fear of crime, anger at criminals, and sympathy for victims.

> QUESTION Why did a certain movie have such a powerful effect on you and your friends?
>
> THESIS SENTENCE The film is a unique and important statement of the private terrors of adolescence.

Note that all three thesis statements imply an explanatory purpose—an effort to understand something and share that understanding. The third thesis sentence, however, suggests a persuasive purpose as well: the writer hopes that readers will accept her evaluation of the film.

A well-focused thesis sentence benefits not only your readers but also you as a writer, because it gives you a yardstick to judge the completeness, consistency, and supportiveness of your analysis. Don't be discouraged, though, if your thesis sentence doesn't come to you until *after* you've written a first draft and had a chance to focus your ideas. Writing about your subject may be the best way to find its meaning and significance.

▶ Organizing

In the **introduction** to your essay, let readers know why you are bothering to analyze your subject: Why is the subject significant? How might the essay relate to the experiences of readers or be useful to them? A subject unfamiliar to readers might be summarized or described, or some part of it (an anecdote or a quotation, say) might be used to grab readers' interest. A familiar subject might be introduced with a surprising fact or an unusual perspective. An evaluative analysis might open with reference to an opposing viewpoint.

In the **body** of the essay, you'll need to explain your principle of analysis. The arrangement of elements and analysis should suit your subject and purpose: you can describe the elements and then offer your analysis, or you can introduce and analyze elements one by one. You can arrange the elements themselves from most to least important, least to most complex, most to least familiar, spatially, or chronologically. Devote as much space to each element as it demands: there is no requirement that all elements be given equal space and emphasis if their complexity or your framework dictates otherwise.

Most analysis essays need a **conclusion** that reassembles the elements, returning readers to a sense of the whole subject. The conclusion can restate the thesis, summarize what the essay has contributed, consider the influence of the subject or its place in a larger picture, or (especially in an evaluation) assess the effectiveness or worth of the subject.

▶ Drafting

If the subject or your view of it is complex, you may need at least two rough drafts of an analysis essay—one to work out what you think and one to clarify your principle, cover each element, and support your points with concrete details and vivid examples (including quotations if the subject is a written work). Plan on two drafts if you're uncertain of your thesis when you begin; you'll save time in the long run by attending to one goal at a time. Especially because an analysis essay says something about a subject by explaining its structure, you need to have a clear picture of the whole and how each part relates to it.

As you draft, be sure to consider your readers' needs as well as the needs of your subject and your own framework:

- *If the subject is unfamiliar to your readers*, you'll need to carefully explain your principle of analysis, define all specialized terms, distinguish the parts from one another, and provide ample illustrations.

- *If the subject is familiar to readers*, your principle of analysis may not require much justification (as long as it's clear), but your details and examples must be vivid and convincing.

- *If readers may dispute your way of looking at your subject*, be careful to justify as well as explain your principle of analysis.

Whether readers are familiar with your subject or not, always account for any evidence that may seem not to support your opinion—either by showing why, in fact, the evidence is supportive or by explaining why it is unimportant. (If contrary evidence refuses to be dispensed with, you may have to rethink your approach.)

▶ Revising and Editing

When you revise and edit your essay, use the following questions and the Focus box on the next page to uncover any remaining weaknesses.

- *Is your principle of analysis clear?* The significance of your analysis and your view of the subject should be apparent throughout your essay.

- *Is your analysis complete?* Have you identified all elements according to your principle of analysis and determined their relations to one another and to the whole? If you have omitted some elements from your discussion, will the reason for their omission be clear to readers?

- *Is your analysis consistent?* Have you applied your principle of analysis to the entire subject (including any elements you have omitted)? Do all elements reflect the same principle, and are they clearly separate rather than overlapping? You may find it helpful to check your draft against your list of elements or to outline the draft itself.

- *Is your analysis well supported?* Is the thesis supported by clear assertions about parts of the subject, and are the assertions supported by concrete, specific evidence (sensory details, facts, quotations, and so on)? Do not rely on your readers to prove your thesis.

- *Is your analysis true to the subject?* Is your thesis unforced, your analysis fair? Is your new whole (your reassembly of the elements) faithful to the original?

FOCUS ON COHERENCE

With several elements that contribute to the whole of a subject, an analysis will be easy for your readers to follow only if you frequently clarify what element you are discussing and how it fits with your principle of analysis. To help readers keep your analysis straight, rely on transitions and repetition to achieve coherence.

- **Transitions** such as those listed in the Glossary act as signposts to tell readers where you, and they, are headed. Some transitions indicate that you are shifting between subjects, either finding resemblances between them (*also, like, likewise, similarly*) or finding differences (*but, however, in contrast, instead, unlike, whereas, yet*). Other transitions indicate that you are moving on to a new point (*in addition, also, furthermore, moreover*). Consider, for example, how transitions keep readers focused in the following paragraph from "The Distorting Mirror of Reality TV," an essay by Sarah Coleman:

   > Let's start with the contestants. Most producers of reality TV shows would like you to believe they've picked a group of people who span a broad spectrum of human diversity. But if you took the demographics of an average reality show and applied them to the population at large, you'd end up with a society that was ninety percent white, young, and beautiful. In fact, though reality TV pretends to hold up a mirror to society, its producers screen contestants in much the same way as producers of television commercials and Hollywood movies screen their actors. For ethnic minorities, old people, the un-beautiful, and the disabled, the message is harsh: even in "reality" you don't exist.

- **Repetition and restatement** of labels for your principle of analysis or for individual elements make clear the topic of each sentence. In the preceding passage, the repetition of *contestants* and *producers* and the substitution of *people* and *they* for each emphasize the elements under discussion. The restatement of *reality, TV/television*, and *diversity/demographics/population* clarifies the principle of analysis (the unreality of reality show contestants).

See pages 37–38 for additional discussion of these two techniques.

The most wasted of all days is one without laughter.   —E. E. Cummings

There is a thin line that separates laughter and pain, comedy and tragedy, humor and hurt.   —Erma Bombeck

Analyzing humor is like dissecting a frog. Few people are interested and the frog dies of it.   —E. B. White

JOURNAL RESPONSE   Reflect for a moment on your favorite source of humor: a particular comedian, perhaps, or a television show, a Web site, a comic strip. Write a journal entry explaining what you like about this source of comedy, trying to pin down as many details as you can.

Scott Adams

Scott Adams (born 1957) is best known for his cubicle-bound comic strip, *Dilbert*, which dissects the painfully hilarious minutiae of office culture. Raised in upstate New York, Adams earned a BA in economics from Hartwick College and an MBA from the University of California at Berkeley. He started his career as a programmer for a bank and then for a telephone company in the San Francisco area; the day jobs served as early inspirations for *Dilbert*, which Adams began publishing while still employed full time. He made the innovative decision in 1994 to provide his e-mail address in the panels, and the feedback from readers helped him to refine the strip into the acclaimed office staple it is today. Adams is the author of nearly four dozen books of comics, self-help, and business advice, most recently *Dilbert Gets Re-accommodated* (2017) and *Win Bigly: Persuasion in a World Where Facts Don't Matter* (2017). He is also the co-owner of a small restaurant in California and a certified hypnotist.

Funny Business

What makes a piece of writing funny? In this 2010 essay for the esteemed business newspaper the *Wall Street Journal*, Adams sets out to explain while he demonstrates.

Last weekend a French fry got lodged in my sinus cavity.   1

   I suppose it all started when I was eleven years old. Two of my school   2
buddies and I were huddled on the schoolyard, whisper-sharing everything we knew about the mysteries of the human reproductive process.

We patched together bits and pieces of what we had heard from our older brothers. This was problematic, because two of our brothers were unreliable, and one was a practical joker. And to be fair, my friends and I were poor listeners.

As I later learned, we got a fairly important part of the reproductive puzzle wrong. I can't be more specific about our faulty information, at least not in the *Wall Street Journal*, so instead I will tell you a story about golf. If you choose to draw any parallels, that's your own fault.

Okay, so this golfer hits a majestic drive, and follows it up with an awesome chip and an improbable putt. The golfer pumps his fist and dances a little jig. He turns to his caddy for a high-five and gets no response. "Wasn't that some great golfing?" the golfer asks. The caddy says, "Yes . . . but it was the wrong hole."

Last weekend, I was visiting my tiny hometown of Windham, New York, enjoying dinner out with my parents, my sister, and two eighty-ish widows who are longtime family friends. One of the ladies mentioned running into an old schoolmate of mine who was part of the misinformed schoolyard troika of way-back-then. When I heard my schoolmate's name, I flashed back to that day, vividly recalling the key bit of information we got wrong, and I wondered how long it took my buddies to correct their mistaken understandings. I took a bite of my French fry and listened to the rest of the story about how this fellow hadn't changed much since he was a kid. And then one of the widows added, sort of as an afterthought, "He never had any children."

Let me tell you that this was a bad time for me to have food in my mouth. The situation demanded a spit-take, but this was a nice restaurant, and I was sitting directly across from the two innocent widows. I clamped my lips shut and hoped for the best. Something sneeze-like exploded inside me. It was an unholy combination of saliva, potato, laughter and compressed air. I squeezed my sphincter shut, closed my eyes, and well, I don't remember much after that. I think the French fry hit the top of my sinus cavity and caused some sort of concussion.

Anyway, the reason we're here today is so I can give you valuable writing tips. My specialty is humor, so let's stick with that slice of the assignment.

The topic is the thing. Eighty percent of successful humor writing is picking a topic that is funny by its very nature. My story above is true, up until the exaggeration about the French fry in the sinus cavity. You probably assumed it was true, and that knowledge made it funnier.

Humor likes danger. If you are cautious by nature, writing humor probably isn't for you. Humor works best when you sense that the writer

is putting himself in jeopardy. I picked the French-fry story specifically because it is too risqué for the *Wall Street Journal*. You can't read it without wondering if I had an awkward conversation with my editor. You might wonder if the people in my story will appreciate seeing my version of events in the *Wall Street Journal*. I wonder that too.

In the early days of my cartooning career, as the creator of *Dilbert*, part of the strip's appeal was that I was holding a day job while mocking the very sort of company I worked for. If you knew my backstory, and many people did, you could sense my personal danger in every strip. (My manager eventually asked me to leave. He said it was a budget thing.)   10

Humor is about people. It's impossible to write humor about a concept or an object. All humor involves how people think and act. Sometimes you can finesse that limitation by having your characters think and act in selfish, stupid or potentially harmful ways around the concept or object that you want your reader to focus on.   11

Exaggerate wisely. If you anchor your story in the familiar, your readers will follow you on a humorous exaggeration, especially if you build up to it. My story was true and relatable until the French-fry exaggeration.   12

Let the reader do some work. Humor works best when the reader has to connect some dots. Early in my story I made you connect the golf story to the playground story. The smarter your audience, the wider you can spread the dots. I used this method again when I said of my aborted spit-take, "I don't remember much after that." Your mind might have filled in a little scene in which, perhaps, my eyes bugged out, my cheeks went all chipmunk-like, and I fell out of my chair.   13

Animals are funny. It's a cheap trick, but animal analogies are generally funny. It was funnier that I said, "my cheeks went all chipmunk-like" than if I had said my cheeks puffed out.   14

Use funny words. I referred to my two schoolmates and myself as a troika because the word itself is funny. With humor, you never say "pull"   15 when you can say "yank." Some words are simply funnier than others, and you know the funny ones when you see them. (Pop Quiz: Which word is funnier, observe or stalk?)

Curiosity. Good writing makes you curious without being too heavy-handed about it. My first sentence in this piece, about the French fry lodged in my sinus cavity, is designed to make you curious. It also sets the tone right away.   16

Endings. A simple and classic way to end humorous writing is with a call-back. That means making a clever association to something especially humorous and notable from the body of your work. I would give you an example of that now, but I'm still having concentration issues from the French fry.   17

Meaning

1. What is the thesis of "Funny Business"? Does Adams state it explicitly? Try to summarize the central meaning of his analysis in a sentence or two of your own.

2. How does the *Dilbert* cartoon on the opposite page illustrate Adams's ideas about humor?

3. Why is the essay's last sentence particularly effective as a conclusion? Point to evidence from the text to support your answer.

4. If you are uncertain of the meanings of any of the words listed below, try to guess them from the context of the essay. Then look them up to see how close your definitions were to those in the dictionary. Test out the new words by using each of them in a sentence or two of your own.

parallels (3)	putt (4)	risqué (9)
majestic (4)	troika (5, 15)	finesse (11)
chip (4)	jeopardy (9)	analogies (14)

Purpose and Audience

1. What is Adams's purpose in writing this essay? How do you know?

2. What assumptions does Adams make about his audience? Where are those assumptions most clearly expressed?

Method and Structure

1. How does Adams use the method of analysis for comic effect? In what ways does analysis lend itself particularly well to a humorous subject such as this one?

2. What is Adams's principle of analysis, and into what elements does he divide his subject? Be specific, supporting your answer with examples from the text.

3. What do the first sentences of paragraphs 8, 9, and 11–17 have in common?

4. How does Adams organize his ideas?

5. OTHER METHODS   The first six paragraphs of the essay use **narration** to tell a joke. How is this **example** essential to Adams's analysis?

Language

1. Answer the "Pop Quiz" Adams poses in paragraph 15: "Which word is funnier, observe or stalk?" What other words in the essay strike you as inherently funny? Why does Adams repeat several of them?

2. What is Adams's **tone**? How seriously does he take his subject?

Writing Topics

1. JOURNAL TO ESSAY   In your journal response (p. 156), you reflected on your favorite source of comedy. Now write a more formal essay in which you describe that source of comedy and explain what makes it so funny to you. You might cite Adams's elements of humor to explain your enjoyment, if you find them useful, or develop your own principle of analysis to assess just what it is that makes people laugh.

2. Adams claims that it is "impossible to write humor about a concept or an object" (paragraph 11). Is that true, in your experience? Drawing on the principles of humor that Adams outlines in his essay, try your hand at writing something funny. You might write about people or animals if you like, but feel free to choose as your topic a concept or an object that you find amusing on its own.

3. CULTURAL CONSIDERATIONS   Based on the examples Adams uses in this essay, what can you infer about his age, background, and economic status? Does Adams seem to assume his audience is similar to him? (Remember, this essay first appeared in the *Wall Street Journal*.) Are readers who don't match his assumptions (perhaps you yourself) likely to enjoy the essay as much as those who do match? Write an essay in which you analyze the writer's apparent assumptions, explaining how they strengthen the essay, weaken it, or don't affect it at all.

4. **CONNECTIONS**   Apply Adams's analysis to one or more of the other humorous essays in this book: Amy Tan's "The Darkest Moment of My Life" (p. 100), David Sedaris's "Me Talk Pretty One Day" (p. 131), Olivia Melendez's "The Chinese Kindergartener" (p. 139), and Jonathan R. Gould's "The People Next Door" (p. 185). Then write an essay that examines how these writers develop humor. Address as many of Adams's elements of humor as seem fitting, but consider especially what is gained from exaggeration and what qualities exaggeration often has. How does each writer make his readers laugh? Use quotations and paraphrases from "Funny Business" and the other essays as your support.

Television—teacher, mother, secret lover!
—Homer Simpson

Television is chewing gum for the eyes.
—Frank Lloyd Wright

All television is educational television. The question is: What is it teaching?
—Nicholas Johnson

JOURNAL RESPONSE Reflect for a few moments on your favorite show on TV. Write a journal entry explaining what you like about the show, trying to get down as many details as you can. (Alternatively, think of a television program that you object to because it is offensive or annoying in some way and write about why it bothers you so much.)

Leslie Jamison

Hailed by one critic as "very much the next thing in nonfiction," Leslie Jamison is known for crafting strongly emotive writing that blends personal memoir, objective reporting, and critical analysis. She was born in 1983 in Washington, DC, grew up in Los Angeles, and received a bachelor's degree from Harvard, a master's in fine arts from the University of Iowa, and a PhD from Yale. A former baker, innkeeper, and medical actor paid to mimic symptoms for the sake of testing doctors-in-training, Jamison first came to national attention with *The Empathy Exams* (2014), an acclaimed collection of long-form essays that all examine some aspect of human pain. She is also the author of a novel, *The Gin Closet* (2010); a memoir, *The Recovering: Intoxication and Its Aftermath* (2018); and of essays for periodicals ranging from *Harper's Magazine* and *Believer* to *Virginia Quarterly Review*. In 2017, Jamison was selected to be the guest editor for the annual series *Best American Essays*. She currently teaches creative nonfiction in the MFA program at Columbia University, where she also leads the Marian House Project, a residential writing program for women transitioning from addiction. She lives in Brooklyn, New York.

Sublime, Revised

In this self-contained extract from a longer essay in *The Empathy Exams*, Jamison draws on the academic theories of philosopher Edmund Burke (1729–97) to understand the disturbing pleasures of watching the reality television program *Intervention*. When viewers indulge such satisfactions, Jamison worries, they feed their own addictions.

The warning, as ever, is also a promise: *This program contains subject matter* 1
and language that may be disturbing to some viewers. It's a promise the same
way an ambulance is a promise, or a scar, or a freeway clogged around an
accident.

The show is called *Intervention*, and each episode is named for its addict: 2
Jimbo, Cassie, Benny, Jenna. Danielle lines up twelve prescription bottles
on the coffee table while her eight-year-old says, "I know real mommy is
just waiting to come out." Sonia and Julia are anorexic twins who follow
each other around the house so that one won't burn more calories than the
other. Everyone has a wound: Gloria drinks because of her breast cancer.
Danielle takes her mother's Percocet because her father is a drunk. Marci
drinks because she lost custody of her kids because she drinks.

Andrea is twenty-nine. She hasn't lived with her husband and chil- 3
dren for nine months. She spends her days drinking rum carefully rationed
by her mother. She takes a drink and tells her mother, "This one is because
you never got me counseling." She keeps a bottle of Captain Morgan in
one hand and a liter of Pepsi in the other. She has bruises all over her body
from where she's tripped over chairs, fallen into door frames, landed on
the floor. Excessive bruising can be a sign of compromised liver function,
the show tells us. We are given scientists' eyes. We can see the purpling
damage for ourselves.

The camera work is an experiment in turning monotony into some- 4
thing interesting. The fatigue and stamina of addiction are kept electric
by compression: time-lapse shots of a bottle's sinking line of whiskey; a
cancerous pile of empties in the corner; a timeline of photos that ticks off
stations of the cross, sinner to martyr to corpse: smiling baby gives way to
pockmarked meth ghoul gives way to sullen mug shot.

Sober Andrea talks about her responsibilities. Drunk Andrea talks 5
about her afflictions. She toasts the twin nodes of trauma that constitute
her life: an absent alcoholic father and a rape at fourteen. When she is
drunk, she doesn't believe she can do anything but hurt.

The structure of the show implicitly endorses her narrative of victim- 6
hood. It needs a story to tell, after all, and she's fashioned one — a story
patterned by the saving, satisfying grace of cause-and-effect: get raped, get
silenced, get abandoned, get drunk. The television program needs a gene-
alogy for her dysfunction. Getting drunk is more interesting when it can
be read as a ledger of traumas rather than their source. Recovering alcoholics sometimes talk about feeling like they never got the Life Instruction
Manual everyone else got. Here's a substitute set of imperatives: lose a job,
get drunk; lose a child, get drunker. Lose everything. Andrea has. So get
sober. Maybe she will.

The father of her children, Jason, barely greets her when she comes to   7
visit the kids each month. She still calls him the love of her life. He says,
"What's up?" and keeps cooking lunch. He declines to be interviewed by
the program. He doesn't participate in the intervention. He's given up.
He's not crying on the other side of the bathroom door, or yanking the
bottle from her hands. He's just gone.

We're not gone, though, we viewers. We stay with Andrea after she   8
tells her children good-bye. We see her get drunk, again. We see why it
might have been hard for Jason to stay.

The shows takes care to emphasize, over and over again, that the   9
participants have agreed to be on a reality TV show about addiction but
don't know they will face an intervention. Given that the biggest reality
TV show about addiction in America today is *Intervention*, this is a bit difficult to believe. But the point is, people want to believe it. They want to
know something the addict doesn't. They want the intervention to be
climactic, surprising, and powerful. They want to be in on it. *Don't throw
your life away, Andrea*, they'd say, if they were in the room. *I think you can
make it.*

In his theory of the sublime, eighteenth-century philosopher Edmund   10
Burke proposes the notion of "negative pain": the idea that a feeling of
fear—paired with a sense of safety, and the ability to look away—can
produce a feeling of delight. One woman can sit on her couch with a glass
of Chardonnay and watch another woman drink away her life. The TV is
a portal that brings the horror close, and a screen that keeps it at bay—
revising Burke's sublime into a sublime voyeurism, no longer awe at the
terrors of nature but fascination at the depths of human frailty.

The professionals who moderate the show's interventions are called   11
"Interventionists," a title that seems better suited to a blockbuster film
about the Apocalypse. I imagine a slick troop of heroes, clad in black,
giving an ultimatum to the world about its addiction to capitalism or oil.
These Interventionists are mild-mannered grandparents dressed in business
casual. They almost always stress the singularity of the intervention—"You
will never get another chance like this," they say. They mean what they
hope: this moment will divide the addict's life into a cleanly spliced
Before and After.

It's true, of course: the addict will probably never get another interven-   12
tion like this—which is to say, on reality TV—but this is precisely the difference between the addict and his audience. For the regular viewer, the
once-in-a-lifetime intervention happens every Monday night at nine. The
unrepeatable is repeated. Every week is a relapse, the viewer thrown back
into addiction after last week's vow to stay clean. Epiphany is succeeded by

another intoxication. A grown woman throws up on her mother's couch once more. A needle jams into the same junked vein. Disturbance is promised, recorded, dissolved—then resurrected, so it can be healed again.

Meaning

1. *Intervention*'s content advisory warning "is also a promise," Jamison writes in her first paragraph, "the same way an ambulance is a promise, or a scar, or a freeway clogged around an accident." What does she mean? What is being promised?

2. What exactly is an intervention? Does Jamison explain the practice adequately for readers to understand?

3. What is Jamison's thesis? Where does she state it explicitly? Try to explain her principle of analysis in a sentence or two of your own.

4. If you are uncertain of the meanings of any of the words listed below, try to guess them from the context of the essay. Then look them up to see how close your definitions were to those in the dictionary. Test out the new words by using each of them in a sentence or two of your own.

ghoul (4)	voyeurism (10)	singularity (11)
nodes (5)	Apocalypse (11)	epiphany (12)
genealogy (6)	ultimatum (11)	resurrected (12)
portal (10)		

Purpose and Audience

1. What do you think Jamison's purpose was in writing this essay: to get more people to watch *Intervention*? to explain why the show appeals to viewers? to convince addicts to change their ways? to do something else?

2. What assumptions does Jamison make about her audience? Does she assume that readers are familiar with *Intervention*? with Edmund Burke's theory of the sublime? How familiar with the show (or the theory) would readers have to be in order to understand Jamison's analysis?

Method and Structure

1. Notice the distinctive strategy Jamison uses in the **introduction** to her essay. How does she capture readers' attention?

2. Why do you think Jamison chose the method of analysis to talk about the role of pain and trauma in the appeal of *Intervention*? How does the method help Jamison achieve her purpose?

3. What elements of *Intervention* does Jamison examine? How does she organize her analysis? How does she reassemble the elements into a new whole?

4. OTHER METHODS   As her title suggests, Jamison attempts in this essay to craft a revised **definition** of *sublime*. What makes a person feel sublime, as Edmund Burke defines it? as Jamison does? How does she apply the philosopher's concept to her viewing habits?

Language

1. Identify several instances of religious or spiritual **images** in this essay. Why do you suppose Jamison uses such imagery? What is the effect?

2. How would you characterize the **tone** of Jamison's essay? Support your answer with examples from the text.

3. Explain the **irony** of Jamison's concluding observation.

Writing Topics

1. JOURNAL TO ESSAY   In your journal response (p. 162) you reflected on a favorite (or detested) television show. Now write a more formal essay in which you describe that TV show and explain what makes it so enjoyable (or not) for you. Just as Jamison took *Intervention* apart to understand its allure, explain what elements contribute to the appeal (or offensiveness) of the show you selected. Does its popularity rest mostly on the people involved, the places depicted, the story line, or other features? Does it make you think about who you are as a person or change your view of the world? Does it make viewers feel sublime? If it is merely good (or bad) "entertainment," describe what makes it so.

2. As the family members of the addicts portrayed on *Intervention* could attest, loving another person can often bring both great joy and great suffering. In fact, most people have probably had at least one family or romantic relationship that didn't work out the way they would have liked. Write an essay about a difficult or disappointing relationship you have had. Describe the ups and downs of the relationship, from feelings of support and tenderness to moments of conflict and anger, and consider what you have learned from the experience.

3. CULTURAL CONSIDERATIONS   In the Western world, we watch a lot of television: some of us watch it every day. Some people feel that TV can expand our vision of the world by showing us different people and places and exposing us to new ideas and issues. Others argue that TV narrows our views, inundating us with shallow content designed to please the crowd. What is your opinion about the effects of TV? Do you think that your viewing habits have an essentially positive or negative effect on you? Write an essay in which you explain how you think TV affects you.

4. **RESEARCH** Jamison notes in paragraph 2 that one of the addicts on *Intervention* takes her mother's Percocet, a prescription painkiller. Starting with the Centers for Disease Control and Prevention Web site (*cdc.gov/ rxawareness/*), do some research to learn about the opioid drug crisis currently plaguing the country and then write an essay that explores your thoughts on the issue. Should everyone have access to effective pain medications, regardless of the risk of addiction or social cost? Should some drugs be made available to all while others should be restricted? Are doctors at fault for overprescribing painkillers, or are victims to blame for demanding the drugs? How does reasonable use of opioids turn to abuse? Do pharmaceutical companies have an obligation to make drugs safe, or do they have a right to profit from the fruits of their research and development efforts? What, if anything, can be done to help people recover from addiction? Who should be helping them?

5. **CONNECTIONS** Amy Tan, in "The Darkest Moment of My Life" (p. 100), describes a moment of revelation while deep in a natural cave. In a brief essay, apply Edmund Burke's concept of the sublime, as Jamison explains it, to Tan's flash of insight. What would Jamison say were the factors in Tan's experience that brought her to reverie? How do you understand it?

If Barbie is so popular, why do you have to buy her friends?   —Steven Wright

I think they should have a Barbie with a buzz cut.   —Ellen DeGeneres

Barbie is just a doll.   —Mary Schmich

JOURNAL RESPONSE Think of a toy or game that you played with as a child (Barbie, GI Joe, *Star Wars* action figures, Risk, Monopoly) that may have had other meanings besides pure entertainment. Make a list of messages that the makers of the toy or game might intentionally or unintentionally have been sending to children—for example, Monopoly could be seen as teaching the values of capitalism, and Barbie is often criticized for setting unrealistic standards of beauty.

Saanya Ojha

Saanya Ojha grew up in Chandigarh, India, where she was a merit scholar at Vivek High School. While pursuing a dual degree in international studies and finance and decision making at the University of Pennsylvania, she studied abroad in France and worked as a nonprofit social impact consultant and student advisory council member. She graduated in 2016 and is now a hedge-fund analyst at an international investment firm. Ojha reports that her interests include practicing yoga, reading, writing poetry, drinking tea, and traveling. She lives in Hong Kong.

Plastic Perfection: A Closer Look at Barbie
(Student Essay)

In this careful analysis of an enduring yet controversial toy for girls, Ojha offers detailed examples and evidence from several sources to support a fresh take on Barbie dolls. She wrote this essay as a review of the literature for a writing seminar, and then submitted it to *3808*, a journal of critical writing at the University of Pennsylvania. She revised the essay for *The Compact Reader*, tightening the focus, strengthening her voice, and converting the source citations to MLA style.

Barbie, one of the most popular cultural icons of our time, is at the heart   1
of controversy. Many people have been socially conditioned to believe that there is true evil lurking behind that pretty plastic face that figures prominently in their childhood memories. They are told that Barbie sets unrealistic expectations, breeds low self-esteem, and places undue

stress on young girls. As they grow older, the insistent drone of the anti-Barbie brigade grows even louder, tainting their innocent childhood memories with smears of doubt and suspicion. However, is the 11.5–inch plastic doll really evil incarnate? The effects of this contentious doll on the lives of millions of girls around the world have been documented and debated in countless research texts. But not all scholars outright condemn the doll. Many acknowledge that, in fact, Barbie sends what one pair of researchers describe as "complex and contradictory" messages for girls (Urla and Swedlund 284). And while Barbie is perceived by many as the symbol of a consumerist culture, unmitigated materialism, regressive gender stereotypes, and a hegemonic vision of heterosexuality (Ockman 85), accepting these flaws should not deter us from digging deeper to find the lesser-known constructive lessons this doll might impart. The truth is that Barbie conveys several positive messages to young girls.

First, the wide range of professions that Barbie can have allows young girls to envision a future for themselves in which they can realize all their dreams. They are not restricted by the ideas of the traditional roles of women in society. As writer and women's studies professor Sherrie Inness points out in "Barbie Gets a Bum Rap: Barbie's Place in the World of Dolls," Barbie's various jobs are not restricted to traditionally female ones such as nurse, stewardess, or primary school teacher; Barbie allows young girls to imagine themselves as paleontologists, pilots, dentists, and even racecar drivers (174). She opens up a whole plethora of opportunities for young girls and shows them that they are within reach. Similarly, journalist Susan Shapiro notes in "My Mentor, Barbie" that Barbie teaches girls that "it's cool to have many careers" and active lifestyle choices (122). And children's author Yona Zeldis McDonough argues in "Barbie (Doll)" that options like Tennis Anyone, Ski Queen, Icebreaker, Career Girl, and Graduation Barbies began to challenge established notions of femininity and provided an alternate narrative that was refreshing and encouraging. Ruth Handler, one of Mattel's founders and the doll's creator, even asserted that she "designed Barbie with a blank face" so that every girl "could project her own dreams of the future onto Barbie" (qtd. in Ockman 81). Barbie allows girls to picture themselves in a range of different professions, ranging from astronaut to doctor to fashion model.

Moreover, Barbie contradicts the traditional feminine image of women as self-sacrificing nurturers. Barbie's existence is not centered on raising her family, bringing up babies, or tending to her husband. She understands "family is fundamental," as evidenced by her many close cousins, sisters, and range of friends, but Barbie pursues her passions without any inhibitions (Shapiro 121, 122). Ken, Barbie's boyfriend, is

2

3

present only as a peripheral part of her life. Shapiro quips that her Barbie taught her that "a shortage of men won't ruin the party" (122). On a similar note, Inness observes that Barbie does not convey a message of "maternity and domesticity," while most other dolls on the market overwhelm young girls with a singular message that "babies are all a woman (or a girl) needs for complete bliss" and showcase the joys of motherhood (180). In contrast, Barbie teaches young girls the importance of pursuing their dreams. McDonough adds that Barbie has never taken on "the role of a wife" and instead acts as a "singular sensation." Thus Barbie breaks free from the traditional expectations of a woman to marry, have babies, and devote herself selflessly to family life.

Further, Barbie advocates to young girls the thrill of adventure and   4
exploration, in direct contrast to the passive, almost decorative role women are stereotypically expected to have in society. She is in fact centered on bringing to young girls the joys of exploration whether in exploration of her own identity, her many professions, or the world in general. While Malibu Barbie goes to the beach to get her tan, Paleontologist Barbie decks up in khakis to go digging for fossils; while Astronaut Barbie flies to the moon, Veterinarian Barbie makes the sick dog feel better. Barbie seems to be telling girls that the world is their oyster. As Inness puts it, "Barbie is about movement and action. She tells young girls that it is fun and exciting for them to have adventures, even hopping on their Hot

Keith Homan/Alamy Stock Photo

Stylin' Motorcycles and heading for the open road" (179). In what Shapiro calls "professional soul-searching," Barbie explores different facets of her own personality (123). McDonough similarly sees her as "living her own life" and "forging her own destiny."

Finally, Barbie teaches self-reliance to young girls. From a young age, girls are fed traditional gender stereotypes and presented with the ideal image of a shy, submissive, acquiescent woman who is forever dependent on a man, whether her father, brother, or husband. These regressive ideas are firmly shown the door in Barbie-land. Art historian Carol Ockman quotes a consumer who describes the lessons Barbie imparts: "She owns a Ferrari and doesn't have a husband; she must be doing something right" (74). And literary critic M. G. Lord explains how Barbie taught "first-generation Barbie owners" like herself the important lesson of independence: in stark contrast to all the other dolls they had played with before her, she is not defined by her relationships with men (9). Barbie carved her own distinct identity. Ken, her love interest, does not have much say in her life. She is young, fun, feisty, and takes care of herself. Barbie makes herself the top priority in her life and does not regret it.

While it's important to recognize and in some measure sympathize with the almost vituperative criticism that has been leveled against Barbie, we should not discount her positive aspects. Barbie is ambitious, goal oriented, adventurous, independent, and focused on personal growth. In many ways she is a positive influence on the lives of young children. The question, however, remains: do the positive messages do enough to balance and even counteract the negative messages that Barbie seems to convey? On the one hand, Barbie helps girls and young women break free of social stereotypes and regressive gender prejudices, while on the other, she snares them in a personal hell of negative self-image and poor self-esteem. A doll that combined the positives of Barbie and stayed away from her negatives would go a long way in preserving the innocence of childhood and ensuring that Barbie's constructive lessons are not lost in the conflicting messages she conveys.

Works Cited

Innes, Sherrie A. "Barbie Gets a Bum Rap: Barbie's Place in the World of Dolls." *The Barbie Chronicles: A Living Doll Turns Forty*, edited by Yona Zeldis McDonough, Simon and Schuster, 1999, pp. 175–81.

Lord, M. G. *Forever Barbie: The Unauthorized Biography of a Real Doll.* William Morrow, 1994.

McDonough, Yona Zeldis, editor. *Barbie Chronicles: A Living Doll Turns Forty.* Simon and Schuster, 1999.

_ _ _. "Barbie (Doll)." *New York Times Magazine*, 25 Jan. 1998, www.nytimes .com/1998/02/15/magazine/1-what-barbie-really-taught-me-491365 .html.

Ockman, Carol. "Barbie Meets Bouguereau: Constructing an Ideal Body for the Late Twentieth Century." *The Barbie Chronicles: A Living Doll Turns Forty*, edited by Yona Zeldis McDonough, Simon and Schuster, 1999, pp. 73–88.

Shapiro, Susan. "My Mentor, Barbie." *The Barbie Chronicles: A Living Doll Turns Forty*, edited by Yona Zeldis McDonough, Simon and Schuster, 1999, pp. 121–24.

Urla, Jacqueline and Alan C. Swedlund. "The Anthropometry of Barbie: Unsettling Ideals of the Feminine Body and Popular Culture." *Deviant Bodies: Critical Perspectives on Difference in Science and Popular Culture*, edited by Jennifer Terry and Jacqueline Urla, Indiana UP, 1995, pp. 277–313.

Meaning

1. In your own words, explain Ojha's thesis. Where does she state it explicitly?

2. Why do many critics condemn Barbie? What are the "positive messages" that she sends to girls, as Ojha sees it?

3. Look again at the concluding paragraph. What is Ojha proposing in her answer to the question she poses?

4. If you are uncertain of the meanings of any of the words listed below, try to guess them from the context of the essay. Then look them up to see how close your definitions were to those in the dictionary. Test out the new words by using each of them in a sentence or two of your own.

brigade (1)	hegemonic (1)	peripheral (3)
incarnate (1)	paleontologists (2)	acquiescent (5)
contentious (1)	plethora (2)	vituperative (6)
regressive (1)		

Purpose and Audience

1. What seems to be the writer's purpose in this essay: to explain the effects Barbie has on girls' self-image? to defend the doll from her critics? to do something else?

2. What assumptions does Ojha seem to make about her readers—their gender or age, their attitudes toward Barbie, their attitudes toward feminism, and so on?

Method and Structure

1. What principle of analysis does Ojha apply to her examination of Barbie? Why is that principle particularly well suited to her subject?

2. Throughout her essay, Ojha cites quotations, ideas, and opinions from **sources**. What does this material contribute to her analysis?

3. What does Ojha accomplish with the first word and the first sentence of paragraphs 2, 3, 4, and 5?

4. OTHER METHODS   Ojha's analysis presents an **argument** in support of Barbie. Why, then, does she start by listing criticisms of the doll?

Language

1. How would you describe Ojha's **tone**? How seriously does she take her subject? Is the tone appropriate, given her purpose?

2. What strategy does Ojha use to establish the credibility of the scholars whose work she cites? Why do you suppose she does it?

Writing Topics

1. JOURNAL TO ESSAY   Using "Plastic Perfection" as a model, write an analysis of the toy or game you explored in your journal (p. 168). What meanings besides pure entertainment, if any, did it carry? Your essay may be based on research or on your own observations, but it should include plenty of description so that readers unfamiliar with the toy or game can picture it in their minds, and it should carefully examine each element of your analysis for its contribution to the intentional or unintentional messages you identified.

2. How did you react to Ojha's essay? Did it have any effect on your opinion of Barbie dolls? Do you agree with her assessment of the positive messages they send? Do you believe that the negative messages cited by critics outweigh anything good about the franchise? Or do you find the subject irrelevant and not worthy of analysis? Why? Write an essay that responds to Ojha's conclusions. Be sure to include evidence to support your view.

3. CULTURAL CONSIDERATIONS   It may surprise you to learn that the inspiration for Barbie was a racy adult doll from World War II–era Germany; Mattel specifically adapted it for American girls in the late 1950s. What characteristics of Barbie and her friends strike you as especially American? How might the dolls be different if they were designed for children in or from

other countries? Why do you think so? The characteristics you identify may come from Ojha's observations or your own experience, but be sure to explain why you think they are distinctly American.

4. **CONNECTIONS**   Like Ojha, Antonio Ruiz-Camacho, in "Souvenirs" (p. 244), explores the cultural significance of objects marketed to children — in his case, Kermit the Frog timepieces and Mexican folklore whistles. In an essay, compare and contrast how popular culture has affected these two writers. How do their respective points of view affect their experiences and attitudes? You might consider, for example, how and why each writer first encountered the objects, the countries they grew up in, or the meanings they see in their toys. Be sure to include examples from both essays to support your conclusions.

WRITING WITH THE METHOD

▶

DIVISION OR ANALYSIS

Select one of the following topics, or any other topic they suggest, for an essay developed by analysis. Be sure to choose a topic you care about so that analysis is a means of communicating an idea, not an end in itself.

People, Animals, and Objects

1. The personality of a friend or relative
2. The personality of a typical politician, teacher, or other professional
3. An animal such as a cat, dog, horse, cow, spider, or bat
4. A machine or an appliance, such as a solar panel, hybrid engine, harvesting combine, smartphone, tablet, hair dryer, or toaster
5. A nonmotorized vehicle, such as a skateboard, inline skates, bicycle, or sailboat
6. A building such as a hospital, theater, or sports arena

Ideas

7. The perfect marriage
8. The perfect crime
9. A theory or concept in a field such as psychology, sociology, economics, biology, physics, engineering, or astronomy
10. The evidence in a political argument (written, spoken, or reported in the news)
11. A liberal arts education

Aspects of Culture

12. A stereotype
13. A style of dress or "look," such as that associated with the typical hipster, body-builder, or outdoors enthusiast
14. A typical hero or villain in children's movies, science fiction, or romance novels
15. A popular Web site or Internet meme
16. A literary work: short story, novel, poem, essay
17. A visual work: painting, sculpture, building
18. A musical work: song, concerto, symphony, opera
19. A performance: sports, acting, dance, music, speech
20. The slang of a particular group or occupation

WRITING ABOUT THE THEME

LOOKING AT POPULAR CULTURE

1. The selections by Moises Velasquez-Manoff (p. 150), Luci Tapahonso (p. 150), Scott Adams (p. 156), Leslie Jamison (p. 162), and Saanya Ojha (p. 168) all include the theme that what you see — whether in entertainment, advertising, or consumer products — is not all you get. Think of something you have used, heard, seen, or otherwise experienced in popular culture that made you suspect a hidden message or agenda. Consider, for example, a childhood toy, a popular breakfast cereal, a political speech, a magazine, a textbook, a video game, a movie, or a visit to a theme park. Using the paragraphs and essays in this chapter as models, write an analysis of your subject, making sure to divide it into distinct elements and to conclude it by reassembling those elements into a new whole.

2. Leslie Jamison and Saanya Ojha both refer to popular culture's power to make us feel better about ourselves. At the same time, both writers suggest that such feelings are superficial at best, maybe even harmful on a deeper level. Write an essay in which you analyze the effects of popular culture on self-esteem, drawing on both essays and your own understanding of the issue. Consider, for instance, the role of advertising in exploiting insecurities to sell products, or recent findings that heavy users of social media tend to find the experience depressing. How does popular culture affect you?

3. Moises Velasquez-Manoff, Luci Tapahonso, Leslie Jamison, and Saanya Ojha all write seriously about popular culture, a subject that some people would consider trivial and unworthy of critical attention. How informative and useful are such analyses? Where does each selection tell us something significant about ourselves, or in contrast, where does it fail in trying to make the trivial seem important? Is popular culture — music, television, film, books, restaurant chains — best looked at critically, best ignored, or best simply enjoyed? Explain your answer in an essay, using plenty of examples to support your thesis.

9

CLASSIFICATION

▶

DISTINGUISHING OURSELVES FROM OTHERS

We classify when we sort things into groups: kinds of cars, styles of writing, types of customers. Because it creates order, **classification** helps us make sense of our experiences and our surroundings. With it, we see the correspondences among like things and distinguish them from unlike things, similarities and distinctions that can be especially helpful when making a decision or encouraging others to see things from a new perspective. You use classification when you prioritize your bills, sort your laundry, or organize your music collection; you might also draw on the method to choose among types of data plans, to propose new pay scales at your workplace, or to argue at a town meeting that some types of community projects are more valuable than others. Because classification helps us name things, remember them, and discuss them with others, it is also a useful method for developing and sharing ideas in writing.

Writers classify people more than any other subject, perhaps because the method gives order and even humor to our sense of humanity. The authors in this chapter explore and celebrate the distinctions among us that create diversity. In a paragraph, Scaachi Koul asserts that only two kinds of people believe traditional weddings in India are enjoyable. On a more serious note, Joyce Carol Oates, in another paragraph, sorts those who have left their home countries by their reasons for leaving. Then, in essays, Jonathan R. Gould identifies four kinds of neighborly personalities, David Brooks examines several characteristics of communities to argue that American society isn't as diverse as we like to think, and Harrison Candelaria Fletcher considers variations of skin tone and ethnic identity among his family and his peers.

Reading Classification

Writers classify primarily to explain a pattern in a subject that might not have been noticed before: a sportswriter, for instance, might observe that great basketball defenders tend to fall into one of three groups based on their style of play: the shot blockers, the stealers, and the brawlers. Sometimes, writers also classify to persuade readers that one group is superior: the same sportswriter might argue that shot blockers are the most effective defenders because they not only create turnovers like the stealers do, but they also intimidate the opponent like the brawlers do.

Classification involves a three-step process:

1. Separate things into their elements, using the method of **division or analysis** (previous chapter).
2. Isolate the similarities among the elements.
3. Group or classify the things based on those similarities, matching like with like.

The following diagram illustrates a classification essay that appears later in this chapter, "The People Next Door" by Jonathan R. Gould Jr. Gould's subject is neighbors, and he sees four distinct kinds:

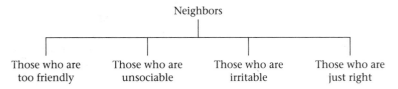

All the members of Gould's overall group share at least one characteristic: they have been his neighbors. The members of each subgroup also share at least one characteristic: they are too friendly, for instance, or unsociable. The people in each subgroup are independent of one another, and none of them is essential to the existence of the subgroup: the kind of neighbor would continue to exist even if, at the moment, Gould didn't live next door to such a person.

The number of groups in a classification scheme depends entirely on the basis for establishing the classes in the first place. There are two systems:

- In a *complex classification* like that used for neighbors, each individual fits firmly into one class because of at least one distinguishing feature shared with all members of that class but not with any members of any other classes. All the too-friendly neighbors are overly friendly, but none of the unsociable, irritable, or just-right neighbors shares this characteristic.

■ In a *binary* or *two-part classification*, two classes are in opposition to each other, such as constructive and destructive neighbors. Often, one group has a certain characteristic that the other group lacks. For instance, neighbors could be classified into those who respect your privacy and those who don't. A binary scheme is useful to emphasize the possession of a particular characteristic, but it is limited if it specifies nothing about the members of the "other" class except that they lack the trait.

Sorting items demands a **principle of classification** that determines the groups by distinguishing them. For instance, Gould's principle in identifying four groups of neighbors is their behavior toward him and his family. Principles for sorting a year's movies might be genre (action-adventure, comedy, drama), place of origin (domestic, foreign), or cost of production (low-budget, medium-budget, high-budget). The choice of a principle depends on the writer's main interest in the subject.

Although a writer may emphasize one class over the others, the classification itself must be complete and consistent. A classification of movies by genre would be incomplete if it omitted comedies. It would be inconsistent if it included action-adventures, comedies, dramas, low-budget films, and foreign films: such a system mixes *three* principles (genre, cost, origin); it omits whole classes (what about high-budget domestic dramas?); and it overlaps other classes (a low-budget foreign action-adventure would fit in three different groups).

Analyzing Classification in Paragraphs

Scaachi Koul is a humorist and critic whose work often focuses on the tribulations and hilarities of being Indian in Canada. Born in Calgary, Alberta, in 1991, she was raised there by her immigrant parents and now lives in Toronto, where she is a culture writer for *BuzzFeed*. This paragraph is from her first book, *One Day We'll All Be Dead and None of This Will Matter* (2017).

<u>There are two types of people who insist that Indian weddings are fun.</u> The first are white people, who are frequently well-meaning but stupid and enjoy things vaguely different from themselves by exoticizing them. . . . The second type are any people who have never actually been to an Indian wedding in India with Indian people. Or, at least, have never been to the entirety of an Indian wedding, the full five to seven days, the multiple outfits, the familial requirements that forfeit your time and independence. No, these people swoop in for the ceremony and reception, they eat some pakoras and talk about how "cute" it is when little girls have unibrows, maybe they show up early for the henna ceremony and ask for a lower-back tat, and then we never see them again. Indian weddings are a lot of things, but "fun" has never been their purpose.

Principle of classification (topic sentence underlined): people who think Indian weddings are fun

1. White people who are misinformed

2. Indian people who attend only the fun parts

Joyce Carol Oates (born 1938) is a prolific and award-winning writer who has published many dozens of novels, stories, plays, poems, essays, and critical analyses. In this paragraph from "Refugees in America," her review of Viet Thanh Nguyen's short story collection *The Refugees* (2017), Oates classifies men who, like Nguyen, have left their home countries.

Consider the distinctions between the words *expat, immigrant, refugee*. "Expat" suggests a cosmopolitan spirit and resources that allow mobility; to be an "immigrant" suggests some measure of need. A "refugee" is, by definition, desperate: he has been displaced from his home, has been rendered stateless, has few or no resources. The expat retains an identity as he retains his citizenship, his privileges; the refugee loses his identity amid the anonymity of many others like him. In the way that enslaved persons are truncated by the term *slaves*, defined by their condition, there's a loss of identity in the category term *refugees*. It might seem to be more humane, and accurate, to give someone who is forced to seek refuge a more expansive designation: "displaced person."

Principle of classification: circumstances of leaving home

1. Expat: voluntary adventure; retains identity

2. Immigrant: voluntary, some need; implied identity

3. Refugee: involuntary, desperate need; loses identity

Implications of classification

Developing an Essay by Classification

▶ Getting Started

Classification essays are often assigned in college: you might be asked to identify the major branches of government for a political science class, for instance, or to categorize difficult personality types for a business communication course. When you need to develop your own subject for a classification essay, think of one large class of things whose members you've noticed fall into subclasses, such as study habits, midnight shoppers, or charity fundraising appeals. Be sure that your general subject forms a class in its own right—that all its members share at least one important quality. Then look for your principle of classification, the quality or qualities that distinguish some members from others, providing poles for the members to group themselves around. One such principle for charity fundraising appeals might be the different methods of delivery, such as telephone calls, public gatherings, advertisements, and social media campaigns.

While generating ideas for your classification, keep track of them in a list, diagram, or outline to ensure that your principle is applied thoroughly (to all classes) and consistently (each class relating to the principle). Fill in the list, diagram, or outline with the distinguishing features of each class and with examples that will clarify your scheme.

▶ Forming a Thesis

You will want to state your principle of classification in a thesis sentence so that you know where you're going and your readers know where you're taking them. Be sure the sentence also conveys a *reason* for the classification so that the essay does not become a dull list of categories. The following tentative thesis sentence is mechanical; the revision below it is more interesting.

TENTATIVE THESIS SENTENCE   Charity fundraising requests are delivered in many ways.

REVISED THESIS SENTENCE   Of the many ways to deliver charity fundraising requests, the three that rely on personal contact are generally the most effective.

(Note that the revised thesis sentence implies a further classification based on whether the requests involve personal contact or not.)

▶ Organizing

The **introduction** to a classification essay should make clear why the classification is worthwhile: What situation prompted the essay? What do readers already know about the subject? What use might they make of the information you will provide? Unless your principle of classification is self-evident, you may want to explain it briefly—but save extensive explanation for the body of the essay.

In the **body** of the essay, the classes may be arranged in order of decreasing familiarity or increasing importance or size—whatever pattern provides the emphasis you want and clarifies your scheme for readers. You should at least mention each class, but some classes may demand considerable space and detail.

A classification essay often ends with a **conclusion** that restores the wholeness of the subject. Among other uses, the conclusion might summarize the classes, comment on the significance of one particular class in relation to the whole, or point out a new understanding of the whole subject gained from the classification.

▶ Drafting

For the first draft of your classification, your main goal will be to establish your scheme: spelling out the purpose and principle of classification and defining the groups so that they are complete and consistent, covering the subject without mixing principles or overlapping. The more you've been able to plan your scheme, the less difficult the draft will be. If you can also fill in the examples and other details needed to develop the groups, do so.

Be sure to consider your readers' needs as you draft. For a subject familiar to readers, such as study habits, you probably wouldn't need to justify your principle of classification, but you would need to enliven the classes themselves with vivid details. For an unfamiliar subject, in contrast, you might need to take considerable care in explaining the principle of classification as well as in detailing the classes.   ·

▶ Revising and Editing

The following questions and the information in the Focus box on the next page can help you revise and edit your classification.

   ■ *Will readers see the purpose of your classification?* Let readers know early on why you are troubling to classify your subject, and keep this purpose evident throughout the essay.

FOCUS ON PARAGRAPH DEVELOPMENT

A crucial aim of revising a classification is to make sure each group is clear: what's counted in, what's counted out, and why. It's not unusual to get so focused on identifying and sorting categories during the draft stage that you neglect the details. In that case, you'll need to go back and provide examples, comparisons, and other particulars to make the groups clear as you develop the paragraph(s) devoted to each group.

The following undeveloped paragraph gives just the outline of one group in a four-part classification of ex-smokers into zealots, evangelists, the elect, and the serene:

> The second group, evangelists, does not condemn smokers but encourages them to quit. Evangelists think quitting is easy, and they preach this message, often earning the resentment of potential converts.

Contrast this bare-bones adaptation with the actual paragraphs written by Franklin E. Zimring in his essay "Confessions of a Former Smoker":

> By contrast, the antismoking evangelist does not condemn smokers. Unlike the zealot, he regards smoking as an easily curable condition, as a social disease, and not a sin. The evangelist spends an enormous amount of time seeking and preaching to the unconverted. He argues that kicking the habit is not *that* difficult. After all, *he* did it; moreover, as he describes it, the benefits of quitting are beyond measure and the disadvantages are nil.
>
> The hallmark of the evangelist is his insistence that he never misses tobacco. Though he is less hostile to smokers than the zealot, he is resented more. Friends and loved ones who have been the targets of his preachments frequently greet the resumption of smoking by the evangelist as an occasion for unmitigated glee.

In the second sentence of both paragraphs, Zimring explicitly contrasts evangelists with zealots, the group he previously discussed. And he does more, as well: he provides specific examples of the evangelist's message (first paragraph) and of others' reactions to him (second paragraph). These details pin down the group, making it distinct from other groups and clear in itself.

For more advice on developing paragraphs through specifics, see pages 35–36.

- *Is your classification complete?* Your principle of classification should create categories that encompass every representative of the general subject. If some representatives will not fit the scheme, you may have to create a new category or revise the existing categories to include them.

- *Is your classification consistent?* Consistency is essential to save readers from confusion or irritation. Make sure all the classes reflect the same principle and do not overlap. Remedy flaws by adjusting the classes or creating new ones.

We make our friends; we make our enemies; but God makes our next-door neighbor.
—G. K. Chesterton

Good fences make good neighbors.
—Proverb

For what do we live, but to make sport for our neighbors, and laugh at them in our turn?
—Jane Austen

JOURNAL RESPONSE Jot down a list of neighbors you have now and have had in the past. Then write a short journal entry about the different kinds of neighbors you have encountered.

Jonathan R. Gould Jr.

Jonathan R. Gould Jr., was born in 1968 in Little Falls, New York, and grew up on a dairy farm in nearby Fort Plain. After graduating from Little Falls Baptist Academy as valedictorian of his class, he served three years in the US Army, specializing in administration and computer programming. At the State University of New York (SUNY) at Oneonta, Gould was an honors student, received the Provost Award for academic distinction, and obtained a BS in mathematics education.

The People Next Door
(Student Essay)

From his experiences in many different settings, Gould identifies four types of neighbors, only one of which could be considered truly neighborly. Gould wrote this essay in 1994 for a writing course at SUNY.

I have moved more often than I care to remember. However, one thing always stays the same no matter where I have been. There is always a house next door, and that house contains neighbors. Over time, I have begun putting my neighbors into one of four categories: too friendly, unsociable, irritable, and just right.

Neighbors who are too friendly can be seen just about anywhere. I mean that both ways. They exist in every neighborhood I have ever lived in and seem to appear everywhere I go. For some strange reason these people become extremely attached to my family and stop in as many as eight to ten times a day. No matter how tired I appear to be, nothing short

185

of opening the door and suggesting they leave will make them go home at night. (I once told an unusually friendly neighbor that his house was on fire, in an attempt to make him leave, and he still took ten minutes to say goodbye.) What is truly interesting about these people is their strong desire to cook for us even though they have developed no culinary skill whatsoever. (This has always proved particularly disconcerting since they stay to watch us eat every bite as they continually ask if the food "tastes good.")

The unsociable neighbor is a different story altogether. For reasons of   3 his own, he has decided to pretend that we do not exist. I have always found that one or two neighbors of this type are in my neighborhood. It is not easy to identify these people, because they seldom leave the shelter of their own house. To be honest, the only way I know that someone lives in their building is the presence of a name on the mailbox and the lights shining through the windows at night. My wife often tries to befriend these unique people, and I have to admire her courage. However, even her serenity is shaken when she offers our neighbors a fresh-baked apple pie only to have them look at her as if she intended to poison them.

Probably the most difficult neighbor to deal with is the irritable   4 neighbor. This individual probably has several problems, but he has reduced all those problems down to one cause—the proximity of my family to his residence. Fortunately, I have only encountered this type of neighbor in a handful of settings. (He is usually too busy with one group of "troublemakers" to pick up a new set.) The times that I have encountered this rascal, however, have proved more than enough for my tastes. He is more than willing to talk to me. Unfortunately, all he wants to tell me is how miserable my family is making him. Ignoring this individual has not worked for me yet. (He just adds my "snobbishness" to his list of faults that my family displays.) Interestingly, this fellow will eat anything my wife (bless her soul) might make in an attempt to be sociable. Even though he never has anything good to say about the food, not a crumb will be left on the plate when he is finished (which leads me to wonder just how starved and impoverished he must be).

At the risk of sounding like Goldilocks, there is also a neighbor who   5 is "just right." One of the most wonderful things about this neighbor is that there has always been at least one everywhere I have gone. We meet often (though not too often), and our greetings are always sincere. Occasionally, our families will go out to eat or to shop, or just sit and talk. We tend to spend as much time at their house as they do at ours (two to three times a month), and everyone knows just when it is time to say goodnight.

For some reason, this neighbor knows how to cook, and we frequently exchange baked goods as well as pleasantries. For obvious reasons, this type of neighbor is my favorite.

As I mentioned before, each type of neighbor I have encountered is a 6 common sight in any neighborhood. I have always felt it was important to identify the type of neighbors that were around me. Then I am better able to maintain a clear perspective on our relationship and understand their needs. After all, people do not really change; we just learn how to live with both the good and the bad aspects of their behavior.

Meaning

1. Where does Gould state his thesis?

2. What is the difference between unsociable and irritable neighbors in Gould's classification?

3. If you are uncertain of the meanings of any of the words listed below, try to guess them from the context of the essay. Then look them up to see how close your definitions were to those in the dictionary. Test out the new words by using each of them in a sentence or two of your own.

culinary (2)	proximity (4)	pleasantries (5)
disconcerting (2)	impoverished (4)	

Purpose and Audience

1. Why do you suppose Gould wrote this essay? Where does he give the clearest indication?

2. Does Gould make any assumptions about his audience? Does he seem to be writing for a certain type of reader?

Method and Structure

1. Why do you think Gould chose the method of classification to write about the subject of neighbors? How does the method help him achieve his purpose?

2. What is Gould's principle of classification? Do you think his classification is complete and consistent? How else might the author have sorted neighbors?

3. Why do you think Gould stresses the fact that he has encountered most of these types of neighbors everywhere he has lived?

4. What does Gould accomplish in his conclusion?

5. **OTHER METHODS**   Gould's categories lend themselves to **comparison and contrast**. Based on his descriptions, what are the differences between the too-friendly neighbor and the just-right neighbor?

Language

1. What is Gould's tone? How seriously does he take the problem of difficult neighbors?

2. Point out several instances of **hyperbole** or overstatement in the essay. What effect do these have?

Writing Topics

1. **JOURNAL TO ESSAY**   In your journal response (p. 185) you began a process of classification by focusing on neighbors you have had. Now think of a group to which you belong — a religious organization, your family, a club or committee, even a writing class. Write a classification essay in which you sort the group's members into categories according to a clear principle of classification. Be sure to label and define each type for your readers, to provide examples, and to position yourself in one of the categories. What does your classification reveal about the group as a whole?

2. Most of us have had at least one colorful or bothersome neighbor at some time or another — a busybody, a recluse, a borrower. Write a descriptive essay (with some narration) about an interesting neighbor you have known or a narrative essay (with some description) about a memorable run-in with a neighbor.

3. **CULTURAL CONSIDERATIONS**   "Good fences make good neighbors," says a character in Robert Frost's poem "Mending Wall," and many people in our live-and-let-live society would seem to agree. Is the best neighbor an invisible one? Or do we lose something when we ignore those who are literally closest to us? Write an essay giving a definition of what it means to be a good neighbor. Or, if you prefer, write an essay in which you compare and contrast neighboring habits in different types of communities you have lived in or know of.

4. **CONNECTIONS**   Both Gould and David Brooks, in "People Like Us" (next page), classify communities: Gould distinguishes four categories of neighbors, while Brooks focuses on the kinds of neighborhoods people share. Write an essay in which you compare the two essays. How persuasive do you find each writer's groups? Which comes closest to your own experiences with neighborhoods? Why?

No two people are alike and both of them are glad of it.   —*Farmers' Almanac*

We are a multicultural country—always have been, and to our credit, always will be. It is something that we should be very proud of and embrace.
                                                                        —Cheech Marin

I think the expression "It's a small world" is really a euphemism for "I keep running into people I can't stand."
                                                                        —Brock Cohen

JOURNAL RESPONSE   Take a few minutes to describe the people in the place where you grew up. Was everybody in your neighborhood alike—economically, racially, academically, and so forth? Or did the people around you represent a mix of classes, colors, education levels, types of employment? How did your family fit in?

David Brooks

A distinguished journalist, political analyst, and moderate conservative, David Brooks has engaged readers across the political spectrum for three decades. He was born in 1961 in Toronto, Ontario, grew up in New York City and a Philadelphia suburb, and graduated from the University of Chicago in 1983. He began his journalism career as a police reporter for the Chicago City News Bureau, and in 1984 he moved to the *Washington Times*, writing editorials and movie reviews. Brooks has since worked as an international reporter and contributing editor for the *Wall Street Journal*, the *Weekly Standard*, *Newsweek*, and the *Atlantic*. In 2003 he launched a regular column for the *New York Times*, now appearing twice weekly on the op-ed page. He is the author of four books of what he calls "comic sociology": *Bobos in Paradise: The New Upper Class and How They Got There* (2000), *On Paradise Drive: How We Live Now (and Always Have) in the Future Tense* (2004), *The Social Animal: The Hidden Sources of Love, Character, and Achievement* (2011), and *The Road to Character* (2015). Brooks is a media personality as well, regularly appearing as a commentator on the NPR program *All Things Considered* and the PBS show *NewsHour*.

People Like Us

The United States is often described as a multicultural "melting pot," in which people with diverse backgrounds come together and form a shared American identity. Examining the populations of several US communities, Brooks disputes this notion. "People Like Us" first appeared in the *Atlantic* in 2003.

Maybe it's time to admit the obvious. We don't really care about diversity   1
all that much in America, even though we talk about it a great deal. Maybe
somewhere in this country there is a truly diverse neighborhood in which
a black Pentecostal minister lives next to a white anti-globalization activist, who lives next to an Asian short-order cook, who lives next to a professional golfer, who lives next to a postmodern-literature professor and a
cardiovascular surgeon. But I have never been to or heard of that neighborhood. Instead, what I have seen all around the country is people making strenuous efforts to group themselves with people who are basically
like themselves.

Human beings are capable of drawing amazingly subtle social distinc-   2
tions and then shaping their lives around them. In the Washington, DC,
area Democratic lawyers tend to live in suburban Maryland, and Republican lawyers tend to live in suburban Virginia. If you asked a Democratic
lawyer to move from her $750,000 house in Bethesda, Maryland, to a
$750,000 house in Great Falls, Virginia, she'd look at you as if you had
just asked her to buy a pickup truck with a gun rack and to shove chewing
tobacco in her kid's mouth. In Manhattan the owner of a $3 million SoHo
loft would feel out of place moving into a $3 million Fifth Avenue apart-
ment. A West Hollywood interior decorator would feel dislocated if you
asked him to move to Orange County. In Georgia a barista from Athens
would probably not fit in serving coffee in Americus.

It is a common complaint that every place is starting to look the   3
same. But in the information age, the late writer James Chapin[1] once told
me, every place becomes more like itself. People are less often tied down
to factories and mills, and they can search for places to live on the basis
of cultural affinity. Once they find a town in which people share their
values, they flock there, and reinforce whatever was distinctive about the
town in the first place. Once Boulder, Colorado, became known as conge-
nial to politically progressive mountain bikers, half the politically progressive mountain bikers in the country (it seems) moved there; they
made the place so culturally pure that it has become practically a parody
of itself.

But people love it. Make no mistake—we are increasing our happi-   4
ness by segmenting off so rigorously. We are finding places where we
are comfortable and where we feel we can flourish. But the choices
we make toward that end lead to the very opposite of diversity. The

----

[1] A progressive Democrat, Professor Chapin (1942–2002) was a political analyst,
a writer for United Press International, and an author of history textbooks. [Editors'
note.]

United States might be a diverse nation when considered as a whole, but block by block and institution by institution it is a relatively homogeneous nation.

When we use the word "diversity" today we usually mean racial integration. But even here our good intentions seem to have run into the brick wall of human nature. Over the past generation reformers have tried heroically, and in many cases successfully, to end housing discrimination. But recent patterns aren't encouraging: according to an analysis of the 2000 census data, the 1990s saw only a slight increase in the racial integration of neighborhoods in the United States. The number of middle-class and upper-middle-class African American families is rising, but for whatever reasons—racism, psychological comfort—these families tend to congregate in predominantly black neighborhoods.

In fact, evidence suggests that some neighborhoods become more segregated over time. New suburbs in Arizona and Nevada, for example, start out reasonably well integrated. These neighborhoods don't yet have reputations, so people choose their houses for other, mostly economic reasons. But as neighborhoods age, they develop personalities (that's where the Asians live, and that's where the Hispanics live), and segmentation occurs. It could be that in a few years the new suburbs in the Southwest will be nearly as segregated as the established ones in the Northeast and the Midwest.

Even though race and ethnicity run deep in American society, we should in theory be able to find areas that are at least culturally diverse. But here, too, people show few signs of being truly interested in building diverse communities. If you run a retail company and you're thinking of opening new stores, you can choose among dozens of consulting firms that are quite effective at locating your potential customers. They can do this because people with similar tastes and preferences tend to congregate by ZIP code.

The most famous of these precision marketing firms is Claritas, which breaks down the US population into sixty-two psycho-demographic clusters, based on such factors as how much money people make, what they like to read and watch, and what products they have bought in the past. For example, the "suburban sprawl" cluster is composed of young families making about $41,000 a year and living in fast-growing places such as Burnsville, Minnesota, and Bensalem, Pennsylvania. These people are almost twice as likely as other Americans to have three-way calling. They are two and a half times as likely to buy Light n' Lively Kid Yogurt. Members of the "towns & gowns" cluster are recent college graduates in places such as Berkeley, California, and Gainesville, Florida. They are big consumers of Dove Bars and *Saturday Night Live*. They tend to drive small foreign cars and to read *Rolling Stone* and *Scientific American*.

Looking through the market research, one can sometimes be amazed by how efficiently people cluster—and by how predictable we all are. If you wanted to sell imported wine, obviously you would have to find places where rich people live. But did you know that the sixteen counties with the greatest proportion of imported-wine drinkers are all in the same three metropolitan areas (New York, San Francisco, and Washington, DC)? If you tried to open a motor-home dealership in Montgomery County, Pennsylvania, you'd probably go broke, because people in this ring of the Philadelphia suburbs think RVs are kind of uncool. But if you traveled just a short way north, to Monroe County, Pennsylvania, you would find yourself in the fifth motor-home-friendliest county in America.

Geography is not the only way we find ourselves divided from people unlike us. Some of us watch Fox News, while others listen to NPR. Some like David Letterman, and others—typically in less urban neighborhoods—like Jay Leno.[2] Some go to charismatic churches; some go to mainstream churches. Americans tend more and more often to marry people with education levels similar to their own, and to befriend people with backgrounds similar to their own.

My favorite illustration of this latter pattern comes from the first, noncontroversial chapter of *The Bell Curve*.[3] Think of your twelve closest friends, Richard J. Herrnstein and Charles Murray write. If you had chosen them randomly from the American population, the odds that half of your twelve closest friends would be college graduates would be six in a thousand. The odds that half of the twelve would have advanced degrees would be less than one in a million. Have any of your twelve closest friends graduated from Harvard, Stanford, Yale, Princeton, Caltech, MIT, Duke, Dartmouth, Cornell, Columbia, Chicago, or Brown? If you chose your friends randomly from the American population, the odds against your having four or more friends from those schools would be more than a billion to one.

9

10

11

---

[2] David Letterman (born 1947) hosted the subversive late-night talk shows *Late Night with David Letterman* and *The Late Show with David Letterman* from 1982 to 2015; Jay Leno (born 1950), hosted the more traditional rivals *The Tonight Show* and *The Jay Leno Show* from 1992 to 2014. [Editors' note.]

[3] Published in 1994, the book uses statistical analysis to argue that IQ is inherited and to warn that the American population will become less intelligent (and less affluent) if college graduates continue having fewer children than less educated people do—both controversial claims that upset many readers. [Editors' note.]

Cartoon by Steve Brodner, 2003.

Many of us live in absurdly unlikely groupings, because we have orga-   12
nized our lives that way.

It's striking that the institutions that talk the most about diversity   13
often practice it the least. For example, no group of people sings the diversity anthem more frequently and fervently than administrators at just
such elite universities. But elite universities are amazingly undiverse in
their values, politics, and mores. Professors in particular are drawn from a
rather narrow segment of the population. If faculties reflected the general
population, thirty-two percent of professors would be registered Democrats
and thirty-one percent would be registered Republicans. Forty percent
would be evangelical Christians. But a recent study of several universities
by the conservative Center for the Study of Popular Culture and the
American Enterprise Institute found that roughly ninety percent of those
professors in the arts and sciences who had registered with a political
party had registered Democratic. Fifty-seven professors at Brown were
found on the voter-registration rolls. Of those, fifty-four were Democrats. Of the forty-two professors in the English, history, sociology, and
political-science departments, all were Democrats. The results at Harvard,
Penn State, Maryland, and the University of California at Santa Barbara
were similar to the results at Brown.

What we are looking at here is human nature. People want to be   14
around others who are roughly like themselves. That's called community.

It probably would be psychologically difficult for most Brown professors to share an office with someone who was pro-life, a member of the National Rifle Association, or an evangelical Christian. It's likely that hiring committees would subtly—even unconsciously—screen out any such people they encountered. Republicans and evangelical Christians have sensed that they are not welcome at places like Brown, so they don't even consider working there. In fact, any registered Republican who contemplates a career in academia these days is both a hero and a fool. So, in a semi-self-selective pattern, brainy people with generally liberal social mores flow to academia, and brainy people with generally conservative mores flow elsewhere.

The dream of diversity is like the dream of equality. Both are based on 15
ideals we celebrate even as we undermine them daily. (How many times have you seen someone renounce a high-paying job or pull his child from an elite college on the grounds that these things are bad for equality?) On the one hand, the situation is appalling. It is appalling that Americans know so little about one another. It is appalling that many of us are so narrow-minded that we can't tolerate a few people with ideas significantly different from our own. It's appalling that evangelical Christians are practically absent from entire professions, such as academia, the media, and filmmaking. It's appalling that people should be content to cut themselves off from everyone unlike themselves.

The segmentation of society means that often we don't even have 16
arguments across the political divide. Within their little validating communities, liberals and conservatives circulate half-truths about the supposed awfulness of the other side. These distortions are believed because it feels good to believe them.

On the other hand, there are limits to how diverse any community 17
can or should be. I've come to think that it is not useful to try to hammer diversity into every neighborhood and institution in the United States. Sure, Augusta National[4] should probably admit women, and university sociology departments should probably hire a conservative or two. It would be nice if all neighborhoods had a good mixture of ethnicities. But human nature being what it is, most places and institutions are going to remain culturally homogeneous.

It's probably better to think about diverse lives, not diverse institu- 18
tions. Human beings, if they are to live well, will have to move through

---

[4]Located in Georgia, the private Augusta National Golf Club hosts the prestigious annual Masters tournament; until August 2012, it excluded women from membership. [Editors' note.]

a series of institutions and environments, which may be individually homogeneous but, taken together, will offer diverse experiences. It might also be a good idea to make national service a rite of passage for young people in this country: it would take them out of their narrow neighborhood segment and thrust them in with people unlike themselves. Finally, it's probably important for adults to get out of their own familiar circles. If you live in a coastal, socially liberal neighborhood, maybe you should take out a subscription to *The Door*, the evangelical humor magazine; or maybe you should visit Branson, Missouri.[5] Maybe you should stop in at a megachurch. Sure, it would be superficial familiarity, but it beats the iron curtains that now separate the nation's various cultural zones.

Look around at your daily life. Are you really in touch with the broad diversity of American life? Do you care? 19

Meaning

1. Can you find a statement of Brooks's thesis anywhere in his essay? Try to express the author's main idea in your own words.

2. What are "psycho-demographic clusters" (paragraph 8)? What do they have to do with Brooks's thesis?

3. What useful purposes are served by segregation, according to Brooks? What are the negative consequences of people choosing to live in areas where the neighbors are similar?

4. If you are uncertain of the meanings of any of the words listed below, try to guess them from the context of the essay. Then look them up to see how close your definitions were to those in the dictionary. Test out the new words by using each of them in a sentence or two of your own.

globalization (1)	congenial (3)	charismatic (10)
postmodern (1)	segmenting (4)	mores (13)
strenuous (1)	homogeneous (4, 17, 18)	evangelical (13, 18)
dislocated (2)	demographic (8)	renounce (15)

Purpose and Audience

1. Does Brooks make any assumptions about his audience? Where does he give the clearest indication of the type of person he imagines reading his essay?

---

[5]A tourist destination that features amusement parks, wax museums and similar attractions, and more than fifty theaters and music venues showcasing country-and-western acts and pop stars from the 1950s, '60s, and '70s. [Editors' note.]

2. What seems to be Brooks's purpose for writing "People Like Us"? Does he want to inform, persuade, or entertain his readers? How can you tell?

3. How does the cartoon by Steve Brodner (p. 193) relate to Brooks's essay? Why do you suppose the *Atlantic* included it with the article?

Method and Structure

1. What principle of classification does Brooks use to examine American society?

2. What kinds of diversity does Brooks consider in his classification? Diagram or outline his categories. Do any of them overlap?

3. Examine the examples and details Brooks uses to develop his classification. Where did this information come from? What **sources** does Brooks cite, and what evidence does he draw from them? How does he use the evidence he cites?

4. OTHER METHODS   At several points in his essay, Brooks uses **comparison and contrast** to shape his ideas. Locate two or three uses of this method, and explain what they contribute to the author's point.

Language

1. How would you characterize Brooks's **tone**? Why is the tone crucial in helping him achieve his purpose for writing?

2. Point out several **metaphors** in the essay. What effect do they have?

Writing Topics

1. JOURNAL TO ESSAY   How accurately do Brooks's classifications represent your experience? Starting with the description of your home town that you drafted in your journal (p. 189), write an essay that responds to Brooks, answering the two questions he poses in his final paragraph: "Are you really in touch with the broad diversity of American life? Do you care?"

2. Brooks encourages readers to seek out diversity in their experiences by interacting with people who are not like them—to find a way to connect with strangers. What, in your view, is the appropriate way to interact (or not interact) with a stranger? In answering, exclude situations that might be risky, such as deserted nighttime streets or strangers who appear clearly threatening. Think instead of a safe situation, such as a long line at the grocery store or coffee shop or the waiting room of a doctor's office. What are your "rules" for initiating conversation and for responding to a

stranger's overtures? What informs your rules: experience? personality? upbringing? How can readers apply your rules to make diverse acquaintances in their own lives?

3. **RESEARCH**   Brooks notes in paragraph 5 that "according to an analysis of the 2000 census data, the 1990s saw only a slight increase in the racial integration of neighborhoods in the United States." Visit the Web site of the US Census Bureau (*census.gov*) and find more recent information on racial integration in your local area. How has the shape of your community changed? Is it more diverse, or less, than it was a decade ago—or a generation ago? Write an essay analyzing the state of diversity in your community, considering how recent changes have affected the ways people relate to one another.

4. **CONNECTIONS**   Like "People Like Us," "Funny Business" by Scott Adams (p. 156) uses a cartoon to help illustrate the author's point. Both cartoons might be considered offensive to some readers. Why include them, then? Examine the visual elements of these two essays, and, in an essay of your own, assess the risks and rewards of using cartoons as evidence. Consider each author's purpose for writing and the overall tone of his essay, as well as the effectiveness (or lack thereof) of the visual presented. Do both writers mean to amuse, for instance, or do the cartoons serve other purposes?

America is a country founded by people from someplace else on ideas borrowed from someplace else, ultimately to try to distinguish itself from everyplace else. It is a fraught balance of identity.   —Jeb Lund

No Statue of Liberty ever greeted our arrival in this country . . . we did not, in fact, come to the United States at all. The United States came to us.   —Luis Valdez

In this country *American* means white. Everybody else has to hyphenate.   —Toni Morrison

JOURNAL RESPONSE   How does your ethnic, racial, religious, or cultural background influence your everyday life? Write a short journal entry to explore the answer to this question.

Harrison Candelaria Fletcher

The son of a Midwestern pharmacist and a New Mexican artist, Harrison Candelaria Fletcher (born 1962) is a former journalist who writes creative nonfiction about memory and the blending of cultures. He explored the depths of his parents' lives and their influences on his own identity in the prize-winning memoirs *Descanso for My Father: Fragments of a Life* (2012) and *Presentimiento: A Life in Dreams* (2016) — about his father and mother, respectively (*descanso* is Spanish for "resting place"; a *presentimiento* is a premonition). Fletcher grew up in Albuquerque, New Mexico, graduated from the University of New Mexico in 1985, and worked as a newspaper reporter and columnist for eighteen years before receiving an MFA in creative writing from the Vermont College of Fine Arts in 2006. His essays and prose poems have been published in literary journals such as *New Letters*, *Fourth Genre*, and *Puerto del Sol* and recognized with multiple awards, including a Pushcart Prize special mention. Fletcher teaches writing in the graduate program at Colorado State University and is the editor of *Shadowbox* magazine. He lives in Fort Collins, Colorado.

White

In this essay, abridged from a chapter in *Descanso for My Father*, Fletcher, who was not yet two when his father died, draws on his personal experience and his sense of irony to examine the degrees of paleness he inherited from a ghost.

CREAM

With a cup of strong coffee and five packets of creamer, I can approximate   1
the skin tone of the nine members of my mother's family.

MILK

I never see the shadow or the red carton flash, and even when the pint of   2
milk explodes against the head of my wheat-haired friend I'm late to
understand what the Chicano boy means when he curses from the sidewalk of my junior high cafeteria, "Shit. Missed that honky."

EGGSHELL

Ricky Sandoval pins me by the throat against a C-Building locker, the   3
combination lock spinning beside my head, and slaps me on one cheek,
then the other, until my composure cracks, my eyes water, and my face
burns red.

"See?" he says. "That's all you need. A little color."   4

SCAR

The razor is too dull to cut, so I scratch a fingernail on the back of my   5
left hand hoping my big brother will see. He yanks me off the front
porch anyway and into the kitchen where he and his fatherless friends
have found a better way to scar—a curtain pin heated orange on the gas
range and pressed to the tender fold between thumb and forefinger, into
the shape of a cross, into the symbol of belonging he's seen on brown
Chicano fists. He holds my arm tight against the Formica counter while
I close my eyes and still see the blue flame. A vodka shot. A cold water
blast. I stand beside him as our matching crucifixes swell with blood.
Afterward, we raid vegetable gardens, set pampas plumes alight, and
bust phonebooths until glass drips from our denim jackets like rain.
I pick the scab to keep the scar alive, but my cross fades first, swallowed
by pale skin.

LIQUID PAPER

"No. We are in *not* Mexican," my mother says.   6
　　"Chicano?" I ask.   7
　　"No," she says, snickering.   8
　　"Spanish?"   9
　　"No."   10

"Then what do I say on my report?"   11
"Don't say anything."   12
"How about Irish? Like Dad."   13
"He wasn't Irish. He was Scottish-French."   14
"Wasn't your grandmother Italian? I thought that's where I got my   15
red hair."
"Your hair isn't red. It's auburn. And if you want to know the truth,   16
my family's Basque."
"How do you spell it?"   17

ASPIRIN

Fourteen in the backyard weeds among the horseflies and cicadas with   18
my bath towel and baby oil, shirtless under the hundred-degree sun. It's
late August, two weeks to remake myself for my sophomore year at Valley
High. My head pounds. My ears buzz. My navel pools with sweat.

An hour later, a rash breaks across my torso. Second-degree burns, the   19
doctor tells my mother on the phone. An allergic reaction to the sun. His
prescription: ice cubes, a cold compress, Noxzema, and Bayer tablets for
the pain.

I spend two days in bed raking my fingernails over itchy lubricated   20
skin. It's okay, I tell my mother and snickering sisters. When the swelling
stops, maybe I'll tan.

FLUORESCENT

Brendon Jefferson is the only black kid in tenth grade PE. He dribbles two   21
basketballs simultaneously, leaps above the rim, dunks them both. I watch
from the sidelines, envious.

One morning during wrestling, we sit side by side on the mat with   22
the soccer captain and the driver of a low-slung Monte Carlo, hugging
our knees while the coach pairs us into matches. Brendon looks at each
of us, then pokes his thigh, the soccer player's thigh, and the low-rider's
thigh.

"Check this out," he says. "I'm black. He's yellow. He's brown. And   23
you . . ."
He jabs my skin, bloodless under fluorescent lights.   24
"You're just white!"   25
He rolls onto his back, laughing.   26
We wrestle to a draw.   27

GHOST

After college I attend a National Association of Hispanic Journalists con-   28
vention in Dallas. I linger among the beige cubicles while other reporters
and editors brush past me with résumés and business cards. When
I approach, they study my face, squint at my nametag, and turn away.
Several hours into the job fair, with few interviews and even fewer prospects, I duck into a men's room, flip over my badge, and scribble in my
mother's maiden name, Candelaria. Back in the main arena, recruiters
smile, hands extend, appointments open.

I walk through walls.   29

LIGHTBULB

"A Chicano," explains the sculptor, the activist, the co-founder of the   30
Denver multicultural arts council, "is someone who is born in the
United States but has a blood mixture of Aztec and Spanish. A Chicano
is a person with one foot in one culture and one foot in another culture
who resists being forced to choose. A Chicano is a person trying to
define themselves for themselves. A Chicano is a person seeking their
true identity."

"I guess that makes me a Chicano," I say, touching my pale check.   31

"Me, too," she says laughing. "And I was born in Mexico."   32

BLANK

NOTE: Please answer BOTH questions, numbers 7 *and* 8.   33

    7) Are you Spanish/Hispanic/Latino? (Mark the "no" box if not
       Spanish/Hispanic/Latino)
       ☐ No, not Spanish/Hispanic/Latino
       ☐ Yes, Puerto Rican
       ☐ Yes, Cuban
       ☐ Yes, Mexican, Mexican-American, Chicano
       ☐ Yes, other Spanish/Hispanic/Latino—Print here: _____

    8) What is your race? Mark one
       ☐ Black, African-American, Negro
       ☐ American Indian, Alaskan Native
      ☐ Pacific Islander, Asian
       ☐ White
       ☐ Some other race. Print here: _____

Meaning

1. Does "White" have a thesis? Try to express Fletcher's main idea in your own words.

2. In his introduction Fletcher notes that he was "late to understand what the Chicano boy" meant when he said, after hitting another boy with a carton of milk, "Missed that honky" (paragraph 2). What *did* the boy mean? Why did Fletcher miss his meaning?

3. Why did Fletcher, along with his older brother and his friends, burn a cross into his hand when he was young? How was it a "symbol of belonging" (paragraph 5)? Belonging to what?

4. If you are uncertain of the meanings of any of the words listed below, try to guess them from the context of the essay. Then look them up to see how close your definitions were to those in the dictionary. Test out the new words by using each of them in a sentence or two of your own.

honky (2)	pampas (5)	cicadas (18)
composure (3)	Basque (16)	Aztec (30)
Formica (5)		

Purpose and Audience

1. What do you think might have prompted Fletcher to write so personally about the color of his skin? What evidence from the text can you use to support your answer?

2. What assumptions does Fletcher make about the readers of his essay? Are those assumptions correct in your case?

Method and Structure

1. Consider the labels Fletcher devises for each section of his essay. What function do these labels serve? How do they contribute to his overall point?

2. Does "White" present a complex classification or a binary one? What categories does Fletcher examine? Explain your answer.

3. What is Fletcher's principle of classification?

4. The structure of this classification is unusual in that it does not have a formal introduction or conclusion. How does Fletcher's final section restore the wholeness of his subject?

5. OTHER METHODS   Where in this essay do you find a **definition** of *Chicano*? What does Fletcher understand the term to mean? How do you understand it?

Language

1. Why, according to Fletcher, has he adopted his mother's maiden name as part of his own? What effect has it had for him?

2. What does Fletcher accomplish in quoting other people throughout his essay? What does the **dialogue** contribute to his classification?

3. Examine Fletcher's **tone**. How would you characterize his attitude toward his subject? Is he angry, resigned, hopeful, something else? Does his overall tone strengthen his essay or weaken it? Why?

Writing Topics

1. JOURNAL TO ESSAY   In your journal response (p. 198), you considered the effect of your cultural heritage on your everyday experiences. Now develop your ideas into an essay in which you evaluate the importance you assign to any outward symbols of your inheritance: food, music, holidays, customs, religious services, clothing, and the like. For example, do such signs serve to strengthen your cultural identity? If you don't have such signs, how important is their absence?

2. Think of a relative or close friend who has physical or personality traits noticeably different from yours. Write an essay in which you explore the differences, focusing on how the two of you behave in particular circumstances or respond to specific experiences. How do you account for these differences?

3. CULTURAL CONSIDERATIONS   Many scientists and cultural critics argue that there are no significant biological differences between people of varying colors and ethnicities. Race, they say, is a *social construct*: in other words, our understanding of racial difference is the result of what we're taught by society, not scientific truth. Fletcher's narrative explores one instance of this kind of cultural education: as a child he did not understand that others considered him to be white, and he continues to wrestle with the labels available to him. Write an essay in which you explore your own understandings of race and try to pinpoint where they came from. When did you first learn that skin color matters in American culture? Do you believe that there are real differences between races, or do you lean toward the idea that skin color is irrelevant? Explain your answer, giving plenty of details from your own experiences.

4. CONNECTIONS   Like Fletcher, Lisa Richardson, in "Notes from a Black Daughter of the Confederacy" (p. 376), writes poignantly about the frustrations of being classified by skin color. The two writers address similar issues, but their perspectives and their purposes for writing are quite different. In an essay of your own, compare the tones and viewpoints of these two authors.

WRITING WITH THE METHOD

▶

CLASSIFICATION

Select one of the following topics, or any other topic they suggest, for an essay developed by classification. Be sure to choose a topic you care about so that classification is a means of communicating an idea, not an end in itself.

People

1. Boring people
2. Laundromat users
3. Politicians
4. Passengers on public transportation

Psychology and Behavior

5. Punishments
6. Obsessions
7. Medical patients
8. Dreams

Things

9. Buildings on campus
10. Junk foods
11. Games
12. Mobile devices

Sports and Leisure

13. Gym members
14. Campers
15. Styles of baseball pitching, tennis serving, or another sports skill
16. Styles of dance, guitar playing, acting, or another performance art

Communications Media

17. Talk-show hosts
18. Blogs
19. Sports announcers
20. Advertisements

WRITING ABOUT THE THEME

DISTINGUISHING OURSELVES FROM OTHERS

1. Write a brief essay in which you classify students at your college or university or at a competing school. You may devise your own classification system, if you wish, or you might try adapting the categories of any of the writers in this chapter to this subject. Do some of them fit Scaachi Koul's depiction of well-meaning white people who nonetheless exoticize cultural differences (p. 179)? How many come from other countries, like the expats, immigrants, and refugees Joyce Carol Oates (p. 180) describes? Do they exhibit, like Jonathan R. Gould Jr.'s neighbors, behaviors that seem "too friendly, unsociable, irritable, and just right" (p. 185)? Do they, like the subjects of David Brooks's "People Like Us" (p. 189), fit into a particular "psycho-demographic cluster"? Are they, like Harrison Candelaria Fletcher and his friends (p. 198), ethnically diverse? How else might you distinguish them from each other?

2. Scaachi Koul and Jonathan R. Gould Jr. both classify and label people with some intention to amuse their readers. However, as Joyce Carol Oates, Harrison Candelaria Fletcher, and David Brooks suggest, not all labels used to classify people are harmless. Consider, for example, labels based on gender or race or sexual orientation. Write an essay in which you discuss both the benefits and the costs of assigning labels to people — for those using the labels, for those being labeled, and for society as a whole. Give plenty of specific examples.

3. All of the authors in this chapter suggest that stereotypes play a significant part in our perceptions of others and ourselves. Scaachi Koul finds humor in some people's mistaken assumptions that Indian weddings are fun, while Joyce Carol Oates expresses concern that the very term *refugees* dehumanizes people. Jonathan R. Gould Jr. deliberately stereotypes his neighbors so he can "maintain a clear perspective on our relationship and understand their needs"; David Brooks insists that Americans benefit from considering ethnic, political, and cultural affinities when choosing their neighborhoods; and Harrison Candelaria Fletcher struggles to reconcile other people's beliefs that he is white with his sense that he is Chicano. To what extent, if at all, are such stereotypes the result of media hype or distortion, whether in advertising, news stories, television programming, movies, or elsewhere? What else might contribute to popular assumptions in each case? Write an essay explaining how stereotypes arise in the first place. You could use the misconceptions identified by the authors in this chapter for your examples, or you could supply examples of your own.

10

PROCESS ANALYSIS

▶
CONSIDERING THE NATURAL ENVIRONMENT

Game rules, repair manuals, cookbooks, science textbooks—these and many other familiar works are essentially process analyses. They explain how to do something (play Dungeons and Dragons, patch a hole in the wall), how to make something (an omelet), or how something happens (how hormones develop, how a computer stores and retrieves data). That is, they explain a sequence of actions with a specified result (the **process**) by dividing it into its component steps (the **analysis**). You might use process analysis to explain how a hybrid engine saves gas or how a student organization can influence cafeteria menus. You also use process analysis when you want to teach someone how to do something, such as create a fund-raising Web page or follow a new office procedure.

The authors represented in this chapter all set out to examine the steps involved in maintaining a healthy relationship with the natural environment, and for that purpose process analysis is the logical choice of method. In paragraphs, Miranda Smith provides detailed instructions for planting a tree, while Ted Genoways explains how mining operations extract oil from sand. Brian Doyle, in an essay, recommends a way for readers to engage with nature writing—and for writers to make a difference. Student writer Marina Keegan contemplates the damages inflicted by natural forces. And in a dramatic depiction of the annual spring melts in the Pacific Northwest, Rick Bass makes a poetic plea for conservation.

Reading Process Analysis

Almost always, the purpose of process analysis is to explain, but sometimes a parallel purpose is to prove something about a process or to evaluate it: a writer may want to show how easy it is to change a tire, for instance, or urge aspiring marathon runners to follow a training regimen on the grounds of its safety and effectiveness.

Processes occur in several varieties, including mechanical (a car engine), natural (cell division), psychological (acquisition of sex roles), and political (the electoral college). Process analyses generally fall into one of two types:

- A *directive* process analysis tells how to do or make something: bake a cake, tune a guitar, negotiate a deal, write a process analysis. It outlines the steps in the process completely so that the reader who follows them can achieve the specified result. Generally, a directive process analysis addresses the reader directly, using the second-person *you* ("You should think of negotiation as collaboration rather than competition") or the imperative (commanding) mood of verbs ("Add one egg yolk and stir vigorously").

- An *explanatory* process analysis provides the information necessary for readers to understand the process, but more to satisfy their curiosity than to teach them how to perform it. It may address the reader directly, but the third-person *he, she, it,* and *they* are more common.

Whether directive or explanatory, process analyses usually follow a **chronological order**. Most processes can be divided into phases or stages, and these in turn can be divided into steps. The stages of changing a tire, for instance, may be jacking up the car, removing the flat, putting on the spare, and lowering the car. The steps within, say, jacking up the car may be setting the emergency brake, blocking the other wheels, loosening the lug nuts, positioning the jack, and raising the car. Following a chronological order, a writer covers the stages in sequence and, within each stage, covers the steps in sequence.

To ensure that the reader can duplicate the process or understand how it unfolds, a process analysis must fully detail each step and specify the reasons for it. In addition, the writer must ensure that the reader grasps the sequence of steps, their duration, and where they occur. To this end, **transitions** that signal time and place—such as *after five minutes, meanwhile, to the left,* and *below*—can be invaluable.

Though a chronological sequence is usual for process analysis, the sequence may be interrupted or modified to suit the material. A writer may need to pause in a sequence to provide definitions of specialized terms or to explain why a step is necessary or how it relates to the preceding and following steps. Instructions on how to change a tire, for instance, might stop briefly to explain that the lug nuts should be loosened slightly *before* the car is jacked up in order to prevent the wheel from spinning once the weight is off the tire.

Analyzing Processes in Paragraphs

Miranda Smith (1944–2011), the author of several best-selling gardening books, was a master horticulturalist and an organic farmer. The following instructions are from her comprehensive guide to vegetables, flowers, and private landscapes, *Complete Home Gardening* (2006).

Planting depth is important. You want the plant to grow at the same depth that it did at the nursery. To accomplish this, position the plant so that the former soil mark is an inch or so above the ground when you finish planting. This allows for the inevitable sinking of roots into the soil during the first year or so, without having the plant drop so low that the crown will be suffocated. Add or remove soil as necessary to adjust the level. Now lower the roots or root ball into the hole, and gently backfill the hole with soil. Pack the soil firmly throughout the process to eliminate air pockets. When the hole is half full, water well to make the soil settle. Finish filling the hole with soil, and water again. With fall planting, when the ground is drier, dig the hole a day before, and fill it with water before planting. In the spring, when the ground is already wet, you can skip this step.

Marginal annotations:
Directive process analysis: tells how to plant a tree

Process divided into steps

Reason for step

Reason for step

Reason for step

Reason for step

Transitions (underlined) signal time and place

Sequence altered to offer optional step

Ted Genoways (born 1972) has contributed to several publications, including *Mother Jones*, *onEarth*, and *Best American Travel Writing*. The paragraph presented here comes from "The High Cost of Oil," a 2014 investigative report for *Outside*.

The article explores the impacts on Canada's First Nations people of mining the Alberta tar sands region for bitumen, a controversial form of crude oil.

Seemingly unchecked by regulations, the mines expanded into giant black caverns, where massive shovel loaders <u>now scoop</u> the coal-like rock, <u>seventy tons at a time</u>, into dump trucks three stories tall. Heavy haulers deliver mined material into a double-roll crusher, <u>then</u> a conveyor system carries the ground-up rock into a cyclo-feeder. <u>In sprawling</u> coking and refining facilities, hot water melts the tar sands into a slurry, sending clouds of thick smoke and steam across the landscape. <u>What remains</u> is chemically separated to produce a thin top layer of bitumen froth, <u>but everything else</u>—the heavy sand, the toxic wastewater, and the leftover chemicals—is by-product, and it's emptied into tailings ponds the size of enormous lakes.

Explanatory process analysis: tells how oil is extracted from tar sands

Process examined in chronological sequence

Transitions (underlined) signal steps

Result of the process

Developing an Essay by Process Analysis

▶ Getting Started

You'll find yourself writing process analyses for your courses in school (for instance, explaining how a drug alters brain chemistry), in memos at work (recommending a new procedure for approving cost estimates), or in life outside work (sharing a recipe for vegan curry). To find a subject when an assignment doesn't specify one, examine your interests or hobbies or think of something whose workings you'd like to research in order to understand them better. Explore the subject by listing chronologically all the necessary stages and steps.

Remember your readers while you are generating ideas. Consider how much background information they need, where specialized terms must be defined, and where examples must be given. Especially if you are providing instructions, consider what special equipment readers will need, what hitches they may encounter, and what the interim results should be. To build a table, for instance, what tools would readers need? What should they do if the table wobbles even after the corners are braced? What should the table feel like after the first sanding or the first varnishing?

▶ Forming a Thesis

While you are exploring your subject, decide on the point of your analysis and express it in a thesis sentence that will guide your writing and tell your readers what to expect. The simplest thesis states what the process is and outlines its basic stages. For instance:

> Building a table involves a three-stage process of cutting, assembling, and finishing.

You can increase your readers' interest in the process by also conveying your reason for writing about it. You might assert that a seemingly difficult process is actually quite simple, or vice versa:

> Changing a tire does not require a mechanic's skill or strength; on the contrary, a ten-year-old child can do it.

> Windsurfing may look easy, but it demands the knowledge of an experienced sailor and the balance of an acrobat.

You might show how the process demonstrates a more general principle:

> Getting a bill through Congress illustrates majority rule at work.

Or you might assert that a process is inefficient or unfair:

> The state's outdated licensing procedure forces new drivers to waste hours standing in line.

Regardless of how you structure your thesis sentence, try to make it clear that your process analysis has a point. Usually you will want to include a direct statement of your thesis in your introduction so that readers know what you're writing about and why the process should matter to them.

▶ Organizing

Many successful process analyses begin with an overview of the process to which readers can relate each step. In such an **introduction** you can lead up to your thesis sentence by specifying when or where the process occurs, why it is useful or interesting or controversial, what its result is, and the like. Especially if you are providing instructions, you can also use the introduction (perhaps a separate paragraph) to provide essential background information, such as the materials readers will need.

After the introduction, you should present the stages distinctly, perhaps one or two paragraphs for each, and usually in chronological order.

Within each stage, you then cover the necessary steps, also chronologically. This chronological sequence helps readers understand how a process unfolds or how to perform it themselves. Try not to deviate from it unless you have good reason to—perhaps because your process requires you to group simultaneous steps or your readers need definitions of terms, reasons for steps, connections between separated steps, and other explanations.

A process essay may end simply with the result. But you might also provide a formal **conclusion** with a summary of the major stages, a comment on the significance or usefulness of the process, or a recommendation for changing a process you have criticized. For a directive process essay, you might state the standards by which readers can measure their success or give an idea of how much practice may be necessary to master the process.

▶ Drafting

While drafting your process analysis, concentrate on getting in as many details as you can: every step, how each relates to the one before and after, how each contributes to the result. In revising you can always delete unnecessary details and digressions if they seem cumbersome, but in the first draft it's better to overexplain than underexplain.

Drafting a process analysis is a good occasion to practice a straightforward, concise writing style, as clarity is more important than originality of expression. Stick to plain language and uncomplicated sentences. If you want to dress up your style a bit, you can always do so after you have made yourself clear.

▶ Revising and Editing

When you've finished your draft, ask a friend to read it. If you have explained a process, he or she should be able to understand it. If you have given instructions, he or she should be able to follow them or imagine following them. Then examine the draft yourself against the following questions and Focus box.

■ *Have you adhered to a chronological sequence?* Unless there is a compelling and clear reason to use some other arrangement, the stages and steps of your analysis should proceed in chronological order. If you had to depart from that order—to define or explain or to sort out simultaneous steps—the reasons should be clear to your readers.

■ *Have you included all necessary steps and omitted any unnecessary digressions?* The explanation should be as complete as possible but not cluttered with information, however interesting, that contributes nothing to the readers' understanding of the process.

■ *Have you accurately gauged your readers' need for information?* You don't want to bore readers with explanations and details they don't need. But erring in the other direction is even worse, for your essay will achieve little if readers cannot understand it.

■ *Have you shown readers how each step fits into the whole process and relates to the other steps?* If your analysis seems to break down into a multitude of isolated steps, you may need to organize them more clearly into stages.

■ *Have you used plenty of informative transitions?* Transitions such as *at the same time* and *on the other side of the machine* indicate when steps start and stop, how long they last, and where they occur. (A list of such expressions appears in the Glossary under *transitions*.) The expressions should be as informative as possible; signals such as *first . . . second . . . third . . . fourteenth,* and *next . . . next* do not help indicate movement in space or lapses in time, and they quickly grow tiresome.

FOCUS ON CONSISTENCY

While drafting a process analysis, you may start off with subjects or verbs in one form and then shift to another form because the original choice feels awkward.

■ In *directive* analyses that tell readers how to do something, shifts occur most often with the subjects *one* or *a person*:

> INCONSISTENT   To keep the car from rolling while changing the tire, <u>one</u> should first set the car's emergency brake. Then <u>you</u> should block the other three tires with objects like rocks or chunks of wood.

To repair the inconsistency here, you could stick with *one* for the subject (*one should block*), but that usually sounds stiff. It's better to revise the earlier subject to be *you*:

> CONSISTENT   To keep the car from rolling while changing the tire, <u>you</u> should first set the car's emergency brake. Then <u>you</u> should block the other three tires with objects like rocks or chunks of wood.

Sometimes, writers try to avoid *one* or *a person* or even *you* by shifting to passive verbs that don't require actors:

INCONSISTENT   To keep the car from rolling while changing the tire, <u>you</u> should first set the car's emergency brake. . . . Before the car <u>is raised</u>, the lug nuts of the wheel <u>should be loosened</u>. . . .

But the passive voice is wordy and potentially confusing, especially when directions should be making it clear who does what. (See p. 49 for more on passive verbs.)

The easiest solution to the problem of inconsistent subjects and voices is to use the imperative, or commanding, form of verbs, in which *you* is understood as the subject:

CONSISTENT   To keep the car from rolling while changing the tire, first <u>set</u> the car's emergency brake. Then <u>block</u> the other three tires with objects like rocks or chunks of wood.

■ In *informative* analyses that explain how something happens, passive verbs may be necessary if you don't know who the actor is or want to emphasize the action over the actor. But identifying the actor is generally clearer and more concise:

CONSISTENT   A <u>mechanic</u> always <u>loosens</u> the lug nuts of the wheel before raising the car.

Imperative and active verbs should be consistent, too. Don't shift back and forth between *block* and *you should block* or between *is raised* and *loosens*.

See pages 47–48 for more on shifts and how to avoid them.

LearningCurve   To practice editing for consistency, visit *LaunchPad Solo for Readers and Writers* > LearningCurve > Sentences > Active and Passive Voice

If you only read [what] everyone else is reading, you can only think
what everyone else is thinking.   —Haruki Murakami

If there's a book you really want to read, but it hasn't been written yet,
then you must write it.   —Toni Morrison

Until I feared I would lose it, I never loved to read. One does not love
breathing.   —Harper Lee

JOURNAL RESPONSE   What do you read for pleasure, and how do you tend
to read it? That is, do you read in any particular way? In your journal,
identify the kinds of writing that most appeal to you (true crime, mysteries, poetry, biography, celebrity magazines, and so forth), and list the steps
in the reading process you usually undertake. If you don't read for pleasure, list the steps you take to avoid reading.

Brian Doyle

A writer and an editor, Brian Doyle (1956–2017) was known for his breathtaking
reflections on faith, human connection, and the natural world. He was born in New
York City and graduated from the University of Notre Dame in 1978. He was the
award-winning editor of *Portland* magazine and a regular contributor to the
Atlantic Monthly, *Harper's*, *Orion*, and *The Sun*, among others. A person deeply
affected by matters of family, Doyle wrote his first book, *Two Voices* (1996), in collaboration with his father and his second, *The Wet Engine* (2005), in exploration of
his infant son's heart condition. He also published two novels and several critically
acclaimed collections of essays, fiction, and poetry, including *Leaping* (2003),
Epiphanies and Elegies (2006), *Grace Notes* (2011), and *Children and Other Wild Animals* (2014). Doyle was the recipient of three Pushcart Prizes, six *Best American
Essays* designations, and a John Burroughs Award for nature writing. In his spare
time he enjoyed playing basketball.

How to Read a Nature Essay

"The best writers," Doyle once said, "are the best listeners." In this unusual take on
how-to, he explores his idea of what goes into good environmental writing while
at the same time explaining how readers should let themselves be affected by
someone else's work. Doyle's "greatest nature essay *ever*" first appeared in *Orion*
in 2008.

The greatest nature essay *ever* would begin with an image so startling and ①
lovely and wondrous that you would stop riffling through the rest of the
mail, take your jacket off, sit down at the table, adjust your spectacles, tell
the dog to lie *down*, tell the kids to make their *own* sandwiches for heav-
enssake, that's why God gave you *hands*, and read straight through the
piece, marveling that you had indeed seen or smelled or heard *exactly*
that, but never quite articulated it that way, or seen or heard it articulated
that way, and you think, *Man, this is why I read nature essays, to be startled
and moved like that, wow.*

The next two paragraphs would smoothly and gently move you into a ②
story, seemingly a small story, a light tale, easily accessed, something personal but not self-indulgent or self-absorbed on the writer's part, just sort of
a cheerful nutty everyday story maybe starring an elk or a mink or a child,
but then there would suddenly be a sharp sentence where the dagger enters
your heart and the essay spins on a dime like a skater, and you are plunged
into waaay deeper water, you didn't see it coming at *all*, and you actually
shiver, your whole body shimmers, and much later, maybe when you are in
bed with someone you love and you are trying to evade his or her icy feet,
you think, *My God, stories do have roaring power, stories are the most crucial
and necessary food, how come we never hardly say that out loud?*

The next three paragraphs then walk inexorably toward a line of ③
explosive Conclusions on the horizon like inky alps. Probably the sentences get shorter, more staccato. Terser. Blunter. Shards of sentences. But
there's no opinion or commentary, just one line fitting into another, each
one making plain inarguable sense, a goat or even a senator could easily
understand the sentences and their implications, and there's no shouting,
no persuasion, no eloquent pirouetting, no pronouncements and accusa-
tions, no sermons or homilies, just calm clean clear statements one after
another, fitting together like people holding hands.

Then an odd paragraph, this is a most unusual and peculiar essay, for ④
right here where you would normally expect those alpine Conclusions,
some Advice, some Stern Instructions & Directions, there's only the quiet
murmur of the writer tiptoeing back to the story he or she was telling you
in the second and third paragraphs. The story slips back into view gently,
a little shy, holding its hat, nothing melodramatic, in fact it offers a few
gnomic questions without answers, and then it gently slides away off the
page and off the stage, it almost evanesces or dissolves, and it's only later
after you have read the essay three times with mounting amazement that
you see quite how the writer managed the stagecraft there, but that's the
stuff of another essay for another time.

And finally the last paragraph. It turns out that the perfect nature ⑤
essay is quite short, it's a lean taut thing, an arrow and not a cannon, and

here at the end there's a flash of humor, and a hint or tone or subtext of sadness, a touch of rue, you can't quite put your finger on it but it's there, a dark thread in the fabric, and there's also a shot of espresso hope, hope against all odds and sense, but rivetingly there's no call to arms, no clarion brassy trumpet blast, no Web site to which you are directed, no hint that you, yes you, should be ashamed of how much water you use or the car you drive or the fact that you just turned the thermostat up to seventy, or that you actually have not voted in the past two elections despite what you told the kids and the goat. Nor is there a rimshot ending, a bang, a last twist of the dagger. Oddly, sweetly, the essay just ends with a feeling eerily like a warm hand brushed against your cheek, and you sit there, near tears, smiling, and then you stand up. Changed.

Meaning

1. Does Doyle mean for readers to accept this particular essay as the "greatest nature essay *ever*" (paragraph 1)? Why do you think so? Examine the essay closely before you answer. (Hint: start by comparing the number of paragraphs in Doyle's essay with the number of paragraphs in the essay he describes.)

2. What is the main point of Doyle's process analysis? Can you find a direct statement of his thesis?

3. Of the sentences in a perfect nature essay, Doyle says that "a goat or even a senator could easily understand" (paragraph 3). Where in Doyle's essay does this **image** reappear? Why a goat?

4. If you are uncertain of the meanings of any of the words listed below, try to guess them from the context of the essay. Then look them up to see how close your definitions were to those in the dictionary. Test out the new words by using each of them in a sentence or two of your own.

articulated (1)	homilies (3)	taut (5)
inexorably (3)	alpine (4)	clarion (5)
staccato (3)	gnomic (4)	
pirouetting (3)	evanesces (4)	

Purpose and Audience

1. What, according to Doyle, is the purpose of reading? of writing?

2. This piece was originally written for *Orion*, a literary magazine focused on nature, environment, and politics. What, then, could Doyle assume about his readers? What else does he seem to assume about them? How are those assumptions reflected in his essay? (You might want to look at the magazine's mission statement, available at *orionmagazine.org*, for more clues.)

Method and Structure

1. Doyle identifies five main stages in reading an effective nature essay. What are these stages, and do they necessarily occur in a sequence? Support your answer with evidence from the essay.

2. How does Doyle organize his process analysis? Point to the transitional phrases that lend his essay **coherence**.

3. Doyle's first paragraph is one long sentence, and his essay contains many **comma splices** and **sentence fragments**. Identify at least two examples of each. Is this sloppy writing, or does Doyle break the rules of sentence grammar for a reason? What do Doyle's sentence faults contribute to (or take away from) his essay? Explain your answer.

4. **OTHER METHODS** Doyle's process analysis depends on **division or analysis** of "the perfect nature essay" (paragraph 5). What, according to Doyle, are the elements of an effective essay? What does a good essay *not* do?

Language

1. Doyle frequently switches point of view between third person (*it*) and second person (*you*). Why? Are these **shifts** purposeful? distracting? Why do you think so?

2. Doyle uses several figures of speech in his essay—for example, "a sharp sentence where the dagger enters your heart" (paragraph 2), a **metaphor**. Find other examples of metaphor, as well as **simile** and **personification**. What do these nonliteral expressions contribute to the essay? Do any strike you as particularly inventive or effective?

3. In paragraphs 3 and 4 Doyle capitalizes words that do not normally require capitals: "Conclusions, . . . Advice, . . . Stern Instructions & Directions." Why? What point is he making by employing this device?

4. Doyle uses many **colloquial** expressions, such as "tell the dog to lie *down*" (paragraph 1). Identify a few other expressions common to everyday speaking. Why are they appropriate (or not), given Doyle's purpose for writing?

Writing Topics

1. **JOURNAL TO ESSAY** You may have a particular method of reading, writing, or studying that works or doesn't work for you. In your journal you listed the steps you normally take when reading or when avoiding reading (p. 214). Now, take that list, or another like it, and transform it into a how-to or how-not-to guide for other students. Be sure your essay clearly outlines the materials your readers will need, outlines the steps they will

need to take to successfully follow your instructions, and specifies the result they can expect to achieve.

2. Write a directive process analysis explaining how to do something that is important to you but that others may not know about. For instance, you might tell readers how to thwart identity thieves, how to build a birdhouse, or how to reduce their carbon footprints. Be sure to explain why your subject is meaningful and to identify all the steps involved.

3. Doyle says that "it's only later after you have read [an] essay three times with mounting amazement that you see quite how the writer managed the stagecraft there, but that's the stuff of another essay for another time" (paragraph 4). Write that essay at this time. Reread "How to Read a Nature Essay" at least twice, and then analyze Doyle's "stagecraft." How do the parts of his essay work individually and together to move readers?

4. RESEARCH   Doyle is critical of writers who lecture people busy with family responsibilities about changing their habits for the sake of the environment, but his references to behaviors such as wasting water, raising the thermostat, and neglecting to vote deliberately invoke many people's concerns that American lifestyles have significant environmental consequences. Locate and read a few essays, articles, or books that argue for reducing personal consumption. (*Orion* magazine would be a useful starting point.) Then write a serious argumentative essay that addresses some aspect of limited natural resources, such as water or fossil fuels. Do Americans take more than their fair share of such resources? How does American consumption compare to that in other countries, such as Sweden or China? Under what circumstances, if any, should personal choice be limited in the name of global responsibility? Be sure to include examples to support your opinions, and be careful to cite your sources (see Part Three).

5. CONNECTIONS   Like Doyle, Scott Adams offers tips for writers who seek to have an emotional impact on their readers. Read "Funny Business" (p. 156) if you haven't already, and then compare Adams's purpose, structure, and advice with Doyle's. What assumptions do the two writers share, and where do their perspectives diverge? How do they use similar methods to achieve their goals? What might humorists learn from naturalists, and vice versa? Do you find one essay more useful than the other? Why, or why not?

It's the great gift of human beings that we have this power of empathy. . . .
We can all sense a mysterious connection with each other.   —Meryl Streep

This is a wonderful planet, and it is being completely destroyed by people
who have too much money and power and no empathy.   —Alice Walker

The quality of mercy is not strain'd, / It droppeth as the gentle rain
from heaven / Upon the place beneath.   —William Shakespeare

JOURNAL RESPONSE   Have you ever been confronted with the problem of a
sick or injured animal—an ailing family pet, perhaps, a bird fallen from a
nest, or an unexpected deer on a back road? What happened, and what
did you do? How did the incident make you feel? Write about the experience in your journal.

Marina Keegan

While still a college student, Marina Keegan gained national attention as a promising—and devastatingly insightful—writer. She worked as a staff writer for the *Yale
Daily News*, interned at the *Paris Review*, blogged for *The New Yorker*, published a
stinging critique of Wall Street in the *New York Times*, and staged a reading of one
of her plays at a major drama festival. Born in Wayland, Massachusetts, in 1989,
Keegan spent her summers on the beaches of Cape Cod and sailed competitively
throughout her youth. She completed her bachelor's degree at Yale University in
2012 and had an entry-level job with *The New Yorker* lined up, but she was killed in a
car accident five days after graduation. *The Opposite of Loneliness* (2014), an anthology of Keegan's best short stories and essays, was published posthumously.

Why We Care about Whales
(Student Essay)

The following selection from *The Opposite of Loneliness* traces a heartbreaking pro-
cess to explore the cruelties of nature and the inadequacies of human response.
Keegan wrote this essay when she was a sophomore; it was first published in the
Yale Daily News in 2009.

When the moon gets bored, it kills whales. Blue whales and fin whales and   1
humpback, sperm, and orca whales; centrifugal forces don't discriminate.

With a hushed retreat, the moon pulls waters out from under fins and   2
flippers, oscillating them backward and forward before they slip outward.
At nighttime, the moon watches its work. Silver light traces the strips of
lingering water, the jittery crabs, the lumps of tangled seaweed.

Slowly, awkwardly, the whales find their footing. They try to fight the   3
waves, but they can't fight the moon. They can't fight the world's rota-
tion or the bathymetry of oceans or the inevitability that sometimes
things just don't work out.

More than two thousand cetaceans die from beaching every year.   4
Occasionally they trap themselves in solitude, but whales are often
beached in groups, huddled together in clusters and rows. Whales feel
cohesion, a sense of community, of loyalty. The distress call of a lone
whale is enough to prompt its entire pod to rush to its side—a gesture
that lands them nose to nose in the same sand. It's a fatal symphony of
echolocation; a siren[1] call to the sympathetic.

The death is slow. As mammals of the Cetacea order, whales are con-   5
scious breathers. Inhalation is a choice, an occasional rise to the ocean's
surface. Although their ancestors lived on land, constant oxygen expo-
sure overwhelms today's creatures.

Beached whales become frantic, captives to their hyperventilation.   6
Most die from dehydration. The salty air shrinks their oily pores, captur-
ing their moisture. Deprived of the buoyancy water provides, whales can
literally crush themselves to death. Some collapse before they dry
out—their lungs suffocating under their massive bodies—or drown when
high tides cover their blowholes, filling them slowly while they're too
weak to move. The average whale can't last more than twenty-four hours
on land.

In their final moments, they begin belching and erupting in violent   7
thrashing. Finally, their jaws open slightly—not all the way, but just
enough that the characteristic illusion of a perpetual smile disappears.
This means it's over. I know this because I watched as twenty-three whale
mouths unhinged. As twenty-three pairs of whale eyes glazed over.

I had woken up that morning to a triage center outside my win-   8
dow. Fifty or so pilot whales were lying along the stretch of beach in front
of my house on Cape Cod, surrounded by frenzied neighbors and animal
activists. The Coast Guard had arrived while I was still sleeping, and
guardsmen were already using boats with giant nets in an attempt to pull

---

[1] In Greek mythology, sirens are sea nymphs whose irresistible singing lures
sailors to their deaths against a rocky shoreline. [Editors' note.]

the massive bodies back into the water. Volunteers hurried about in groups, digging trenches around the whales' heads to cool them off, placing wet towels on their skin, and forming assembly lines to pour buckets of water on them. The energy was nervous, confused, and palpably urgent.

Pilot whales are among the most populous of the marine mammals in the cetacean order. Fully grown males can measure up to twenty feet and weigh three tons, while females usually reach sixteen feet and 1.5 tons. 9

Their enormity was their problem. Unlike the three dolphins that had managed to strand themselves near our house the previous summer, fifty pilot whales were nearly impossible to maneuver. If unfavorable tidal currents and topography unite, the larger species may be trapped. Sandbars sneak up on them, and the tides tie them back. 10

People are strange about animals. Especially large ones. Daily, on the docks of Wellfleet Harbor, thousands of fish are scaled, gutted, and seasoned with thyme and lemon. No one strokes their sides with water. No one cries when their jaws slip open. 11

Pilot whales are not an endangered species, yet people spend tens of thousands of dollars in rescue efforts, trucking the wounded to aquariums and in some places even airlifting them off of beaches. Perhaps the whales' sheer immensity fosters sympathy. Perhaps the stories of Jonah or Moby Dick[2] do the same. Or maybe it's that article we read last week about that whale in Australia understanding hand signals. Intelligence matters, doesn't it? Brain size is important, right? Those whales knew they were dying. They have some sort of language, some sort of emotion. They give birth, for God's sake! There aren't any pregnant fish in the Wellfleet nets. No communal understanding of their imminent fatality. 12

I worry sometimes that humans are afraid of helping humans. There's less risk associated with animals, less fear of failure, fear of getting too involved. In war movies, a thousand soldiers can die gruesomely, but when the horse is shot, the audience is heartbroken. It's the *My Dog Skip*[3] effect. The *Homeward Bound*[4] syndrome. 13

---

[2] In the Old Testament of the Bible, the prophet Jonah is swallowed by a whale as punishment for disobeying God; he spends three days in the creature's belly before it spits him out and he repents. Moby Dick is the great white whale obsessively hunted by Captain Ahab in Herman Melville's 1851 novel of the same name. [Editors' note.]

[3] A sentimental 2000 movie, based on Willie Morris's 1995 memoir, about a boy's relationship with his dog. [Editors' note.]

[4] A 1993 remake of a 1963 movie that follows two dogs and a cat as they travel across the United States to reunite with their human family. [Editors' note.]

When we hear that the lady on the next street over has cancer, we   14
don't see the entire town flock to her house. We push and shove and wet
whales all day, then walk home through town past homeless men curled
up on benches—washed up like whales on the curbsides. Pulled outside
by the moon and struggling for air among the sewers. They're suffocating
too, but there's no town assembly line of food. No palpable urgency, no
airlifting plane.

Fifty stranded whales are a tangible crisis with a visible solution.   15
There's camaraderie in the process, a *Free Willy*[5] fantasy, an image of Flipper[6] in everyone's mind. There's nothing romantic about waking up a
man on a park bench and making him walk to a shelter. Little self-righteous
fulfillment comes from sending a check to Oxfam International.

Would there be such a commotion if a man washed up on the beach?   16
Yes. But stranded humans don't roll in with the tide—they hide in the
corners and the concrete houses and the plains of exotic countries we've
never heard of, dying of diseases we can't pronounce.

In theory I can say that our resources should be concentrated on sav-   17
ing human lives, that our "Save the Whales" T-shirts should read "Save
the Starving Ethiopians."[7] Logically, it's an easy argument to make. Why
do we spend so much time caring about animals? Yes, their welfare is
important, but surely that of humans is more so.

Last year a nonprofit spent $10,000 transporting a whale to an aquar-   18
ium in Florida, where it died only three days after arriving. That same
$10,000 could have purchased hundreds of thousands of food rations. In
theory, this is easy to say.

But when I was looking in the eye of a dying pilot whale at four in   19
the morning, my thoughts were not so philosophical. Four hours until high
tide. Keep his skin moist. Just three hours now. There wasn't time for logic.
My rationality had slipped away with the ebbing dance of the waves.

I had helped all day. We had managed to save twenty-seven of the   20
fifty whales, but twenty-three others were deemed too far up shore, too
old, or already too close to death. That night, after most of the volunteers had gone home, I went back outside my bedroom to check on the
whales.

---

[5] A 1993 family movie about a troubled boy's efforts to release a performing
whale from captivity. [Editors' note.]

[6] *Flipper* was a popular television program in the sixties about a dolphin who
could communicate with its park-ranger friend. [Editors' note.]

[7] Ethiopia, an independent but impoverished country in northeast Africa, has
long been plagued by drought and famine. [Editors' note.]

It was mid-tide, and the up-shore seaweed still crunched under my 21
bare feet. The water was rising. The moonlight drifted down on the salt-
caked battlefield, reflected in the tiny pools of water and half-shell oysters.

It was easy to spot the living whales. Their bodies, still moist, shined 22
in the moonlight. I weaved between carcasses, kneeling down beside an
old whale that was breathing deeply and far too rapidly for a healthy pilot.

I put my hands on his nose and placed my face in front of his visible 23
eye. I knew he was going to die, and he knew he was going to die, and we
both understood that there was nothing either of us could do about it.

Beached whales die on their sides, one eye pressed into the sand, the 24
other facing up and forced to look at the moon, at the orb that pulled the
water out from under its fins.

There's no echolocation on land. I imagined dying slowly next to my 25
mother or a lover, helplessly unable to relay my parting message. I remember trying to convince myself that everything would be fine. But he
wouldn't be fine. Just like the homeless man and the Ethiopian aren't fine.

Perhaps I should have been comforting one of them, placing my 26
hands on one of their shoulders. Spending my time and my money and
my life saving those who walked on two legs and spoke without echoes.

The moon pulled the waters forward and backward, then inward 27
and around my ankles. Before I could find an answer, the whale's jaw
unclenched, opening slightly around the edges.

Meaning

1. Summarize the gist of the process Keegan analyzes. How do whales end
   up on shore? How do they die?
2. Why, according to Keegan, are whales "often beached in groups" (paragraph 4)? What point is she making here?
3. What would you say is Keegan's thesis? Why *do* we care about whales, in
   her estimation?
4. If you are uncertain of the meanings of any of the words listed below, try
   to guess them from the context of the essay. Then look them up to see
   how close your definitions were to those in the dictionary. Test out the
   new words by using each of them in a sentence or two of your own.

centrifugal (1)	buoyancy (6)	camaraderie (15)
oscillating (2)	triage (8)	romantic (15)
bathymetry (3)	palpable (8, 14)	exotic (16)
cetaceans (4, 9)	topography (10)	ebbing (19)
echolocation (4, 25)	tangible (15)	

Purpose and Audience

1. Why do you think Keegan chose this topic for her essay? Does she have a reason for writing beyond explaining whale rescue? How does her process analysis help to accomplish this purpose?

2. Keegan poses two questions in paragraph 12 but doesn't answer them. What is the purpose of these questions? What do they reveal about how Keegan imagines her audience?

Method and Structure

1. Keegan's process analysis does not follow a strictly chronological order. Trace the organization of her essay. Where does the process analysis begin and end? Why does Keegan deviate from the process analysis when she does? What is the effect of her deviations?

2. Point out transitional words, phrases, and sentences that Keegan uses as guideposts in her process analysis.

3. Weigh the evidence that Keegan gives to support her ideas. Which evidence is personal, and which is not? Are both the personal and the nonpersonal equally effective? Why, or why not?

4. OTHER METHODS   Where and how does Keegan use **comparison and contrast** to establish the significance of her subject?

Language

1. What effect does Keegan achieve with her opening sentence? How does the moon function as a **symbol** throughout the essay?

2. How would you describe Keegan's **tone**? How can you tell that the author is personally invested in the process she is explaining?

Writing Topics

1. JOURNAL TO ESSAY   Our attitudes toward the natural world are often influenced by the family, community, or larger culture in which we grew up. Building on your journal entry (p. 219), write an essay in which you examine the feelings that you have had about a particular sick or injured animal. To what extent were your reactions to the animal's plight at least partly due to other people? Describe the animal and your emotions, and explain the origins of your feelings as best you can. If you wish, you may incorporate information about the animal gleaned from your reading, as Keegan does in her essay.

2. Reread Keegan's essay for instances of **personification** in her descriptions of the moon and of the whales. Starting with your response to the first question on language, write an essay analyzing Keegan's use of personification, concentrating on how that figure of speech in particular contributes to the overall effect of her essay.

3. CULTURAL CONSIDERATIONS   Look again at the quotations preceding Keegan's essay. Does our culture encourage empathy, or does it reward selfishness? What do communities do for people, and what do people owe their communities in return? How much can one person do? In an essay, examine the relationship between the community and the individual in American society, drawing a conclusion about the importance, relevance, or practicality of volunteering one's time, money, or talents.

4. CONNECTIONS   Keegan means to teach her readers about whales and whale rescue, certainly, but she also attempts to persuade readers to examine their assumptions about human poverty as an overwhelming problem without "a visible solution" (paragraph 15). In "Where's the Empathy"? (p. 357), Nicholas Kristof also writes about our attitudes toward poor people and our failures to help those in need. In an essay, compare and contrast Keegan's and Kristof's positions on the need for charity and government assistance in a civilized society. Consider not only what each writer says about the social responsibilities and personal benefits of helping others, but also his or her tone and assumptions about how readers might respond. Which author is more successful at persuading readers to empathize with those less fortunate, and why?

We abuse land because we regard it as a commodity belonging to us. When we see land as a community to which we belong, we may begin to use it with love and respect.
— Aldo Leopold

I am I plus my surroundings, and if I do not preserve the latter, I do not preserve myself.
— José Ortega y Gasset

If we had no winter, the spring would not be so pleasant; if we did not sometimes taste of adversity, prosperity would not be so welcome.
— Anne Bradstreet

JOURNAL RESPONSE   Write a journal entry about a natural phenomenon that affected you, such as a lightning storm, a hurricane, or a blizzard. How did the event make you act and feel?

Rick Bass

Born in Texas in 1958, Rick Bass is a fiction writer, a naturalist, and a teacher. For almost a decade he worked as a petroleum geologist, figuring out where to drill for oil and natural gas. He was educated at Utah State University and earned a BS in geology and wildlife management in 1979. Bass's stories and essays have appeared in the *Paris Review, Esquire, Outside, Tricycle: The Buddhist Review, The Best American Short Stories, The Lives of Rocks* (2006), *For a Little While* (2016), and many other periodicals and anthologies. His novels include *Nashville Chrome* (2010), *All the Land to Hold Us* (2013), and *Where the Sea Used to Be* (2014). Bass has also written several award-winning books about the natural world, among them *The Deer Pasture* (1985), *Oil Notes* (1989), *Why I Came West* (2009), and *The Black Rhinos of Namibia: Searching for Survivors in the African Desert* (2013). He lives on a ranch in northern Montana, where he works to protect his adopted home from logging.

Gardens of Ice and Stone

First published in the *Southern Review* in 2009, "Gardens of Ice and Stone" portrays a gloriously violent natural event in action. In the process, Bass tries to explain why it's important to defend what's left of the wilderness from human activity.

The last bridges and cornices of ice cave in alongside the river, floating   1
downstream like rafts or leisure boats, stacking up at the bend or against
a logjam, piling high into a hastily constructed but impressive piece of

jumbled architecture, forcing the little rushing river to build and build and then at last overflow the ice, swelling and rising and broadening out across the floodplain until, over the course of a few magical days, the little river appears to be as wide and brown and ambitious as the great Missouri or the Mississippi: a giant that sprawls through and across our valley.

And in those shallow, spreading floodwaters, a shimmering glitter of silt and all kinds of other organic matter—bear dung and rotting log mulch and deer pellets and dead trout and winter-killed elk and everything else within the river's hungry reach—sparkles suspended, and is distributed far and wide, into the forest and across the brown and sullen floodplain.   2

The river will keep rising, choosing at first the myriad paths of least resistance, carrying the richness of its casually spreading breadth into all the places that are so hungry for that distribution of wealth.   3

But beneath the easygoing demeanor, beneath the gentle, sleepy, wandering flood, a desire is quivering, and an anxiousness. This river is running late now. Its destined path runs to the great curve of the Kootenai, which receives the straight-running river, notched with its feathery side tributaries, as the arc of a bow cradles a drawn arrow. The Kootenai then sends these waters into the greatest American river of the Pacific Northwest, the Columbia, which follows its mandate to the ocean, and to the salmon, and the sturgeon, and the cedars. . . .   4

The old saw about a sculptor looking at a piece of wood or a chunk of marble and somehow seeing the buried shape within is a hackneyed artistic cliché, an oversimplification of the mysteries of the creative process. And yet so often, particularly when measured against the scale of history or landscape, an observer of that process can see the emergence of repeating patterns, some simple and others complex, which in the cumulative, laid out on the table like cards dealt—hearts, clubs, diamonds, spades— one through ten, and jack, queen, king, ace—reveal but a slight recasting of the same story, more or less familiar with each passing shuffling and playing, assembly and disassembly and reassembly.   5

The specifics change, or against a tiny human scale they *seem* to change—a three is played instead of a four, a two instead of a five—but the game itself is always intimately familiar, and so very much the same, if rarely quite predictable; and in this manner of a story that must get told, a story that cannot help but be told, the strength of the river backed up behind and underlying the ice jam must always be released: sometimes sooner, other times later, but always.   6

For a while, then, before that release, the jammed river meanders, spreading nutrients and richness to the most unlikely places. It reaches   7 into distant nooks and crevices, a digressive storytelling that ignores the pressure continuing to build and strain against the thickened bridge of milk-colored ice.

The story must be told, however, must and will be completed.   8

One day the ice begins to tremble. Not noticeably, at first, but faintly.   9
Trembling, then stilling itself, trembling, then stilling. It might only be one's imagination. Perhaps nothing of consequence is occurring.

A few days later, however, the trembling is more pronounced, and   10
noticeable—a visible shuddering. And at night, as the day's surge of high-mountain meltwater finally makes its way down to the ice bridge on the valley floor below, all the way down from the tops of the mountains that had been bathed in May sun twelve hours earlier—at night, then, the first melodies of cracking or straining ice can be heard, sounding at first like a perfunctory stroke of a fiddler's bow drawn once or twice across the quivering, taut strings of the instrument: the warming up, the preparation.

Beyond that first draw of the bowstring, it will sometimes take a full   11
week before all the sound is engaged: before the gates of ice crash open, and the river is born or resurrected again, and goes hurtling, singing, calling down its old waiting stone canyons, leaping and shouting and carrying along in its roar the xylophonic arrangement of a winter's worth of driftwood, entire forests bobbing and surging along in wild and clattering arrhythmia.

The Kootenai River near Libby, Montana.

David R. Frazier Photolibrary, Inc./Alamy Stock Photo

Every year, that story gets told. And every year, the sun returns and   12
dries out the coat of mud slime that was deposited on the floodplain,
leaving rich gardens of river dirt that speak in a mosaic to where the ice
bridges were.

In subsequent years, rich willow and verdant meadows will encroach   13
upon the new soil; and in late May, and on into the calm of summer,
moose and deer and elk will wander out into those wild and seemingly
random gardens to graze upon the fruits that are the flood's bounty, and
the same story will be told over and over again, up and down the length
of the wild river, the locations of the new gardens shifting only slightly,
like waves. . . .

In this valley, we have but fifteen of these wild gardens—officially called   14
"roadless areas"—left. They require a minimum size of one thousand
acres to be classified as such, and in order to qualify, they must never have
been invaded by any roads.

Such has been the frenzy of extraction in this forest, the subsidized   15
liquidation of the biggest and best of the timber—well over a million
loaded logging trucks have rolled out of this forest, out of this valley, and
out of this impoverished county—Where did all the money go? Was
there ever any money, or was it all simply given or traded away?—that in
the million or so acres lying between the Canadian border and the curve
of the Kootenai River, spanning east of Idaho to west of Lake Koocanusa,
virtually none remain.

Heroically, this gasping strand of wild archipelago provides refuge not   16
only to the last of many threatened and endangered species, such as
wolves and grizzlies and caribou and wolverines, but also to reservoirs of
spirit. Fifteen: and worse yet, not a single one of them has any form of
permanent legal protection whatsoever. Despite the living, pulsing, breathtaking wildness of this landscape—a biological wildness, rather than a
recreational wildness—perhaps the wildest valley in the lower forty-eight,
in that regard—there's still not a single acre—*not one acre*—of protected
public land.

It's a big injustice.   17

I didn't mean to get back into any of this. All I wanted to do with   18
this essay was to paint; and since it's May, to paint with the color green,
the forms and swirls of motion that emerge so dramatically in this season. Too, I know that my yowling about environmental justice can be
counterproductive; that it jars the composition, that it makes a part of
me awaken from what can be—what *is*—otherwise a splendid, even
phenomenal, dream.

And far more effective here might be a simple presentation of beauty, 19
so that you, gentle reader, would come on your own initiative, unsummoned, to love this landscape.

I should remind you, however, that this valley isn't a tourist destina- 20
tion filled with glamorous lakes and majestic spines of rock and ice. It's
not really a place to come to. It's a place to dream of. It's a biological wilderness, full of frog-roar and swamp-muck and tangled blowdown[1] and
mosquitoes and deeply angry, suspicious people, none of whom would be
pleased to see your shining, happy-vacationing face.

This is a place of mud and mire, a celebration of the rank and the 21
fecund, the cold and the uncomfortable, the frayed and the wild. This is
a place whose last wild gardens should be protected for their own sake,
not yours or mine.

And they are gardens. In May, while much of the world is puttering 22
about in the warming black earth, coaxing carrot seeds and lettuce sprouts
into the bright new world, the gardens I am most interested in have been
planted by no hand of man or woman but are instead bulging, swelling,
shifting, on the verge of delivering spotted elk calves from their mothers
and delivering bears back into the world, bears ascending once more to
the surface from their earthen burrows like astronauts returning from the
strangest of journeys.

More gardening: the mountains delivering torrents of rushing water, 23
recharging the buried aquifers between immense slabs of tilted stone; the
fossils of ancient sea creatures tumbling with the season's new talus down
into the bed of bright glacier lilies below: trilobites, fenestellids, cephalopods, and ostracods[2] on the prowl once more, and the earth itself stretching and yawning like a wildcat, supple and hungry, awakened, youthful,
vibrant.

Swirling bouquets of dragonflies rising from the waving marsh fronds 24
like sun-lit jewels summoned by no gardener we will ever meet in this life,
though perhaps the next. . . .

Meaning

1. What do you make of the title of this essay? What are the gardens to
   which Bass refers? How are they created, and why are they important?

2. Examine the author's depiction of a game of cards in paragraphs 5 and 6.
   What point is Bass making with this **analogy**?

---

[1] Trees and branches knocked to the ground by wind. [Editors' note.]

[2] Bass lists here four common types of fossils that might be found among the
talus, or a pile of fallen rocks at the bottom of a cliff. [Editors' note.]

3. What does Bass mean by "a tiny human scale" in paragraph 6? What attitude toward human beings and their activities does he go on to convey in paragraphs 20–22?

4. Does Bass have a thesis? What does he suggest the annual spring melt in Montana can teach us about the threat of climate change in general?

5. If you are uncertain of the meanings of any of the words listed below, try to guess them from the context of the essay. Then look them up to see how close your definitions were to those in the dictionary. Test out the new words by using each of them in a sentence or two of your own.

cornices (1)	xylophonic (11)	fecund (21)
silt (2)	arrhythmia (11)	ascending (22)
tributaries (4)	verdant (13)	torrents (23)
hackneyed (5)	encroach (13)	aquifers (23)
perfunctory (10)	archipelago (16)	talus (23)

Purpose and Audience

1. What seems to be Bass's main purpose in writing this essay? What does he want for the Kootenai River watershed? What passages support your interpretation?

2. What assumptions does Bass make about his audience? Does he assume his readers will agree with his ideas, or is he also writing for people who might disagree? How can you tell?

Method and Structure

1. Why do you think Bass chose to write a process analysis instead of simply narrating one of his experiences of the spring melt or arguing his point directly? In other words, what does he gain by emphasizing the yearly repetition and the stages of the process?

2. Bass's essay is divided into two sections: paragraphs 1–13 and 14–24. Consider the different focus of each section. How does this structure serve Bass's purpose?

3. **OTHER METHODS** Bass's essay is full of rich, telling **description**. How many senses does he appeal to? (Give examples.) How do these sensory details play an important part in the essay, given the subject matter?

Language

1. Bass uses several figures of speech, such as the **simile** of chunks of ice "floating downstream like rafts or leisure boats" (paragraph 1). Find two or three other figures of speech—such as **metaphor**, **personification**,

hyperbole, or **paradox**—and analyze how each one contributes to Bass's meaning and helps convey his attitude toward his subject.

2. Each of the first three paragraphs of this essay consists of one long sentence. What effect does Bass create by writing this way?

3. Three times in the essay Bass ends the last sentence of a paragraph with an ellipsis mark (". . .") instead of a period, question mark, or exclamation mark. Why? What could be the purpose of trailing off the way he does?

Writing Topics

1. **JOURNAL TO ESSAY**   Using Bass's essay as a model, write a contemplative process analysis of something that fascinates you, frightens you, or upsets you. Your subject could be a natural phenomenon you recounted in your journal (p. 226), or an instance of environmental injustice, such as those Bass portrays, or something else: visiting a health-care clinic, meeting a deadline for an important project, obtaining a permit through a government agency. You may use examples from your own experience and observation, from experiences you have read or heard about, or from both sources.

2. Think of a time when you felt that you experienced in nature "a story that must get told" (paragraphs 6, 8, 12, and 13)—perhaps on a hike or a camping trip, on a vacation, or even on your street. Write an essay trying to re-create this experience, using concrete language and figures of speech to make your readers feel, hear, see, taste, or smell what you did.

3. **CULTURAL CONSIDERATIONS**   Do you agree with Bass that human activities damage the wilderness but nature will regenerate itself? Or do you think he overlooks positive contributions that humans have made to the earth? Write an essay in which you agree or disagree with Bass's assumptions, citing specific examples to support your opinion. How does your response to Bass lead you to answer his claim of "injustice" in paragraph 17?

4. **CONNECTIONS**   Both Bass and Marta Taylor, in "Desert Dance" (p. 96), depict dramatic natural phenomena that occur in the American West. Compare the way Taylor describes a desert lightning storm in paragraphs 5 and 6 of her essay to Bass's description of a mountain river melt in paragraphs 1–4 and 9–11 of his essay. How does each writer combine striking images and original figures of speech to convey a strong sense of mood and a feeling in the reader that he or she is there? Do you think one author's description is more successful than the other's? Why?

WRITING WITH THE METHOD

PROCESS ANALYSIS

Select one of the following topics, or any other topic they suggest, for an essay developed by process analysis. Be sure to choose a topic you care about so that process analysis is a means of communicating an idea, not an end in itself.

Technology

1. How an engine or other machine works
2. How to guard privacy online
3. How to get through an automated voice-recognition system
4. How to recover lost or damaged digital files
5. How wind can be converted into electricity

Education and Career

6. Training an animal, such as a dog, a horse, or a flea
7. Learning a new language
8. Interviewing for a job
9. Succeeding in biology, history, computer science, or another course
10. Coping with a difficult boss

Entertainment and Hobbies

11. Performing a magic trick
12. Throwing a really *bad* party
13. Playing a sport or a musical instrument
14. Making great chili or some other dish

Health and Appearance

15. Getting physically fit
16. Climbing a mountain
17. Falling down gracefully
18. Treating a sprained ankle or wrist

Family and Friends

19. Offering constructive criticism
20. Driving your parents, brother, sister, friend, or roommate crazy
21. Assigning chores fairly
22. Making new friends in a new place

WRITING ABOUT THE THEME

▶

CONSIDERING THE NATURAL ENVIRONMENT

1. All of the writers in this chapter are concerned in some way with how humans affect the earth, whether positively or negatively. Miranda Smith (p. 208) encourages gardeners to plant trees, while Ted Genoways (p. 208) investigates how fossil fuels are extracted from the soil. Brian Doyle (p. 214) worries about the impact of daily activities like raising the thermostat, Marina Keegan (p. 219) wonders why some people put more effort into helping animals than each other, and Rick Bass (p. 226) rails against the logging industry. Write an essay of your own about harming or protecting some aspect of the environment. Do you regard climate change, pollution, or extinction as critical problems, for instance? Do you believe the government is taking adequate steps to protect the planet? Do you believe that the actions of individuals can make a difference? Your essay may but need not be an argument: that is, you could explain your answer to any of these questions, or you could argue a specific point. Either way, use examples and details to support your ideas.

2. Although we tend to think of nature as unspoiled wilderness, some of the authors in this chapter recognize that the natural world can be both beautiful and harsh. Marina Keegan's portrayal of the moon as a killer and Rick Bass's celebration of the violence of the Montana spring melt are most notable in this respect, but even Brian Doyle's examination of nature writing praises "a subtext of sadness," while Miranda Smith acknowledges that plantings can suffocate and Ted Genoways portrays ponds filled with toxic runoff. Write a process analysis about a natural phenomenon that has made an impression on you, emphasizing its blemishes rather than its beauty.

3. Apply Brian Doyle's ideas about the "greatest nature essay *ever*" to the other two essays in this chapter. How well do Marina Keegan's "Why We Care about Whales" and Rick Bass's "Gardens of Ice and Stone" adhere to Doyle's standards? Does either qualify as a "perfect nature essay"? Why, or why not? Write an essay using Doyle's principles to analyze one or both of these selections. Quote Doyle's analysis and passages from the other writers as appropriate, being sure to use proper citation format (see pp. 214–218) to acknowledge your sources.

11

COMPARISON AND CONTRAST

▶

FEELING AT HOME

An insomniac watching late-night television faces a choice between two vampire movies broadcasting at the same time. To make up her mind, she uses the dual method of **comparison and contrast.**

- *Comparison* shows the similarities between two or more subjects: the similar broadcast times and topics of the two movies force the insomniac to choose between them.

- *Contrast* shows the differences between subjects: the different actors, locations, and reputations of the two movies make it possible for the insomniac to choose one.

As this example suggests, comparison and contrast usually work together because any subjects that warrant side-by-side examination usually resemble each other in some respects and differ in others. You use the method instinctively whenever you need to choose among options — for instance, two political candidates, four tiers of health coverage, or several pairs of running shoes. You might also use comparison to make sense of competing proposals for calming traffic in a congested neighborhood, to explain how nursing has changed in the past decade, or to determine whether you should be more concerned about the sun's harmful rays or the chemicals in sunscreen.

Writers, too, often draw on the method, especially when a comparison can explain something that may be unfamiliar to their readers. All of the writers presented in this chapter, for instance, use comparison and contrast to examine their personal concepts of home. A paragraph by Maya Angelou notes the differences between her grandmother's house and her mother's. Another paragraph, by Iranian American writer Firoozeh

Dumas, contrasts attitudes toward serious students in the two countries where she grew up. Antonio Ruiz-Camacho finds surprising parallels in his youthful visions of the United States and his American sons' impressions of his home country of Mexico. Brian Jaehyung Kim tries to determine whether he's more himself with his family in Seoul or his friends in Massachusetts. And Barbara Lazear Ascher contrasts assumptions about people without homes with the dignity she observes in one homeless man's behavior.

Reading Comparison and Contrast

Writers generally use comparison and contrast for one of two purposes:

- To *explain* the similarities and differences between subjects so as to make either or both of them clear.
- To *evaluate* subjects so as to establish their advantages and disadvantages, strengths and weaknesses.

The explanatory comparison does not take a position on the relative merits of the subjects; the evaluative comparison does, and it usually concludes with a preference or a suggested course of action. An explanatory comparison in a consumer magazine, for example, might show the similarities and differences between two digital music services; an evaluative comparison on the same subject might argue that one service is better than the other.

Whether explanatory or evaluative, comparisons treat two or more subjects in the same general class or group: tax laws, religions, attitudes toward marriage, diseases, advertising strategies, diets, contact sports, friends. A writer may define the class to suit his or her interest—for instance, a television critic might focus on crime dramas, on cable news programs, or on classic situation comedies. The class likeness ensures that the subjects share enough features to make comparison worthwhile. With subjects from different classes, such as an insect and a tree, the similarities are so few and differences so numerous—and both are so obvious—that explaining them would be pointless.

In putting together a comparison, a writer selects subjects from the same class and then, using division or analysis, identifies the features shared by the subjects. These **points of comparison** are the characteristics of the class and thus of the subjects within the class. For instance, the points of comparison for digital music services may be music selection, pricing, and device compatibility; for air pollutants they may be sources and dangers to plants, animals, and humans. These points help to arrange similarities and differences between subjects, and, more important, they ensure direct comparison rather than a random listing of unrelated characteristics.

In an effective comparison, a thesis or controlling idea governs the choice of class, points of comparison, and specific similarities and differences, while also making the comparison worthwhile for the reader. Clearly, comparison requires a firm organizational hand. Writers have two options for arranging a comparison:

- *Subject-by-subject*, in which the points of comparison are grouped under each subject so that the *subjects* are covered one at a time.

- *Point-by-point*, in which the subjects are grouped under each point of comparison so that the *points* are covered one at a time.

The brief outlines that follow illustrate the different arrangements as they might be applied to digital music services:

Subject-by-subject	*Point-by-point*
Tunelet	Music selection
Music selection	Tunelet
Pricing	Spindle
Device compatibility	Pricing
Spindle	Tunelet
Music selection	Spindle
Pricing	Device compatibility
Device compatibility	Tunelet
	Spindle

Since the subject-by-subject arrangement presents each subject as a coherent unit, it is particularly useful for comparing impressions of subjects: the dissimilar characters of two people, for instance. However, covering the subjects one at a time can break an essay into discrete pieces and strain readers' memories, so this arrangement is usually confined to essays that are short or that compare several subjects briefly. For longer comparisons requiring precise treatment of the individual points—say, an evaluation of two proposals for a new student-aid policy—the point-by-point arrangement is more useful. Its chief disadvantage is that the reader can get lost in the details and fail to see any subject as a whole. Because each arrangement has its strengths and weaknesses, writers sometimes combine the two in a single work, using the divided arrangement to introduce or summarize overall impressions of the subjects and using the alternating arrangement to deal specifically with the points of comparison.

Analyzing Comparison and Contrast in Paragraphs

Maya Angelou (1928–2014) was a revered writer whose poems, novels, and autobiographies were filled with joy and hope despite a tumultuous youth spent shuttled between the homes of her grandmother and her divorced parents. This paragraph is from *Letter to My Daughter* (2008), a book of essays and advice dedicated to a girl Angelou wanted but never had.

When I was thirteen, my grandmother took me back to California to join my mother, and she returned immediately to Arkansas. The California house was a world away from that little home in which I grew up in Arkansas. My mother wore her straight hair in a severe stylish bob. My grandmother didn't believe in hot curling women's hair, so I had grown up with a braided natural. Grandmother turned our radio on to listen to the news, religious music, *Gang Busters,* and *The Lone Ranger.* In California my mother wore lipstick and rouge and played loud blues and jazz music on a record player. Her house was full of people who laughed a lot and talked loudly. I definitely did not belong. I walked around in that worldly atmosphere, with my hands clasped behind my back, my hair pulled back in a tight braid, humming a Christian song.

Point-by-point organization

Comparison clarified by topic sentence (underlined once) and repetition (underlined twice)

1. Appearances

2. Sounds

Firoozeh Dumas (born 1966), a humorist who emigrated to California from Iran with her family at the age of seven, hopes to dispel Americans' fears of Iranians by revealing their "shared humanity." The following paragraph is adapted from her essay collection *Laughing without an Accent* (2008).

Good old Iranian or American qualities such as aiming high and striving despite difficulties have been replaced with everyone receiving a trophy for participating, but that's not the only obstacle. In Iran, we celebrated the math geniuses, the ones with neat

Subject-by-subject organization

1. Iranian students

handwriting, the <u>ones who tried to excel in school</u>, the <u>ones who spent a lot of time on their homework</u>. They received <u><u>prizes</u></u>. Their names were in the newspaper. We applauded them and wished our children could be like them. <u>Here</u>, those kids are called <u><u>nerds</u></u> and <u><u>geeks</u></u> and dorks. This may be the only country where people make fun of the <u><u>smart</u></u> kids. Now *that's* <u><u>stupid</u></u>. I only hope that the engineer who built the bridge that I drive across or the nurse who administers our vaccines or the teacher who teaches my kids was a <u><u>total nerd</u></u>.

2. American students

Comparison clarified by transitions (underlined once) and repetition (underlined twice)

Developing an Essay by Comparison and Contrast

▶ Getting Started

Whenever you observe similarities or differences between two or more members of the same general class—activities, people, ideas, things, places—you have a possible subject for comparison and contrast. Just be sure that the subjects are worth comparing and that you can do the job in the space and time allowed. For instance, if you have a week to complete a three-page paper, don't try to show all the similarities and differences between country music and rhythm and blues. The effort can only frustrate you and irritate your readers. Instead, limit the subjects to a manageable size—for instance, the lyrics of a representative song in each type of music—so that you can develop the comparisons completely and specifically.

To generate ideas for a comparison, explore each subject separately to pick out its characteristics, and then explore the subjects together to see what characteristics one suggests for the other. Look for points of comparison. Early on, you can use **division or analysis** to identify points of comparison by breaking the subjects' general class into its elements. A song lyric, for instance, could be divided into story line or plot, basic emotion, and special language such as dialect or slang. After you have explored your subjects fully, you can use **classification** to group your characteristics under the points of comparison. For instance, you might classify characteristics of two proposals for a new student-aid policy into qualifications for eligibility, minimum and maximum amounts to be made available, and repayment terms.

As you gain increasing control over your material, consider also the needs of your readers:

- Do they know your subjects well, or will you need to take special care to explain one or both of them?
- Will your readers be equally interested in similarities and differences, or will they find one more enlightening than the other?

▶ Forming a Thesis

While you are shaping your ideas, you should also begin formulating your controlling idea, your thesis. The first thing you should do is look over your points of comparison and determine whether they suggest an evaluative or explanatory approach.

The thesis of an evaluative comparison will generally emerge naturally because it coincides with your purpose of supporting a preference for one subject over another:

THESIS SENTENCE (EVALUATION)   Both services offer a wide range of music, but Spindle is less expensive and more flexible than Tunelet.

In an explanatory comparison, however, your thesis will need to do more than merely reflect your general purpose in explaining. It should go beyond the obvious and begin to identify the points of comparison. For example:

TENTATIVE THESIS SENTENCE (EXPLANATION)   Rugby and American football are the same in some respects and different in others.

REVISED THESIS SENTENCE (EXPLANATION)   Though rugby requires less strength and more stamina than American football, the two games are very much alike in their rules and strategies.

These examples suggest other decisions you must make when formulating a thesis:

- Will you emphasize both subjects equally or stress one over the other?
- Will you emphasize differences, similarities, or both?

Keeping your readers in mind as you make these decisions will make it easier to use your thesis to shape your essay. For instance, if you decide to write an evaluative comparison and your readers are likely to be biased against your recommendation, you will need to support your case with plenty of specific reasons. If the subjects are equally familiar to your readers (as the music services are in the previous examples), you'll want to give them equal emphasis, but if one subject is unfamiliar (as rugby is in the United States), you will probably need to stress it over the other.

Knowing your audience will also help you decide whether to focus on similarities, differences, or both. Generally, you'll stress the differences between subjects your readers consider similar (such as music services) and the similarities between subjects they are likely to consider different (such as rugby and American football).

▶ Organizing

Your readers' needs and expectations can also help you plan your essay's organization. An effective **introduction** to a comparison often provides some context for readers—the situation that prompts the comparison, for instance, or the reason you see a need for it. Placing your thesis sentence in the introduction also informs readers of your purpose and point, and it may help keep you focused while you write.

For the **body** of the essay, choose the arrangement that will present your material most effectively. Remember that the subject-by-subject arrangement suits brief essays comparing dominant impressions of the subjects, whereas the point-by-point arrangement suits longer essays requiring emphasis on individual points of comparison. If you are torn between the two—wanting both to sum up each subject and to show them side by side—then a combined arrangement may be your wisest choice.

A rough outline like the models shown earlier (p. 237) can help you plan the basic arrangement of your essay as well as the order of the subjects and points of comparison. If your subjects are equally familiar to your readers and equally important to you, then it may not matter which you treat first. But if one subject is less familiar or if you favor one, then that one should probably come second. You can also arrange the points themselves to reflect their importance and your readers' knowledge: from least to most significant or complex, from most to least familiar. Be sure to use the same order for both subjects.

Most readers know intuitively how comparison and contrast works, so they will expect you to balance your comparison feature for feature as well. In other words, all the features mentioned for the first subject should be mentioned as well for the second, and any features not mentioned for the first subject should not suddenly materialize for the second.

The **conclusion** to a comparison essay can help readers see the whole picture: the chief similarities and differences between subjects compared in a divided arrangement, or the chief characteristics of subjects compared in an alternating arrangement. In addition, you may want to comment on the significance of your comparison, advise readers on how they can use the information you have provided, or recommend a specific course of action for them to follow. As always, the choice of conclusion should reflect the impression you want to leave with readers.

▶ Drafting

Drafting your essay gives you the chance to spell out your comparison so that it supports your thesis or, if your thesis is still tentative, to discover what you think by writing about your subject. You can use **paragraphs** to help manage the comparison as it unfolds:

- In a *subject-by-subject* arrangement, if you devote two paragraphs to the first subject, try to do the same for the second subject. For both subjects, try to cover the points of comparison in the same order, and group the same ones in paragraphs.

- In a *point-by-point* arrangement, balance the paragraphs as you move back and forth between subjects. If you treat several points of comparison for the first subject in one paragraph, do the same for the second subject. If you apply a single point of comparison to both subjects in one paragraph, do the same for the next point.

This way of drafting will help you achieve balance in your comparison and see where you may need more information to flesh out your subjects and your points. If the finished draft seems too rigid in its pattern, you can always loosen things up when revising.

▶ Revising and Editing

When you are revising and editing your draft, use the following questions and the information in the Focus box on the next page to be certain that your essay meets the principal requirements of the comparative method.

- *Are your subjects drawn from the same class?* The subjects must have notable differences *and* notable similarities to make comparison worthwhile — though, of course, you may stress one over the other.

- *Does your essay have a clear purpose and say something significant about the subject?* Your purpose of explaining or evaluating and the point you are making should be evident in your thesis *and* throughout the essay. A vague, pointless comparison will quickly bore readers.

■ *Do you apply all points of comparison to both subjects?* Even if you emphasize one subject, the two subjects must match feature for feature. An unmatched comparison may leave readers with unanswered questions or weaken their confidence in your authority.

■ *Does the pattern of comparison suit readers' needs and the complexity of the material?* Although readers will appreciate a clear organization and roughly equal treatment of your subjects and points of comparison, they will also appreciate some variety in the way you move back and forth. You needn't devote a sentence to each point, first for one subject and then for the other, or alternate subjects sentence by sentence through several paragraphs. Instead, you might write a single sentence on one point or subject but four sentences on the other—if that's what your information requires.

FOCUS ON PARALLELISM

With several points of comparison and alternating subjects, a comparison will be easier to follow if you emphasize likenesses and differences in your wording. Take advantage of the technique of parallelism to help readers keep your subjects straight. **Parallelism**—the use of similar grammatical structures for elements of similar importance—balances a comparison and clarifies the relationship between elements. At the same time, lack of parallelism can distract or confuse readers.

As you edit, look for groups of related ideas. To make elements parallel, repeat the forms of related words, phrases, and sentences:

NONPARALLEL   Both music services allow subscribers to listen to songs on their computers, phones, or a smart speaker.

PARALLEL   Both music services allow subscribers to listen to songs on their computers, phones, or smart speakers.

NONPARALLEL   Tunelet sells songs individually, but Spindle users can get unlimited streaming for a monthly subscription fee.

PARALLEL   Tunelet sells songs individually, but Spindle allows unlimited streaming for a monthly subscription fee.

For more on parallelism, see page 50.

LearningCurve   To practice editing for parallel structure, visit *LaunchPad Solo for Readers and Writers* > LearningCurve > Parallelism

Your responsibility as a parent is not as great as you might imagine. . . .
If your child simply grows up to be someone who does not use the word
collectible as a noun, you can consider yourself an unqualified success.

—Fran Lebowitz

Junk is the ideal product . . . the ultimate merchandise. No sales talk
necessary. The client will crawl through a sewer and beg to buy.

—William S. Burroughs

Toys were lots of fun before they became capitalist tools. —Beth Copeland Vargo

JOURNAL RESPONSE Many people derive comfort from a childhood object
throughout life: they may no longer sleep with a teddy bear, but the sight
of it on the shelf provides security and a connection with the past. Think
of such an object that exists for you—a favorite toy, a model ship or car,
a pillow, a ball, something one of your parents gave you. Describe the
object as specifically as you can.

Antonio Ruiz-Camacho

Storyteller Antonio Ruiz-Camacho was born in 1973 in Toluca, Mexico, and graduated from Universidad Iberoamericana, in Mexico City, in 1996. He worked as a journalist in Mexico City and in Madrid, Spain, for several years before settling in Texas
with his family. He earned a master's degree in fine arts from the University of Texas
at Austin, where he now teaches creative writing; he has also managed online news
and personal finance sites and occasionally teaches bilingual writing workshops for
elementary schoolchildren. Ruiz-Camacho's reporting and fiction have appeared in
both English and Spanish in the *New York Times*, *Kirkus Reviews*, *Poets and Writers*,
Etiqueta Negra, *Texas Monthly*, and other publications. His first compilation of short
stories, *Barefoot Dogs*, was published in 2015 to critical and popular acclaim.

Souvenirs

In this 2014 essay for the *New York Times*'s "Private Lives" series, Ruiz-Camacho contrasts his own childhood vacations in the United States with his sons' recent vacations in Mexico. The keepsakes each child chose to remember his visit strikes the
author with a nostalgia for home, wherever that may be.

It was the summer of 1980, and I was seven years old, when I traveled to   1
America for the first time. I came to Los Angeles with my mom. The trip,

which included visits to Disneyland and Sea World and Knott's Berry Farm,[1] was the reward my parents gave me for finishing first grade with honors. The Mexican middle class has always been as pampering in its affections as aspirational in its customs, and my family was no exception.

We came to California from another galaxy. We lived in a town 2 called Toluca. It was only forty miles from Mexico City, but felt light years away from any form of civilization. Five channels on TV, only one of them for kids, which I'd watch from the moment I came back from school until I had to go to bed. (I know; my kids now hear this and gasp.) *El Pájaro Loco* and *Don Gato*[2] would air early in the afternoon, while *Los Picapiedra* and *Los Supersónicos*—the Flintstones and Jetsons[3]— the absolute prime timers, would come on later. In between cartoons, American ads dubbed in Spanish would sell otherworldly toys local stores hardly ever carried—the Elastic Man, the Duncan yo-yo, the Millennium Falcon Spaceship from *Star Wars*. My seven-year-old self firmly believed that life Up North was better, more advanced and irresistibly alluring.

Upon landing in Los Angeles I was a bit disappointed that cars didn't 3 glide along the streets as I'd imagined, but everything else seemed to confirm my theories about America. The control tower at LAX[4] looked exactly like a house from *Los Supersónicos*, the milk I had for breakfast at the hotel—served in half-pint cartons, as if in a Hollywood movie!—tasted so delicious and real-milk-like, and the avenues were decorated with palm trees, something back home I had seen only in Acapulco.

I came back from California with my first wristwatch. The strap was 4 white and the dial black, decorated with Mickey Mouse as Tony Manero[5]—Mickey's hands, *Saturday Night Fever*-style, pointed to the minutes and the hours.

After that first trip, we traveled to America every year. We went to 5 Orlando and Miami, then to New York City and Niagara Falls. It was during that trip to the Northeast that I got my most treasured memento

---

[1] Three popular theme parks in Southern California. [Editors' note.]

[2] *Woody Woodpecker* and *Top Cat*. [Editors' note.]

[3] Both Hanna-Barbera cartoons with similar story lines and with multiple voice actors in common, *The Flintstones* centers on a Stone Age family, and *The Jetsons* takes place one hundred years in the future. [Editors' note.]

[4] Los Angeles International Airport. [Editors' note.]

[5] Played by John Travolta, Tony Manero is the hero of the 1977 disco movie *Saturday Night Fever*. The still image of Travolta poised in a dance move—one arm pointing up, the other down—is iconic. [Editors' note.]

from those early expeditions to the Better North. It's an apple-green plastic alarm clock that features Kermit the Frog[6] as a film director, sitting on his director's chair, holding a megaphone.

I lost that groovy watch long ago, but the apple-green alarm clock   6
stayed with me, tagging along as I left my hometown and ultimately my home country, moving from Toluca to Mexico City, then to Madrid, then to Austin. Last year, the alarm system on the clock started to get faulty, and I, with a heavy heart, had to start using a different device to wake up in the mornings. But Kermit and his megaphone still sit on my bedside table, like a keepsake from the time I dreamed of going to more intriguing and far-off lands.

My kids were nine and twelve when they visited Mexico for the first   7
time. I wanted to do that trip before, but it wasn't possible for many reasons, including time, money, green-card procedures and the wave of violence that struck my home country soon after I left.

But last summer we went to the Yucatán Peninsula, one of the safest   8
regions in the country, among the least impacted by the drug and extortion and kidnapping wars of recent years. We spent the first couple of days in Tulum, then paid visits to the archaeological zones of Chichén Itzá, Uxmal and Coba.

Before the trip, I was jittery. Despite the reassurances of friends and   9
relatives from Mexico, I was concerned about our safety. But it wasn't only that. I was secretly afraid my kids wouldn't connect with the place I came from. I was afraid they'd compare Mexico and America the same way I had as a kid.

And they did. The Yucatán Peninsula blew their minds just as Cali-   10
fornia did mine thirty-three years before. At a small restaurant by the beach in Tulum called Zamas, they had the best chicken tacos of their lives. At a supermarket outside Merida, they had the most delicious *pan dulce*[7] ever. Above absolutely everything else, they fell in love with the Maya pyramids.

We were on our way back to Austin when my older son, Emiliano,   11
asked why we live where we live. Why can't we live in Mexico?

In December, my family and I went back, and spent Christmas in   12
Toluca, my hometown, for the first time. It was a more sobering experience for my kids, as Central Mexico showed them a side of the country

---

[6] A popular Muppet character, Kermit was the on-screen director of *The Muppet Show* (1976–81). [Editors' note.]

[7] "Sweet bread," or pastry. [Editors' note.]

Yucatán hadn't—the wild gap between rich and poor, slums alongside skyscrapers, kids their own age begging at the stoplights.

During that trip, they implored that we pay a visit to Teotihuacán, about an hour and a half away. We were atop the Pyramid of the Sun, along with dozens of other visitors, when it started to pour heavily, in typical Mexico City fashion. The people around us were less preoccupied with keeping themselves from the rain, though, than they were with waiting their turn to touch the very center point of the pyramid, marked by a minute metallic knob, for a chance to absorb the pyramid's mythic energy. We were no exception.   13

Back on the ground, my younger son, Guillermo, spent part of his trip allowance on two ocarinas—traditional wind instruments—made out of clay by local craftsmen. One, bright brown and white, has the shape of an eagle; the other, more colorful and with a rougher finish, resembles the head of a jaguar warrior from Aztec mythology. If you blow through them at the right angle, they are supposed to reproduce these symbolic figures' calls.   14

Those were the kinds of souvenirs the Mexican middle-class kid that I was, fascinated by all things Up North, infused with prejudices about my own country, would dismiss as too rustic, too dull, too low-class.   15

But there they are, those clay ocarinas, handmade and otherworldly, alongside Guillermo's Kindle, sitting every night on his bedside table.   16

Meaning

1. Ruiz-Camacho explores differences between American and Mexican cultures. What is his main idea? Try to express his implied thesis in your own words.

2. Why do you suppose Ruiz-Camacho translates the titles of *Los Picapiedra* and *Los Supersónicos* but not *El Pájaro Loco* or *Don Gato* (paragraph 2)? What makes the Flintstones and the Jetsons particularly significant to his comparison?

3. Why was Ruiz-Camacho worried that his sons would "compare Mexico and America the same way [he] had as a kid" (paragraph 9)? What impression did Mexico actually make on them?

4. If you are uncertain of the meanings of any of the words listed below, try to guess them from the context of the essay. Then look them up to see how close your definitions were to those in the dictionary. Test out the new words by using each of them in a sentence or two of your own.

aspirational (1)	memento (5)	archaeological (8)
alluring (2)	expeditions (5)	rustic (15)

Purpose and Audience

1. Is Ruiz-Camacho's comparison explanatory or evaluative? Does he conclude that one country is better than the other? Draw evidence from the essay to support your answer.

2. The author refers at several points to violence and poverty in Mexico, but he doesn't elaborate. Does it seem, then, that he is writing primarily to an American audience, to a Mexican audience, or to any reader, regardless of country of origin?

Method and Structure

1. Is "Souvenirs" arranged point-by-point or subject-by-subject? What are the main points of comparison?

2. Does the author focus on similarities or differences in his comparison? Why do you think he chose one emphasis over the other?

3. OTHER METHODS   Ruiz-Camacho uses **narration** and **examples** to develop his comparison. Locate specific uses of these methods, and explain what they contribute to the essay.

Language

1. "We came to California from another galaxy," Ruiz-Camacho writes in paragraph 2. Locate other words and phrases that invoke outer space or a futuristic world. What does this use of **metaphor** and **hyperbole** contribute to the author's meaning?

2. Why does Ruiz-Camacho capitalize "Up North" in paragraph 2? Where else does he use capital letters in unconventional ways? What is the effect?

3. What key terms does Ruiz-Camacho repeat or restate to help give his essay **coherence?** Identify those that seem most significant.

Writing Topics

1. JOURNAL TO ESSAY   In your journal entry (p. 244), you described an object of attachment from your childhood. Expand that description into an essay that explores its significance for you. How did you acquire it? Why is it special? What does it mean to you? Consider both the positive and negative associations the object holds for you.

2. Recall a time when you accompanied a parent or other adult (aunt, uncle, grandparent, and so on) to a place he or she knew well but you were seeing for the first time. It could be a place where the person grew up,

went to school, lived for a time, or vacationed. Write an essay in which you compare your reactions to the place with what you remember of the adult's reactions or what, with hindsight, you think the adult's reactions might have been.

3. RESEARCH Ruiz-Camacho refers to the Yucatán Peninsula as a region of Mexico "among the least impacted by the drug and extortion and kidnapping wars of recent years" (paragraph 8). What is he talking about? Research the current situation of violent unrest in Mexico, considering especially the impact of the drug trade on politics and daily life. Then write an essay in which you present your findings.

4. CONNECTIONS In "Double Identity" (next page), student writer Brian Jaehyung Kim also examines some of the prejudices he holds about his home country, announcing he "takes pride in the fact that he isn't like the 'other Koreans' and that he 'doesn't seem Korean at all.'" And like Ruiz-Camacho, Kim experiences feelings of ambivalence when he returns to visit. Read his essay, and compare and contrast Kim's examination of identity with Ruiz-Camacho's assessment of place. Whose concept of cultural influence strikes you as more realistic or insightful? Why would either writer harbor negative perceptions of the lands of their birth or the people who remain there? Explain your answer, using plenty of details from both readings to support your thesis. If you have left home yourself and have mixed feelings about it, you may include your personal experiences in your essay as well.

There's no place like home. There's no place like home. There's no place like home.
— Dorothy Gale

Where we love is home — home that our feet may leave, but not our hearts.
— Oliver Wendell Holmes, Sr.

You can keep my things; they've come to take me home.   — Peter Gabriel

JOURNAL RESPONSE   Where do you call home? Is it the place where your family is from? where you were born? where you grew up? where you live now? What makes a place a home? And how does your idea of home affect your sense of who you are? Ponder these questions in your journal.

Brian Jaehyung Kim

Brian Jaehyung Kim was born in South Korea in 1995. He moved to Moscow, Russia, in 2002 and spent most of his childhood there attending an international school before moving to the United States as a teenager. A student at the University of Massachusetts, Amherst, Kim is looking to graduate with a degree in biochemistry. His eyes are set on medical school and a future in the medical field, particularly ophthalmology.

Double Identity
(Student Essay)

Kim wrote "Double Identity" for his first-year course in College Writing; it was then selected for inclusion in UMass Amherst's annual collection of excellent work, *The Student Writing Anthology*. The university writing course, explains the chair of the anthology committee, "begins by asking students to examine the 'self,' or one of our many selves, as a text." In doing just that with competing national identities as his subject, Kim evaluates the meanings of a name.

Amherst, Massachusetts: September 2014
The whole campus seemed to be in a rush. Movers were carrying boxes   1
left and right; students were saying goodbyes to their families and hellos to their new roommates. As I stood in front of the door of what would become my new home, I frowned at the name that was stuck on the door: Jaehyung. I immediately put down my backpack, took out a pen and

scribbled over the name tag. It no longer read Jaehyung, but instead had a new name: Brian.

Seoul, South Korea: March 2010
I was finally back in my home country after seven years in a foreign coun-   2
try. Was school here going to be as hard as the numerous tales had made it out to be? Was I going to have trouble fitting in? Was I going to survive the competition and the endless hours of studying that was required of every student in the country? I had no idea. All I knew was that I was ready for the challenge. As I got dressed in the newly purchased school uniform, I couldn't help but smile. I had always been disgusted at the idea of wearing a uniform to school, but it didn't look too bad. I put on the shirt, the jacket, and the dull gray pants. Finally, I pinned my name tag on the left side of my chest. The name tag read Jaehyung Kim. Or more accurately, 김재형.

Moscow, Russia: August 2002
"If you don't understand what they're saying, just say 'Pardon me?'" my   3
mom reminded me as she helped me get on the bus. Today was the big day. Jaehyung Kim, a little boy who was born and raised in Korea for the past eight years of his life, was in another country, boarding a bus that would take him to a school that would speak another language. As the bus approached the school, I could read the sign: "Anglo American School of Moscow." I was going to meet kids from all over the world here, all united in one school, all speaking one language: English. As I found my way into the classroom and settled down, the teacher required us to take part in the usual, boring, introduce-yourself-to-the-class ordeal. However, I was excited. I was excited to set foot into a new school, excited to be sur-rounded by people from all across the globe, and excited to introduce myself to those people. When my turn came, I stood up, full of energy, and announced, "Hi, my name is Brian Kim!"

A name carries more meaning than a combination of letters you write on   4
the top right portion of your test or a sequence of sounds that you respond to. A name is something that represents you and who you are. You can find out quite a bit about a person just by their name. For example, let's take my name: Brian. If Jake from Texas, the quintessential American col-lege student, sees or hears my name, he can safely assume that I am also a male, as opposed to if he heard the name Brianna, in which case he would infer that I was a female. If Jake were to come across the name Jaehyung, he would know that I am from a different country than he is, for as of yet, to my limited knowledge, there have been not too many American babies named Jaehyung.

Just like that, a name can give out information such as one's gender ⁵ and which region of the world one is from. In most cases, a name can guide you to find out information about someone before even meeting them. However, for me, my name can be misleading and misguiding. When Jake hears the name Brian, he might not immediately match it with a tall, black haired, Asian boy with glasses, and he might not assume right away that I was from the other side of the world. I have two names—Brian and Jaehyung—and I have two identities—Brian and Jaehyung.

Jaehyung was born in Korea. He comes back from school every day. ⁶ He eats dinner with his family and watches TV with them. On the weekends, he likes to play tennis with his dad. Jaehyung goes to Korea during vacations and visits his family. Every lunar New Year, he dresses up in formal, traditional Korean attire and performs the traditional bow to his grandparents, parents, uncles, and aunts, wishing them all a healthy and fruitful year. He speaks Korean, eats Korean food, and practices Korean culture. Jaehyung is Korean.

Brian was never born, but technically created. He goes to school every ⁷ day. He eats lunch with his friends and enjoys playing sports with them. On the weekdays, he enjoys calling his friends for a game of basketball or a night at the movies. During the school year, Brian engages himself in his academics: participating in group projects, writing essays, and taking exams. He likes to take the train to Boston and walk around the city, exploring different shops and different restaurants. He speaks English, eats American food, and likes what American culture has to offer. Brian is American.

Brian will never visit his grandparents during vacations and wear tra- ⁸ ditional Korean clothes. Brian does not speak Korean and does not practice the Korean culture. Whenever his friends ask him to teach them how to speak Korean, he laughs it off and tries to change the subject. When fellow Korean students approach him and try to start a conversation in Korean, he responds in English and tries his best to avoid them. Brian takes pride in the fact that he isn't like the "other Koreans" and that he "doesn't seem Korean at all." Whenever he and his non-Korean friends engage in a conversation about his home country, it would go something like this:

"Do you listen to K-Pop?" ⁹

"No." ¹⁰

"Why do Korean people like to wear such tight-fitting clothes then?" ¹¹

"I wouldn't know." ¹²

"But you're Korean?" ¹³

"Yeah, not really. Whatever." ¹⁴

Brian has always attended an international school where not many 15 people were Korean. He is used to making friends with people who speak English, and it feels awkward to him and makes him uncomfortable when he has to become Korean in front of them. Brian isn't Korean. He doesn't know how to be, and he doesn't want to be.

Jaehyung will not present his group project to his classmates; he will 16 not walk around the city of Boston, visiting shops and buying video games. Jaehyung does not speak English and does not endorse the American culture. Whenever he returns to Korea to visit his family, he is the center of attention. They crowd around him, asking what life is like in a foreign country. They ask him to say something in English, and are impressed when they find out that he can roll his r's. Jaehyung understands that most of his family members are jealous of the fact that he is near-fluent in English—something every Korean wants these days. However, he feels alienated. He feels like they're treating him like someone from another planet, gathering around him and asking him to perform tricks that they cannot. Ever since he was born, Jaehyung has been raised in a Korean family, speaking Korean and practicing Korean culture. Jaehyung isn't American. He doesn't know how to be, and he doesn't want to be.

These two identities are both present in one body: me. I am both a 17 Korean and an American. I speak their languages, understand and practice their cultures. Sometimes I'm Brian: English is the more comfortable language for me, I enjoy being American, and I want to be treated like other Americans. I don't want to stand out just because my looks suggest that I might be from another country. Other times, I'm Jaehyung. Korean is my native language, and I do everything a Korean would do. When I am with my family and my Korean friends, I want to fit in, to be one of them. I don't want to stand out because I know how to speak English or because I've spent time with people from all over the world. Did I prefer being one identity over the other? Not necessarily. However, when I was Brian, I wanted to be Brian. When I was Jaehyung, I wanted to be Jaehyung. But which one was the real me? Did I have to pick one over the other? Would one have to be the dominant identity and the other take the back seat? Was it even possible to live with two identities?

There was one little fact that I missed when I was struggling to find 18 out which one was the real me. Both Brian and Jaehyung have the same last name: Kim. Both Brian and Jaehyung are in me: two seemingly different people sharing one body, taking turns to express themselves. At first it was confusing. It always seemed like I was in conflict with myself, unsure about who I was, until I realized that these two identities aren't in conflict, but coexisting in a certain harmony that only I can produce. Not many people in this world have the name Brian. Fewer people have the name Jaehyung, and even fewer people have both names. I am both Brian and Jaehyung. I am the tall, dark-haired, Asian boy who can be seen walking among a group of friends, laughing and pushing one another around. I am also the tall, dark-haired, Asian boy who can be seen sitting among his family members, dressed up nicely in traditional clothing, enjoying the sweetness of freshly sliced fruit. I am both Brian and Jaehyung Kim.

Meaning

1. What is the significance of a person's name, as Kim sees it? What do his names reveal about him?

2. "Brian was never born," Kim writes in paragraph 7. What does he mean? How, then, did he come into existence?

3. Does Kim have a thesis? Where in the essay does he make his point clear?

4. If you are uncertain of the meanings of any of the words listed below, try to guess them from the context of the essay. Then look them up to see how close your definitions were to those in the dictionary. Test out the new words by using each of them in a sentence or two of your own.

quintessential (4)	lunar (6)	coexisting (18)
infer (4)	alienated (16)	harmony (18)

Purpose and Audience

1. Whom does Kim assume as his audience? How do his subject, evidence, and **tone** reflect his assumptions?

2. Does Kim's purpose in comparing his Korean and American identities strike you as explanatory or evaluative? Why? What evidence from the text can you use to support your opinion?

Method and Structure

1. Why is comparison and contrast particularly well suited to Kim's subject and purpose?

2. What quality or qualities do both subjects of Kim's essay share? What points of comparison does he use to contrast them?

3. How does Kim organize his comparison? Where in the essay does he focus on similarities between Brian and Jaehyung? Where does he focus on differences? Why do you think he might have chosen to organize his essay as he does?

4. OTHER METHODS "Double Identity" opens with three vignettes. What seems to be the purpose of these short **narratives**? What is their effect?

Language

1. How would you characterize Kim's **point of view** in this essay? How does his **style** reflect the fact that Kim is comparing versions of himself?

2. What do you make of the conversation Kim cites in paragraphs 9–14? What is the effect of this **dialogue**?

3. How does Kim use **parallel structure** to support his comparison? Give some examples from his essay.

Writing Topics

1. JOURNAL TO ESSAY   In your journal response (p. 250), you explored what home means to you. Now expand your thoughts into an essay-length **definition** of *home*, making sure to use plenty of examples and details to show your readers what the word means to you. Does your definition correspond to traditional assumptions about family and nationality, or is it unconventional? What characteristics does your definition not include? How does your sense of home define *you*?

2. CULTURAL CONSIDERATIONS   Contemporary American society places great importance on the individual, encouraging people to "be themselves," to develop original insights and tastes, and to voice their own opinions. In contrast, many other cultures emphasize conformity for the greater good. Write an essay in which you explain how either the pressure to be yourself or the pressure to conform with others has affected you in a personal way. For example, how have these pressures affected your college experience in situations such as classroom participation or writing term papers? Do you often feel compelled to be different or conform? How do you tend to react to these pressures?

3. RESEARCH   Kim mentions traveling home to Korea to celebrate the lunar new year with his family (paragraph 6), but he doesn't offer much detail about the occasion. Using the Web and perhaps an encyclopedia, gather information on the Korean new year, or *Seollal*. (See Part Three for tips on

finding and using sources.) When is it celebrated, and by whom? What are some traditions and customs associated with it? What makes it a particularly Korean holiday? How is it similar to, and different from, New Year's celebrations in North America? Write a brief essay reporting your findings.

4. CONNECTIONS   Jennifer Finney Boylan, in her essay "In the Early Morning Rain" (p. 73) also writes about struggling with issues of identity. How do she and Brian Jaehyung Kim both manage to capture and hold readers' interest in deeply personal essays about themselves? Write an essay that examines the strategies these two writers use to make their own experiences relevant and relatable to highly specific audiences.

You are where you live.
—Anna Quindlen

People who are homeless are not social inadequates. They are people without homes.
—Sheila McKechnie

How does it feel / To be without a home / Like a complete unknown / Like a rolling stone?
—Bob Dylan

JOURNAL RESPONSE   In your journal write briefly about how you typically feel when you encounter a person who appears to be homeless. Are you sympathetic? disgusted? something in between?

Barbara Lazear Ascher

Born in 1946, American writer Barbara Lazear Ascher is known for her insightful, inspiring essays. She obtained a BA from Bennington College in 1968 and a JD from Cardozo School of Law in 1979. After practicing law for two years, Ascher turned to writing full time. Her work has appeared in a diverse assortment of periodicals, including the *New York Times*, *Vogue*, the *Yale Review*, *Redbook*, and *National Geographic Traveler*. Ascher has also published a memoir of her brother, who died of AIDS, titled *Landscape without Gravity: A Memoir of Grief* (1993), and several collections of essays: *Playing after Dark* (1986), *The Habit of Loving* (1989), and *Dancing in the Dark: Romance, Yearning, and the Search for the Sublime* (1999). She lives in New York City.

The Box Man

In this classic essay from *Playing after Dark*, the evening ritual of a homeless man prompts Ascher's reflection on the nature of solitude. By comparing the Box Man with two other solitary people, Ascher distinguishes between chosen and unchosen loneliness.

The Box Man was at it again. It was his lucky night.   1

The first stroke of good fortune occurred as darkness fell and the night   2
watchman at 220 East Forty-fifth Street neglected to close the door as he slipped out for a cup of coffee. I saw them before the Box Man did. Just inside the entrance, cardboard cartons, clean and with their top flaps intact. With the silent fervor of a mute at a horse race, I willed him toward them.

It was slow going. His collar was pulled so high that he appeared   3
headless as he shuffled across the street like a man who must feel Earth
with his toes to know that he walks there.

Standing unselfconsciously in the white glare of an overhead light,   4
he began to sort through the boxes, picking them up, one by one, inspect-
ing tops, insides, flaps. Three were tossed aside. They looked perfectly
good to me, but then, who knows what the Box Man knows? When he
found the one that suited his purpose, he dragged it up the block and
dropped it in a doorway.

Then, as if dogged by luck, he set out again and discovered, behind   5
the sign at the parking garage, a plastic Dellwood box, strong and clean,
once used to deliver milk. Back in the doorway the grand design was
revealed as he pushed the Dellwood box against the door and set its cardboard cousin two feet in front—the usual distance between coffee table
and couch. Six full shopping bags were distributed evenly on either side.

He eased himself with slow care onto the stronger box, reached into   6
one of the bags, pulled out a *Daily News*, and snapped it open against his
cardboard table. All done with the ease of IRT Express passengers whose
white-tipped, fair-haired fingers reach into attaché cases as if radar-
directed to the *Wall Street Journal*. They know how to fold it. They know
how to stare at the print, not at the girl who stares at them.

That's just what the Box Man did, except that he touched his tongue   7
to his fingers before turning each page, something grandmothers do.

One could live like this. Gathering boxes to organize a life. Wander-   8
ing through the night collecting comforts to fill a doorway.

When I was a child, my favorite book was *The Boxcar Children*. If   9
I remember correctly, the young protagonists were orphaned, and rather
than live with cruel relatives, they ran away to the woods to live life on
their own terms. An abandoned boxcar was turned into a home, a bubbling
brook became an icebox. Wild berries provided abundant desserts and days
were spent in the happy, adultless pursuit of joy. The children never worried where the next meal would come from or what February's chill might
bring. They had unquestioning faith that berries would ripen and streams
run cold and clear. And unlike Thoreau,[1] whose deliberate living was
self-conscious and purposeful, theirs had the ease of children at play.

Even now, when life seems complicated and reason slips, I long to   10
live like a Boxcar Child, to have enough open space and freedom of

---

[1] Henry David Thoreau (1817–62) was an American essayist and a poet who for
two years lived a solitary and simple life in the woods. He wrote of his experiences
in *Walden* (1854). [Editors' note.]

movement to arrange my surroundings according to what I find. To turn streams into iceboxes. To be ingenious with simple things. To let the imagination hold sway.

Who is to say that the Box Man does not feel as Thoreau did in his doorway, not "crowded or confined in the least," with "pasture enough for . . . imagination." Who is to say that his dawns don't bring back heroic ages? That he doesn't imagine a goddess trailing her garments across his blistered legs?

His is a life of the mind, such as it is, and voices only he can hear. Although it would appear to be a life of misery, judging from the bandages and chill of night, it is of his choosing. He will ignore you if you offer an alternative. Last winter, Mayor Koch[2] tried, coaxing him with promises and the persuasive tones reserved for rabid dogs. The Box Man backed away, keeping a car and paranoia between them.

He is not to be confused with the lonely ones. You'll find them everywhere. The lady who comes into our local coffee shop each evening at five-thirty, orders a bowl of soup and extra Saltines. She drags it out as long as possible, breaking the crackers into smaller and smaller pieces, first in halves and then halves of halves and so on until the last pieces burst into salty splinters and fall from dry fingers onto the soup's shimmering surface. By 6 p.m., it's all over. What will she do with the rest of the night?

You can tell by the vacancy of expression that no memories linger there. She does not wear a gold charm bracelet with silhouettes of boys and girls bearing grandchildren's birthdates and a chip of the appropriate birthstone. When she opens her black purse to pay, there is only a crumpled Kleenex and a wallet inside, no photographs spill onto her lap. Her children, if there are any, live far away and prefer not to visit. If she worked as a secretary for forty years in a downtown office, she was given a retirement party, a cake, a reproduction of an antique perfume atomizer and sent on her way. Old colleagues—those who traded knitting patterns and brownie recipes over the water cooler, who discussed the weather, health, and office scandal while applying lipstick and blush before the ladies' room mirror—they are lost to time and the new young employees who take their places in the typing pool.[3]

---

[2] Edward Koch was the mayor of New York City from 1978 to 1989. [Editors' note.]

[3] Before personal computers became commonplace, many businesses hired people—usually women—to type the handwritten letters, memos, and other documents prepared by higher-level employees. The group of secretaries was known as a typing pool. [Editors' note.]

Each year she gets a Christmas card from her ex-boss. The envelope is   15
canceled in the office mailroom and addressed by memory typewriter.[4]
Within is a family in black and white against a wooded Connecticut landscape. The boss, his wife, who wears her hair in a gray page boy, the three
blond daughters, two with tall husbands and an occasional additional
grandchild. All assembled before a worn stone wall.

Does she watch game shows? Talk to a parakeet, feed him cuttlebone,   16
and call him Pete? When she rides the buses on her Senior Citizen pass,
does she go anywhere or wait for something to happen? Does she have a
niece like the one in Cynthia Ozick's story "Rosa," who sends enough
money to keep her aunt at a distance?

There's a lady across the way whose lights and television stay on all   17
night. A crystal chandelier in the dining room and matching Chinese
lamps on Regency end tables in the living room. She has six cats, some
Siamese, others Angora and Abyssinian. She pets them and waters her
plethora of plants—African violets, a ficus tree, a palm, and geraniums in
season. Not necessarily a lonely life except that 3 a.m. lights and television seem to proclaim it so.

The Box Man welcomes the night, opens to it like a lover. He moves   18
in darkness and prefers it that way. He's not waiting for the phone to ring
or an engraved invitation to arrive in the mail. Not for him a PO number.
Not for him the overcrowded jollity of office parties, the hot anticipation
of a singles' bar. Not even for him a holiday handout. People have tried
and he shuffled away.

The Box Man knows that loneliness chosen loses its sting and claims   19
no victims. He declares what we all know in the secret passages of our
own nights, that although we long for perfect harmony, communion, and
blending with another soul, this is a solo voyage.

The first half of our lives is spent stubbornly denying it. As children we   20
acquire language to make ourselves understood and soon learn from the
blank stares in response to our babblings that even these, our saviors, our
parents, are strangers. In adolescence when we replay earlier dramas with
peers in the place of parents, we begin the quest for the best friend, that person who will receive all thoughts as if they were her own. Later we assert that
true love will find the way. True love finds many ways, but no escape from
exile. The shores are littered with us, Annas and Ophelias, Emmas and Juliets,[5]

---

[4] An early word processor. [Editors' note.]

[5] These are all doomed heroines of literature. Anna is the title character of Leo
Tolstoy's novel *Anna Karenina* (1878). Emma is the title character of Gustave Flau-
bert's novel *Madame Bovary* (1856). Ophelia and Juliet are in Shakespeare's plays—
the romantic partners, respectively, of Hamlet and Romeo. [Editors' note.]

all outcasts from the dream of perfect understanding. We might as well draw the night around us and find solace there and a friend in our own voice.

One could do worse than be a collector of boxes.   21

Meaning

1. What is the **subject** of "The Box Man"? Is Ascher writing primarily about homelessness or something else?

2. What is the main idea of Ascher's essay—the chief point the writer makes about her subject, to which all the other ideas and details in the essay relate?

3. What are the subordinate ideas that contribute to Ascher's main idea? That is, how does Ascher support her thesis?

4. Ascher mentions several works of literature in this essay. Make a list of these **allusions**. What do they contribute to Ascher's meaning? Is familiarity with these works essential to understanding her point?

5. If you are uncertain of the meanings of any of the words listed below, try to guess them from the context of the essay. Then look them up to see how close your definitions were to those in the dictionary. Test out the new words by using each of them in a sentence or two of your own.

fervor (2)	coaxing (12)	cuttlebone (16)
dogged (5)	vacancy (14)	plethora (17)
attaché (6)	silhouettes (14)	jollity (18)
ingenious (10)	atomizer (14)	solace (20)

Purpose and Audience

1. What seems to be Ascher's reason for writing this piece? Does she simply want to express her admiration for a homeless person she encountered, or is she trying to do something else here? What does she seem to hope readers will gain from her essay?

2. What does Ascher assume about the characteristics, knowledge, and interests of her readers? How are these assumptions reflected in her essay?

Method and Structure

1. Ascher compares a solitary homeless man with two solitary women. What are her points of comparison? How do these points lead up to her evaluation of chosen versus unchosen loneliness?

2. Sketch an informal outline of "The Box Man." How does Ascher organize the ideas in her comparison? How does the organization serve her subject and purpose?

3. **OTHER METHODS**   In developing her comparison, Ascher draws on several methods, including **narration**, **description**, **example**, and **analysis**. Locate instances of each of these methods, and comment on their effectiveness.

Language

1. Examine closely the words Ascher uses in her depictions of the Box Man and the two women. What does her language reveal about her attitudes toward these people?

2. Ascher occasionally uses incomplete sentences, such as "To turn streams into iceboxes" (paragraph 10). Identify some of the other **sentence fragments** in her essay. What effect does Ascher achieve with them?

3. Where and how does Ascher use parallelism to emphasize ideas of equal importance?

Writing Topics

1. **JOURNAL TO ESSAY**   In your journal you recorded your thoughts on how you typically respond to the sight of a homeless person (p. 257). Now that you've read Ascher's thoughts after seeing one homeless man, respond to her essay, particularly her assumptions. Does anyone really *choose* homelessness, as Ascher suggests in paragraph 12? What is a home, in her estimation? How might a person end up living on the street? Can a homeless person really be as content as she says? Why do you think so?

2. With Ascher's essay as a model, write an essay of your own that uses examples and comparison to explain why you admire another person. You might write about a stranger, as Ascher does, or about anyone who has had a positive influence on your outlook on life.

3. **CULTURAL CONSIDERATIONS**   To some degree, Ascher's essay attempts to counter misperceptions of homeless people held by the majority of society. Think of a minority group to which you belong. It could be based on housing, income, race, ethnicity, language, sexual orientation, religion, physical disability, or any other characteristic. How is your minority perceived in the dominant culture, and how does this perception resemble or differ from the reality as you know it? Write an essay comparing the perception of and the reality of your group.

4. **RESEARCH** If you live in or have visited an urban area, you have probably seen people sleeping in doorways or scavenging for food. And you have almost certainly seen homelessness and extreme poverty discussed in the news and depicted in the media. Research the problem of homelessness and any solutions that have been proposed or attempted, whether locally or on a national level. Then, considering the information you find, your own experiences, and the observations in Ascher's essay, write an essay proposing a solution to the problem.

5. **CONNECTIONS** In "Why We Care about Whales" (p. 219), Marina Keegan also writes about homelessness and human dignity, but she comes at the problem from a very different perspective than Ascher does. Consider your own experiences and observations as well as the ideas in Ascher's and Keegan's essays, and then write an essay in which you examine your assumptions about homeless people. Describe both personal encounters and media stereotypes, and discuss how these experiences led to your beliefs.

WRITING WITH THE METHOD

COMPARISON AND CONTRAST

Select one of the following topics, or any other topic they suggest, for an essay developed by comparison and contrast. Be sure to choose a topic you care about so that the comparison and contrast is a means of communicating an idea, not an end in itself.

Experience

1. Two jobs you have held or are considering
2. High school and college
3. Your own version of an event you witnessed or participated in and someone else's view of the same event (perhaps a friend's or a reporter's)

People

4. A vegetarian and an omnivore
5. Gender roles
6. Two or more candidates for public office
7. The homes of two friends

Places and Things

8. City and country
9. Public and private transportation
10. Contact lenses and Lasik surgery
11. Print and electronic books

Art and Entertainment

12. The work of two artists, or two works by the same artist
13. Broadcast television and streaming media
14. A college sports game and a professional game in the same sport
15. Vampires and zombies

Education and Ideas

16. Talent and skill
17. Learning and teaching
18. Poverty and wealth
19. Your study method and that of a classmate

WRITING ABOUT THE THEME

FEELING AT HOME

1. All of the authors in this chapter suggest that feeling at home is largely a matter of fitting in with others. Maya Angelou (p. 238) concludes she doesn't "belong" in her mother's house, and Firoozeh Dumas (p. 238) is astonished by Americans' disdain for "nerds and geeks and dorks." Antonio Ruiz-Camacho (p. 244) refers to his lingering "prejudices" about his home country of Mexico, Brian Jaehyung Kim (p. 250) recalls adjusting to three new schools in three new places, and Barbara Lazear Ascher (p. 257) rejects assumptions that living alone is better than living on the street. Write an essay in which you offer your definition of *community*. Consider not only what constitutes a group identity but also why people might seek (or reject) a connection with others. What do communities offer their members, and what do they demand of individuals in return?

2. Several of the authors in this chapter emigrated from another country. Firoozeh Dumas was born in Iran, Brian Jaehyung Kim comes from Korea by way of Russia, and Antonio Ruiz-Camacho grew up in Mexico and worked in Spain before he landed in Texas. As they could all attest, the United States is a country of immigrants, and each group has made an indelible mark on American society. For example, consider just foods: salsa outsells ketchup, curries are offered everywhere, and cappuccino and sushi are everyday indulgences for many Americans who have no Italian or Japanese heritage. Write an essay about the effects of immigration on your daily life: the food you consume, the music you listen to, the clothing you prefer, and so forth. Include personal examples and historical information to bring your ideas to life.

3. Every writer in this chapter wrestles with questions of identity, addressing issues as diverse as the emotional impact of racial stereotypes (Dumas, Kim), cultural attitudes toward intelligence and education (Dumas, Kim, Ruiz-Camacho), the role of peers and family in the development of one's self-esteem (Angelou, Dumas, Kim, Ruiz-Camacho, Ascher), and the importance of a sense of home (Angelou, Kim, Ruiz-Camacho, Ascher). All five authors rely on comparison and contrast, but otherwise they go about their tasks very differently. Most notably, perhaps, their **tones** vary widely, from irony to vulnerability to frustration. Choose the two works that seem most different in this respect, and analyze how the tone of each helps the author achieve his or her purpose. Give specific examples to support your ideas. Does your analysis lead you to conclude that one tone is likely to be more effective than another in addressing sensitive issues?

12

DEFINITION

▶

PURSUING HAPPINESS

Definition sets the boundaries of a thing, a concept, an emotion, or a value. In answering "What is it?" and also "What is it *not*?" definition specifies the main qualities of a subject and its essential nature. Since words are only symbols, pinning down their precise meanings is essential for us to understand ourselves and one another. Thus we use definition constantly, whether we are explaining a new word like *youthquake* to someone who has never heard it, specifying what we're after when we say we want to do something *fun*, or clarifying the diagnosis of a child as *hyperactive*. Definition is, in other words, essential whenever we want to be certain that we are understood.

We often use brief definitions to clarify the meanings of words—for instance, taking a few sentences to explain a technical term in an engineering study. But we may also need to define concepts at length, especially when they are abstract, complicated, or controversial. Drawing on other methods of development, entire definition essays might be devoted to debated phrases (such as *fake news*), to the current uses of a word (*monopoly* in business), or to the meanings of a term in a particular context (like *personality* in psychological theory). *Happiness* is the core topic of this chapter: the authors represented here all offer their own perspectives on a feeling that many of us take for granted. In paragraphs, Carlin Flora explains the meaning of happiness as most psychologists understand it, and Dagoberto Gilb outlines the sources of pride for one Latino community. Then in essays, Augusten Burroughs writes about the satisfaction to be found in accepting unhappiness as a natural state, Jessica Sayuri Boissy finds joy in adhering to a Zen principle of living in the moment, and Julia Alvarez extols the benefits of practicing gratitude as a way of being.

Reading Definition

There are several kinds of definition, each with different uses. One is the **formal definition**, usually a statement of the general class of things to which the word belongs, followed by the distinction(s) between it and other members of the class. For example:

	General class	*Distinction(s)*
A submarine is	a seagoing vessel	that operates underwater.
A parable is	a brief, simple story	that illustrates a moral or religious principle.
Pressure is	the force	applied to a given surface.
Insanity is	a mental condition	in which a defendant does not know right from wrong.

A formal definition usually gives a standard dictionary meaning of the word (as in the first two examples) or a specialized meaning agreed to by the members of a profession or discipline (as in the last two examples, from physics and criminal law, respectively). Writers use formal definition to explain the basic meaning of a term so that readers can understand the rest of a discussion. Occasionally, a formal definition can serve as a springboard to a more elaborate, detailed exploration of a word. For instance, an essay might define *pride* simply as "a sense of self-respect" before probing the varied meanings of the word as people actually understand it and then settling on a fuller and more precise meaning of the author's own devising.

This more detailed definition of *pride* could fall into one of two other types of definition: stipulative and extended. A **stipulative definition** clarifies the particular way a writer is using a word: it stipulates, or specifies, a meaning to suit a larger purpose; the definition is part of a larger whole. For example, to show how pride can destroy personal relationships, a writer might first stipulate a meaning of *pride* that ties in with that purpose. Though a stipulative definition may sometimes take the form of a brief formal definition, most require several sentences or even paragraphs. In a physics textbook, for instance, the physicist's definition of *pressure* quoted earlier probably would not suffice to give readers a good sense of the term and eliminate all the other possible meanings they may have in mind.

Whereas a writer may use a formal or stipulative definition for some larger purpose, he or she would use an **extended definition** for the sake of defining—that is, for the purpose of exploring a thing, quality, or idea in its full complexity and drawing boundaries around it until its meaning is complete and precise. Extended definitions usually treat subjects so complex, vague, or laden with emotions or values that people misunderstand or disagree over their meanings. The subject may be an abstract concept like *patriotism*, a controversial phrase like *beginnings of life*, a colloquial or slang expression like *hype*, a thing like *drone*, a scientific idea like *neural plasticity*, even an everyday expression like *nagging*. Besides defining, the purpose may be to persuade readers to accept a definition (for instance, that life begins at conception, or at birth), to explain (what is neural plasticity?), or to amuse (nagging as exemplified by great nags).

As the variety of possible subjects and purposes may suggest, an extended definition may draw on whatever methods will best accomplish the goal of specifying what the subject encompasses and distinguishing it from similar things, qualities, or concepts. Several strategies are unique to definition:

- **Synonyms**, or words of similar meaning, can convey the range of the word's meanings. For example, a writer could equate *misery* with *wretchedness* and *distress*.

- **Negation**, or saying what a word does not mean, can limit the meaning, particularly when a writer wants to focus on only one sense of an abstract term, such as *love*, that is open to diverse interpretations.

- The **etymology** of a word—its history—may illuminate its meaning, perhaps by showing the direction and extent of its change (*pride*, for instance, comes from a Latin word meaning "to be beneficial or useful") or by uncovering buried origins that remain implicit in the modern meaning (*patriotism* comes from the Greek word for "father"; *happy* comes from the Old Norse word for "good luck").

These strategies of definition may be used alone or together, and they may occupy whole paragraphs in an essay-length definition; but they rarely provide enough range to surround the subject completely. That's why most definition essays draw on at least some of the other methods discussed in this book. One or two methods may predominate: an essay on nagging, for instance, might be developed with brief **narratives**. Or several methods may be combined: a definition of *patriotism* might **compare** it with *nationalism*, analyze its **effects** (such as the actions people take on its behalf), and give **examples** of patriotic individuals. By drawing on the appropriate methods, a writer defines and clarifies a specific perspective on the subject so that the reader understands the meaning exactly.

Analyzing Definition in Paragraphs

Carlin Flora (born 1975) is a science journalist and the author of *Friendfluence: The Surprising Ways Friends Make Us Who We Are* (2013). The following paragraph is from "The Pursuit of Happiness," an article she wrote for the magazine *Psychology Today*.

What *is* happiness? The most useful definition—and it's one agreed upon by neuroscientists, psychiatrists, behavioral economists, positive psychologists, and Buddhist monks—is more like satisfied or content than "happy" in its strict bursting-with-glee sense. It has depth and deliberation to it. It encompasses living a meaningful life, utilizing your gifts and your time, living with thought and purpose. It's maximized when you also feel part of a community. And when you confront annoyances and crises with grace. It involves a willingness to learn and stretch and grow, which sometimes involves discomfort. It requires acting on life, not merely taking it in. It's not joy, a temporary exhilaration, or even pleasure, that sensual rush—though a steady supply of those feelings course through those who seize each day.

> Question introduces concept to be defined
>
> Synonyms
>
> Factors that contribute to happiness:
> meaningful life
> community
> positive attitude
> activity
>
> Concluding sentence states what happiness is not

Dagoberto Gilb (born 1950) is a fiction writer and an essayist. Raised in Southern California by Mexican and German American parents, Gilb often celebrates the lives of working-class Latinos in his work. This paragraph is from his essay "Pride," first published in the *Texas Observer*.

Pride hears gritty dirt blowing against an agave whose stiff fertile stalk, so tall, will not bend—the love of land, rugged like the people who live on it. Pride sees the sunlight on the Franklin Mountains in the first light of morning and listens to a neighbor's gallo—the love of culture and history. Pride smells a sweet, musky drizzle of rain and eats huevos con chile in corn tortillas heated on a cast iron pan—the love of heritage. Pride is the fearless reaction to disrespect and disregard. It is knowing the future will prove that wrong.

> Definition by description:
> Sound and touch
>
> Sight and sound (a *gallo* is a rooster)
>
> Smell and taste (*huevos* are eggs)
>
> Explanations (underlined once) and topic sentence (underlined twice) clarify meaning

Developing an Essay by Definition

▶ Getting Started

You'll sometimes be asked to write definition essays, as when a psychology exam asks for a discussion of *schizophrenia* or a political science assignment calls for an explanation of the term *totalitarianism*. To come up with a subject on your own, consider words that have complex meanings and are either unfamiliar to readers or open to varied interpretations. The subject should be something you know and care enough about to explore in great detail. An idea for a subject may come from an overheard conversation (for instance, a reference to someone as "too patriotic"), a personal experience (an accomplishment that filled you with pride), or something you've seen or read (another writer's definition of *jazz*).

Begin exploring your subject by examining and listing its conventional meanings (consulting an unabridged dictionary may help here, and the dictionary will also give you synonyms and etymology). Also examine the differences of opinion about the word's meanings—the different ways, wrong or right, that you have heard or seen it used. Run through the other methods to see what fresh approaches to the subject they open up:

- How can the subject be described?
- What are some examples?
- Can the subject be divided into qualities or characteristics?
- Can its processes help define it?
- Will comparing and contrasting it with something else help sharpen its meaning?
- Do its causes or effects help clarify its sense?

Some of the questions may turn up nothing, but others may open your eyes to meanings you had not seen.

▶ Forming a Thesis

When you have generated a good list of ideas about your subject, settle on the purpose of your definition. Do you mostly want to explain a word that is unfamiliar to readers? Do you want to express your own view so that readers see a familiar subject from a new angle? Do you want to argue in favor of a particular definition or perhaps persuade readers to look more critically at themselves or their surroundings? Try to work your purpose into a thesis sentence that summarizes your definition and—just as important—asserts something about the subject. For example:

> TENTATIVE THESIS STATEMENT   The prevailing concept of *patriotism* is danger-ously wrong.

> REVISED THESIS STATEMENT   Though generally considered entirely positive in meaning, *patriotism* in fact reflects selfish, childish emotions that have no place in a global society.

(Note that the revised thesis statement not only summarizes the writer's definition and makes an assertion about the subject but it also identifies the prevailing definition she intends to counter in her essay.)

With a thesis sentence formulated, reevaluate your ideas in light of it and pause to consider the needs of your readers:

- *What do readers already know about your subject,* and what do they need to be told in order to understand it as you do?

- *Are your readers likely to be biased for or against your subject?* If you were defining *patriotism,* for example, you might assume that your readers see the word as representing a constructive, even essential value that contributes to the strength of a country. If your purpose were to con-test this view, as implied by the revised thesis statement above, you would have to build your case carefully to win readers to your side.

▶ Organizing

The **introduction** to a definition essay should provide a base from which to expand and at the same time explain to readers why the forthcom-ing definition is useful, significant, or necessary. You may want to report the incident that prompted you to define, say why the subject itself is important, or specify the common understandings, or misunderstand-ings, about its meaning. Several devices can serve as effective beginnings: the etymology of the word; a quotation from another writer supporting or contradicting your definition; or an explanation of what the word does *not* mean (negation). (Try to avoid the overused opening that cites a dic-tionary: "According to *Webster's Dictionary,* _____ means. . . ." Your readers have probably seen this opening many times before.) If it is not implied in the rest of your introduction, you may want to state your thesis so that readers know precisely what your purpose and point are.

The **body** of the essay should then proceed, paragraph by paragraph, to refine the characteristics or qualities of the subject, using the arrangement and methods that will distinguish it from anything similar and provide your perspective. For instance, you might try any of the following approaches:

- *Draw increasingly tight boundaries around the subject,* moving from broader, more familiar meanings to the one you have in mind.
- *Arrange your points in order of increasing drama.*
- *Begin with your own experience of the subject* and then show how you see it operating in your surroundings.

The **conclusion** to a definition essay is equally a matter of choice. You might summarize your definition, indicate its superiority to other definitions of the same subject, quote another writer whose view supports your own, or recommend that readers make some use of the information you have provided. The choice depends—as it does in any kind of essay—on your purpose and the impression you want to leave with readers.

▶ Drafting

While drafting your extended definition, keep your subject vividly in mind. Say too much rather than too little about it to ensure that you capture its essence; you can always cut when you revise. And be sure to provide plenty of details and examples to support your view. Such evidence is particularly important when, as in the earlier example of patriotism, you wish to change readers' perceptions of your subject.

   In definition, the words you use are especially important. Abstractions and generalities cannot draw precise boundaries around a subject, so your words must be as **concrete** and **specific** as you can make them. You'll have chances during revising and editing to work on your words, but try during drafting to pin down your meanings. Use words and phrases that appeal directly to the senses and experiences of readers. When appropriate, use **figures of speech** to make meaning inescapably clear; instead of "Patriotism is childish," for example, you might write "The blindly patriotic person is like a small child who sees his or her parents as gods, all-knowing, always right." The **connotations** of words—the associations called up in readers' minds by words like *home, ambitious,* and *generous*—can contribute to your definition as well. But be sure that connotative words trigger associations suited to your purpose. And when you are trying to explain something precisely, rely most heavily on words with generally neutral meanings.

▶ Revising and Editing

When you are satisfied that your draft is complete, revise and edit it against the following questions and the information in the Focus box.

■ *Have you defined your subject completely and tightly?* Your definition should not leave gaps, nor should the boundaries be so broadly drawn that the subject overlaps something else. For instance, a definition of *hype* that focuses on exaggerated and deliberately misleading claims should include all such claims (some political speeches, say, as well as some advertisements), and it should exclude appeals that do not fit the basic definition (some public-service advertising, for instance).

■ *Does your definition reflect the conventional meanings of the word?* Even if you are providing a fresh slant on your subject, you can't change its meaning entirely, or you will confuse your readers and undermine your own credibility. *Patriotism*, for example, could not be defined from the first as "hatred of foreigners," because that definition strays into an entirely different realm. The conventional meaning of "love of country" would have to serve as the starting point, though your essay might interpret the meaning in an original way.

FOCUS ON UNITY

When drafting a definition, you may find yourself being pulled away from your subject by the descriptions, examples, comparisons, and other methods you use to specify meaning. Let yourself explore byways of your subject — doing so will help you discover what you think. But in revising you'll need to direct all paragraphs to your thesis, and within paragraphs you'll need to direct all sentences to the paragraph topic, generally expressed in a **topic sentence**. In other words, you'll need to ensure that your essay and its paragraphs have **unity**.

One way to achieve unity is to focus each paragraph on some part of your definition and then focus each sentence within the paragraph on that part. If parts of your definition require more than a single paragraph, by all means expand them. But keep the group of paragraphs focused on a single idea. Jessica Sayuri Boissy's essay "One Cup at a Time"

LearningCurve To practice revising for unity, visit *LaunchPad Solo for Readers and Writers* > LearningCurve > Topic Sentences and Supporting Details

(p. 281) proceeds in just such a pattern, as the following outline shows. The first paragraph concludes with Boissy's thesis. Then topic sentences in paragraphs 2–9 specify the paragraphs' topics. A look at Boissy's essay will show you that each of her paragraphs elaborates on its specific topic.

THESIS   For me, this phrase [*ichigo ichie*] has brought awareness of the value of living each day, hour, minute, and second to the fullest and seizing each chance encounter that life unexpectedly brings.

PARAGRAPH 2   Although *ichigo ichie* can be written with the English alphabet, in Japanese, the phrase is written as 一期一会, giving a more visual representation of the meaning.

PARAGRAPH 4   However, the simplicity of meaning shatters when translated into English.

PARAGRAPH 6   In fact, . . . Zen thinking lies at the heart of *chado*, the Japanese tea ceremony.

PARAGRAPH 7   It wasn't until I attended my first tea ceremony in my first year of middle school that I actually experienced *ichigo ichie* in its fullest sensory delight.

PARAGRAPH 8   In that moment, this mixing of sensory impressions . . . helps to create the feeling of *ichigo ichie*.

PARAGRAPH 9   Even before you knew the phrase *ichigo ichie*, you were living this word in your life, because life is about the coming and going — about the changes.

For more on unity in essays and paragraphs, see pages 36–37.

We are happy when we have family, we are happy when we have friends, and almost all the other things we think make us happy are just ways of getting more family and friends.

— Daniel Gilbert

You cannot protect yourself from sadness without protecting yourself from happiness.

— Jonathan Safran Foer

I do not think we have a "right" to happiness. If happiness happens, say thanks.

— Marlene Dietrich

JOURNAL RESPONSE Have you ever said, "I just want to be happy"? Most of us have at some point, whether out loud to a friend or family member or silently to ourselves. Take a few moments to write in your journal about what happiness means to you. What do you want out of life? How do you plan to get it?

Augusten Burroughs

Augusten Burroughs was born Christopher Robinson in 1965 and legally changed his name when he turned eighteen, an effort to distance himself from a traumatic youth. He has held a variety of positions, including advertising copywriter, dog trainer, and commentator for National Public Radio, but Burroughs is best known for a series of painfully open memoirs about his struggles with abuse and addiction: *Running with Scissors* (2002), an examination of parental abandonment and an unwelcome relationship with a pedophile; *Dry* (2003), a personal study of alcoholism; and *A Wolf at the Table* (2008), an indictment of the author's father. Burroughs has also written a novel and several collections of essays and stories, and in 2012 he published *This Is How: Proven Aid in Overcoming Shyness, Molestation, Fatness, Spinsterhood, Grief, Disease, Lushery, Decrepitude and More*, a self-help book he says he "was born to write." Recently the recipient of a Lambda Literary Award as well as an honorary doctorate of letters from the Savannah College of Art and Design, Burroughs lives with his husband in rural Connecticut.

Unhappily Ever After

In this self-contained chapter from *This Is How*, Burroughs draws on personal experience and a dark sense of humor to advise readers on the perils of pursuing happiness. Wanting to be happy, he cautions, is a sure-fire way to make yourself miserable.

"I just want to be happy."   1

I can't think of another phrase capable of causing more misery and per-   2
manent unhappiness. With the possible exception of, "Honey, I'm in love
with your youngest sister and she's agreed to marry me so I'd like a divorce."

Yet at first glance, it seems so guileless. Children just want to be   3
happy. So do puppies and some middle-aged custodians.

Happy seems like a healthy, normal desire. Like wanting to breathe   4
fresh air or shop only at Whole Foods.

But "I just want to be happy" is a hole cut out of the floor and cov-   5
ered with a rug.

Here's the problem: when you say to yourself or somebody else,   6
"I just want to be happy," the implication is that you're not.

So what you want is something you don't have.   7

That's a mole behind your ear. Maybe it's just a mole and that's all it   8
is. Wanting health insurance when you don't have it, wanting your kids
to get a good education—nothing troubling about that.

But maybe that mole is something worse that's going to spread. And   9
you become a person who moves frantically through life grabbing things
off the shelf—the dark-haired boyfriend with the great parents since the
blond musicians haven't worked out so well, the breast implants because
then you'll like your body, the law degree that will make your father so
proud of you and maybe you'll learn to like the law—but never managing
to find the right thing, the one thing that will finally make you feel you
aren't missing something essential, such as the point.

The "I just want to be happy" bear trap is that until you define   10
precisely, just exactly what "happy" is, you will never feel it.

By defining what "happy" means to you in absolutely concrete terms   11
you can then see what actions you need to take—or subtractions you
need to make—to be able to say, "Yup, okay. This is the happy I was looking
for. I've got it now. It's safe to get the breast implants."

If you're not a bespoke sort of person, you could use the standard,   12
off-the-shelf definition.

Happiness is "a state of well-being characterized by emotions ranging   13
from contentment to intense joy."

It's probably far-fetched to think you could be in a state of intense joy   14
for most of the day. But maybe you could be mostly content.

Whatever being happy means to you, it needs to be specific and also   15
possible. Maybe if you didn't have to go to work every day at a job you
only tolerate but instead started your own online jewelry business. Maybe
this would make you happy because you love jewelry; you find it interesting,
you like to make it, you like the people who like it.

When you have a blueprint for what happiness is, lay it over your life 16
and see what you need to change so the images are more aligned.

This recipe of defining what happiness means to you and then 17
fiddling with your life to make the changes needed to make yourself
happy will work for some people. But not for others.

I am one of the others. 18

I am not a happy person. 19

There are things that do make me experience joy. But joy is a fleeting 20
emotion, like a very long sneeze.

I feel contentment rarely, but I do feel it. 21

A lot of the time what I feel is interested. Or I feel melancholy. And 22
I also frequently feel tenderness, annoyance, confusion, fear, hopelessness, friskiness.

It doesn't all add up to anything I would call happiness. 23

What I'm thinking is, is that so terrible? 24

I used to say "I just want to be happy" all the time. I said it so fre- 25
quently and without care that I forgot to refill the phrase with meaning,
so it was just a shell of words.

When I said these words, I had only a vague sense of what happiness 26
even meant to me.

I can see it in others. I even know one person who is happy ninety-five 27
percent of the time, seriously. He's not stupid. As a matter of fact, he's
right here beside me as I write, his own computer on his own lap organizing his playlist. And he makes me happy more often than I have ever been
happy. But I will never be as happy as he is. And I don't mind this because
I might not appreciate his happiness so much if I had it, too.

Also, I know a physicist who loves his work. People mistake his con- 28
stant focus and thought with unhappiness. But he's not unhappy. He's
busy. I bet when he dies, there will be a book on his chest.

Happiness is a wonderful goal for those who are inclined on a genetic 29
level toward that emotional end of the spectrum.

Happiness is a treadmill of a goal for people who are not happy by 30
nature.

Being an unhappy person does not mean you must be sad or dark. You 31
can be interested instead of happy. You can be fascinated instead of happy.

Meaning

1. What is wrong, in Burroughs's estimation, with saying "I just want to be
   happy" (paragraph 1)? What's the harm in expressing a universal human
   desire?

2. In your own words, **paraphrase** Burroughs's understanding of the "standard, off-the-shelf definition" of happiness (paragraph 12). How would he like to see happiness defined instead?

3. The title of this essay is an **allusion**, a reference to something else that Burroughs assumes his readers know of. What does the title refer to? How does the allusion reinforce his meaning?

4. If you are uncertain of the meanings of any of the words listed below, try to guess them from the context of the essay. Then look them up to see how close your definitions were to those in the dictionary. Test out the new words by using each of them in a sentence or two of your own.

guileless (3)	contentment (13, 21)	friskiness (22)
bespoke (12)	melancholy (22)	spectrum (29)

Purpose and Audience

1. Burroughs identifies two kinds of people: those who are happy and those who are not. Which of these groups (if either) do you think Burroughs is addressing, and why?

2. What assumptions does Burroughs make about his audience? How do those assumptions influence his purpose? Support your response with evidence from the essay.

3. What is your attitude toward happiness? Did Burroughs's essay change your way of thinking? If so, how? If not, why not? Use specific examples from the essay to support your answer.

Method and Structure

1. "Unhappily Ever After" identifies several potential synonyms for *happiness*. Make a list of those synonyms, both the "standard" ones (paragraph 12) and Burroughs's own. Which ones come closest to your own understanding of what happiness is? What other synonyms would you propose?

2. Consider how Burroughs uses negation to develop his definition. Why does he focus on unhappiness to the extent that he does?

3. This essay contains many short paragraphs. Do you find the short paragraphs more or less readable than the longer paragraphs used by most of the other writers included in this book? As an exercise in revision, try linking Burroughs's short paragraphs into longer paragraphs wherever such links seem sensible. What specific reasons can you give for each of your changes?

4. **OTHER METHODS**   As writers often do, Burroughs employs several methods to develop his definition, including **division or analysis, cause-and-effect analysis, process analysis, comparison and contrast, classification**, and **example**. What do the examples of happy people he cites in paragraphs 27 and 28 have in common?

Language

1. In several places throughout his essay, Burroughs uses **metaphors** to add depth to his definition. Locate two examples that you find especially striking, and explain their meaning and their effect.

2. Burroughs generally uses the second-person *you* or the first-person *I*. Do you think the essay would have been more or less effective if he had stuck with less intimate alternatives, such as *he, she, they*, or *the unhappy person* throughout? Why?

3. "Unhappily Ever After" contains many vague pronoun references, **comma splices**, and, most notably, **sentence fragments**. Identify at least three instances. (Refer to pp. 44–48 if you need help.) Is this sloppy writing, or does Burroughs break the rules of grammar and punctuation for a purpose? What do the sentence errors contribute to (or take away from) his essay? Explain your answer.

Writing Topics

1. **JOURNAL TO ESSAY**   Burroughs claims that "until you define precisely, just exactly what 'happy' is, you will never feel it" (paragraph 10). In your journal entry (p. 275), you pondered what happiness means to you. Now, build on that entry to write an extended definition of *happiness*. As Burroughs does, present a wide range of examples to suggest various aspects of your subject, and be careful that your personal definition is "specific and also possible," as Burroughs advises (15). Does your definition correspond to conventional assumptions about happiness, or is it more like Burroughs's definition? What characteristics does your definition *not* include?

2. Think of a person you know or know of whose life is unhappy by contemporary standards but satisfying by Burroughs's standards. Write an essay describing this person's personality, interests, and accomplishments in detail, showing how his or her personal values and goals ensured contentment despite pressure from society to be externally happy. Be sure to include plenty of concrete details and examples.

3. **RESEARCH**   Burroughs insists that some people are simply unhappy by nature. Do some library research on the psychological problem of depression. (A periodicals database or the *Diagnostic and Statistical Manual of Mental Disorders* can give you a start, and many books have been written on the subject.) Write a brief essay outlining the contemporary definition of depression and explaining some of its treatments, including therapy and medication. How common is the problem, and what can be done about it?

4. **CONNECTIONS**   Leslie Jamison, in "Sublime, Revised" (p. 162), also writes about unhappiness. Unlike Burroughs, however, Jamison suggests that misery can be an unexpected source of pleasure. Read or reread her essay, and consider how these two writers characterize the notion of desire and its effects. As they explain it, what are the risks and rewards of seeking pleasure? What happens to people who *want* to be happy? to those around them? How might Burroughs and Jamison respond to each other's essays? In an essay of your own, compare their perspectives. Does one seem more on target than the other, in your opinion? Why?

We're all so busy chasing the extraordinary that we forget to stop and be grateful for the ordinary.   —Brené Brown

What I regret most in life are failures of kindness.   —George Saunders

We are cups, constantly and quietly being filled. The trick is knowing how to tip ourselves over and let the beautiful stuff out.   —Ray Bradbury

JOURNAL RESPONSE   How do you cope with the stress of college? of life in general? In your journal, make a list of the activities and mental strategies you use to keep yourself calm and centered. Do some efforts work better than others? Why do you think that is?

Jessica Sayuri Boissy

Jessica Sayuri Boissy was born in 1988 and raised in a bilingual household in San Francisco. The product of a cross-cultural marriage in a highly diverse city, she often found herself effortlessly switching between English and Japanese in order to communicate with her American-born father and her Japanese-born mother. Boissy graduated in 2010 from the University of California, Davis. Two years later she achieved her "childhood dream" of living in Japan, where she teaches English, writes for *Japan Today* and other blogs, and practices Bikram yoga. She spends her free time exploring the museums of modern Tokyo and the shrines and temples of ancient Kyoto.

One Cup at a Time
(Student Essay)

Boissy wrote "One Cup at a Time" for her first-year writing class in response to a prompt asking students to examine a language barrier they had experienced with a single word or phrase. Of *ichigo ichie*, the Japanese proverb the assignment inspired her to translate, Boissy says it reminds us "to cherish even the most seemingly mundane days, for these days will only occur once, never to happen again." Her essay was first published in *Prized Writing,* an anthology of the best student work to come out of the writing program at the University of California, Davis.

Ichigo ichie conveys a Japanese aesthetic ideal relating to transience that,   1
when translated into English, literally signifies "one encounter, one chance." The philosophy behind it is that one should always do one's best

when meeting someone, treasuring each encounter as a once-in-a-lifetime event, even if it is a friend whom one sees often. For me, this phrase has brought awareness of the value of living each day, hour, minute, and second to the fullest and seizing each chance encounter that life unexpectedly brings. Though the ritual of meeting people follows a regular routine, this phrase stresses that each moment is a unique meeting to be lived intently, never to be repeated, as if today were the last time you might meet—in other words, this phrase teaches one to live his or her whole life now—the fullest in the moment.

Unlike the English alphabet, the Japanese writing system is composed of *kanji*, characters that embody the meanings in graphic forms. Although *ichigo ichie* can be written with the English alphabet, in Japanese, the phrase is written as 一期一会, giving a more visual representation of the meaning. The first part of the word, *ichigo* or 一期, symbolizes one period, in the terms of *ichigo ichie*, one lifetime. The second part, *ichie* or 一会, symbolizes one meeting. Thus, when put together the phrase *ichigo ichie* is formed, a phrase that easily rolls out of my mouth. Each character has three syllables, and the *ichi*, signifying the number one, at the beginning of each character gives a particular ring to the phrase, a consistency if not an echo—stressing the importance of only *"one* meeting" in our *"one* lifetime."

Also, because the meaning of *ichigo ichie* can be comprehended visually, nothing impinges on one's understanding. It is as though no interpretation is needed because the visual representation of the characters gives the reader the feeling of the word through the characters. Thus, the reader can be the sole interpreter of what *ichigo ichie* means to him or her.

Jessica Sayuri Boissy

However, the simplicity of meaning shatters when translated into English. Instead, the English language suggests a blizzard of wordy interpretations, such as "with every departure there is an encounter" or "one chance in a lifetime" or "treasure every meeting, for it will never reoccur"—phrases that sound nice but still cannot communicate the simplicity and wholeness of the original phrase.

Phrases and words can be translated into many different languages, but the culture still plays a significant role in understanding not just the literal meaning but also the roots of words. The English equivalents lack the Zen spirit that permeates this phrase. Much like the Zen teachings, *ichigo ichie* teaches the importance of living in the present moment.

In fact, this Zen thinking lies at the heart of *chado*, the Japanese tea   6
ceremony. By concentrating on making tea inside a quiet tearoom, participants in the Japanese tea ceremony can reach a calm state of mind and reflect on themselves, cultivating a serene and mindful attitude towards each ceremony and towards life outside the tearoom. This attitude demands the awareness that although the steps of the ritual have not changed over the centuries, every time people come together over a bowl of tea, they create an original experience. In this context *ichigo ichie* retains the meaning of "one encounter, one chance," but also acquires another meaning—"one cup, one moment." In this context, *ichie* maintains the meaning of "one encounter" but *ichigo* becomes "one bowl of tea."

It wasn't until I attended my first tea ceremony in my first year of   7
middle school that I actually experienced *ichigo ichie* in its fullest sensory delight. I can remember slowly sliding the door to the tearoom and being showered by an abundance of sensations . . .

> . . . *from the fragrance of the sandalwood incense set into the charcoal beneath the hot water kettle to the aroma of freshly whisked green tea* . . .
>
> . . . *from the sound of water coming to a boil to the sound of soft cotton socks gliding over tatami* . . .
>
> . . . *from the handling of the* yakimono, *pottery streaked with ash glaze, to the small wooden lacquer-ware plates* . . .
>
> . . . *from the visual beauty of the calligraphy hanging beside the flower arrangement and, ultimately, from the taste of sweet bean cakes to the flavor of bitter green tea* . . .

In that moment, this mixing of sensory impressions—whereas in   8
everyday life one at a time will do—helps to create the feeling of *ichigo ichie*. Although incense smoke always rises and the water in the kettle eventually boils, the combination of sounds, tastes, smells, textures, and visual pleasures of the day's tea ceremony will never be reproduced exactly that way again. This reflection brings to mind another aspect of the physical nature of the tea ceremony—the interrelationship of three basic elements: *monosuki, furumai,* and *chashitsu,* or things, behavior, and setting. The tea ceremony that I experienced on that day when I was twelve will never be relived in a tea ceremony when I am eighteen. And the same

philosophy can be applied to each day we experience in a lifetime—one should always do one's best, whether it is making tea for another or simply meeting up with a friend, treasuring each encounter as a once-in-a-lifetime event.

Even before you knew the phrase *ichigo ichie*, you were living this   9 word in your life, because life is about the coming and going—about the changes. These changes can take on many forms: our first tea ceremony, high school graduation, twenty-first birthday, or receiving our PhD. And even if we meet each other in class every Tuesday and Thursday, I am not the same student and you are not the same teacher, because we are all participants in this inevitable change. But it is through these changes that *ichigo ichie* stresses the importance of treating each encounter as a once-in-a-lifetime event and focusing on the details of each occasion, the particular people and things involved daily. In other words, living fully in the present—*ichigo ichie*—drinking life, and tea, to its fullest—one cup at a time.

Meaning

1. What is the "cup" to which the title of this essay refers? What is Boissy's main idea?

2. What is the meaning of *Zen* as Boissy uses it in paragraphs 5 and 6? (If necessary, look up the word in an encyclopedia or unabridged dictionary.) How do Zen teachings relate to Boissy's thesis?

3. If you are uncertain of the meanings of any of the words listed below, try to guess them from the context of the essay. Then look them up to see how close your definitions were to those in the dictionary. Test out the new words by using each of them in a sentence or two of your own.

aesthetic (1)	permeates (5)	tatami (7)
transience (1)	serene (6)	lacquer (7)
impinges (3)		

Purpose and Audience

1. What is Boissy's purpose or purposes in writing this essay: to express herself? to explain something? to persuade readers of something? Support your answer by referring to passages from the essay.

2. How can you tell that Boissy wrote this essay for her teacher and her classmates at the University of California, Davis? How do you think her original readers may have responded to her ideas? How do *you* respond? Why?

Method and Structure

1. Why is definition particularly well suited to Boissy's subject and purpose? In what ways is the literal translation of *ichigo ichie* inadequate to explain its meaning?

2. What is the function of the hand-painted Japanese characters Boissy includes with her essay? What additional meanings does the calligraphy impart?

3. Why do you suppose Boissy uses italics and ellipses so extensively in paragraph 7? What is their effect?

4. OTHER METHODS   Explain the tea ceremony Boissy depicts in paragraphs 6–8. How does this use of **process analysis** and **description** help to develop her definition?

Language

1. In addition to *ichigo ichie*, Boissy uses several other Japanese words in her essay. How does she ensure that readers understand their meaning? What do they contribute to her main idea?

2. How would you characterize the overall **tone** of the essay? How does Boissy achieve it?

Writing Topics

1. JOURNAL TO ESSAY   In your journal response (p. 281), you listed some of your strategies for managing stress. How do you react to Boissy's essay? Do you agree with her that life is an endless series of changes and so we must take care to live in the moment? Or do you find her philosophy impractical, her suggestions overly idealistic? Write an essay of your own responding to Boissy's ideas and advice. Be sure to include examples to support your view.

2. Boissy writes that the ritual of a traditional Japanese tea ceremony teaches a lesson that "can be applied to each day we experience in a lifetime — one should always do one's best, whether it is making tea for another or simply meeting up with a friend, treasuring each encounter as a once-in-a-lifetime event" (paragraph 8). Think of some rituals that are important to you and your friends or your family — for instance, a holiday celebration, a vacation activity, a way of decompressing after a difficult week. Choose one such ritual and, in a brief essay, explain it to outsiders. Focus on the details and steps of the ritual as well as on the significance it has for you and other members of your group.

3. **CULTURAL CONSIDERATIONS**   Boissy wrote her essay in response to a prompt asking her to examine a language barrier she had experienced with a single word or phrase. Try your hand at a similar essay of your own. Start by recalling a language barrier you have encountered. It may have involved a language other than English, a regional dialect, a slang term, workplace or academic jargon, or perhaps a generation gap. Focusing on a single word or phrase, examine the misunderstandings you have experienced. You might choose to define the term, as Boissy did, or you could narrate a representative incident involving it or compare and contrast your understanding with other people's comprehension. Whatever approach you choose, be sure to use concrete and specific words as well as vivid descriptions and plenty of detail to ensure that readers understand your meaning.

4. **CONNECTIONS**   While Boissy writes about the pleasures to be found in even the most mundane personal interactions, Barbara Lazear Ascher, in "The Box Man" (p. 257), asserts that we should learn to appreciate our own company, to find "a friend in our own voice." In an essay, compare these two writers' assumptions about relationships, and then draw your own conclusions about the value of friends and family. Consider, for instance, in what ways Ascher's "Box Man" and two lonely women might be said to have embraced or rejected Boissy's notion of *ichigo ichie*, as well as what we stand to gain—or lose—by treasuring each encounter with another person, as Boissy advises. What role do other people play in building and maintaining a happy life?

Gratitude is the fairest blossom which springs from the soul.

—Henry Ward Beecher

Perfection is out of reach. But grace—grace you can reach for.

—Elizabeth Scott

Barn's burnt down—now I can see the moon.

—Mizuta Masahide

JOURNAL RESPONSE   What are you grateful for? Most of us can name at least a few things for which we give thanks, even if we rarely express such appreciation to ourselves or to others. Take a few minutes to jot down in your journal a tally of your blessings.

Julia Alvarez

Julia Alvarez is a novelist, poet, essayist, and teacher who often writes about the complexities of immigration and bicultural identity. She was born in New York City in 1950 and raised in the Dominican Republic until the age of ten, when political upheaval—her father had been part of a failed effort to oust the brutal dictator Rafael Trujillo—forced her family to flee. Alvarez attended Connecticut College, graduated from Middlebury College, and then completed a master's degree in creative writing from Syracuse University in 1975. She traveled the United States teaching poetry and creative writing workshops until she published her first novel, *How the García Girls Lost Their Accents* (1991)—a critical and popular success. Her prolific output since then has spanned several genres, including the novels *In the Time of the Butterflies* (1994), *Saving the World* (2006), and *Return to Sender* (2009); poetry in volumes such as *Seven Trees* (1998) and *The Woman I Kept to Myself* (2004); essays collected in *Something to Declare* (1998); children's novels and picture books like *The Secret Footprints* (2000) and *How Tía Lola Came to Stay* (2001); and the nonfiction study *Once Upon a Quinceañera: Coming of Age in America* (2007). Also a writer-in-residence teaching at Middlebury College, Alvarez lives with her husband on a small working farm in Vermont.

The Practice of Gracias

A little over a decade ago, Alvarez and her husband started Alta Gracia, a literacy and sustainable agriculture initiative in the Dominican Republic. As part of that mission, she regularly travels to the island to advocate on behalf of farm workers. In this 2015 article for *Orion* magazine, she reports on her meetings with one of those workers. Jailed for his own advocacy, he astonishes Alvarez with his capacity for cheer in the worst of circumstances.

One of the things that kept surprising me about Jhonny Rivas was his 1 sense of gratitude.

Jhonny, a Haitian living in the Dominican Republic, a country not 2 known for its kindness toward its neighbor, was arrested almost two years ago on charges of having murdered a witch. But you can't hide the sun with a finger, as the Dominican saying goes: everyone knew that Jhonny was framed for organizing his fellow Haitian workers to demand their rights from the big landowners. Imprisonment was a way of taking him out of circulation and teaching him a lesson.

When I visited him at *la fortaleza*,[1] the dungeon-type fort that also 3 serves as a jail, Jhonny had already been held without a hearing for eight months. The guard at the entrance opened the metal door wide enough for me to step through, then clanged it shut behind me. A stocky, shirtless prisoner with a Hello Kitty[2] locket on a chain around his neck led me down a dim, tunnel-like hallway lined with prisoners. We stopped at what could only be described as a slot in the wall just large enough for a plank with a thin mat on top. A gaunt, dark-skinned man stepped forth and embraced me. The first word out of his mouth was, "Gracias."

A moment before, I had been as close to a circle in hell as I'd ever 4 experienced, except in books. But Jhonny's welcome transformed that world into one of hospitality and warmth.

Under his pillow, Jhonny kept a cell phone. It turned out there was an 5 underground market whereby you could purchase contraband articles from the Hello Kitty guy, who paid the guards to look the other way. When the phone was charged and the winds were blowing in the right direction, I could reach him all the way from Vermont. The weariness in his voice at times bordered on despair. His baby son had died; his wife was sick; no money was coming in; his small plot of land had been razed by intruders.

But invariably, at the end of our conversations, Jhonny would express 6 his gratitude: God had given him the fortitude to get through another day. He thanked me for the call; he asked me to thank my husband; he sent blessings to my children and their children, good health to my friends and their families. Our goodbyes lasted minutes, sometimes trailing off when the wind started blowing in the wrong direction.

[1] Spanish: fortress. [Editors' note.]

[2] A cartoon character featured on a line of products made by the Japanese novelties company Sanrio. [Editors' note.]

I was stunned. Jhonny should be cursing, not blessing, his lot in life. 7
What made him so grateful? His faith? His poverty, so that he was thankful for the least kindness that came his way?

If so, he was far richer than most of us. He had mastered the art of 8
gratitude.

This was a revelation to me. I've always thought of gratitude as oblig- 9
atory good manners in response to getting something you want, or at
least that the giver thought you wanted. Sometimes gratitude wells up
spontaneously as we drink from an overflowing cup of the good things in
life. But it's not that gratitude I'm talking about here. Nor is it the inspirational-poster variety, whereby you talk yourself or more likely someone
else tries to talk you into seeing the glass as half full. The problem with
that kind of gratitude is that you've already taken out the measuring stick.

I'm talking about gratitude when the glass seems completely empty. 10
When you don't even have a glass to your name. Gratitude as an attitude
you cultivate, a practice, a way of life.

Jhonny's gratitude went deeper than his immediate circumstances 11
and recalled a world in which kindness operated and courtesy flowed. He
was able to step outside the oppressive paradigm he was in and keep a
liberating knowledge alive in himself and those around him. Later,
I learned that both Haitian and Dominican prisoners had asked him to be
their chaplain. They wanted access to a valuable asset that couldn't be
purchased on Hello Kitty's black market.

What Karen Armstrong[3] writes about religion is also true of Jhonny's 12
kind of gratitude: "Religion isn't about believing things. It's ethical
alchemy. It's about behaving in a way that changes you, that gives you
intimations of holiness and sacredness."

"Gracias," Jhonny would say, and a whole chain reaction of sweet- 13
ness and light would flood into the very place that seemed to negate such
qualities. No wonder the word for expressing gratitude in Spanish, *gracias*,
is also the word for grace.

And many saving graces do come to those who practice Jhonny's 14
kind of gratitude:

You get to be here now. How else will you notice that someone got 15
here a moment before you, shoveled the path to your office building,
made sure the heat was turned on? Henry James's[4] advice to young writers

---

[3] Karen Armstrong (born 1944) is a British theologian and former nun who has
written several books of comparative religion. [Editors' note.]
[4] Henry James (1843–1916) was an influential American novelist and brother of
philosopher/psychologist William James (1842–1910). [Editors' note.]

is good advice for all of us: "Be him on whom nothing is lost." You gain the whole world, and a soul besides.

You get to live in a bigger world than just your circumstance, that   16
imprisoning and sometimes entitled gated community of self. You are large, you contain multitudes, and how![5] You realize that whatever has helped you become who you are has been made possible by a whole root system of family, friends, strangers, history. Your life doesn't belong just to you, but also to all those who have invested in you.

And because you feel grateful, you are better able to manage the things   17
you aren't grateful for—including being locked up for one year, seven months, and two days, which is how long Jhonny was jailed before he was finally released, all charges dropped. When I spoke to him just after he was freed, Jhonny expressed his gratitude to his lawyers, a mother-daughter team who had defended him pro-bono; to his wife, who had endured so many hardships during his absence; to all of us who had stood by him. He felt grateful, he said, for the opportunity to continue to struggle for the rights of those still behind bars, awaiting their own moment of grace.

Meaning

1. Explain the meaning of the Dominican saying "you can't hide the sun with a finger" (paragraph 2). Why do you suppose Alvarez uses the phrase in her introduction?

2. In one or two sentences, summarize Alvarez's definition of gratitude. Consider not only the functions she mentions but also the relationships she portrays.

3. What does *gracias* mean? Alvarez doesn't offer an English translation, but she does note that it "is also the [Spanish] word for grace" (paragraph 13). So what is *grace*? What other synonyms does Alvarez provide?

4. If you are uncertain of the meanings of any of the words listed below, try to guess them from the context of the essay. Then look them up to see how close your definitions were to those in the dictionary. Test out the new words by using each of them in a sentence or two of your own.

contraband (5)	obligatory (9)	intimations (12)
razed (5)	cultivate (10)	multitudes (16)
fortitude (6)	paradigm (11)	pro-bono (17)
revelation (9)	alchemy (12)	

---

[5]Alvarez alludes here to a famous line from Walt Whitman's poem "Song of Myself," in *Leaves of Grass* (1855): "I am large, I contain multitudes." [Editors' note.]

Purpose and Audience

1. Why do you think Alvarez wrote this essay? Was her purpose to explain her reasons for visiting the Dominican Republic, to report on what she found there, to protest Jhonny Rivas's imprisonment, to persuade readers to examine their own attitudes, or something else? What passages in the essay support your answers?

2. What does Alvarez seem to assume about her readers, particularly regarding their age groups, nationalities, or social and economic backgrounds? In answering these questions, cite specific passages from the essay.

Method and Structure

1. Where and how does Alvarez stipulate the meaning of gratitude as she understands it?

2. Why does Alvarez repeat the words of Karen Armstrong and Henry James in paragraphs 12 and 15? What is the effect of quoting these people?

3. Analyze Alvarez's essay as a piece of definition, considering its thoroughness, its specificity, and its effectiveness in distinguishing the subject from anything similar.

4. **OTHER METHODS** Alvarez develops her definition primarily by **example** and by **cause-and-effect analysis**. What does she identify as the causes of gratitude, and what are the effects of embracing it "as a way of life" (paragraph 10)? What does Jhonny Rivas's experience contribute to the essay?

Language

1. After noting Jhonny Rivas's poverty, Alvarez writes that "he was far richer than most of us" (paragraph 8). Explain the **paradox** of this statement.

2. A poet and novelist, Alvarez enlivens her prose with **metaphors** and literary **allusions**. Find some examples and comment on their effectiveness.

Writing Topics

1. **JOURNAL TO ESSAY** In your journal entry (p. 287) you listed a few things for which you are grateful. Now that you've read Alvarez's essay, do you have any misgivings about your response? Was your list of the "getting something you want" or the "good things in life" types she criticizes (paragraph 9)? Or is your sense of gratitude already of the sort Alvarez praises? Has she inspired you to change the way you look at life, to try to

think and behave more like Jhonny Rivas, perhaps? Why, or why not? Explain your answers in a brief essay.

2. Alvarez tries to explain gratitude academically in paragraphs 12 to 15 as something to do with religion and faith. But she admits that she doesn't know how the psychology works. To what extent do you think our moods can be explained by science? Are our emotions simply the by-products of brain chemistry, as some scientists would suggest? Are they influenced by external factors? Or are they, as Alvarez hopes, attitudes that we can choose? Write an essay, using description and narration, about someone you know (or know of) whose moods are affected by forces beyond his or her control. Be sure to include enough detail to create a vivid portrait for your readers.

3. **CULTURAL CONSIDERATIONS**   As Alvarez suggests, our assessment of the present and our dreams for the future are often influenced by the family, community, or larger culture in which we grew up. Think of a personal goal that seems to have come at least partly from other people. In an essay describe the goal and your feelings about it, and explain the origins of your feelings as best you can.

4. **RESEARCH**   Alvarez acknowledges that the Dominican Republic is "not known for its kindness toward its neighbor" Haiti (paragraph 2), but offers no specifics. In your library or an online periodicals database, research the history of and current state of affairs for Haitians living in their neighboring country. What is their immigration status, for instance, and what rights and responsibilities do they have as residents? Why would Jhonny Rivas need to advocate for Haitian workers, and why would he be jailed for doing so? What could or should be done to improve the lives of people living in the Dominican Republic? Report your findings.

5. **CONNECTIONS**   To what extent, if at all, does Alvarez's idea of *gracias* resemble the concept of *ichigo ichie*, as discussed by Jessica Sayuri Boissy in "One Cup at a Time" (p. 281)? After reading Boissy's essay, list the purposes she believes living in the moment serves. Does feeling gratitude serve similar or different purposes for Jhonny Rivas? What else do Boissy's and Alvarez's definitions have in common? Spell your answer out in an essay, drawing on Boissy's and Alvarez's essays as well as your own experience for evidence.

WRITING WITH THE METHOD

DEFINITION

Select one of the following topics, or any other topic they suggest, for an essay developed by definition. Be sure to choose a topic you care about so that definition is a means of communicating an idea, not an end in itself.

Personal Qualities

1. Intelligence
2. Introversion or extroversion
3. Empathy
4. Responsibility
5. Hypocrisy

Experiences and Feelings

6. A nightmare
7. Love
8. Parenthood
9. An emotion such as fear, excitement, or shame

Social Concerns

10. Charity
11. Homelessness
12. Domestic violence
13. Addiction
14. Racism

Art and Entertainment

15. Dubstep or some other kind of music
16. Steampunk
17. Abstract expressionism or some other art movement

Ideas

18. Freedom
19. Respect
20. Feminism
21. Success or failure
22. A key concept in a course you're taking

WRITING ABOUT THE THEME

▶

PURSUING HAPPINESS

1. The authors in this chapter approach the subject of happiness from very different angles, and each offers a unique definition as a result. Carlin Flora (p. 269) offers a clinical explanation of a psychological state, while Dagoberto Gilb (p. 269) considers the emotional benefits of a tight-knit community. Augusten Burroughs (p. 275) reflects on the sources of unhappiness, Jessica Sayuri Boissy (p. 281) draws on personal experience and cultural tradition to find pleasure in each moment, and Julia Alvarez (p. 287) shows that gratitude, even in the face of adversity, helps to overcome such adversity. How do these writers' perspectives influence their ideas? What do their definitions have in common, and where do they disagree? How do *you* define happiness? Answer in an essay, citing as examples the paragraphs and essays in this chapter and your own experiences and desires.

2. Many of the writers in this chapter identify education as a prerequisite to a happy life. Carlin Flora cites the importance of "a willingness to learn and stretch and grow." Augusten Burroughs notes that the happiest people he knows are also the smartest, Jessica Sayuri Boissy treasures the twice-weekly meetings of her college English class, and Julia Alvarez speaks of "liberating knowledge." What, in your mind, constitutes a good education? Has school been a positive or a negative experience for you? How can you get the most out of your time as a student? Write an essay analyzing the role you think education will play in your potential for success and happiness in the future.

3. In an epigraph on page 275, psychologist Daniel Gilbert asserts, "We are happy when we have family, we are happy when we have friends, and almost all the other things we think make us happy are just ways of getting more family and friends." Most of the writers in this chapter would seem to agree. Dagoberto Gilb, Augusten Burroughs, Julia Alvarez, and Jessica Sayuri Boissy all write of the impact that loved ones have on a person's satisfaction with life, and even Carlin Flora stresses that happiness is enhanced "when you also feel part of a community." How important is family (immediate or extended) in shaping our sense of who we are and what we want? To what extent does the larger community — friends, teachers, neighbors — also play a significant role in forming a person's identity? Answer in an essay, citing as examples the selections in this chapter and observations of your own.

13

CAUSE-AND-EFFECT ANALYSIS

UNDERSTANDING SCIENCE AND TECHNOLOGY

Why did free agency become so important in professional baseball, and how has it affected the sport? What caused the recent warming of the Pacific Ocean, and how did the warming affect the earth's weather? We answer questions like these with **cause-and-effect analysis**, the method of dividing occurrences into their elements to find relationships among them. Like everyone else, you probably consider causes and effects many times a day: Why is the traffic so heavy today? What will happen if I major in art history rather than business? In writing you'll also draw often on cause-and-effect analysis, perhaps explaining why the school's basketball team has been so successful this year, making sense of what made a bridge collapse, or arguing that adult illiteracy threatens American democracy.

Because cause-and-effect analysis attempts to answer *why* and *what if*—two of the most basic questions of human experience—you'll find the method often in your reading as well. The selections in this chapter all attempt to pinpoint a cause-and-effect relationship between recent scientific developments and their consequences, intended or not. In one paragraph, Ross Anderson considers the geopolitical dangers of a warming climate. In another paragraph, Diane Ackerman asserts that electronic gadgets are shifting our vision. In essays, James Kakalios uses physics to explain how traffic jams form, Derek Thompson asks how the emergence of smartphones will shape popular entertainment, and Kaitlyn Haskie considers how twenty-first-century communication tools are both benefiting and undermining traditional indigenous communities.

Reading Cause-and-Effect Analysis

Cause-and-effect analysis is found in just about every discipline and occupation—not just the natural sciences but also social science, history, engineering, medicine, law, business, sports, and more. In any of these fields, as well as in writing done for college courses, the purpose in analyzing may be to explain or to persuade. In explaining why something happened or what its outcome was or will be, writers try to order experience and pin down connections. In arguing with cause-and-effect analysis, they try to demonstrate why one explanation of causes is more accurate than another or how a proposed action will produce desirable or undesirable results.

When writers analyze *causes*, they try to discover which of the events preceding a specified outcome actually made it happen: What factors led to Adolf Hitler's rise in Germany? Why have essential oils become so popular with consumers?

When writers analyze *effects*, they try to discover which of the events following a specified occurrence actually resulted from it: What do we do for (or to) drug addicts when we imprison them? What happens to our foreign policy when the president's advisers disagree over its conduct? These are existing effects of past or current situations, but effects are often predicted for the future: How would a cure for cancer change the average life expectancy of men and women? How might your decision to take family leave impact your future job prospects?

Causes and effects can also be analyzed together, as the questions opening this chapter illustrate.

The possibility of arguing about causes and effects points to the main challenge of this method. Related events sometimes overlap, sometimes follow one another immediately, and sometimes connect over gaps in time. They vary in their duration and complexity. They vary in their importance. Analyzing causes and effects thus requires not only identifying them but also discerning their relationships accurately and weighing their significance fairly.

Causes and effects often do occur in a sequence, each contributing to the next in what is called a *causal chain*. For instance, an unlucky man named Jones ends up in prison, and the causal chain leading to his imprisonment can be outlined as follows: Jones's neighbor, Smith, dumped trash on Jones's lawn. In retaliation, Jones set a small brush fire in Smith's yard. A spark from the fire accidentally ignited Smith's house. Jones was prosecuted for the fire and sent to jail. In this chain each event is the cause of an effect, which in turn is the cause of another effect, and so on to the unhappy conclusion.

Identifying a causal chain partly involves sorting out events in time:

- *Immediate* causes or effects occur nearest an event. For instance, the immediate cause of a town's high unemployment rate may be the closing of a large manufacturing plant where many townspeople work.

- *Remote* causes or effects occur further away in time. The remote cause of the town's unemployment rate may be a drastic decline in the manufacturing company's sales or (more remote) a weak regional or national economy.

Analyzing causes also requires distinguishing their relative importance in the sequence:

- *Major* causes are directly and primarily responsible for the outcome. For instance, if a weak economy is responsible for low sales, it is a major cause of the manufacturing plant's closing.

- *Minor* causes (also called *contributory* causes) merely contribute to the outcome. The manufacturing plant might have closed for the additional reason that the owners could not afford to replace or repair its aging machinery.

As these examples illustrate, time and significance can overlap in cause-and-effect analysis: a weak economy, for instance, is both a remote and a major cause; the lack of funds for repairs is both an immediate and a minor cause.

Since most cause-and-effect relationships are complex, several pitfalls can weaken an analysis or its presentation. One is a confusion of coincidence and cause—that is, an assumption that because one event preceded another, it must have caused the other. This error is nicknamed **post hoc**, from the Latin *post hoc, ergo propter hoc,* meaning "after this, therefore because of this." Superstitions often illustrate post hoc: a basketball player believes that a charm once ended her shooting slump, so she now wears the charm whenever she plays. But post hoc also occurs in more serious matters. For instance, the office of a school administrator is vandalized, and he blames the incident on a recent speech by the student-government president criticizing the administration. But the administrator has no grounds for his accusation unless he can prove that the speech incited the vandals. In the absence of proof, the administrator commits the error of post hoc by asserting that the speech caused the vandalism simply because the speech preceded the vandalism.

Another potential problem to watch for in cause-and-effect writing is the error of **oversimplification**. An effective analysis must consider not just the causes and effects that seem obvious or important but *all* the possibilities: remote as well as immediate, minor as well as major. One form of oversimplification confuses a necessary cause with a sufficient cause:

■ A *necessary* cause, as the term implies, is one that must happen in order for an effect to come about. Note that an effect can have more than one necessary cause: for example, if emissions from a factory cause a high rate of illness in a neighborhood, the emissions are a necessary cause.

■ A *sufficient* cause, in contrast, is one that brings about the effect *by itself.* The emissions are not a sufficient cause of the illness rate unless all other possible causes—such as water pollution or infection—can be eliminated.

Oversimplification can also occur if opinions or emotions are allowed to cloud the interpretation of evidence. Suppose that a writer is examining the reasons a gun-control bill she opposed was passed by the state legislature. Some of the evidence strongly suggests that a member of the legislature, a vocal supporter of the bill, was unduly influenced by lobbyists. But if the writer attributed the passage of the bill solely to this legislator, she would be exaggerating the significance of a single legislator and ignoring the opinions of the many others who also voted for the bill. To achieve a balanced analysis, she would have to put aside her personal feelings and consider all possible causes for the bill's passage.

Analyzing Causes and Effects in Paragraphs

Ross Andersen is a senior editor at *The Atlantic*, in charge of the magazine's science, technology, and health coverage. This paragraph is from "Pleistocene Park," a 2017 feature article on an experimental nature reserve in the Arctic Circle.

If this intercontinental ice block warms too quickly,   Cause: warming
climate
its thawing will send as much greenhouse gas into the

atmosphere each year as do all of America's SUVs, airliners, container ships, factories, and coal-burning plants combined. It could throw the planet's climate into a calamitous feedback loop, in which faster heating begets faster melting. The more apocalyptic climate-change scenarios will be in play. Coastal population centers could be swamped. Oceans could become more acidic. A mass extinction could rip its way up from the plankton base of the marine food chain. Megadroughts could expand deserts and send hundreds of millions of refugees across borders, triggering global war.

Effects:

rising sea levels

acidic oceans

mass extinction

drought

migration

war

Diane Ackerman (born 1948) is a poet and essayist who writes extensively on the natural world. The following paragraph comes from *The Human Age: The World Shaped by Us* (2014), a prose exploration of human civilization and its impact on the planet.

Near- or farsightedness was always assumed to be hereditary. No more. In the United States, one-third of all adults are now myopic, and nearsightedness has been soaring in Europe as well. In Asia, the numbers are staggering. A recent study testing the eyesight of students in Shanghai and young men in Seoul reported that ninety-five percent were nearsighted. From Canberra to Ohio, one finds similar myopia, a generation of people who can't see the forest for the trees. This malady, known as "urban eyes," stems from spending too much time indoors, crouched over small screens. Our eyeballs adjust by changing shape, growing longer, which is bad news for those of us squinting to see far away. For normal eye growth, children need to play outside, maybe watching how a squirrel's nest, high atop an old hickory tree, sways in the wind, then zooming down to the runnel-rib on an individual blade of grass. Is that brown curtsey at the bottom of the yard a wild turkey or a windblown chrysanthemum?

Effect: myopia, or nearsightedness

Causes:

too much screen time indoors

eyeballs adjust by lengthening

not enough time outdoors

Developing an Essay by Cause-and-Effect Analysis

▶ Getting Started

Assignments in almost any course or line of work ask for cause-and-effect analysis: What caused the Vietnam War? In the theory of sociobiology, what are the effects of altruism on the survival of the group? Why did costs exceed the budget last month? You can find your own subject for cause-and-effect analysis from your experiences, from observation of others, from your course work, or from your reading outside school. Anytime you find yourself wondering what happened or why or what if, you may be onto an appropriate subject.

Remember that your treatment of causes or effects or both must be thorough; thus your subject must be manageable within the constraints of time and space imposed on you. Broad subjects like those in the following examples must be narrowed to something whose complexities you can cover adequately.

BROAD SUBJECT   Causes of the decrease in American industrial productivity

NARROWER SUBJECT   Causes of decreasing productivity on one assembly line

BROAD SUBJECT   Effects of cigarette smoke

NARROWER SUBJECT   Effects of parents' secondhand smoke on small children

Whether your subject suggests a focus on causes or effects or both, list as many of them as you can from memory or from further reading. If the subject does not suggest a focus, then ask yourself questions to begin exploring it:

- Why did it happen?
- What contributed to it?
- What were or are its results?
- What might its consequences be?

One or more of these questions should lead you to a focus and, as you explore further, to a more complete list of ideas.

But you cannot stop with a simple list, for you must arrange the causes or effects in sequence and weigh their relative importance. Do the events break down into a causal chain? Besides the immediate causes and effects, are there also less obvious, more remote ones? Besides the major causes or effects, are there also minor ones? At this stage, you may find that diagraming relationships helps you see them more clearly. The follow-ing diagram illustrates the earlier example of the plant closing:

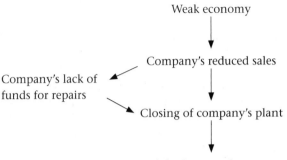

Though uncomplicated, the diagram does sort out the causes and effects and shows their relationships and sequence.

While you are developing a clear picture of your subject, you should also be anticipating the expectations and needs of your readers. As with the other methods of essay development, consider especially what your readers already know about your subject and what they need to be told:

- Do readers require background information?
- Are they likely to be familiar with some of the causes or effects you are analyzing, or should you explain every one completely?
- Which causes or effects might readers already accept?
- Which ones might they disagree with?

If, for instance, the plant closing affected many of your readers — putting them or their relatives out of work — they might blame the company's owners rather than economic forces beyond the owners' control. You would have to address these preconceptions and provide plenty of evidence for your own interpretation.

▶ Forming a Thesis

To help manage your ideas and information, try to develop a working thesis sentence that states your subject, your perspective on it, and your purpose. For instance:

> EXPLANATORY THESIS SENTENCE Unemployment has affected not only my family's finances but also our relationships.

PERSUASIVE THESIS SENTENCE   Contrary to local opinion, the many people put out of work by the closing of Windsor Manufacturing were victims not of the owners' incompetence but of the nation's weak economy.

Notice that these thesis sentences reflect clear judgments about the relative significance of possible causes or effects. Such judgments can be difficult to reach and may not be apparent when you start writing. Often you will need to complete a draft of your analysis before you are confident about the relationship between cause and effect. And even if you start with an idea of how cause and effect are connected, you may change your mind after you've mapped out the relationship in a draft. That's fine: just remember to revise your thesis sentence accordingly.

▶ Organizing

The **introduction** to a cause-and-effect essay can pull readers in by describing the situation whose causes or effects you plan to analyze, such as the passage of a bill in the legislature or a town's high unemployment rate. The introduction may also provide background, such as a brief narrative of a family quarrel; or it may summarize the analysis of causes or effects that the essay disputes, such as townspeople blaming owners for a plant's closing. If your thesis is not already apparent in the introduction, stating it explicitly can tell readers exactly what your purpose is and which causes or effects or both you plan to highlight. But if you anticipate that readers will oppose your thesis, you may want to delay stating it until the end of the essay, after you have provided the evidence to support it.

The arrangement of the **body** of the essay depends primarily on your material and your emphasis. If events unfold in a causal chain with each effect becoming the cause of another effect, and if stressing these links coincides with your purpose, then a simple chronological sequence will probably be clearest. But if events overlap and vary in significance, their organization will require more planning. Probably the most effective way to arrange either causes or effects is in order of increasing importance. Such an arrangement helps readers see which causes or effects you consider minor and which major, while it also reserves your most significant (and probably most detailed) point for last. The groups of minor or major events may then fit into a chronological framework.

To avoid being preoccupied with organization while you are drafting your essay, prepare some sort of outline before you start writing. The outline need not be detailed so long as you have written the details elsewhere or can retrieve them easily from your mind. But it should show all the causes or effects you want to discuss and the order in which you will cover them.

In the **conclusion** to your essay, you may want to restate your thesis—or state it, if you deliberately withheld it for the end—so that readers are left with the point of your analysis. If your analysis is complex, readers may also benefit from a summary of the relationships you have identified. And depending on your purpose, you may want to specify why your analysis is significant, what use your readers can make of it, or what action you hope they will take.

▶ Drafting

While drafting your essay, strive primarily for clarity—sharp details, strong examples, concrete explanations. To make readers see not only *what* you see but also *why* you see it, you can draw on just about any method of writing discussed in this book. For instance, you might **narrate** the effect of a situation on one person, analyze a **process**, or **compare** and **contrast** two interpretations of cause. Particularly if your thesis is debatable (like the earlier example asserting the owners' blamelessness for the plant's closing), you will need accurate, representative facts to back up your interpretation, and you may also need quotations from experts such as witnesses and scholars. If you do not support your assertions specifically, your readers will have no reason to believe them. (For more on evidence in persuasive writing, see the next chapter. For more on finding and documenting sources, refer to Part Three.)

▶ Revising and Editing

While revising and editing your draft, consider the following questions and the Focus box on the next page to be sure your analysis is sound and clear.

- *Have you explained causes or effects clearly and specifically?* Readers will need to see the pattern of causes or effects—their sequence and relative importance. And readers will need facts, examples, and other evidence to understand and accept your analysis.

- *Have you demonstrated that causes are not merely coincidences?* Avoid the error of post hoc, of assuming that one event caused another just because it preceded the other. To be convincing, a claim that one event caused another must be supported with ample evidence.

■ *Have you considered all the possible causes or effects?* Your analysis should go beyond what is most immediate or obvious so that you do not over-simplify the cause-and-effect relationships. Your readers will expect you to present the relationships in all their complexity.

■ *Have you represented the cause-and-effect relationships honestly?* Don't deliberately ignore or exaggerate causes or effects in a misguided effort to strengthen your essay. If a cause fails to support your thesis but still does not invalidate it, mention the cause and explain why you believe it to be unimportant. If a change you are proposing will have bad effects as well as good, mention the bad effects and explain how they are outweighed by the good. As long as your reasoning and evidence are sound, such admissions will not weaken your essay; on the contrary, readers will appreciate your fairness.

■ *Have you used transitions to signal the sequence and relative importance of events?* **Transitions** between sentences can help you pinpoint causes or effects (*for this reason, as a result*), show the steps in a sequence (*first, second, third*), link events in time (*in the same month*), specify duration (*a year later*), and indicate the weights you assign events (*equally important, even more crucial*).

FOCUS ON CONCISENESS

While drafting a cause-and-effect analysis, you may need to wander a bit to discover just what you think about the sequence and relative importance of reasons and consequences. As a result, your sentences may wander a bit, too, reflecting your need to circle around your ideas in order to find them. The following draft passage reveals such difficulties:

> WORDY   Employees often worry about suggestive comments from others. The employee may not only worry but feel the need to discuss the situation with coworkers. One thing that is an effect of sexual harassment, even verbal harassment, in the workplace is that produc-tivity is lost. Plans also need to be made to figure out how to deal with future comments. Engaging in these activities is sure to take time and concentration from work.

Drafting this passage, the writer seems to have built up to the idea about lost productivity (third sentence) after providing support for it in the first two sentences. The fourth sentence then adds more support. And sentences 2–4 all show a writer working out ideas: sentence subjects and verbs do not focus on the main actors and actions of the sentences, words repeat unnecessarily, and word groups run longer than needed for clarity.

These problems disappear from the edited version below, which moves the main ideas up front, uses subjects and verbs to state what the sentences are about, and cuts unneeded words.

> CONCISE   Even verbal sexual harassment in the workplace causes loss of productivity. Worrying about suggestive comments, discussing those comments with coworkers, planning how to deal with future comments — all these activities take a harassed employee's time and concentration away from work.
>
> For more on editing for conciseness, see pages 48–49.

The purpose of life is to produce and consume automobiles.　　—Jane Jacobs

It is only here, in your very own castle of rubber and steel, that you can for a short but blissful time throw off the cloak of civilizations and be the raging Hun you always wanted to be.　　—Adair Lara

Have you ever noticed that anybody driving slower than you is an idiot, and anybody going faster than you is a maniac?　　—George Carlin

JOURNAL RESPONSE　What kind of vehicle do you drive: a hand-me-down wreck? a sporty convertible? an environmentally friendly hybrid? an occasional rental? Write about your first or current car, describing why you chose it, what you use it for, and the reasons you like or dislike it. If you don't have access to a car, do you hope to acquire one someday? What, when, and why—or why not?

James Kakalios

Physicist James Kakalios (born 1958) grew up reading comic books, graduated from the City College of New York, and took his PhD at the University of Chicago in 1982. A professor at the University of Minnesota, he noticed that first-year students were not engaged with his introductory course, so he refashioned it around comic characters, using physics to explain their superpowers. The course was a hit and captured international media attention, encouraging Kakalios to write *The Physics of Superheroes* (2005, second edition 2009), a best-selling volume of popular science that has been translated into six languages. He followed that volume with *The Amazing Story of Quantum Mechanics* (2010), an effort to illuminate the subject without any math, and *The Physics of Everyday Things* (2017), another book of science for laypeople. Kakalios has also served as the science consultant for the movies *The Watchmen* (2007) and *The Amazing Spiderman* (2012) and as an associate fellow at the Minnesota Supercomputing Institute. He lives in Minneapolis with his wife and three children.

The Physics of Everyday Traffic

In *The Physics of Everyday Things*, Kakalios lightheartedly guides readers through the "extraordinary science of an ordinary day": waking up, going to work, keeping a doctor's appointment, flying to a business meeting, giving a presentation, and staying the night in a hotel. In this passage from the book, he has readers imagine themselves stuck in a traffic jam, then uses basic physics to explain how it might have happened. Notice that in providing footnotes, Kakalios does not follow any particular documentation system such as the MLA style explained later in this book (pp. 399–419), but he nonetheless clearly identifies the sources of his information.

Traffic seems to be going at a decent pace, and you begin to wonder if you might 1
actually arrive early to your appointment. Spotting some gaps in the traffic flow, you switch lanes twice, trying to advance and make better time. You glance away from the road for an instant and turn on the radio to check the weather and traffic reports. A nice, partly cloudy day with no significant storms or wind—looks like there won't be any problems with your flight departure. The traffic report is equally positive, with no reports of any significant road construction or automobile accidents during the morning rush hour. Suddenly you see a series of brake lights ahead. You quickly step on the brakes to avoid rear-ending the car in front of you. There is an actual traffic jam that seems to have popped out of nowhere. You smack the steering column in frustration, wishing you could levitate over the stopped cars.

As the density of cars per mile of highway increases, the "flux"—that is, 2
the number of cars passing a given point per hour—will grow. But if the density of cars becomes too large, the flux actually decreases, and a lower flux translates to a longer travel time.[1] Physics says that traffic would be forever smooth and easy, if only we could get rid of the drivers.

When the density of cars on the highway is low, the motion of each 3
one can be treated independently, its speed set by road conditions but not constrained by other vehicles. This is not unlike a very dilute gas of atoms, where the chance of two atoms meeting each other is small. The situation changes as the density of cars increases, when the motion of cars is more like the atoms in a liquid, where movement is limited by their interactions with neighboring atoms. At rush hour, when the density of cars on the road is highest, you can become stuck in a traffic jam that seems to have no obvious cause. These jams are not always caused

---

[1] Books that describe models of traffic flow for a general readership include Mitchel Resnick, *Turtles, Termites and Traffic Jams: Explorations in Massively Parallel Microworlds* (MIT Press, 1994); and Tom Vanderbilt, *Traffic: Why We Drive the Way We Do (and What It Says about Us)* (Knopf, 2008). Those looking for more mathematical discussions should start with Dirk Helbing, "Traffic and Related Self-Driven Many-Particle Systems," *Reviews of Modern Physics* 73, 1067 (2001), and references therein.

by construction or an accident; they are, in fact, an intrinsic instability of the traffic itself.[2]

For higher car densities, the flow of traffic can be described as a   4 collective phenomenon, not unlike when water molecules interact with other nearby molecules to form a large-scale disturbance, such as a wave. In the case of highway traffic, when drivers spot a gap in traffic ahead, they typically do not slow down to increase the spacing between their car and those in front of them, but rather speed up to decrease this separation. Each driver deliberately, though independently, packs his or her car closer to those ahead, forming a cluster. As faster cars meet the rear edge of the cluster, they must slow down; they can speed up again only when they move through the high-density pack and reach the cluster's front edge.[3]

Two factors play a key role in smooth traffic flow: your awareness of   5 the buildup of cars ahead of you, and your response time to any change in the density of cars.[4] A long response time means that it takes longer for drivers to respond to changes in density in front of them, and instead of smooth flow, the clusters will grow larger and larger.

An analogous situation is a sandpile that is built up by dropping dry   6 grains of sand on top of each other, until an unstable cone is formed. If one more grain is added, it can cause an avalanche down the side of the pile.[5] Similarly, at rush hour, cars pack themselves into evergrowing clusters, and then all that is needed for a jam to form is one person at the front edge of the pack tapping on the brakes or just easing off the gas pedal, slowing down slightly. This initiates a backward-propagating avalanche of stopped cars that spontaneously forms a traffic jam. Only those cars on the front line are able to take advantage of the now-lower density

---

[2] These intrinsic jams can cost us real money—a 2011 "Urban Mobility Report" from the Texas Transportation Institute estimated the economic impact of traffic jams on the US economy to be roughly $100 billion per year, equivalent to $750 per commuter.

[3] B. S. Kerner and P. Konhauser, "Cluster Effect in Initially Homogeneous Traffic Flow," *Physical Review E* 48, 2335 (1993); Kai Nagel and Maya Paczuski, "Emergent Traffic Jams," *Physical Review E* 51, 2909 (1995); H. Y. Lee, H.-W. Lee, and D. Kim, "Origin of Synchronized Traffic Flow on Highways and Its Dynamic Phase Transition," *Physical Review Letters* 81, 1130 (1998); B. S. Kerner, "Experimental Features of Self-Organization in Traffic Flow," *Physical Review Letters* 81, 3797 (1998).

[4] Robert E. Chandler, Robert Herman, and Elliott W. Montroll, "Traffic Dynamics: Studies in Car Following," *Operations Research* 6, 163 (1958).

[5] While there is considerable overlap between the dynamics of granular media and traffic flow (see, for example, the proceedings of the International Workshop on Traffic and Granular Flow, held every two years for the past two decades), the equations describing a sandpile's instability differ from those modeling the spontaneous formation of traffic jams.

of cars ahead of them and accelerate out of the jam. Those in the middle and back end of the stalled pack must wait for this leading edge to diffuse back to them before they can resume their journey. Even when the car in front has moved on, the next car does not instantly start accelerating, as its driver also has a finite response time.[6] Of course, while the stopped cars are waiting for the unblocked front edge of the cluster to reach them, new cars are stopping and joining the jam from the rear.

If you were to drive at a steady, uniform speed, keeping pace with the average flow of traffic, then not only would your chances of getting stopped in a spontaneous jam diminish, but you would actually make it easier for the drivers following you. By driving at a steady speed and deliberately *not* shrinking any gaps, you will avoid joining a dense cluster of cars ahead; and if a jam does form, you will give it time to evaporate before you reach it.[7] In essence, you should elect to drop out of the tail end of a traffic wave, smoothing out the density of cars on the road. If all cars drove at the posted speed limit, or at the same average velocity, then the numbers of cars that a highway could carry would climb to the theoretical maximum, and you, along with every other driver, would reach your destination faster.

Meaning

1. Describing a typical drivers' behavior, Kakalios writes, "you switch lanes twice, trying to advance and make better time" (paragraph 1). Does he approve of this habit?

2. Does this essay have a thesis? What (or who) is to blame for traffic back-ups that "have no obvious cause" (paragraph 3), according to Kakalios?

3. What is "flux" (paragraph 2), as Kakalios defines it? Why is it important to his explanation of traffic jams?

4. If you are uncertain of the meanings of any of the words listed below, try to guess them from the context of the essay. Then look them up to see how close your definitions were to those in the dictionary. Test out the new words by using each of them in a sentence or two of your own.

levitate (1)	dilute (3)	diffuse (6)
density (2)	intrinsic (3)	finite (6)
constrained (3)	propagating (6)	velocity (7)

---

[6] Takashi Nagatani, "Traffic Jams Induced by Fluctuation of a Leading Car," *Physical Review E* 61, 3534 (2000).

[7] Junfang Tian, Rui Jiang, Geng Li, Martin Treiber, Bin Jia, and Chenqiang Zhu, "Improved 2D Intelligent Driver Model in the Framework of Three-Phase Traffic Theory Simulating Synchronized and Concave Growth Patterns of Traffic Oscillations," *Transportation Research Part F: Traffic Psychology and Behavior* 41, 55 (2016).

Purpose and Audience

1. Is the author's purpose in this piece to explain or to persuade? What does he hope readers will do or believe as a result of reading his cause-and-effect analysis?

2. Who is the "you" being addressed in the opening and closing paragraphs? What do these paragraphs and the rest of the essay tell you about the author's conception of his audience?

Method and Structure

1. How do traffic jams happen, absent accidents or construction? Explain the causal chain as Kakalios outlines it.

2. The author opens and closes his essay by having readers imagine driving in heavy traffic. What is the effect of this scenario?

3. A college professor, Kakalios is careful to cite the sources of his information. What does this material contribute to his analysis?

4. OTHER METHODS   Where in the essay does Kakalios use **comparison and contrast** to explain the physics of traffic? Does anything about these **analogies** strike you as unusual? Why, or why not?

Language

1. Why do you suppose the entire first paragraph of this essay is printed in italics? Do you find the author's strategy here effective, or not? Why?

2. How would you characterize Kakalios's **tone**? How seriously does he take his subject? Support your answer with specific details, sentence structures, and phrases from the essay.

Writing Topics

1. JOURNAL TO ESSAY   Building on your journal response (p. 306), write an essay in which you **analyze** the benefits and drawbacks of your current mode of transportation. Make a list of all the elements that constitute a particular vehicle or public conveyance (such as a bus or subway). In your essay examine each element to show what it contributes to the whole. Be sure your principle of analysis is clear to readers.

2. How successfully does Kakalios explain physics to an audience of non-scientists? Was his meaning clear to you? Write an essay identifying the strategies he uses to connect with readers and assessing their effectiveness. What, if anything, might he have done to better explain his specialized subject to regular people? Why do you think so?

3. RESEARCH Kakalios jokes in paragraph 2 that "traffic would be forever smooth and easy, if only we could get rid of the drivers," but some would say that getting rid of drivers is not only desirable but also possible, even inevitable. Look into the efforts some automotive manufacturers and technology companies are putting into developing driverless cars. Who is attempting to make autonomous vehicles, and why? How would they work? What are some of the controversies surrounding their invention? Do you applaud the idea of driverless cars, or do you object to it? Why? Write an argumentative essay that addresses the issue of autonomous vehicles seriously. To what extent, and where, should automotive manufacturers and tech giants be allowed to test them? How safe can they be? Under what circumstances, if any, should drivers be able to override their features? How likely are they to be sold to the public any time soon? Be sure to include examples to support your opinions.

4. CONNECTIONS While Kakalios uses science and objective analysis to urge readers to change their individual driving habits for the greater good, Julia Alvarez, in "The Practice of Gracias" (p. 287), takes a very different approach to persuasion, focusing emotionally on one person's habits of mind to nudge readers to shift their own attitudes for personal benefit. Write an essay in which you compare and contrast the tone, style, and approach in each essay. Which author's approach do you find more effective in convincing readers to change their behaviors, and why?

What the mass media offers is not popular art, but entertainment
which is intended to be consumed like food, forgotten, and replaced
by a new dish.
                                                    —W. H. Auden

The medium is the message.
                                                    —Marshall McLuhan

I'm in the middle of my life, and I just don't have enough years left
to spend a large proportion of them inside an iPhone.   —Zadie Smith

JOURNAL RESPONSE   What kind of media do you regularly consume: movies? cable shows? network news? music? magazines? social network feeds? game apps? something else? And how do you access your news and entertainment: broadcast to a television? on DVD or Blu-ray? streaming to a device? housed on a Web site? on the radio? through print? some other way? Write about the mass media products you most enjoy, describing when and how often you watch or read and the reasons you do so. (Alternatively, write about the mass media products you find most troublesome. What problems do you have with them?)

Derek Thompson

Called "one of the brightest new voices in American journalism" and named to both *Inc.* and *Forbes* magazines' "Thirty under Thirty" lists of promising talent, Derek Thompson has quickly established a distinguished career as a writer and speaker. Born in 1986 and raised in Washington, DC, he earned a bachelor's degree with a triple major in journalism, political science, and legal studies from Northwestern University in 2008 and immediately landed a position at the *Atlantic*, where he is now a senior editor. Thompson's insightful explorations of economics, technology, and the media have also appeared in *Slate*, *Business Week*, *Business Insider*, and the *Daily Beast*. He is a weekly guest on National Public Radio's *Here and Now* and makes frequent appearances on television news discussion panels. Thompson's first book, *Hit Makers: The Science of Popularity in an Age of Distraction* (2017), was, fittingly, an instant bestseller. He lives in New York City.

The Making of Hits

Thompson is highly regarded for his skill at constructing sophisticated and uncannily astute analyses of millennial culture, connecting dots that others might not even see. In this essay adapted from the introduction to *Hit Makers*, he starts with a story about the runaway success of Brahms's lullaby in the nineteenth century to show how distribution technologies shape the forms of entertainment we consume today.

Johannes Brahms, born in 1833 in Hamburg, was one of the most well-known composers of his time. "Wiegenlied"—"Lullaby and goodnight, with roses bedight. . ."—was his most immediate success. Published at the height of his popularity in 1868, the song was written as a lullaby for an old friend to sing to her new baby boy. But it soon became a hit throughout the continent, and the world. . . . 1

In Brahms's time, if you wanted people to hear your symphony, you needed to find musicians and a concert hall. Commercial music was scarce, and the music business belonged to the people who controlled the halls and the printing presses. 2

But today, something interesting is happening. Scarcity has yielded to abundance. The concert hall is the Internet, the instruments are cheap, and anybody can write their own symphony. The future of hits will be democratic, chaotic, and unequal. Millions will compete for attention, a happy few will go big, and a microscopic minority will get fantastically rich. 3

The revolution in media is clearest in the last sixty years in moving pictures and video. When the biblical blockbuster *Ben-Hur* premiered on November 18, 1959. before a celebrity audience of more than 1,800 at Loew's State Theatre in New York City, the movie industry was the third-largest retail business in the United States, after groceries and cars (Epstein 6). The movie set Hollywood records for the largest production budget and the most expensive marketing campaign ever, and it became the second-highest-grossing movie in history at that time, behind *Gone with the Wind*. 4

The twinkling of camera flashes at that premiere might have blinded some movie executives to the fact that Americans' monogamous relationship with the silver screen was already ending. Television proved an irresistible seductress. By 1965, more than ninety percent of households had a television set, and they were spending more than five hours watching it every day (Gordon 418). The living room couch replaced the movie theater seat as the number of movie tickets bought per adult fell from about twenty-five in 1950 to four in 2015 (Orbach and Einav 137). 5

Television replaced film as the most popular medium of visual storytelling, along with a massive shift in attention and dollars—from weekly movie tickets to cable bills, whose monthly payments have supported a vast ecosystem of live sports, both brilliant and formulaic dramas, and endless reality shows. The most famous moviemaking corporations in the 6

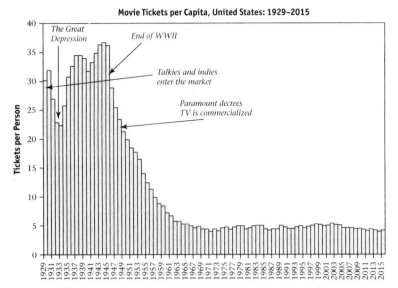

Movie Tickets per Capita, United States: 1929–2015

*Source: Barak Orbach (2016).

world, like the Walt Disney Company and Time Warner, have for years made more profit from cable channels like ESPN and TBS than from their entire movie divisions (Thompson 22). In the early twenty-first century, every movie company is not so secretly in the television business.

But today television is merely the largest screen in a glittering world of glass. In 2012, for the first time ever, Americans spent more time interacting with digital devices like their laptops and phones than with television (Meeker, "2013 Internet"). In 2013, the world produced almost four billion square feet of LCD screens, or about eighty square inches for every living human being ("Spread"). In developing regions—like China, Indonesia, and sub-Saharan Africa—audiences skipped the era of desktops and laptops altogether and started with computers in their pockets.

In the big picture, the world's attention is shifting from content that is *infrequent, big,* and *broadcast* (i.e., millions of people going to the movies once a week) to content that is *frequent, small,* and *social* (i.e., billions of people looking at social media feeds on their own glass-and-pixel displays every few minutes).

As late as 2000, the media landscape was dominated by one–to–one-million productions. on movie screens, television screens, and car radios. But ours is a mobile world, where hits, like *Angry Birds,* and empires, like *Facebook,* thrive on tiny glassy plates. In 2015, the technology analyst

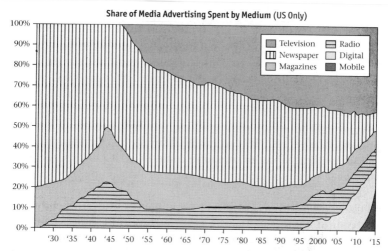

Share of Media Advertising Spent by Medium (US Only)

Bloomberg eMarketer. Author's analysis | Matthew Ball.

Mary Meeker reported that one quarter of America's media attention is devoted to mobile devices that did not exist a decade ago ("2016 Internet"). Television is not dying so much as it is pollinating a billion video streams on a variety of screens, most of which people can carry in their hands. Television once freed "moving images" from the clutches of the cineplex; in the historical sequel, mobile technology is emancipating video from the living room.

As the medium changed, so have the messages. Traditional broadcast 10 television was live, ad supported, and aired once a week. This made it a perfect home for dramas and crime procedurals that relied on several cliff-hangers per episode (to extend viewership throughout the commercials) and pat endings. But streaming television, which is often commercial-free, rewards audiences who watch for several hours at a time. People don't have to stop after one episode of *House of Cards* on Netflix or *Downton Abbey* on Amazon Video; they can watch as much as they want. Combining the aesthetic of film, the episodic nature of traditional television, and the "binge" potential of a novel or Wagnerian[1] opera, the near future of television isn't bound by the straitjacket of one-hour blocks. It's "long-form"—or, perhaps, *any-form.*

Meanwhile, smaller content is eroding television from the bottom. 11 In April 2013, Robby Ayala, a Florida Atlantic University senior, posted

---

[1] Richard Wagner (1813–83) was a German composer. [Editors' note.]

several videos making fun of the campus's abundance of raccoons on *Vine*, a defunct social network of six-second loops that, for millions of young people, made for better television than television. When he amassed more than one million followers a few months later, he dropped out of law school and went to work for a Twitter-owned network for *Vine* stars. He amassed 3.4 million followers and a billion total views of his videos and earned a living by performing in sponsored posts for companies like HP.[2] Actors used to go to Los Angeles or New York because those cities housed the gatekeepers who owned the distribution of media. But now any person with a phone or computer could be next week's viral sensation. In this moment of gate-crashers and global attention, anybody can be a hit maker.

Technology has always shaped entertainment—and our expectations   12
of what sort of content is "good." In the eighteenth century, audiences who attended symphonies paid for a long evening's performance. In the early twentieth century, the music industry moved into the business of radio and vinyl. The first ten-inch vinyl records could comfortably hold about three minutes of music, which helped shape expectations that a modern pop single shouldn't be more than 240 seconds. Today, a *Vine* is just six seconds.

Is six-second entertainment ludicrously brief? It is—if you were raised   13
on Schubert,[3] Brahms, and concert halls. It's not—if you were raised on Robby Ayala, *Facebook*, and the 3.5-inch screen of a smartphone. For better and for worse, people tend to gravitate toward the familiar, and technology shapes these familiarities.

The screens are getting smaller, and they're also getting smarter. We   14
used to merely consume content. Now the content consumes us too—our behaviors, our rituals, and our identities. Before the 1990s, the music industry had no daily information on who was listening to songs in their homes and on the radio. Today, every time you play a song on your phone, the music industry is listening, too, and using your input to guide the next hit. Facebook, Twitter, and digital publishers have tools that tell them not only what story you click on, but also how far you read and where you click next. We used to just play the hits; now the hits play us back.

These smart devices have injected a measure of science into the work   15
of building hits and helping companies crack that ultimate code for consumers and audiences: what do we pay attention to, and why?

---

[2] HP, formerly known as Hewlett Packard, is a technology company that manufactures and sells computers, tablets, and printers. [Editors' note.]

[3] Franz Schubert (1797–1828) was an Austrian composer. [Editors' note.]

Works Cited

Epstein, Edward Jay. *The Big Picture: Money and Power in Hollywood.* Random House, 2005.

Gordon, Robert. *The Rise and Fall of American Growth: The US Standard of Living Since the Civil War.* Princeton UP, 2016.

Meeker, Mary. "2013 Internet Trends Report." *KPCB*, Kleiner Perkins Caulfied Byers, 31 May 2013, www.kpcb.com/blog/2013-internet-trends.

– – –. "2016 Internet Trends Report." *KPCB*, Kleiner Perkins Caulfied Byers, 1 June 2016, www.kpcb.com/blog/2016-internet-trends-report.

Orbach, Barak Y. and Liran Einav. "Uniform Prices for Differentiated Goods: The Case of the Movie-Theater Industry." *International Review of Law and Economics*, 27, 2007, pp. 129–53.

"The Spread of Glass." *Benedict Evans Blog*, Slack, 3 Jan. 2014, ben-evans .com/benedictevans/2014/1/3/the-spread-of-glass.

Thompson, Derek. "The Most Valuable Network." *The Atlantic*, Sept. 2013, pp. 22–24.

Meaning

1. Does Thompson have a thesis? Try to express his main idea in your own words.

2. "As the medium changed," Thompson writes, "so have the messages" (paragraph 10). What does he mean? To what famous statement is he **alluding** here? (Hint: take another look at the quotations preceding the essay on p. 312.)

3. How, according to Thompson, did advertising affect the content of "[t]raditional broadcast television" (paragraph 10)? How does he believe the recent shift to streaming will shape such programming moving forward?

4. What does the entertainment industry stand to gain from recent advances in "smart" mobile technology, as Thompson sees it? How, that is, will they see to it that "the hits play us back" (paragraph 14)?

5. If you are uncertain of the meanings of any of the words listed below, try to guess them from the context of the essay. Then look them up to see how close your definitions were to those in the dictionary. Test out the new words by using each of them in a sentence or two of your own.

monogamous (5)	pollinating (9)	defunct (11)
seductress (5)	cineplex (9)	gatekeepers (11)
medium (6)	emancipating (9)	ludicrously (13)
ecosystem (6)	procedurals (10)	
formulaic (6)	aesthetic (10)	

Purpose and Audience

1. What seems to be Thompson's primary purpose in this piece? Does he want to express his opinion about technology and popular entertainment? explain the demise of television? persuade readers to upgrade their phones? something else? Why do you think so?

2. For whom is Thompson writing? How can you tell?

Method and Structure

1. What specific cause does Thompson examine in this piece? What does he say will be its effects?

2. Take a close look at the two graphs Thompson provides. What is the purpose of these visuals? Where did they come from? What do they contribute to his analysis?

3. A journalist, Thompson supports his ideas with information from published studies. Locate at least three instances. How effective do you find this evidence? Is it more, or less, persuasive than the examples he takes from his own experience? Why do you think so?

4. OTHER METHODS   Thompson provides many **examples** of new technologies changing entertainment, and he uses **division or analysis** to assess the nature of these changes. What does he accomplish by using these methods?

Language

1. Thompson uses several **figures of speech**, such as "today television is merely the largest screen in a glittering world of glass" (paragraph 7), a **metaphor**. Find two or three other figures of speech, and analyze how they contribute to Thompson's meaning and help convey his attitude toward popular media.

2. How would you characterize Thompson's **style**? Is it appropriate, given his purpose and his audience?

Writing Topics

1. JOURNAL TO ESSAY   Building on your journal response (p. 312), analyze your preferences as a consumer of mass media, answering the question Thompson poses at the end of his essay: "what do [you] pay attention to, and why?" (paragraph 15). Make a list of all the elements that constitute your preferred medium and the setting(s) in which you enjoy it. Why do you prefer the media products that you do? What makes them superior

to the alternatives? In your essay, examine each element to show what it contributes to the whole. Be sure your principle of analysis is clear to readers.

2. "For better and for worse," Thompson writes, "people tend to gravitate toward the familiar, and technology shapes these familiarities" (paragraph 13). What does he mean? And do you agree? In an essay of your own, develop one example of a now familiar media technology — such as radio, film, television, streaming media, smartphones, or tablets — that, in your opinion has (or has not) affected popular entertainment or society in a meaningful way. As you write, consider the original purposes for the technology, the way it came to be used, and its intended and unintended effects on individual behavior.

3. CULTURAL CONSIDERATIONS As Thompson suggests, American television programs are watched all over the world. *House of Cards*, for example, is a big hit in China, and *Baywatch* remains one of the most popular shows in Germany. Many global viewers say they watch such programming to improve their English language skills or to learn about American culture. But what are they learning? Write an essay that focuses on a particular type of show — cable news, for example, or medical dramas — and explores how a non-American viewer might interpret it. Does the program provide an accurate depiction of life in the United States, or does it distort reality?

4. CONNECTIONS Thompson writes of popular music, "every time you play a song on your phone, the music industry is listening, too, and using your input to guide the next hit" (paragraph 14). Similarly, Moises Velasquez-Manoff, in a paragraph from "The Meaning of 'Despacito' in the Age of Trump," analyzes the elements behind one such hit (p. 150). How might Thompson explain the song's success? Building on his and Velasquez-Manoff's assessments of the music industry, write an essay in which you analyze the state of popular music in the United States today. Base your analysis on your own and others' experiences with popular music, on your reading about it, and, if possible, on the experiences of any musicians you know.

Now the cliques are moving online. —Kim Komando

Rather than bringing me closer to others, the time that I spend online isolates me from the most important people in my life: my family, my friends, my neighborhood, my community. —Clifford Stoll

There are three kinds of death in this world. There's heart death, there's brain death, and there's being off the network. —Guy Almes

JOURNAL RESPONSE How do you use your mobile devices? Do you make phone calls with them? send text messages? stick to social media such as *Twitter* or *Instagram*? Write a short journal entry about how you connect with your friends, family, and community online. How would your relationships suffer or improve if you didn't have constant access to the Internet?

Kaitlyn Haskie

Kaitlyn Haskie (born 1995) is a member of the Diné, or Navajo, tribe in Lukachukai, Arizona. As a student at Northern Arizona University, she majored in microbiology and applied indigenous studies, graduating in 2018. Haskie harbors a strong desire to give back to her community and plans to pursue a career in medicine or public health. To that end, she has volunteered at the John Hopkins Center for American Indian Health and the Tse Ho Tso Medical Center, interned with the National Institutes of Health, and produced oral histories with Navajo elders. "Being betwixt and between," Haskie observes, "I am balancing two cultures, my Navajo culture and the Western culture. Keeping equilibrium has proven to be a tumultuous process; however, it has been one of my greatest features."

A Paradigm Shift: Indigenous Peoples in the New Millennium
(Student Essay)

Haskie wrote "A Paradigm Shift" in 2015 for a university-wide scholarship contest, taking first place. Her essay explores the conflict that arises from straddling cultures and examines the far-reaching effects technology is having on American Indian communities and identities. She draws on published materials and personal interviews to support her ideas, and so she documents her sources in MLA style (see pp. 399–419). The explanatory gloss notes are also Haskie's.

Among the Navajo on the reservation where I live, amidst the winter frost 1
and chill, we are engaged in traditional winter storytelling. *Shihastoi*[1]
delight in sharing stories of old, tales of Coyote and his scheming, and
other traditional lore. Once the grandfathers don this persona, no narrative
is left untold; even the *Hajinei*[2] stories are brought forth to tell of the Navajo
"emergence" from world to world. Throughout our journey, the Navajo
people have fashioned traditional tales and accounts revealing our origins,
as well as those of many other creatures and beings. In the *Diné*[3] creation
story, there are four or five worlds: the Black, the Blue, the Yellow, and the
White and/or Glittering world. I have often heard that we are currently
living in the Glittering world (depending on whose *Cheii*[4] is consulted), as
exemplified by the glisten and gleam of modern technology.

While technology was slow to arrive on the reservation, rapid and 2
wide-ranging technological advances have brought the Navajo Nation
swiftly and inexorably to the doorstep of the modern, often-beguiling
Western world. In recent years, these advances have dictated that even
those community members living in the deep recesses of the Navajo
Nation are not immune to technology's wonders. Today, somewhere at
their winter sheep camp, *Shimasani*[5] and *Cheii* are listening to the radio
station KTNN, the voice of the Navajo Nation.

The existence of media like radio, cell phones, and the Internet has 3
brought the Navajo people, along with others around the globe, into the
twenty-first century. In its most useful form, technology has been put to
service revitalizing Navajo and other tribal languages and cultures, acting
as a medium for linguistic and cultural vitality. Continuously threatened
since the colonization of the Americas, notably by government attempts
at forced assimilation during the boarding school era, our traditional languages and practices require our unwavering attention. However, with
the presence of multimedia platforms, preservation is more achievable
and Native issues are increasingly foregrounded.

American Indians are using apps, Web sites, and television programs 4
as vehicles to document, preserve, and share indigenous languages, cultures, and issues. For example, in 2011, First Nations Experience, or FNX,
became the first twenty-four-hour television network geared toward an
indigenous audience (Guskin and Mitchell). The programing includes

---

[1] Navajo male elders.

[2] Emergence.

[3] The Navajo people's name for themselves.

[4] Maternal grandfather; he usually takes on the role of storyteller.

[5] Maternal grandmother.

Native-produced or -themed documentaries, Native arts, and dramatic series, all illustrating the lives and cultures of Native peoples around the world ("About Us"). Another example would be the Rosetta Stone Endangered Language Program, which works to preserve and revitalize indigenous languages. Native communities like the Iñupiaq, Mohawk, Chitimacha, and Navajo have partnered with Rosetta Stone to release customized language software ("Endangered Languages"). Multimedia platforms have opened new spaces for learning indigenous language and culture as well as reaching broader audiences with information about Native issues.

However, the benefits of technology have been accompanied by less   5
positive effects. Like most tribal peoples, the Navajo are animistic believers. Our traditions and culture have been shaped by the presence and awareness of life and spirit all around us and also present in our native language. Language is imbued with a spirit of immense power; to speak a word is to give that word life, and each pronouncement must be instilled with respect. It is here that technology fails us, seeming to belittle the sacredness of language and removing from it the immediacy and intimacy that can only be achieved through living human interaction, often between grandparents, children, grandchildren, and great-grandchildren.

Although groundbreaking technology has allowed for contempo-   6
rary indigenous peoples to reconnect to their Native roots, heritages, and cultures, one of its unintended consequences has been to devalue the human presence in language and culture. Dialog is a staple of indigenous identities. Traditional life lessons passed on orally from Navajo elders to daughters and sons, nieces and nephews, and other family members cannot be separated from the expressions, gestures, laughter, tears, and life experiences that accompany these lessons. It is true that technology has helped contemporary indigenous scholars to engage more fervently in cultural practice, from ceremonies to storytelling. But for many elders, as well as for many young Navajo people who look to them for guidance, technology has created an empty space where physical presence once resided. It is no wonder that some persist in cursing technology under their breaths, as it seems to threaten their very existence. Navajo youth often seem to rely more on googled Web sites than on those whose myriad experiences form the continuity between individuals, generations, and communities.

Presently, there are approximately 370 million indigenous peoples   7
worldwide, each with distinct cultures, traditions, histories, and individual stories. The development of technology has allowed indigenous peoples to reach greater audiences, and those audiences in turn take greater note of indigenous people's knowledge, values, frameworks, and narratives.

Our indigenous knowledge increasingly takes the national and international stage as we participate in global struggles for civil and human rights, environmental sustainability, justice, and equity. We are more visible and our voices resonate with more authority on every continent, as well as here in this country.

Nonetheless, I feel deeply fortunate when I enter the reservation, where service connections grow fainter and technology loses its appeal and sway. Then I experience another, truer connectivity sitting by the fire with my grandfather, listening to his stories. No longer is time of the essence. No longer must e-mails, phone calls, and text messages be promptly answered. A nagging sense of having been rude, disrespectful, or uncooperative by ignoring technology and its demands wanes and disappears. This is a world I cherish, where my ancestors are alive in the sound of my grandfather's voice and where the rush of linear time surrenders to stillness. 8

Indigenous peoples are tasked with navigating two worlds: the Western world and our Native one. As we advance into the future, we are strengthened by the heritage that we carry with us, one that informs our thoughts, words, and actions. The Navajo philosophy of *k'é* guides our relationships and interactions, creating a universe of connectivity. In his book *Navajo Courts and Navajo Common Law: A Tradition of Tribal Self-Governance*, Justice Raymond Austin defines *k'é* as the understanding that "all beings in the universe are interrelated, interconnected, and interdependent; thus, all beings are relatives in a theoretical sense" (83). He explains that our relationships encompass all levels, including the human, the universal, and the spiritual. The Navajo idea of connectivity is transcendent; it is the epitome of genuine connectivity that extends beyond technology to every dimension of the greater world. In a wonderful illustration of the weaving together of the natural world and the world that humans have fashioned, a Navajo elder explained that the "new" technology was not at all surprising to him: the florescent lights of the modern buildings were simply manifestations of the sun, now shining indoors (Begay). 9

Another elder, Miranda Haskie, shares her own view of technology: 10

Before all of this [she gestures to computer and entire room] we lived in a one room Hogan, and we listened to *Cheii* as he told stories through *ma'ii*,[6] about how he's always showing off, in the Coyote and lizard story,[7]

---

[6] Coyote.

[7] In the winter story "Coyote and the Lizards," Coyote wants to join the lizards in sliding down a hill on a rock slab. The lizards tell him that he should not do it; however, Coyote still wants to participate. He tries to sled but gets hurt. Such stories are meant for both entertainment and instruction.

he does it, everyone gets out of the way and then he messes up. He was taught humility. [Nowadays] we live in separate homes. We resort to technology. We don't listen to grandpa or grandma.

For countless generations, Navajos have gathered around fires, listening spellbound to stories both entertaining and instructive, many reserved for winter months when particular animals are deep in hibernation. For us, fire is a source of knowledge, thus making it a prime setting for powerful teachings, one of which is that fire itself, like knowledge, is sacred. Both sustain and enrich life. Treated recklessly, however, both can inflict needless harm. As human beings, whether we fan the sparks of fire or power-on the electronics that surround us, we need to be guided by humility, never forgetting our limits, our responsibility to Mother Earth, and our inextricable bond to one another.

Works Cited

"About Us." *FNX: First Nations Experience*, San Bernardino Community College District, fnx.org/about-fnx. Accessed 26 Jan. 2016.

Austin, Raymond D. *Navajo Courts and Navajo Common Law: A Tradition of Tribal Self-Governance.* U of Minnesota P, 2009.

Begay, Manley. Personal interview. 12 Jan. 2016.

"Endangered Languages." *Rosetta Stone*, 1999–2016, www.rosettastone .com/endangered.

Guskin, Emily and Amy Mitchell. "Innovating News in Native Communities." *The State of the News Media 2012*, The Pew Research Center's Project for Excellence in Journalism, 2012, assets.pewresearch.org /wp-content/uploads/sites/13/2017/05/24141622/State-of-the-News-Media-Report-2012-FINAL.pdf.

Haskie, Miranda. Personal interview. 5 Jan. 2016.

Meaning

1. What do you make of the title of this essay? What is a paradigm, and for whom is it shifting? In what ways?

2. Haskie notes that "the Navajo are animistic believers" (paragraph 5). What does she mean? How is the concept of *animism* related to the "Navajo philosophy of *k'é*" (9), and how are these traditional Navajo ideas distinct from modern Western notions of connectivity?

3. What is wrong, in Haskie's opinion, with relying on "googled Web sites" (paragraph 6) for information? What, or whom, would she prefer that her peers consult instead?

4. What is Haskie's thesis? Where in the essay does she come closest to stating it?

5. If you are uncertain of the meanings of any of the words listed below, try to guess them from the context of the essay. Then look them up to see how close your definitions were to those in the dictionary. Test out the new words by using each of them in a sentence or two of your own.

inexorably (2)	imbued (5)	heritage (9)
beguiling (2)	fervently (6)	transcendent (9)
linguistic (3)	myriad (6)	epitome (9)
assimilation (3)	wanes (8)	manifestations (9)
indigenous (4)	linear (8)	inextricable (10)

Purpose and Audience

1. To whom does Haskie seem to be writing here? What assumptions does she make about her readers and their familiarity with Navajo culture and history? Are those assumptions correct, in your case?

2. What do you imagine is Haskie's purpose in writing this essay? Does she mean primarily to entertain her readers, to educate them, or to persuade them to take some action? Why do you think so?

Method and Structure

1. Why do you think Haskie relies on cause-and-effect analysis to develop her ideas? What are some benefits of new media for indigenous peoples, as she sees it? What have been some "less positive effects"?

2. Which paragraphs fall into the introduction, body, and conclusion of Haskie's essay? What function does each part serve?

3. Examine how Haskie uses information and ideas from sources to develop and support her main idea. What might her analysis have lost without this material?

4. OTHER METHODS Haskie opens and closes her essay by depicting tribal elders in the act of **narrating** traditional stories to younger members. Why does she feel such **dialogue** is so vital to the community? What is the purpose of these stories, as she sees it?

Language

1. What is the overall **tone** of the essay?

2. Haskie uses several difficult words, many of which appear in the vocabulary list above. She also uses complex phrasing, such as "rapid and wide-ranging technological advances have brought the Navajo Nation swiftly and inexorably to the doorstep of the modern, often-beguiling

Western world" (paragraph 2). How would you characterize this language? What does it add to (or take away from) the essay?

3. In her final paragraph, Haskie equates fire with knowledge. What is the point of this **analogy**? Why does Haskie conclude her essay with it?

Writing Topics

1. JOURNAL TO ESSAY   Some people believe that mobile devices can enhance connectivity and community among far-flung friends and relatives, others argue that electronic communication distances us from others and makes us lonely and unhappy, and still others, as Haskie demonstrates, can see some merit in both positions. What is your opinion of the social effects of technology? Do you think that today's communication habits have an overall positive or negative effect? Using your journal response (p. 320) and your reaction to Haskie's essay as a starting point, write an essay of your own in which you explain how you think your mobile devices affect you and your community.

2. Write an essay assessing Haskie's essay. For instance, does the phenomenon she examines apply only to indigenous communities, or is it more universal than she realizes? How persuasive do you find her explanations of connectivity in Navajo culture? Is her cause-and-effect analysis sufficiently thorough? What do you think of her examples? Does she overstate her point? understate it? Are you intrigued by her subject? Agree or disagree with Haskie, supporting your opinion with your own examples.

3. RESEARCH   What do you know of Native American reservation life during the notorious "boarding school era" Haskie mentions in paragraph 3? What, exactly, is she referring to? Do some research on the conditions of reservation life, both at the turn of the twentieth century (1880s to 1920s) and today. Then write an essay that reports your findings and identifies Haskie's position on the issue of cultural assimilation through education in tribal communities, paying close attention to her examples and explaining how she reaches her conclusions.

4. CONNECTIONS   Like Haskie, Harrison Candelaria Fletcher, in "White" (p. 198), and Brian Jaehyung Kim, in "Double Identity" (p. 250), also explore how the experience of inhabiting two cultures contributes to their sense of who they are and to what communities they belong. Though all three authors undoubtedly struggled to forge independent identities, the experiences they describe demonstrate how family relationships play into people's concepts of self. In a brief essay, analyze how these writers convey their feelings about their relatives and the influences those relatives had on them. How, ultimately, do they define themselves?

WRITING WITH THE METHOD

CAUSE-AND-EFFECT ANALYSIS

Select one of the following questions, or any question they suggest, and answer it in an essay developed by analyzing causes or effects. The question you choose should concern a topic you care about so that your cause-and-effect analysis is a means of communicating an idea, not an end in itself.

People and Their Behavior

1. What makes a soldier, police officer, or firefighter a hero?
2. What does a sound body contribute to a sound mind?
3. Why do people root for the underdog?
4. How does a person's alcohol or drug dependency affect others?

Gender and Sexuality

5. Why would a man or woman enter a field that has traditionally been filled by the opposite sex, such as nursing or engineering?
6. What effect has the legalization of gay marriage had on you and your friends?
7. At what age should a person be allowed to seek gender-reassignment surgery, and why?
8. How has feminism changed men's lives, for better or for worse?

Art and Entertainment

9. Why did hip-hop music become so popular both in the United States and abroad?
10. How has the Internet changed the music industry?
11. What makes some professional sports teams succeed year after year while others consistently fail?
12. What impact has a particular television show or movie had on American culture?

Contemporary Issues

13. Why does the United States spend so much money on health care?
14. How will global climate change influence the nature and frequency of extreme weather events?
15. Is a college education worth the expense?
16. Why have political debates become so heated and angry?

WRITING ABOUT THE THEME

▶

UNDERSTANDING SCIENCE AND TECHNOLOGY

1. Many of the writers in this chapter consider the good and bad that have come from recent advances in communication technology, particularly in the form of mobile devices and social media. Derek Thompson's (p. 312) and Kaitlyn Haskie's (p. 320) analyses of the effects smartphones have had on entertainment and community, respectively, are most notable in this respect, but even Diane Ackerman (p. 299) asserts that staring at tiny screens has rendered a generation literally nearsighted. Think of another contemporary product or technology that you believe holds the potential to do unexpected harm — or that could bring unanticipated benefits — and write an essay predicting its consequences. (Be sure to review the cause-and-effect guidelines at the start of this chapter before beginning your analysis.)

2. All of the writers in this chapter draw on some level of research to support their analyses, and three of them formally cite their sources: James Kakalios (p. 306) provides footnotes referring to published research on the physics of traffic and Derek Thompson and Kaitlyn Haskie use the MLA system explained on pages 399–419 of this book. Why do you suppose writing about science and technology, or any similarly academic subject, would inspire someone to conduct research? What is gained, or lost, by consulting the work of others? How important is it to follow a formal documentation system, such as MLA? Why don't Ross Andersen (p. 298) or Diane Ackerman cite sources for their studies of climate and biology, considering that neither is a scientist? Explain your answers in a paragraph or a brief essay, being sure to cite any sources you quote or otherwise consult using MLA style.

3. Although the writers represented in this chapter all touch on matters of science and technology, their tones vary widely, from urgent to ironic to nostalgic. Choose the two selections that seem most different in tone, and analyze how their tones help clarify the authors' points. Is one piece's tone more effective than the other's? If so, why?

14

ARGUMENT AND PERSUASION

▶ SEEKING SOCIAL JUSTICE

Since we argue all the time—with relatives, with friends, with the auto mechanic or a sales associate—a chapter devoted to argument and persuasion may at first seem unnecessary. But arguing with a sales associate over the cost of an extended warranty is quite a different process from arguing with readers over a complex issue. In both cases we are trying to find common ground with our audience, perhaps to change others' views or even to compel them to act as we wish. But the salesperson is in front of us; we can shift our tactics in response to his or her gestures, expressions, and words. The reader, in contrast, is "out there"; we have to anticipate those gestures, expressions, and words in the way we structure the argument, the kinds of evidence we use to support it, even the way we conceive of the subject.

A great many assertions that are worth making are debatable at some level—whether over the facts on which the assertions are based or over the values they imply. Two witnesses to an accident cannot agree on what they saw; two economists cannot agree on what measures will reduce unemployment; two doctors cannot agree on what constitutes life or death. We see such disagreements play out in writing all the time, whether we're reading an accident report, a magazine article claiming the benefits of unemployment rates, or an editorial responding to a Supreme Court decision.

Argument and persuasion is also the ideal method for presenting an opinion or a proposal on a controversial topic, making it a natural choice for the writers in this chapter, all of whom wanted to make a case about social justice. In paragraphs, Jenny Price argues that we should expect gun violence rather than be shocked by it, while Martin Luther King Jr. urges readers to condone nonviolent civil disobedience. In an essay based on research and her own experience as a student journalist, Zoe Krey asserts that better reporting by the mainstream media could help to prevent police brutality. Then, in paired essays, Paul Greenberg and Nicholas Kristof debate the sources and consequences of income inequality in the United States. And the final three essays all touch on the ongoing issue of Confederate memorials: Brent Staples and Ernest B. Furgurson square off on the question of whether statues honoring Southern Civil War leaders should be removed from public spaces, while Lisa Richardson reminds us that the history those monuments represent is more complicated than most people acknowledge.

Reading Argument and Persuasion

Technically, **argument** and **persuasion** are two different processes:

- *Argument* appeals mainly to an audience's sense of reason in order to negotiate a common understanding or to win agreement with a claim. It is the method of a columnist who defends a president's foreign policy on the grounds of economics and defense strategy.

- *Persuasion* appeals mainly to an audience's feelings and values in order to compel some action, or at least to win support for an action. It is the method of a mayoral candidate who urges voters to support her because she is sensitive to the poor.

But argument and persuasion so often mingle that we will use the one term *argument* to mean a deliberate appeal to an audience's reason and emotions in order to create compromise, win agreement, or compel action. Making an effective case for an opinion requires upholding certain responsibilities and attending to several established techniques of argumentation, most of them dating back to ancient Greece.

▶ The Elements of Argument

All arguments share certain elements:

- *The core of any argument is a debatable claim about the subject.* Generally, this **assertion** or **proposition** is expressed as a thesis statement. It may defend or attack a position, suggest a solution to a problem, recommend a change in policy, or challenge a value or belief. Here are a few examples:

  The college should give first priority for on-campus jobs to students who need financial aid.

School prayer has been rightly declared unconstitutional and should not be reinstituted in any form.

Smokers who wish to poison themselves should be allowed to do so, but not in any place where their smoke will poison others.

- *The central assertion is broken down into subclaims,* each one supported by evidence.

- *Significant opposing arguments are raised and dispensed with,* again with the support of evidence.

- *The parts of the argument are organized into a clear, logical structure* that pushes steadily toward the conclusion.

A writer may draw on classification, comparison, or any other rhetorical method to develop the entire argument or to introduce evidence or strengthen the conclusion. For instance, in a proposal arguing for raising a college's standards of admission, a dean might contrast the existing standards with the proposed standards, analyze a process for raising the standards over a period of years, and predict the effects of the new standards on future students' preparedness for college work.

▶ Appeals to Readers

Effective arguments appeal to readers: they ask others to listen to what someone has to say, judge the words fairly, and, as much as possible, agree with the writer. Most arguments combine three kinds of appeals to readers: ethical, emotional, and rational. These appeals are sometimes referred to as *ethos, pathos,* and *logos.*

Ethical Appeal

Known to classical rhetoricians as *ethos* (the Greek word for "character"), the **ethical appeal** is often not explicit in an argument, yet it pervades the whole. It is the sense a writer conveys of his or her expertise and character, projected by the reasonableness of the argument, by the use of evidence, and by tone, as discussed later in this chapter: a rational argument shows readers that the writer is thinking logically and fairly, strong evidence establishes credibility, and a sincere, reasonable tone demonstrates balance and goodwill.

Emotional Appeal

An **emotional appeal** (*pathos* in Greek) aims directly for readers' hearts—for the beliefs, values, and feelings deeply embedded in all of us.

We are just as often motivated by these ingrained ideas and emotions as by our intellects. Even scientists, who stress the rational interpretation of facts above all else, are sometimes influenced in their interpretations by emotions deriving from, say, competition with other scientists. And the willingness of a nation's citizens to go to war may result more from their patriotism and pride than from their reasoned considerations of risks and gains. An emotional appeal in an argument attempts to tap such feelings for any of several reasons:

- To heighten the responsiveness of readers
- To inspire readers to new beliefs
- To compel readers to act
- To assure readers that their values remain unchallenged

A writer's use of *pathos* may be explicit, as when an argument against capital punishment appeals to readers' religious values by citing the Bible's Sixth Commandment, "Thou shalt not kill." But an emotional appeal may also be less obvious, because individual words may have **connotations** that elicit emotional responses from readers. For instance, one writer may characterize an environmental group as "a well-organized team representing diverse interests," while another may call the same group "a hodgepodge of nature lovers and profit-seeking businesspeople." The first appeals to readers' preference for order and balance, the second to readers' fear of extremism and disdain for greed.

The use of *pathos* requires care:

- *An emotional appeal must be directed at the audience's actual beliefs and feelings.*
- *An emotional appeal must be presented calmly* enough that readers have no reason to doubt the fairness in the rest of the argument.
- *An emotional appeal must be appropriate to the subject and to the argument.* For instance, in arguing against a pay raise for city councilors, a legislator might be tempted to appeal to voters' resentment of wealthy people by pointing out that two of the councilors are rich enough to work for nothing. But such an appeal would divert attention from the issue of whether the pay raise is justified for all councilors on the basis of the work they do and the city's ability to pay the extra cost.

Carefully used, *pathos* has great force, particularly when it contributes to an argument based largely on sound reasoning and evidence. The appropriate mix of emotion and reason in a given essay is entirely dependent on the subject, the writer's purpose, and the audience. Emotions are out of place in most arguments in the natural sciences, for instance, where rational interpretations of factual evidence are all that will convince readers of the truth of an assertion. But emotional appeals may be essential to persuade an audience to support or take an action, for emotion is frequently a stronger motivator than reason.

Rational Appeal

A **rational appeal** is one that, as the name implies, addresses the rational faculties of readers—their capacity to reason logically about a problem. It establishes the truth of a proposition or claim by moving through a series of related subclaims, each supported by evidence. In doing so, rational appeals—*logos* to the ancient Greeks—follow processes of reasoning that are natural to all of us. These processes are induction and deduction.

INDUCTION   **Inductive reasoning** moves from the particular to the general, from evidence to a generalization or conclusion about the evidence. It is a process we begin learning in infancy and use daily throughout our lives: a child burns herself the first two times she touches a stove, so she concludes that stoves burn; a moviegoer has liked four movies directed by Guillermo del Toro, so he forms the generalization that Guillermo del Toro makes good movies. Inductive reasoning is also very common in argument: a nurse administrator might offer data to show that two hundred past patients in the psychiatric ward received drugs but no therapy and then conclude that the hospital relies exclusively on drugs to treat mental illness.

The movement from particular to general is called an *inductive leap* because we must make something of a jump to conclude that what is true of some instances (the patients whose records were examined) is also true of all other instances in the class (the rest of the patients). In an ideal world we could perhaps avoid the inductive leap by pinning down every conceivable instance, but in the real world such thoroughness is usually impractical and often impossible. Instead, we gather enough evidence to make our generalizations probable. The evidence for induction may be of several kinds:

- *Facts*: statistics or other hard data that are verifiable or, failing that, have been reliable sources (for instance, the types of drugs prescribed, derived from hospital records)
- *The opinions of recognized experts on the subject*, opinions that are themselves conclusions based on research and observation (for instance, the testimony of an experienced hospital doctor)
- *Examples* illustrating the evidence (for instance, the treatment history of one patient)

DEDUCTION   A sound inductive generalization can form the basis for the second reasoning process, **deductive reasoning**. Working from the general to the particular, we start with such a generalization and apply it to a new situation in order to draw a conclusion about that situation. Like induction, deduction is a process we use constantly to order our experience. The child who learns from two experiences that all stoves burn then sees a new stove and concludes that this stove also will burn. The child's thought process can be written in the form of a **syllogism**, a three-step outline of deductive reasoning:

> All stoves burn me.
> This is a stove.
> Therefore, this stove will burn me.

The first statement, the generalization derived from induction, is called the *major premise*. The second statement, a more specific assertion about some element of the major premise, is called the *minor premise*. And the third statement, an assertion of the logical connection between the premises, is called the *conclusion*. The following syllogism takes the earlier example about a psychiatric ward one step further:

MAJOR PREMISE   The hospital relies exclusively on drugs to treat psychiatric patients.

MINOR PREMISE   Drugs do not cure mental illness.

CONCLUSION   Therefore, the hospital does not cure psychiatric patients.

Unlike an inductive conclusion, which requires a leap, the deductive conclusion derives necessarily from the premises: as long as the reasoning process is valid and the premises are accepted as true, then the conclusion must also be true. To be valid, the reasoning must conform to the process outlined earlier. The following syllogism is *not* valid, even though the premises are true:

> All radicals want to change the system.
> Georgia Allport wants to change the system.
> Therefore, Georgia Allport is a radical.

The flaw in this syllogism is that not *only* radicals want to change the system, so Allport does not *necessarily* fall within the class of radicals just because she wants to change the system. The conclusion, then, is invalid.

A syllogism can be valid without being true if either of the premises is untrue. For example:

All people who want political change are radicals.
Georgia Allport wants political change.
Therefore, Georgia Allport is a radical.

The conclusion here is valid because Allport falls within the class of people who want political change. But the conclusion is untrue because the major premise is untrue. As commonly defined, a radical seeks extreme change, often by revolutionary means. But other forms and means of change are also possible. Allport, for instance, may be interested in improving the delivery of services to the poor and in achieving passage of tougher environmental-protection laws—both political changes, to be sure, but neither radical.

In arguments, syllogisms are rarely spelled out as neatly as in these examples. Sometimes the order of the statements is reversed, as in this sentence paraphrasing a Supreme Court decision:

The state may not imprison a man just because he is too poor to pay a fine; the only justification for imprisonment is a certain danger to society, and poverty does not constitute certain danger.

The buried syllogism can be stated thus:

MAJOR PREMISE   The state may imprison only those who are a certain danger to society.

MINOR PREMISE   A man who is too poor to pay a fine is not a certain danger to society.

CONCLUSION   Therefore, the state cannot imprison a man just because he is too poor to pay a fine.

Often, one of a syllogism's premises or even its conclusion is implied but not expressed. Each of the following sentences omits one part of the same syllogism:

All five students cheated, so they should be expelled. [Implied major premise: cheaters should be expelled.]

Cheaters should be punished by expulsion, so all five students should be expelled. [Implied minor premise: all five students cheated.]

Cheaters should be punished by expulsion, and all five students cheated. [Implied conclusion: all five students should be expelled.]

▶ Fallacies

Inappropriate emotional appeals and flaws in reasoning—called logical **fallacies**—can trap writers as they construct arguments. Watch out for the following errors in particular.

■ *Hasty generalization*: an inductive conclusion that leaps to include *all* instances when at best only *some* instances provide any evidence. Hasty generalizations form some of our worst stereotypes:

> Physically challenged people are mentally challenged, too.
>
> African Americans are good athletes.
>
> Italians are volatile.

■ *Oversimplification*: an inductive conclusion that ignores complexities in the evidence that, if heeded, would weaken the conclusion or suggest an entirely different one. For example:

> The newspaper folded because it couldn't compete with the Internet.

Although the Internet may have taken some business from the newspaper, other newspapers continue to thrive; thus, the Internet could not be the only cause of the newspaper's failure.

■ *Begging the question*: assuming a conclusion in the statement of a premise, and thus begging readers to accept the conclusion—the question—before it is proved. For example:

> We can trust the senator not to neglect the needy because he is a compassionate man.

This sentence asserts in a circular fashion that the senator is not uncompassionate because he is compassionate. He may indeed be compassionate, but the question that needs to be addressed is: what will he do for the needy?

■ *Ignoring the question*: introducing an issue or consideration that shifts the argument away from the real issue. Offering an emotional appeal as a premise in a logical argument is a form of ignoring the question. The following sentence, for instance, appeals to pity, not to logic:

> The mayor was badly used by people he loved and trusted, so we should not blame him for the corruption in his administration.

■ *Ad hominem* (Latin for "to the man"): a form of ignoring the question by attacking the opponent instead of the opponent's arguments. For example:

> O'Brien is married to a convict, so her proposals for prison reform should not be taken seriously.

■ *Either-or*: requiring that readers choose between two interpretations or actions when in fact the choices are more numerous.

> Either we imprison all drug users, or we will become their prisoners.

The factors contributing to drug addiction, and the choices for dealing with it, are obviously more complex than this statement suggests. Not all either-or arguments are invalid, for sometimes the alternatives encompass all the possibilities. But when they do not, the argument is false.

- *Non sequitur* (Latin for "it does not follow"): a conclusion derived illogically or erroneously from stated or implied premises. For instance:

  > Children are too immature to engage in sex, so they should not be taught about it.

  This sentence implies one of two meanings, both of them questionable: only the sexually active can learn anything about sex, or teaching children about sex will cause them to engage in it.

- *Post hoc* (from the Latin *post hoc, ergo propter hoc,* "after this, therefore because of this"): assuming that because one thing preceded another, it must have caused the other. For example:

  > After the town banned smoking in public places, the incidence of vandalism went up.

  Many things may have caused the rise in vandalism, including warmer weather and a climbing unemployment rate. It does not follow that the ban on smoking, and that alone, caused the rise.

Analyzing Argument and Persuasion in Paragraphs

Jenny Price (born 1960) is a public scholar whose research interests include history and the environment. The following paragraph is from "Gun Violence at UC Irvine," a 2009 op-ed article she wrote for the *Los Angeles Times* in response to readers' shock that a woman was shot and killed in a college neighborhood generally considered safe. The paragraph offers an inductive argument.

Twelve thousand people are shot to death in the United States every year—accounting for more than two out of every three killings. That's an average of 33 people daily. An additional 240 people get shot and injured every day, and more than 65 million Americans own a total of 283 million firearms. Where, exactly, do we

Evidence:

Number of gun-related homicides

Number of nonfatal shootings

Extent of gun ownership

expect the 12,000 homicides to happen? Do we really think that the places with gangs and high crime rates are the only places where people are going to use their guns? The widespread numbness to the especially high murder rates in our poor inner-city neighborhoods is egregious enough. But that's matched by the widespread denial that <u>the epidemic of gun violence is playing out every day in every kind of neighborhood across America.</u>

The generalization (underlined): shootings can happen anywhere

Martin Luther King Jr. (1929–68), was a revered and powerful leader of the civil rights movement during the 1950s and 1960s. When leading sit-ins, boycotts, and marches, he always insisted on nonviolent resistance. In this paragraph from "Letter from Birmingham Jail" (1963), King uses deduction to argue in favor of civil disobedience.

You express a great deal of anxiety over our willingness to break laws. This is certainly a legitimate concern. Since we so diligently urge people to obey the Supreme Court's decision of 1954 outlawing segregation in the public schools, at first glance it may seem rather paradoxical for us consciously to break laws. One may well ask: "How can you advocate breaking some laws and obeying others?" The answer lies in the fact that there are two types of laws: just and unjust. I would be the first to advocate obeying just laws. One has not only a legal but a moral responsibility to obey just laws. Conversely, one has a moral responsibility to disobey unjust laws. I would agree with St. Augustine that "an unjust law is no law at all."

Major premise: laws should be obeyed

Minor premise: some laws are unjust and therefore are not laws

Conclusion: unjust laws should not be obeyed

Developing an Argumentative and Persuasive Essay

▶ Getting Started

You will have many chances to write arguments, from defending or opposing a policy such as progressive taxation in an economics course to justifying a new procedure at work to persuading a company to refund your money for a bad product. To choose a subject for an argumentative essay, consider a behavior or policy that irks you, an opinion you want to defend, a change you would like to see implemented, or a way to solve a problem. The subject you pick should meet certain criteria:

- *It should be something you have some knowledge of*—from your own experience or observations, from class discussions, or from reading, although you may need to do further research as well.

- *It should be limited to a topic you can treat thoroughly in the space and time available to you*—for instance, the quality of computer instruction at your school rather than in the whole nation.

- *It should be something that you feel strongly about* so that you can make a convincing case. (However, it's best to avoid subjects that you cannot view with some objectivity, seeing the opposite side as well as your own; otherwise, you may not be open to flaws in your argument, and you may not be able to represent the opposition fairly.)

Once you have selected a subject, do some preliminary research to make sure that you will have enough evidence to support your opinion. This step is especially important with issues that we all tend to have opinions about whether we know the facts or not, such as welfare cheating or tax advantages for the wealthy. Where to seek evidence depends on the nature of your argument.

- *For an argument derived from your own experiences and observations*, such as a recommendation that all students work part-time for the education if not for the money, gathering evidence will be primarily a matter of searching your own thoughts and also uncovering opposing views, perhaps by consulting others.

- *For some arguments derived from personal experience*, you can strengthen your evidence with judicious use of facts and opinions from other sources. An essay arguing in favor of vegetarianism, for instance, could mix the benefits you have felt with those demonstrated by scientific data.

- *For an argument on a nonpersonal or a controversial subject*, you will have to gather the evidence of other sources. Though you might strongly favor or oppose a massive federal investment in solar-energy research, your opinions would count little if they were not supported with facts and the opinions of experts.

For advice on conducting research and using the evidence you find, see Part Three.

In addition to evidence, knowledge of readers' needs and expectations is absolutely crucial in planning an argument. In explanatory writing, detail and clarity alone may accomplish your purpose, but you cannot hope to move readers in a certain direction unless you have some idea of where they stand. You need a sense of their background in your subject, of course. But even more, you need a good idea of their values and beliefs, their attitudes toward your subject—in short, their willingness to be convinced. In a composition class, your readers will probably be your instructor and your classmates, a small but diverse group. A good target when you are addressing a diverse audience is the reader who is neutral or mildly biased one way or the other toward your subject. This person you can hope to influence as long as your argument is reasonable, your evidence is thorough and convincing, your treatment of opposing views is fair, and your appeals to readers' emotions are appropriate to your purpose, your subject, and especially your readers' values and feelings.

▶ Forming a Thesis

With your subject and some evidence in hand, you should develop a tentative thesis. But don't feel you have to prove your thesis at this early stage; fixing it too firmly may make you unwilling to reshape it if further evidence, your audience, or the structure of your argument so demands.

Stating your thesis in a preliminary thesis sentence can help you form your idea. Make this sentence as clear and specific as possible. Don't resort to a vague generality or a nondebatable statement of fact. Instead, state the precise opinion you want readers to accept or the precise action you want them to take or support. For instance:

VAGUE   Computer instruction is important.

NONDEBATABLE   The school's investment in computer instruction is less than the average investment of the nation's colleges and universities.

PRECISE   Money designated for new athletic facilities should be diverted to upgrading computer facilities and hiring first-rate faculty.

VAGUE   Cloning research is promising.

NONDEBATABLE   Scientists have been experimenting with cloning procedures for many years.

PRECISE   Those who oppose cloning research should consider the potentially valuable medical applications.

Since an argumentative thesis is essentially an opinion reached by examining evidence, you will probably need to do some additional reading to ensure that you have a broad range of facts and ideas supporting not only your view of a subject but also any opposing views. Though it may be tempting to ignore your opposition in the hope that readers know nothing of it, it is dishonest and probably futile to do so. Acknowledging and, whenever possible, refuting significant opposing views will enhance your credibility with readers. If you find that some counterarguments damage your own argument too greatly, then you will have to rethink your thesis.

▶ Organizing

Once you have formulated your thesis and evaluated your reasons and evidence against the needs and expectations of your audience, begin planning how you will arrange your argument.

The **introduction** to your essay should draw readers into your framework, making them see how the subject affects them and predisposing them to consider your argument. Sometimes a forthright approach works best, but an eye-opening anecdote or quotation can also be effective. Your thesis sentence may end your introduction. However, if you think readers will not even entertain your thesis until they have seen some or all of your evidence, withhold your thesis for later.

The **body** of the essay consists of your reasons and your evidence for them. The evidence you generated or collected should suggest the reasons that will support the claim of your thesis—essentially the minor arguments that bolster the main argument. In an essay favoring federal investment in solar-energy research, for instance, the minor arguments might include the need for sustainable resources, the feasibility of widespread use of solar energy, and its cost and safety compared with other energy sources. It is in developing these minor arguments that you are most likely to use induction and deduction consciously—generalizing from specifics or applying generalizations to new information. Thus the minor arguments provide the entry points for your evidence, and together they should encompass all the relevant evidence.

Unless the minor arguments form a chain, with each link growing out of the one preceding it, their order should be determined by their potential effects on readers. In general, it is most effective to arrange the reasons in order of increasing importance or strength so as to finish powerfully. But to engage readers in the argument from the start, try to begin with a reason that they will find compelling or that they already know and accept; that way, the weaker reasons will be sandwiched between a strong beginning and an even stronger ending.

The views opposing yours can be raised and refuted wherever it seems most appropriate to do so. If a counterargument pertains to just one of your minor arguments, then dispose of it at that point. But if the counter-arguments are more basic, pertaining to your whole thesis, you should dispose of them either after the introduction or shortly before the conclusion. Bring up counterarguments early if the opposition is particularly strong and you fear that readers will be disinclined to listen unless you address their concerns first. Hold counterarguments for the end when they are generally weak or easily dispensed with once you've presented your case.

In the **conclusion** to your essay, you may summarize the main point of your argument and restate your thesis from your introduction, or state it for the first time if you have saved it for the end. An effective quotation, an appropriate emotional appeal, or a call for support or action can often provide a strong finish to an argument.

▶ Drafting

While you are drafting the essay, work to make your reasoning clear by showing how each bit of evidence relates to the reason or minor argument being discussed and how each minor argument relates to the main argument contained in the thesis. In working through the reasons and evidence, you may find it helpful to state each reason as the first sentence in a paragraph and then support it in the following sentences. If this scheme seems too rigid or creates overlong paragraphs, you can always make changes after you have written your draft. Draw on a range of methods to clarify your points. For instance, define specialized terms or those you use in a special sense, compare and contrast one policy or piece of evidence with another, or carefully analyze causes or effects.

▶ Revising and Editing

When your draft is complete, use the following questions and the Focus box to guide your revision and editing.

- *Is your thesis debatable, precise, and clear?* Readers must know what you are trying to convince them of, at least by the end of the essay if not up front.

- *Is your argument unified?* Does each minor claim support the thesis? Do all opinions, facts, and examples provide evidence for a minor claim? On behalf of your readers, question every sentence you have written to be sure it contributes to the point you are making and to the argument as a whole.

- *Is the structure of your argument clear and compelling?* Readers should be able to follow easily, seeing when and why you move from one idea to the next.

- *Is the evidence specific, representative, and adequate?* Facts, examples, and expert opinions should be well detailed, should fairly represent the available information, and should be sufficient to support your claim.

- *Have you slipped into any logical fallacies?* Detecting fallacies in your own work can be difficult, but your readers will find them if you don't. Look for the fallacies discussed earlier: hasty generalization, oversimplification, begging the question, ignoring the question, ad hominem, either-or, non sequitur, and post hoc.

FOCUS ON TONE

Readers are most likely to be persuaded by an argument when they sense a strong *ethos*, meaning that the writer comes across as reasonable, trustworthy, and sincere. A rational appeal, strong evidence, and acknowledgment of opposing views do much to convey these attributes, but so does **tone**, the attitude implied by word choices and sentence structures.

Generally, you should try for a tone of moderation in your view of your subject and a tone of respectfulness and goodwill toward readers and opponents.

- State opinions and facts calmly:

  OVEREXCITED   One clueless administrator was quoted in the newspaper as saying she thought many students who claim learning disabilities are faking their difficulties to obtain special treatment! Has she never heard of dyslexia, attention deficit disorder, and other well-established disabilities?

  CALM   Particularly worrisome was one administrator's statement, quoted in the newspaper, that many students who claim learning disabilities may be "faking" their difficulties to obtain special treatment.

■ Replace arrogance with deference:

ARROGANT I happen to know that many students would rather party or just bury their heads in the sand than get involved in a serious, worthy campaign against the school's unjust learning-disabled policies.

DEFERENTIAL Time pressures and lack of information about the issues may prevent students from joining the campaign against the school's unjust learning-disabled policies.

■ Replace sarcasm with plain speaking:

SARCASTIC Of course, the administration knows even without meeting students what is best for every one of them.

PLAIN SPEAKING The administration should agree to meet with each learning-disabled student to understand his or her needs.

■ Choose words whose connotations convey reasonableness rather than anger, hostility, or another negative emotion:

HOSTILE The administration coerced some students into dropping their lawsuits. [*Coerced* implies the use of threats.]

REASONABLE The administration convinced some students to drop their lawsuits. [*Convinced* implies the use of reason.]

See pages 39–40 for more on tone and pages 51–52 for more on connotation.

The end must justify the means.

—Matthew Prior

Man is not made better by being degraded; he is seldom restrained from crime by harsh measures, except the principle of fear predominates in his character; and then he is never made radically better for its influence.

—Dorothea Dix

Every society gets the kind of criminal it deserves. What is equally true is that every community gets the kind of law enforcement it insists on.

—Robert Kennedy

JOURNAL RESPONSE Write about a recent time when you were aware of law enforcement in your community—perhaps a noteworthy arrest, a controversy involving police methods, a report of rising or falling crime, even a personal experience. What did you read, hear, or experience, and what did you think about it?

Zoe Krey

Zoe Krey was born in China in 1994 and grew up in Naperville, Illinois. At DePaul University in Chicago, she studied political science, public relations, and advertising and participated in several clubs and activities, including blogging for the school and working on the student newspaper, the *DePaulia*. She graduated in 2016 and continues to live in Chicago, where she found a job in the marketing industry. Beyond writing, which Krey reports she "has always loved," her interests include food and water sports.

Questionable Coverage: Police Brutality Is Only Part of the Problem
(Student Essay)

At the *DePaulia,* Krey served as opinions editor for a year, writing and editing columns on current events while incorporating principles and theories she was studying in her political science and journalism classes. She wrote "Questionable Coverage" for the paper in May of 2015, shortly after protests over the police killings of unarmed black men in Ferguson, Missouri, and Baltimore, Maryland, erupted in riots. "Hyperaware of the way that news is covered" because of her coursework and her own journalistic involvement, Krey argues that the mainstream media can—and should—do a better job.

Police brutality has become a central piece of media coverage in the   1
United States recently, and with the deaths of Eric Garner, Michael Brown,
Tamir Rice, Eric Harris and Freddie Gray,[1] it seems that the problem is at
an all-time high. In the case of Gray, a Baltimore grand jury handed down
indictments against six police officers last week. While some say that justice is being served and that this is a step towards fighting police violence
against citizens, others say that it is not enough.

Is police brutality increasing? Or is it just finally getting the coverage   2
it deserves? CNN reports that society is "seeing more mainstream media
coverage" of police violence for various reasons, one of them being the
increase in citizen journalism, which has been made possible with cell
phones and social media (McLaughlin). Anyone can record a video and
post it online where it might sit in a virtual wasteland, doomed to never
be seen again—or attract the attention of millions and grab national
headlines.

Social media is shifting the agenda-setting roles of politicians and   3
journalists to average citizens. Would the deaths of Michael Brown or
Freddie Gray have sparked as many national protests as they did had
social media and citizen journalism not played a major part? If a picture
is worth a thousand words, a video is worth a million. As videos, such as
of a police officer putting a man in a chokehold or of another officer
denying a request for a medic, circulate in the virtual world they are trans-
ported into a reality that was not quite possible before. CNN reports that
"black newspaper executives feel the videos lend credibility not only to
black victims' versions of events in specific situations, but also to their
versions of events historically. Where a victim's race could affect a story's
perceived veracity, video permits no such prejudice" (McLaughlin). The
videos are shedding light on a problem that has always been there, but
has rarely been believed.

While police brutality is certainly an issue that needs to be addressed,   4
this isn't the only problem at hand in the recent cases. Upon examination
of Michael Brown's death in Ferguson, Missouri, and Freddie Gray's death

---

[1] A closely spaced series of unarmed black males dying at the hands of police. Eric
Garner, 43, died July 17, 2014, after being detained in a chokehold in Long Island,
New York. Michael Brown, 18, was fatally shot during an altercation with police in
Ferguson, Missouri, on August 9, 2014. Tamir Rice, 12, was killed on November 22,
2014, in Cleveland, Ohio, by officers who mistook his toy gun for a real firearm.
Eric Courtney Harris, 44, was accidentally shot and killed by a reserve officer during
an attempted arrest in Tulsa, Oklahoma, on April 22, 2015. Freddie Gray, 25, died
in Baltimore, Maryland, on April 19, 2015, seven days after lapsing into a coma
during transport in a police van. [Editors' note.]

in Baltimore, Maryland, it becomes clear that the looting, rioting and even peaceful protests that followed are symptomatic of a problem that goes deeper.[2]

Ferguson and Baltimore have serious inequality problems that have barely been addressed by the media. After the economic recession of 2008, "the Ferguson and St. Louis region economies were on the upswing, [but] the gains weren't equally shared," *Fortune* magazine reports: "The unemployment rate for African Americans [in the area] . . . was 26 percent in 2012. . ., [while for] white Americans, the unemployment rate was just 6.2 percent" (Gandel). Additionally, a white majority police force was patrolling an area that was largely African American, creating intense racial tensions. Ferguson was crippled by economic and racial inequality, and while this inequality wasn't the direct cause of the protests, it was certainly a factor that was not addressed as much as it should have been by the media.

Media coverage of the Baltimore protests also lacked serious contextual explanations. Michael Fletcher, a reporter for the *Washington Post* and a long-term resident of Baltimore, called the city "a combustible mix of poverty, crime and hopelessness, uncomfortably juxtaposed against rich history, friendly people, venerable institutions and pockets of old-money affluence." Fletcher specifically cites Gray's neighborhood, Sandtown, as an especially poor area, stating, "[m]ore than half of the neighborhood's households earned less than $25,000 a year. . ., and more than one in five adults were out of work—double the citywide average." This is not to suggest that the situations in Baltimore and Ferguson were identical, but to draw attention to the fact that both cities suffer from issues that go deeper than police brutality alone. The media's lack of coverage on the overall contextual situations in these cities results in inaccurate representations of the situation at hand.

Reporting on police brutality has become the way many in the United States learn about problems in cities with intense inequality. Rather than the media playing their investigative role and identifying deeper reasons for social unrest and protests, they have run with the police brutality news frame. Taking the easy way out will have consequences that negatively affect our population as a whole. The American people believe police brutality is the

---

[2]Ferguson experienced weeks of unrest following Brown's death on August 9, 2014; a second wave of protests and riots erupted in November, after a grand jury decided not to indict the shooting officer. In Baltimore, a week of protests spurred by Gray's death turned violent on April 27, 2015, the day of his funeral. [Editors' note.]

issue at hand, when in reality these torn cities' intense racial tensions and inequalities lead to conditions that lend themselves to protests and violence.

The media have a responsibility not only to report facts, but to investigate and analyze events. Reporting on surface issues rather than the root causes of the problem will only perpetuate the cycle of police brutality and protests in cities marked with social and economic unrest. The media are essential to the functioning of democracy, and their lack of investigation is eroding our system of government.   8

When the next round of protests arise, which is bound to happen due to a lack of thoughtful and accurate reporting and policies thus far, the media need to recognize their duty to democracy and to the American people and play their investigative, watchdog role. The fourth estate needs to do what it can to prevent police brutality by identifying the roots of the problem rather than sit back and wait for the next death to highlight a city of inequality. The media need to go beyond the "if it bleeds, it leads" mindset and act like thoughtful reporters and journalists.   9

Works Cited

Fletcher, Michael A. "What You Really Need to Know about Baltimore, from a Reporter Who's Lived There for Over Thirty Years." *The Washington Post*, 28 Apr. 2015, www.washingtonpost.com/news/wonk/wp/2015/04/28/what-you-really-need-to-know-about-baltimore-from-a-reporter-who's-lived-there-for-30-years/.

Gandel, Stephen. "The Economic Imbalance Fueling Ferguson's Unrest." *Fortune*, Time, 15 Aug. 2014, fortune.com/2014/08/15/ferguson-income-inequality/.

McLaughlin, Eliott C. "We're Not Seeing More Police Shootings, Just More Coverage." *CNN*, Turner Broadcasting System, 21 Apr. 2015, www.cnn.com/2015/04/20/us/police-brutality-video-social-media-attitudes/index.html.

Meaning

1. What is the "problem" (paragraph 4) Krey references in her title and addresses in her essay? What is her proposed solution?

2. What does Krey mean by "citizen journalism" (paragraph 2)? How did the practice come about, and how has professional journalism responded?

3. In your own words, explain Krey's thesis. Where does she state it explicitly?

4. If you are uncertain of the meanings of any of the words listed below, try to guess them from the context of the essay. Then look them up to see how close your definitions were to those in the dictionary. Test out the new words by using each of them in a sentence or two of your own.

indictments (1)   contextual (6)   investigative (7)
chokehold (3)   combustible (6)   perpetuate (8)
veracity (3)   juxtaposed (6)
symptomatic (4)   venerable (6)

Purpose and Audience

1. What seems to be Krey's purpose in this argument: to encourage citizens to be more aware of police brutality? to persuade lawmakers to crack down on officers' bad behavior? to do something else?

2. Whom did Krey assume was her audience? (Look back at the note on the essay, p. 345, if you're not sure.) How do her subject, evidence, and tone reflect her assumptions?

Method and Structure

1. Krey's argument is primarily deductive. Express her main idea in the form of a **syllogism**. Do you detect any flaws in her reasoning? If so, what are they?

2. As a whole, is this essay an example of an appeal to emotions or reasoned argument or both? Give evidence for your answer.

3. Examine how Krey uses information and ideas from sources to develop and support her main idea. What might her argument have lost without this material? Why doesn't she cite any page numbers?

4. OTHER METHODS   Krey builds her argument with **examples** and **cause-and-effect analysis**. What examples of police brutality does Krey give? What reason does she provide to explain the public response? Why does she focus on Ferguson, Missouri, and Baltimore, Maryland, in particular?

Language

1. What is the "fourth estate" (paragraph 9)? Why is this **metaphor** particularly well suited to Krey's argument?

2. What **connotations** do the words *brutality* and *inequality* have for you? Why do you suppose Krey repeats these words as often as she does?

Writing Topics

1. JOURNAL TO ESSAY   Starting from your journal response (p. 345), write an essay about the state of law enforcement in your community, as you see it. You could focus on a particular incident involving the police or on more general patterns of action illustrated with examples. Do the police do their jobs effectively and fairly? Do they contribute to easing or to

increasing tensions among groups of people? Do some groups support the police while others don't?

2. Write an essay expressing your opinion of Krey's piece. For instance, how did you react to her implication that "the media's lack of coverage" (paragraph 6) of deeper issues is at least partly to blame for the protests and violence that result from those issues? to her assertion that "police brutality is [not] the issue at hand" (7)? Do you think she is too critical of her journalistic peers? too forgiving of police? Note whether you agree or disagree with Krey, and support your opinion with your own examples.

3. CULTURAL CONSIDERATIONS   The United States is noteworthy among nations for the rights and protections it affords citizens and others suspected of breaking laws, at least on paper. In some other countries, for instance, law-enforcement officers may use almost any means deemed necessary to obtain evidence against a suspected wrongdoer, whereas in the United States not only the Constitution but also federal, state, and local laws protect the rights of individuals and ensure that these protections are enforced equally. Do you think the US system achieves an appropriate balance between fairness to individuals and effectiveness in deterring or stopping illegal activity, or does it lean too far one way or the other? Write an essay stating your opinion and supporting it with examples from your experience, observations, and reading. If you are familiar with individual rights and law-enforcement procedures in another country, you may want to use **comparison and contrast** to help make your point.

4. CONNECTIONS   Like Krey, Leslie Jamison, in "Sublime, Revised" (p. 162) also examines mainstream media. But where Krey blames news outlets for misinforming their audiences, Jamison places at least some fault on reality television viewers for taking pleasure in witnessing the misfortunes of others. What are our responsibilities as consumers of mass media? Are there times when we should look away, for instance, or dismiss accounts as "fake news"? Or should the goal be to think critically about everything we read, see, and hear? Why do you think so? In an essay of your own, criticize or defend some aspect of the media as you see fit. Be sure to include plenty of details and logical reasoning to support your position.

DEBATE: INCOME INEQUALITY

ON WEALTH

It's easy to have principles when you're rich. The important thing is to have principles when you're poor.
— Ray Kroc

Though I am grateful for the blessings of wealth, it hasn't changed who I am. My feet are still on the ground. I'm just wearing better shoes.
— Oprah Winfrey

There's nothing surer / the rich get rich and the poor get poorer.　— Gus Kahn and Raymond B. Egan

JOURNAL RESPONSE   Write a short journal entry about your attitude toward money. How much is enough? Do you consider yourself wealthy? middle class? working class? poor? Why? How do you view people who are better off than you are? How do you view those who are struggling to make ends meet?

Paul Greenberg

Winner of the Pulitzer Prize for editorial writing in 1969, Paul Greenberg writes sharp, provocative columns on subjects ranging from faith to language to international politics. He was born in 1937 in Shreveport, Louisiana, where he grew up in an apartment above his family's second-hand shoe store. After completing a master's degree in journalism and history from the University of Missouri at Columbia, Greenberg began writing editorials for the *Pine Bluff Commercial* while teaching history at the University of Arkansas. He joined the *Arkansas Democrat-Gazette* in 1992, where he directed the editorial page until 2015 and continues to write a nationally syndicated column. Describing himself as "an ideologically unreliable conservative," Greenberg has been awarded multiple honors, but he might be best remembered as the journalist who gave Bill Clinton the moniker "Slick Willie" during the former president's tenure as governor of Arkansas. A regular commentator on CSPAN, Greenberg is also the author of *Resonant Lives: Fifty Figures of Consequence* (1991); *Entirely Personal* (1992), a memoir; and *No Surprises: Two Decades of Clinton Watching (1996)*. He lives in Little Rock, Arkansas.

The Case for Inequality

Greenberg posted this essay to the conservative news and opinion aggregator *Townhall.com* in September of 2015, while a campaign to raise the minimum wage for fast-food workers to $15 was gathering steam in some major cities and leading Congress to debate raising the federal minimum wage as well. Any regulations aimed at lifting some people out of poverty, Greenberg warns, would sink us all.

Would you really like to live in a society in which all are equal—that is, equally poor? Because that is the inevitable result when the goal becomes equalizing everybody's income.

Would you really like to live in a society that sets a minimum wage for all—and so discourages businesses from hiring workers because they can no longer afford to pay them the mandatory wage? In such a system, no wonder jobs for beginners grow scarce. Also, the minimum wage has this way of becoming the maximum wage. For a society cannot put a floor under wages without the risk of making it the ceiling, too.

Would you really like to live in a society without the rich because all must be equal? A society without rich patrons of the arts, for example, or inventors and investors who've struck it rich and so can afford to provide jobs for the rest of us. And buy the goods and services we provide.

Would you really like to live in a society in which you have no incentive to grow rich yourself because all must remain equal? Which means taxes must be set accordingly. So some of us won't rise too far above our neighbors. To ensure that we don't, enact confiscatory income taxes. Or a heavy estate tax, also known as the death tax.

How about a society in which all are equal before the law? Would you be in favor of that kind of equality? Of course you would. Indeed, that was the original meaning of equality and one well worth restoring. But that meaning now has been changed—impoverished, you might say—until now it means only a material equality, not a legal one. Even though a diversity of ideas, origins and, yes, incomes does not weaken our society but strengthens and enhances it. Because it opens up a society to different ways of thinking, acting and earning.

Yet some of our leading or at least loudest politicians have taken to railing against inequality. It's become the grievance du jour. Demagogues aplenty preach against inequality as if they've just discovered it, and are shocked—shocked! And they vow to stamp it out. They feel no need to mention that, in order for everyone to be equal, at least in the material sense, no one must be allowed to have more than his neighbor. When that policy is put into effect, the practical result is that all remain equally poor. That isn't justice; it's envy in action.

Alexis de Tocqueville, our prescient French visitor a couple of centuries ago, described both the promise and danger of *Democracy in America*, the title of his two-volume masterwork.[1] He warned against what he

---

[1] Alexis de Tocqueville (1805–59), a French statesman and historian, toured the United States in 1831 to study the country's prisons and institutions. *Democracy in America* (1835, 1839) recounts the experience and shares the author's candid assessment of a still-young government. [Editors' note.]

called democratic despotism—the leveling instinct that produces a uniform, egalitarian society in which the arts, for example, would perish. And not just the arts. As he put it, "Not only would a democratic people of this kind show neither aptitude nor taste for science, literature, or art, but it would probably never arrive at the possession of them. The law of descent would of itself provide for the destruction of large fortunes at each succeeding generation, and no new fortunes would be acquired. The poor man, without either knowledge or freedom, would not so much as conceive the idea of raising himself to wealth; and the rich man would allow himself to be degraded to poverty, without a notion of self-defense. Between these two members of the community complete and invincible equality would soon be established. No one would then have time or taste to devote himself to the pursuits or pleasures of the intellect, but all men would remain paralyzed in a state of common ignorance and equal servitude."

Winston Churchill[2] said this: "The inherent vice of capitalism is the 8 unequal sharing of blessings; the inherent virtue of socialism is the equal sharing of miseries." When she came along, Margaret Thatcher, the Iron Lady herself,[3] would elaborate on his point: "The statists are making a big issue out of income inequality, hoping to convince ordinary Americans that redistribution is their only hope for a better life. . . . [T]his is horribly misguided because it falsely assumes the economy is a fixed pie. Simply stated, it doesn't make sense—or help anybody—if inequality is reduced by policies that hurt everyone."

Would you really prefer to live in a society that, in its zeal for equality, 9 has forgotten equity? Would you really like to live in such a society, barren of individual distinction and attainment and the wealth they produce for all, because its goal has become equality, not freedom or excellence?

Think about it. Too many of us don't. 10

Meaning

1. "The Case for Inequality" does not include a thesis statement. What is Greenberg's point? Express the author's main idea in your own words.

2. In paragraph 2, Greenberg writes that "the minimum wage has this way of becoming the maximum wage." What does he mean?

---

[2] Sir Winston Churchill (1874–1965) was the liberal prime minister of Great Britain from 1940 to 1945 and again from 1951 to 1955, the author of multiple histories, and the recipient of the 1953 Nobel prize for literature. [Editor's note.]

[3] Margaret Thatcher (1925–2013) was the conservative prime minister of Great Britain from 1979 through 1990. A Soviet journalist nicknamed her the "Iron Lady" for her steely reserve. [Editors' note.]

3. Why is Greenberg so alarmed by attitudes against inequality? Whom does he blame for the problems experienced by the poor?

4. If you are uncertain of the meanings of any of the words listed below, try to guess them from the context of the essay. Then look them up to see how close your definitions were to those in the dictionary. Test out the new words by using each of them in a sentence or two of your own.

inevitable (1)	material (5, 6)	prescient (7)
mandatory (2)	railing (6)	despotism (7)
patrons (3)	du jour (6)	egalitarian (7)
confiscatory (4)	demagogues (6)	inherent (8)

Purpose and Audience

1. What seems to be Greenberg's purpose in writing this essay? Is he writing mainly to express a concern, offer a solution to a problem, influence government decisions, change individuals' attitudes, or do something else? What evidence from the text supports your answer?

2. Who would Greenberg's ideal readers be: workers? employers? lawyers? members of Congress? average Americans? Why do you think so?

3. Whether you are a low-wage worker or not, you probably have some strong responses to this essay. What *are* your responses? Why? Do you think Greenberg intended for at least some readers to respond the way you do? What in the essay supports your answer?

Method and Structure

1. Why does Greenberg repeat the question "Would you really like to live in a society . . ." at the beginning of the first four paragraphs? What does this stylistic device convey about his attitude toward his subject? How does it fit in with Greenberg's main idea and purpose?

2. Is Greenberg's appeal mostly rational or mostly emotional? Explain your answer with examples from the essay.

3. Where in the essay does Greenberg address opposing viewpoints? How fair is his depiction of people with conflicting opinions?

4. What do you take to be Greenberg's purpose in quoting Alexis de Tocqueville, Winston Churchill, and Margaret Thatcher toward the end of his essay (paragraphs 7 and 8)? What is the effect of the quotations?

5. OTHER METHODS   Part of Greenberg's argument hinges on his **definition** of *equality*. What is the proper meaning of the word, as Greenberg sees it? How does he distinguish it from *equity*, and why does it matter?

Language

1. What does Greenberg achieve by addressing the reader directly at the beginning and end of his essay?

2. Notice that paragraphs 3–5 include multiple **sentence fragments**, such as "And buy the goods and services we provide" (3). Trace these fragments, and consider their effect. Is Greenberg writing carelessly here, or does he write in fragments for a purpose? What do the incomplete sentences contribute to, or take away from, his essay? Explain your answer.

3. How would you characterize Greenberg's **tone**? Is he angry, resigned, hopeful, something else? Does his overall tone strengthen his argument or weaken it? Why?

Writing Topics

1. **JOURNAL TO ESSAY** Building on your journal entry about your attitude toward wealth (p. 351), write a response to Greenberg's essay. Does it anger you? frustrate you? reassure you? inspire you? make you feel something else? Do you find Greenberg's examples, claims, and conclusions to be fair? Did he lead you to rethink your own position on inequality? Why, or why not? Support your response with details from Greenberg's essay and examples from your own experience.

2. Greenberg challenges his readers to reject calls for increasing the minimum wage because he believes doing so would discourage employers from hiring. But are minimum-wage jobs really "for beginners" (paragraph 2), as Greenberg suggests? And are they worth having? Write an essay that offers an alternative solution to the employment issue Greenberg describes. Define the problem as you interpret it, and explain its causes. In your proposal, outline the changes you would like to see take place, identify who would have to make them, and predict how your changes would improve things.

3. **CULTURAL CONSIDERATIONS** Contemporary American society places great importance on work, encouraging people to find and devote themselves to jobs that entail responsibility and opportunity for advancement, to put in long hours when required, and to be available and productive at all times. In contrast, many other cultures emphasize leisure (in some European countries, for instance, businesses shut down for a few hours every afternoon; in others, workers are entitled to eight weeks of paid vacation a year). Write an essay in which you consider the benefits and drawbacks of the American work ethic. What do we gain through hard work and determination? What do we lose?

4. **RESEARCH**   Using the library or the Internet, research a political lobbying organization that is concerned with income inequality, such as Occupy Wall Street, Mind the Gap, or Fight for $15. In an essay, summarize the global vision the organization outlines in its mission statement, which may include goals met to date as well as plans for the future. Then discuss whether you agree with the organization's assessment of current economic issues, its proposed solutions, and its methods for achieving those solutions. (You may need to narrow this discussion to a particular issue.)

5. **CONNECTIONS**   Unlike Greenberg, Nicholas Kristof, the author of the next essay ("Where's the Empathy?"), is clearly in favor of taking measures to reduce income inequality. On what major points do the authors agree and disagree? How do the tones of the two essays compare? Does either writer seem more convinced of being in the right? Which essay do you find more convincing, and why?

ON DEATH

The Bustle in a House / The Morning after Death / Is solemnest of industries / Enacted upon Earth.
—Emily Dickinson

Any man's death diminishes me, because I am involved in mankind.
—John Donne

No one on his deathbed has ever said, "I wish I'd spent more time at the office."
—Paul Tsongas

JOURNAL RESPONSE   In your journal, reflect on the purpose of living. What do you hope to accomplish in your lifetime, and where do your priorities lie? Is career most important? family? community? country? service? faith? something else? Why?

Nicholas Kristof

Nicholas Kristof was born in Chicago in 1959 and raised on a farm in rural Yamhill, Oregon. He graduated from Harvard with a degree in government and then studied law at Oxford on a Rhodes scholarship, finishing in 1983. He has been with the *New York Times* ever since, first as an economics reporter, then a correspondent from Los Angeles, Hong Kong, Beijing, and Tokyo, and now a staff writer and twice-weekly columnist. With his wife, former *Times* reporter Sheryl WuDunn, he has written five books that collect individual human-interest stories to examine culture and politics in general, most recently *Half the Sky: Turning Oppression into Opportunity for Women Worldwide* and *A Path Appears: Transforming Lives, Creating Opportunities* (both 2009). Together they won a Pulitzer Prize for international reporting for their coverage of the 1989 Tiananmen Square protests in Beijing; Kristof has also won a Pulitzer for commentary in 2006 and multiple other awards. He travels the world extensively and has lived on four continents, but he currently makes his home in a suburb of New York City.

Where's the Empathy?

Known for his compassionate focus on human rights and injustices in the developing world and at home, Kristof has been called "the moral conscience" of journalism by his peers. In this *New York Times* column from 2015, he demonstrates that conscience in a heartfelt retort to those who would argue that people receiving government benefits have an easy life. The poor, he insists, are being killed by inequality.

The funeral for my high school buddy Kevin Green is Saturday, near the town where we both grew up. The doctors say he died at age fifty-four of multiple organ failure, but in a deeper sense he died of inequality and a lack of good jobs.

Lots of Americans would have seen Kevin—obese with a huge gray beard, surviving on disability and food stamps—as a moocher. They would have been harshly judgmental: *Why don't you look after your health? Why did you father two kids outside of marriage?*

That acerbic condescension reflects one of this country's fundamental problems: an empathy gap. It reflects the delusion on the part of many affluent Americans that those like Kevin are lazy or living cushy lives. A poll released this month by the Pew Research Center found that wealthy Americans mostly agree that "poor people today have it easy because they can get government benefits without doing anything in return."

Lazy? Easy? Kevin used to set out with his bicycle and a little trailer to collect cans by the roadside. He would make about $20 a day.

Let me tell you about Kevin Green. He grew up on a small farm a couple of miles from my family's, and we both attended the same small rural high school in Yamhill, Oregon. We both ran cross country, took welding and agriculture classes and joined Future Farmers of America. After cross country practice, I'd drive him home to his family farm, with its milk cows, hogs and chickens.

Yamhill - Carlton Union High School in the state of Oregon.

Kevin Green, left, and Nicholas Kristof in 1977.

The Greens encapsulated if not the American dream, at least solid upward mobility. The dad, Thomas, had only a third-grade education and couldn't read. But he had a good union job as a cement finisher, paying far above the minimum wage, and he worked hard and made sure his kids did, too. He had no trouble with the law. Kevin and his big sister, Cindy—one of the sweetest girls in school—both earned high school diplomas. Kevin was sunny, cheerful and astonishingly helpful: Any hint that something needed fixing, and he was there with a wrench. But then the dream began to disintegrate.

The local glove factory and feed store closed, and other blue-collar 7 employers cut back. Good union jobs became hard to find. For a while, Kevin had a low-paying nonunion job working for a construction company. After that company went under, he worked as shift manager making trailer homes. He fell in love and had twin boys that he doted on. But because he and his girlfriend struggled financially, they never married.

Then, about fifteen years ago, Kevin hurt his back and was laid off. 8 Soon afterward, his girlfriend moved out, took the kids and asked for child support. The loss of his girlfriend, kids and job was a huge blow. "It knocked him to the dirt," says his younger brother, Clayton, also a pal of mine. "It destroyed his self-esteem."

Kevin's weight ballooned to 350 pounds, and he developed diabetes 9 and had a couple of heart attacks. He grew marijuana and self-medicated with it, Clayton says, and was arrested for drug offenses. My kids would see Kevin and me together and couldn't believe he had run cross country with me, and that he wasn't twenty years older.

Kevin eventually got disability benefits, but he was far behind in 10 child support and was punished by losing his driver's license—which made it pretty much impossible to get a job in a rural area. Disability helped Kevin by providing a monthly check that he desperately needed, but it also hurt him because he might have looked harder for a job if he hadn't been getting those checks, Clayton says.

Susan Seubert/The New York Times/Redux.

Clayton Green, brother of Kevin Green, at his family's farm in Yamhill, Oregon.

*Clayton Green holding a photo on his cell
phone of his brother Kevin Green at his
family's farm in Yamhill, Oregon.*

Yet it's absurd to think that people like Kevin are somehow living it   11
up. After child support deductions, he was living on about $180 a month
plus food stamps and a small income from selling home-grown pot. He
supplemented this by growing a huge vegetable garden and fishing in the
Yamhill River.

Three years ago, Cindy died of a heart attack at fifty-two. Then doc-   12
tors told Kevin a few weeks ago that his heart, liver and kidneys were
failing, and that he was dying. He had trouble walking. He was in pain. He
was also worried about his twin boys. They had trouble in school and
with the law, jailed for drug and other offenses. The upward mobility that
had seemed so promising a generation ago turned out to be a mirage.
Family structure dissolved, and lives become grueling—and shorter.

Kevin wrote a will a few days before he died. He bequeathed his life's   13
savings of $3,500 to his mom for his funeral expenses. Anything left over
is to be divided between his children—and he begs them not to fight over
it. His ashes will be sprinkled on the farm.

I have trouble diagnosing just what went wrong in that odyssey from   14
sleek distance runner to his death at fifty-four, but the lack of good jobs
was central to it. Sure, Kevin made mistakes, but his dad had opportunities
for good jobs that Kevin never had. So, Kevin Green, RIP. You were a good
man—hardworking and always on the lookout for someone to help—yet

you were overturned by riptides of inequality. Those who would judge you don't have a clue. They could use a dose of your own empathy.

Meaning

1. What does Kristof mean by "an empathy gap," and why does he consider it "one of this country's fundamental problems" (paragraph 3)?

2. Where does Kristof place the blame for the Green family's loss of "upward mobility" (paragraph 6) from one generation to the next? What, to his mind, caused the "[American] dream . . . to disintegrate" (6), at least in rural Yamhill, Oregon?

3. What thesis does Kristof attempt to support? Is it stated anywhere?

4. If you are uncertain of the meanings of any of the words listed below, try to guess them from the context of the essay. Then look them up to see how close your definitions were to those in the dictionary. Test out the new words by using each of them in a sentence or two of your own.

acerbic (3)	disintegrate (6)	odyssey (14)
affluent (3)	mirage (12)	riptides (14)
encapsulated (6)	bequeathed (13)	

Purpose and Audience

1. What do you think inspired Kristof to write this essay for his newspaper column? Is he simply expressing his condolences? What else might he be trying to accomplish? What evidence from the text supports your opinion?

2. For whom is Kristof writing: Kevin Green's family? his former employers? the residents of Yamhill, Oregon? other people living on disability and food stamps? someone else? Why do you think so?

Method and Structure

1. As a whole, is "Where's the Empathy?" an example of appeal to emotion, reasoned argument, or both? How would you rate Kristof's ethical appeal? Give evidence for your answer.

2. How does Kristof handle opposing viewpoints? What is the effect of acknowledging that disability benefits might have discouraged his friend from looking for work?

3. Take a close look at the photographs included with this essay. Where do they come from? What do they contribute to Kristof's argument?

4. **OTHER METHODS** What killed Kevin Green, according to his doctors? according to Kristof? How does the author use **cause-and-effect** analysis to build his argument?

Language

1. What is the effect of the two one-word questions that Kristof asks at the start of paragraph 4?

2. Why do you suppose Kristof addresses his friend directly, as "you," in his conclusion?

3. Examine Kristof's tone. How would you characterize his attitude toward his subject?

Writing Topics

1. **JOURNAL TO ESSAY**   Most of us have to work to support ourselves and our families, but as Kristof suggests, an inability to find or keep a good job can overshadow, or even destroy, a person's life. Look again at the quotations preceding his essay and at your journal notes (p. 357), and then compose an essay on the subject of work/life balance. What role does work play in a person's happiness? What role do personal relationships play? How can a person successfully juggle the demands and rewards of both? What if there is no work to be had?

2. In paragraph 6, Kristof notes that Kevin Green's father had a high-paying union job in construction; later he comments that Kevin could only find a "low-paying nonunion job" in the same industry (7). What is your response to these remarks? Write an essay that considers the impact of labor unions on the US job market. What are some sources of friction? What are some advantages? To what extent should the United States encourage unionization, and to what extent should the country restrict it? Why? Use examples from your own experience, observations, and reading.

3. **CULTURAL CONSIDERATIONS**   Kristof's essay questions the foundations of the American dream, which holds that a person from even the most humble circumstances can achieve prosperity through determination and hard work. How realistic, or not, do you think the American dream is today? Write an essay answering this question. As evidence you may want to discuss how, if at all, the American dream applies to you, given your background.

4. **CONNECTIONS**   While Kristof writes with compassion about the struggles experienced by low-wage workers in a weak economy, Paul Greenberg, in the previous essay ("The Case for Inequality," p. 351) writes with admiration of the accomplishments and contributions of the rich. In an essay of your own, consider some aspect of competition and fairness in a capitalistic society. Are executive salaries too high, for instance? Should all workers be guaranteed a living wage? What role should the government play in ensuring citizens' economic well-being? Why do you think so?

ON RACISM

In America there is institutional racism that we all inherit and participate in, like breathing the air in this room—and we have to become sensitive to it.

—Henry Louis Gates Jr.

Racism is man's gravest threat to man—the maximum of hatred for the minimum of reason.

—Abraham Joshua Heschel

An ugly idea left unchallenged begins to turn the color of normal.

—Chimamanda Ngozi Adichie

JOURNAL RESPONSE Prejudice is so pervasive in our society that it can be difficult to avoid. Think of a time when somebody made an assumption about you or treated you badly because of your membership in a group (as a racial, ethnic, religious, or sexual minority; as a science or humanities major; as a club member; as a woman or man; as a "jock," "nerd," or "townie," and so on). Write a journal entry about the incident and how it made you feel.

Brent Staples

Brent Staples was born in 1951 in Chester, Pennsylvania. After receiving a BA from Widener University and a PhD in psychology from the University of Chicago, he began writing on culture and politics for the *New York Times* in 1985. Since 1990, he has been a member of the *Times* editorial board and a contributor to publications including *Ms.*, *Harper's Magazine*, *Slate*, and the *New York Times Magazine*. Staples has also published two books: *Parallel Time: Growing Up in Black and White* (1994), a memoir, and *An American Love Story* (1999), a companion book to the PBS documentary about an interracial family.

Confederate Memorials as Instruments of Racial Terror

How much of a problem is racism in the United States? One area of contentious debate in recent years has concerned the meaning of images honoring the Confederacy — the eleven Southern states that seceded from the Union in 1861, sparking the Civil War and fomenting tensions that linger to this day. While many Southerners defend the Confederate flag and public statues memorializing Confederate leaders as symbols of heritage and regional pride, protestors and some politicians have called for the removal of such symbols on the grounds they celebrate the institution of slavery and purposefully intimidate African Americans. In this essay — published shortly after South Carolina announced the Confederate flag would no longer fly at its statehouse — Staples takes the latter position. "Confederate Memorials as Instruments of Racial Terror" first appeared in the *New York Times* in July 2015.

The Confederate-flag-waving white supremacist charged with murdering   1
nine African Americans in a Charleston, South Carolina, church in June[1] demolished the fiction that the flag was an innocuous symbol of "Southern pride." This barbaric act made it impossible for politicians to hide from the fact that the Confederate banner has been a rallying symbol embraced by racists, night riders and white supremacy groups dating back to the nineteenth century.

This long-denied truth applies as well to Confederate memorials that   2
occupy public space all over the South. Most were erected in the late nineteenth and early twentieth centuries, when the Southern states were eagerly dismantling the rights and liberties that African Americans had enjoyed just after the Civil War, during Reconstruction.[2] These states unleashed a racialized reign of terror and shored up white supremacy by rewriting their Constitutions to disqualify African Americans from full citizenship.

As nonpersons in the eyes of the state, black people had no standing   3
to challenge the rush of Civil War nostalgia that led the South to stock its parks and public squares with symbols that celebrated the Confederate cause of slavery and instilled racial fear. Only in recent decades have black elected officials and some whites started to push back against the Confederate narrative of Southern civic life.

In the wake of the Charleston massacre, for example, the parks and   4
recreation board of Birmingham, Alabama, voted to explore a proposal that would remove a fifty-two-foot Confederate memorial from the entrance of a prominent park and place it with a Confederate heritage group.

---

[1] Staples is referring to Dylan Roof, a self-declared white supremacist who planned and executed a mass shooting in a historically black church for the express purpose of inciting racial violence. His social media accounts at the time were emblazoned with images of the Confederate battle flag. [Editors' note.]

[2] The period following the end of the Civil War (1865–77), during which the federal government held control over the eleven Southern states that had seceded from the Union and granted citizenship, civil liberties, and voting rights to freed slaves. Most states effectively rescinded those freedoms — through intimidation, literacy tests, and poll taxes — when they regained control of their governments. [Editors' note.]

Not all monuments warrant that kind of challenge. But those honoring the Confederate general Nathan Bedford Forrest deserve the backlash they have generated. Forrest presided over the 1864 massacre of Union soldiers, many of them black, at Fort Pillow in Tennessee. He was also a prominent slave trader and served as the first grand wizard of the Ku Klux Klan.[3]

Apologists argue that his involvement with the Klan was unimportant because he later adopted more enlightened views. But as the Forrest biographer Jack Hurst writes, by lending his name to the KKK even temporarily, the general accelerated its development. "As the Klan's first national leader," Mr. Hurst writes, "he became the Lost Cause's avenging angel, galvanizing a loose collection of boyish secret social clubs into a reactionary instrument of terror still feared today."

Protests erupted in Selma, Alabama, in 2000 when a bust of Forrest was unveiled on the grounds of a museum. (One critic likened it to erecting a statue of Hitler in a Jewish neighborhood.) The sculpture was subsequently moved to a cemetery.

Two years ago, the Memphis City Council expunged Confederate names from three parks, one of them named in honor of Forrest. The Council argued that the names were inappropriate for a majority-black

USA TODAY NETWORK/ Sipa USA.

Demonstrators protest at the statue of Nathan Bedford Forrest in Memphis, Tennessee.

---

[3] A secret society formed after the Civil War to assert white supremacy through intimidation, harassment, and violence. [Editors' note.]

city and inconsistent with the cosmopolitan image that Memphis wished to cultivate. The Ku Klux Klan marched in protest.

The Council went further this month, when it voted to begin the process of removing the towering statue of Forrest from what is now known as Health Sciences Park. The plan also calls for removing the remains of Forrest and his wife, which were moved from their original graves and transferred to the park in 1905.   9

Memphis leaders are not alone in their antipathy toward Forrest. Just days after the Charleston killings in June, Bill Haslam, Tennessee's Republican governor, said he supported removing a bust of Forrest from the state Capitol, adding that the general was not someone he would choose to honor.   10

Critics predictably condemn these efforts as bad-faith attempts to rewrite history. But what's happening is that communities that were once bound and gagged on this issue are now free to contest a version of history that was created to reinforce racial subjugation. They are reflecting on how to honor history—including the neglected history of African Americans—and rightly deciding that some figures who were enshrined as heroes in the past do not deserve to be valorized in public places.   11

Meaning

1. What does Staples say was the original purpose in erecting Confederate memorials in Southern communities? Why does it matter when they were created? How does he explain the recent surge in protests of such memorials?

2. Is Staples saying that all Confederate memorials should be taken down? Why do you suppose he focuses on statues of Nathan Bedford Forrest in making his case?

3. Does Staples have a thesis? Where in the essay does he state the gist of his argument most clearly?

4. If you are uncertain of the meanings of any of the words listed below, try to guess them from the context of the essay. Then look them up to see how close your definitions were to those in the dictionary. Test out the new words by using each of them in a sentence or two of your own.

innocuous (1)	galvanizing (6)	subjugation (11)
barbaric (1)	expunged (8)	enshrined (11)
heritage (4)	cosmopolitan (8)	valorized (11)
avenging (6)	antipathy (10)	

Purpose and Audience

1. What seems to have inspired Staples to write this essay? How is "Confederate Memorials as Instruments of Racial Terror" a reaction to a particular cultural moment?

2. Who do you think is the author's target audience? How does Staples engage these readers' support?

Method and Structure

1. If his subject is statues, why does Staples open his essay with a reference to the Confederate flag and the massacre in Charleston? What does he mean when he says "the Confederate banner has been a rallying symbol embraced by racists, night riders, and white supremacy groups dating back to the nineteenth century" (paragraph 1)? To what history is he referring?

2. Staples's argument is based on deduction. Express his reasoning in the form of a syllogism (see pp. 334–335). Do you detect any flaws in his logic? If so, what are they?

3. Why do you think Staples quotes Jack Hurst in paragraph 6? What is the effect of his citing this **source** in particular?

4. Where can you find reference to opposing viewpoints in Staples's essay? How, if at all, does his treatment of alternative perspectives on the issue affect the persuasiveness of his argument?

5. **OTHER METHODS** Staples's argument is based on **examples** of Southern cities that have sought to take down statues of Nathan Bedford Forrest. What does he interpret such efforts to reveal about history?

Language

1. Why does Staples place quotation marks around the phrase "Southern pride" in his introduction (paragraph 1)?

2. Explain the **metaphor** Nathan Bedford Forrest's biographer uses in his assessment of the general's legacy. What does he mean by the "Lost Cause" (paragraph 6)?

3. What is the overall tone of Staples's argument? Is it mainly impassioned or mainly reasoned?

Writing Topics

1. **JOURNAL TO ESSAY** Staples writes about racial prejudices that harm black residents of Southern cities, and in your journal entry (p. 363), you

recorded a personal experience of being prejudged or mistreated for your membership in a group. Now write an essay in which you recount this experience in more detail. What about the prejudgment was inaccurate or unfair? How were you mistreated, and by whom? How did the experience make you feel? Write for a reader who is not a member of the group in question, being sure to include enough detail to bring the experience to life.

2. Think of an issue you feel strongly about, with no hesitation about your point of view being the right one. Write an essay, based largely on emotional appeal, in which you argue your point of view on that issue and state as your thesis the action you think should be taken. Remember that *emotional* does not mean *irrational*: your reasoning must be sound even when you rely on readers' feelings and beliefs, and your appeal must be appropriate to the subject and to the argument (see pp. 330–331).

3. **CULTURAL CONSIDERATIONS**   Staples writes in his conclusion that "what's happening is that communities that were once bound and gagged on this issue are now free to contest a version of history that was created to reinforce racial subjugation" (paragraph 11). What do you think of this statement? Can you think of other forms of racial discrimination that are built into current government policies and practices? And to what extent does it matter whether discrimination is contested or not? Write an essay in which you examine the state of racial discrimination in contemporary politics or culture. You may wish to think broadly about this issue, but bring your essay down to earth by focusing on a specific form of discrimination—perhaps one you've experienced or witnessed in your own life.

4. **CONNECTIONS**   The next two essays, "The End of History?" by Ernest B. Furgurson (p. 369) and "Notes from a Black Daughter of the Confederacy" by Lisa Richardson (p. 376), counter and complicate the argument Brent Staples makes in "Confederate Memorials as Instruments of Racial Terror." Write a response of your own in which you establish your position on the debate over Confederate memorials. Do you agree with Staples that such statues are racist and intimidating and therefore should be taken down, or do you take Furgurson's view that they represent our history and should be respected, even honored? Or does your position fall somewhere between the two extremes, as Richardson's does? Use examples from your own observations and experience (or from the opinions of those you respect) to support your argument.

ON HISTORY

The problem is that my generation was pacified into believing that
racism existed only in our history books.
　　　　　　　　　　　　　　　　　　　　　　　—Chance the Rapper

History is written by the victors.
　　　　　　　　　　　　　　　　　　　　　　　—Proverb

Those who cannot remember the past are condemned to repeat it.
　　　　　　　　　　　　　　　　　　　　　　　—George Santayana

JOURNAL RESPONSE　What does American history mean to you? Is it something you take for granted, a source of pride (or shame), or is it something you hope to learn more about someday? Why? In your journal, reflect on the legacies of our shared past. What privileges and responsibilities come with living in the United States?

Ernest B. Furgurson

Esteemed journalist Ernest B. "Pat" Furgurson (born 1929) grew up in Danville, Virginia, and has spent most of his adult life in and around Washington, DC. He attended Averett College in Danville and spent a few years writing for the *Danville Commercial Appeal,* the Associated Press, the *Roanoke World-News,* and the *Richmond News Leader* before he completed a master's degree at Columbia University in 1953. Furgurson then served for two years in the US Marine Corps and embarked on a decades-long career with the *Baltimore Sun,* working variously as a correspondent, syndicated national affairs columnist, and chief of the Washington Bureau. Furgurson has also published six books of biography and history: *Westmoreland: The Inevitable General* (1968), *Hard Right: The Rise of Jesse Helms* (1986), *Chancellorsville, 1863: The Souls of the Brave* (1992), *Ashes of Glory: Richmond at War* (1996), *Not War but Murder: Cold Harbor, 1864* (2000), and *Freedom Rising: Washington in the Civil War* (2004). Now retired, he continues to write occasional pieces for newspapers and popular magazines.

The End of History?

As a columnist and a historian, Furgurson has long focused his attention on the culture and politics of the American South. In this essay written for the Autumn 2015 issue of *The American Scholar,* a quarterly journal published by the Phi Beta Kappa honor society, he responds directly to Brent Staples's *New York Times* column (p. 363) and similar arguments for removing Confederate memorials from public spaces. Even if they're well intentioned, he cautions, such efforts could quickly get out of hand.

With the lowering of the Confederate battle flag in South Carolina and   1
elsewhere, some diehards still insist that the banner had nothing to do
with race, that it was just a symbol of their Southern heritage. Other
Americans long offended by the Confederate monuments that stand all
across Dixie are urging that those memorials come down along with the
flag. Still others clarify the matter in three words: black lives matter, spray-
painted on monuments north and south. Somewhere amid all this, I am
trying to place myself.

So far, the debate lacks nuance. It seems simple: the Confederate States   2
of America existed to preserve slavery, so anything honoring its memory
should be erased from modern America. But before we send out the wreck-
ing ball, let's do nuance: where do we start, and where do we stop?

What about statues that were cast to mourn for the dead, erected not by   3
the Ku Klux Klan[1] or its descendants, but by grieving widows? Should those
in graveyards be allowed to stand? What about the memorial in Green Hill
Cemetery in my hometown, Danville, Virginia? It's a tall obelisk erected in
1878 by the Ladies Memorial Association, standing in what is today a mostly
black neighborhood. It's a monument to the dead, but it's by no means neutral. It features bas-reliefs of Robert E. Lee and Stonewall Jackson,[2] and says,

> Patriots! Know that these fell in the effort to establish just government
> and perpetuate Constitutional Liberty. Who thus die, will live in lofty
> example.

If it should go, what about the simple government-issued headstone
nearby, which identifies my Civil War great-grandfather as "1st Sgt Co I
53rd Va Infantry," and thousands of others like it?

What about Monument Avenue in Richmond, with its grand like-   4
nesses of Lee, Jackson, Jefferson Davis, J. E. B. Stuart, Matthew Fontaine
Maury?[3] Might we differentiate between fiery politicians such as Davis,
who wasn't even a Virginian, and the generals they dragged into war? If
the generals should go, then what about the privates who marched
because their neighbors did, defending slavery even though they never

---

[1] A secret society formed after the Civil War to assert white supremacy through
intimidation, harassment, and violence. [Editors' note.]

[2] The two best known generals of the Confederate army. Robert E. Lee (1807–70)
surrendered to the Union army's leader Ulysses S. Grant at Appomattox, Virginia,
in 1865. Jackson (1824–63) partnered with Lee and was accidentally shot by his
own troops. [Editors' note.]

[3] Jefferson Davis (1808–89) was president of the Confederacy. General J.E.B.
Stuart (1833–64) led the Confederate troops at the Battle of Gettysburg. Matthew
Fontaine Maury (1806–73) was a Southern naval officer. [Editors' note.]

owned a slave? What about the statues of Confederate soldiers standing before hundreds of county courthouses? Most face north defiantly, muskets at the ready. But others, like the one facing south in the center of Alexandria, Virginia, are unarmed, hats off, heads bowed, clearly mourning fallen comrades. Shall we appoint committees to decide what each sculptor was thinking? You're right: this could get silly.

Detail from the west frieze of the Confederate monument in Arlington National Cemetery.

But suppose we did decide to tear those down—what about all the 5 other reminders of our shameful past? Mount Vernon, Monticello, Montpelier, and the other homes of our slave-owning presidents?[4] What about the statues of Confederate soldiers on every Civil War battlefield site?

To take down every offensive monument in the South willy-nilly 6 reminds me of the wholesale de-Stalinization campaign that I witnessed in the old Soviet Union, and the destruction of ancient monuments by ISIS and Taliban fanatics today.[5] Totalitarian states may decree that the painful past never happened, but any such official effort in our country, even one executed selectively, would be tragic.

---

[4] The mansion at Mount Vernon, Virginia, was home to George Washington. Monticello, in Charlottesville, Virginia, was Thomas Jefferson's estate. James Madison and his wife Dolley lived among several acres and buildings in Montpelier Station, Virginia. All three properties are maintained as historic landmarks and are open to the public for visits and tours. [Editors' note.]

[5] Upon taking office in 1956, Soviet leader Nikita Khrushchev oversaw a campaign to remove public images of and memorials to his predecessor, Josef Stalin. ISIS and Taliban terrorists have in recent years taken to demolishing significant cultural artifacts, among them the Temple of Baal in Palmyra, Syria, the Mosul Museum and Libraries in Iraq, and the Walls of Ninevah in Assyria. [Editors' note.]

Saying all this, and considering my ancestors, I might be shrugged off 7 as just another rearguard Rebel. I qualify four times over for membership in the Sons of Confederate Veterans,[6] vigorous defenders of their heritage and its symbols. Because I'd written Civil War history, I was invited about twenty years ago to speak to the SCV camp in Alexandria. In my talk, I recalled my great-grandfather who died of smallpox in the Yankee prison at Fort Delaware, and the three others who were wounded later in the war. The Sons were impressed. And then I told them that the Confederate battle flag was a provocation that should be retired to the museum. I haven't been invited back.

The punch line of that talk was a pale version of everything I've said 8 and written about race and racism since I did my first column for the late, lamented *Danville Commercial Appeal* at the age of eighteen. Yet, because I remain concerned that I might be misunderstood when I suggest going slow in the current debate, I've let others say what I've been thinking.

Mayor Stephanie Rawlings-Blake of Baltimore, with hard-earned 9 experience trying to cool public anger, has wisely punted these matters by naming a committee to dig into the issue and stir public dialogue. Roger Davidson Jr., a professor at Baltimore's Coppin State University—who, like the mayor, is African American—thinks that demolishing the monuments would be "horrible" because they can be teaching tools about a chapter still misunderstood by too many people.

New York Times editorialist Brent Staples, who has written eloquently 10 about growing up black, strongly supports removing statues of villains like Confederate general Nathan Bedford Forrest,[7] who was a postwar organizer of the Klan. Such efforts are not "bad-faith attempts to rewrite history," he says, but reflections on "how to honor history . . . and rightly deciding that some figures who were enshrined as heroes in the past do not deserve to be valorized in public places."

Interesting that Staples says "some figures," which may suggest just 11 the most egregious offenders, or just Confederates. But neither he nor the mayor nor the professor nor I want to start bulldozing without serious "reflections on how to honor history." For me, that should mean enshrining other heroes at least as conspicuously as the ones who now stir such passions.

---

[6] A private historical society and social club whose membership is limited to the male descendants of Southern Civil War veterans. [Editors' note.]

[7] General Forrest (1821–77) oversaw the massacre of mostly African American Union soldiers at Fort Pillow in 1864. He was the first grand wizard of the Ku Klux Klan. [Editors' note.]

Imagine Martin Luther King, Jr. standing tall in the capital of every   12
state in the old Confederacy, indeed the whole Union . . . Move Arthur
Ashe's token memorial off Monument Avenue and put a grander one on
the broad Boulevard nearby, renaming it Ashe Boulevard. Along it, raise
Powhatan Beaty, Decatur Dorsey, and Edward Ratcliff, who fled slavery to
join the US Colored Troops and won the Medal of Honor fighting for
freedom . . . Erect Thurgood Marshall, Sojourner Truth, Frederick Doug-
lass, Medgar Evers, Crispus Attucks, A. Philip Randolph, Dred Scott, Rosa
Parks, Harriet Tubman . . . The list stretches from 1619 into tomorrow.[8]

If we're going to honor our history, let us honor all of it.   13

Meaning

1. Does this essay have a thesis? Where does the author place himself on the
   issue of Confederate memorials? For instance, does he insist on leaving
   them alone, demand their removal, seek protections for African Americans in the South, or propose an alternate solution to the problem?
   Where does he make his position clear?

2. Why does Furgurson go out of his way to ask about statues "erected not
   by the Ku Klux Klan or its descendants, but by grieving widows" (paragraph 3)? To what argument is he **alluding**?

3. On what grounds does Furgurson oppose removing Confederate memorials? Do you find his reasons convincing? Why, or why not?

4. If you are uncertain of the meanings of any of the words listed below, try
   to guess them from the context of the essay. Then look them up to see
   how close your definitions were to those in the dictionary. Test out the
   new words by using each of them in a sentence or two of your own.

Dixie (1)	totalitarian (6)	lamented (8)
nuance (2)	rearguard (7)	punted (9)
obelisk (3)	Rebel (7)	eloquently (10)
bas-reliefs (3)	Yankee (7)	egregious (11)
willy-nilly (6)	provocation (7)	conspicuously (11)

Purpose and Audience

1. What do you think inspired Furgurson to write this essay in his retirement? Is he simply expressing his frustration? What else might he be
   trying to accomplish? What evidence from the text supports your
   opinion?

---

[8] The people Furgurson lists here are all notable figures in African American history. [Editors' note.]

2. What assumptions does Furgurson make about his readers—their race or ethnicity, their regional affiliations, their political leanings, their knowledge of history and current events, and so on?

3. What effect does Furgurson achieve with the frequent use of first-person pronouns such as *I*, *my*, *we*, and *us*? What does this **point of view** suggest about his relationship to his subject? about his readers' relationship to it?

Method and Structure

1. Does "The End of History?" rely mainly on logical reasoning or emotional appeal? Does the author offer sufficient evidence for his claims, in your view?

2. Where does Furgurson stand on the issue of the Confederate flag? How does it relate to his position on Confederate monuments?

3. Notice that the author cites the opinions of a mayor and a college professor in paragraph 9. Why does he do so? Why has Furgurson been content to "let others say what [he's] been thinking" (8)?

4. Why does Furgurson quote Brent Staples in paragraphs 10 and 11? What function do these passages serve? How are they related to the last line of this essay?

5. **OTHER METHODS**   Examine Furgurson's **descriptions** of memorials throughout the essay. How vivid are they, to your mind? What is their effect?

Language

1. Furgurson poses several questions in this essay, starting with "where do we start, and where do we stop?" (paragraph 2). What is the purpose of such questions?

2. Consider the ellipses (sets of three spaced periods) in paragraph 12. Why do you suppose Furgurson uses them?

3. Furgurson uses many **colloquial** words and expressions, such as *diehards* (paragraph 1), *this could get silly* (4), and *willy-nilly* (6). What similar phrases capture your notice? What is the effect of such language?

Writing Topics

1. **JOURNAL TO ESSAY**   In your journal entry (p. 369), you reflected on what American history means to you. Now that you've read Furgurson's argument against removing Confederate monuments, write a response to his essay. You may find it helpful to do some **freewriting** first to work out what you think about the issue and why. And you may find it helpful

to consider one or more of these questions: Do you find that Furgurson backs up his claims with convincing and sufficient evidence? Do you see any weaknesses in his argument? Does he overstate his case anywhere or neglect to address important points? Do you agree with certain parts of his argument but not others? Or are you in complete agreement with him? How, in your mind, can we "honor all of" (paragraph 13) our history? Support your response with details from Furgurson's essay and examples from your own observation and experience.

2. Choose a social, political, or other kind of problem you care about—it could be the difficulty of obtaining affordable health insurance, over-crowding in public schools, violence in the media, child neglect, or anything else. Describe the problem as you understand it, particularly how it affects people. Then discuss your solution to the problem or some part of it. Be sure to at least acknowledge opposing views.

3. **RESEARCH** Take another look at the list of names Furgurson presents in paragraph 12. How familiar are you with these people and their contributions to American history? Run a quick search, online or using the biographical entries in a college dictionary, to learn the basics about any you don't already know of, then pick a person, or a group of related people (soldiers, for instance, or civil rights leaders of the 1960s), and research their lives. Based on what you learn, write an argument explaining why your chosen subject(s) should (or should not) be memorialized with a public monument such as a statue, a building, or a park or street name. As you compose your argument, consider the following questions: What form should such a monument take, and where should it be located? Who would you have create it? Who will pay for it, and why?

4. **CONNECTIONS** In responding to Brent Staples's argument against the public display of Confederate memorials (p. 363), Ernest Furgurson notes that "the debate lacks nuance" (paragraph 2). How does the next essay, by Lisa Richardson, answer his call? Read "Notes from a Black Daughter of the Confederacy" (next page) and, in a short essay of your own, explain how and why it complicates the issue, not only of the memorials, but also of the history they represent. What can we learn from facing the past, and what should we do with our knowledge?

ON FAMILY

All happy families are alike; each unhappy family is unhappy in its
own way.
—Leo Tolstoy

You don't choose your family. They are God's gift to you, as you are
to them.
—Desmond Tutu

We all grow up with the weight of history on us. Our ancestors dwell
in the attics of our brains as they do in the spiraling chains of knowledge
hidden in every cell of our bodies.
—Shirley Abbott

JOURNAL RESPONSE   Everybody has a history. What is yours? In your journal,
write some notes on your family's backstory based on what you know about
your parents, your grandparents and great-grandparents, or other relatives
who have had an influence on you. Where do they come from, and where
are they now? What obstacles have they overcome, and what have they
achieved? What aspects of your past would you like to know more about?

Lisa Richardson

Lisa Richardson is a former writer for the *Los Angeles Times*. Originally from Boston,
she earned a BA from Dartmouth College in 1986 and has also studied politics and
culture in Spain at the University of Granada and the University of Salamanca. Her
career at the *Times* spanned nearly twenty-five years: she started in 1992 as a
reporter for the South Bay Bureau in Torrance, California, worked her way up to the
Orange County edition, and ultimately landed on the Metro editorial staff, where
she wrote about race, culture, and class, among other contentious topics. Now
head of marketing and communications for a law firm started up by some college
classmates and longtime friends, Richardson lives in Los Angeles but roots for the
Celtics, the Red Sox, and the Patriots.

Notes from a Black Daughter of the Confederacy

The following essay appeared in the *Los Angeles Times* on August 27, 2017, two
weeks after violent protests over the planned removal of a statue of Robert E. Lee
in Charlottesville, Virginia, renewed the national debate over Confederate memorials and brought with it a heightened sense of urgency. In "Notes from a Black
Daughter of the Confederacy," Richardson combines her family's story with a brief
lesson in American history to counter arguments, like those made by Earnest B.

Furgurson in "The End of History?" (p. 369), that the monuments should remain standing because they represent a shared past.

As monuments to the Confederacy are swept away from public spaces, white supremacists, neo-Nazis and the president of the United States have been fretting over the so-called attack on history, presumably their history. Their white history. Attack, assault, erasure, destruction—well, truth and justice in the face of denial and dissembling can certainly feel like that. But there is no such thing as whites-only history; there never was, not even with regard to the Confederacy.

Like millions of African Americans, I am the descendant of a Confederate soldier. True, we are most likely descendants through coerced sex and rape, but we are descendants all the same. According to *Ancestry.com*, the DNA of the average African American is twenty-nine percent European. These bronzed Southern soldiers are literally our forefathers too.

In the peculiar, perverted institution of slavery, white men sired, enslaved and often sold their own children; black nieces and white nephews played together before adulthood drove them to disparate destinies. Whites owned their black siblings. Thomas Jefferson[1] was forty-five when he fathered the first of six children on the fifteen-year-old Sally Hemmings, who was his wife's half sister and also her property. My great-great-grandmother Mary Ellen Fulton was her mistress's niece.

None of this is new or secret information. But the Southern states established powerful "don't ask, don't tell" rules that were essential to both their social structure and the economics of slavery. With power on one side and humiliation on the other, our mythical, segregated history took shape.

Of course, most white Southerners of the period were neither villains nor heroes. The majority did not enslave other people, but neither did they advocate the end of slavery or even the softening of slavery. They did not work to halt the worst practices of the era—the sale of children away from parents, the separation of husbands and wives—nor did they seek to end the concubinage of enslaved girls and women. Many did not own slaves simply because they couldn't afford them.

Blacks and whites will have different perspectives on their entwined history. War victory for my white great-great-great grandfather, Jeremiah H. Dial, who enlisted in the 31st Arkansas infantry regiment and was wounded in the battle of Stone River, Tennessee, in December 1862, would have meant defeat for my great-great-great-grandmother Lavinia

---

[1] Thomas Jefferson (1743–1826) was the third president of the United States and a slaveholder. [Editors' note.]

Fulton and their daughter, Mary Ellen. Instead, Lavinia died a free woman, living to play with her grandchildren and give thanks to God every Sunday in church in Birmingham, Alabama. I thank God my great-great-great-grandfather lost. Every right-thinking person should be glad he lost.

Yet the monuments debate isn't really about the past. It's about a present-day assertion of white supremacy and whether our nation is going to stop making excuses and stare it down. Most of the statues, as has been widely discussed, were erected long after Robert E. Lee surrendered at Appomattox.[2] They were hoisted into view to assert white dominance at specific points in time when African Americans gained a measure of political influence—during Reconstruction[3] and the civil rights era. With the bronzes came domestic terrorism, lynchings, bombings and cross burnings. The current uptick in neo-Nazi and white supremacist activity was entirely predictable. With clockwork precision it surged at the time of the nation's first African American president. 7

So why do some people treat modern icons as if they were ancient relics, like marbles from the Parthenon?[4] 8

Fear. History isn't being erased, but it is being corrected. Relocating a Confederate statue to, say, a museum, is an acknowledgment that we see the naked emperor; we see through the contorted logic that it is possible to separate the Confederacy from the institution of slavery, that it's a whites-only story and slavery is blacks-only, and that treason is the same as patriotism. 9

The president has asked, "Where will it end?" Will the removal of General Lees lead to upheaval for Thomas Jefferson? Trigger the end for George Washington? 10

I would ask, How could a patriot be confused with a traitor? How can leading a war to bring forth a new country be confused with leading a rebellion to tear it in two? 11

The two kinds of monuments do, however, have something in common. The memorialized men serve as avatars, as conduits for the 12

---

[2] The leading general of the Confederate army, Robert E. Lee (1807–70) surrendered to the Union army's leader Ulysses S. Grant at Appomattox, Virginia, in 1865. [Editors' note.]

[3] The period following the end of the Civil War (1865–77), during which the federal government held control over the eleven Southern states that had seceded from the Union and granted citizenship, civil liberties, and voting rights to freed slaves. [Editors' note.]

[4] The Elgin marbles are sculptures created between 447 and 432 BC for the Parthenon, an ancient Greek temple to the goddess Athena. In the early 1800s, an agent for the Ottoman Empire removed about half of the surviving statues and panels to the British Museum in London; Greece has been lobbying for their return ever since. [Editors' note.]

values they espoused. Revolutionary-era monuments lead us to contemplate and revere Revolutionary-era values. Confederate monuments do the same for Confederate ideals. The men of both ages were flawed, but the values of one age bind and sustain us as a nation. The values of the other do not.

As for my Confederate ancestor, I consider him without bitterness. 13
He was a man of his time, his family, his community and his culture. He probably wasn't particularly evil—just an ordinary man, without the advantage we have: 152 years' perspective on the Civil War. I have met a few of his white descendants—my cousins—and we regard each other with genuine affection.

To those who would keep Jeremiah Dial frozen in time, forever trapped 14
at the moment he chose a cause on the wrong side of humanity, I believe you do him a disservice. To those who use him as an excuse to fly the flag of modern-day anti-Semitism, racism and bigotry, you have no right.

To all the bronze Confederate soldiers, in whom I see the image of my 15
great-great-great-grandfather, I would extend this grace. Without resentment or rancor, I would move them into museums and there tell the story of their lives. I would end their utility as flashpoints for racism and division, and, once and for all, allow them to retire from their long service as sentries over a whitewashed history.

Meaning

1. Where does Richardson identify the intertwined problems she intends to address? What solution does she propose?

2. Where, if at all, does Richardson state her thesis? Summarize the point of her argument in your own words.

3. If "the monuments debate isn't really about the past" as Richardson claims in paragraph 7, what *is* it about, in her view? Where in the text does she state the central assumption that grounds her argument?

4. What does Richardson mean by "the flag of modern-day anti-Semitism, racism and bigotry" (paragraph 14)? To what, exactly, is she referring?

5. If you are uncertain of the meanings of any of the words listed below, try to guess them from the context of the essay. Then look them up to see how close your definitions were to those in the dictionary. Test out the new words by using each of them in a sentence or two of your own.

neo-Nazis (1)	disparate (3)	revere (12)
dissembling (1)	concubinage (5)	disservice (14)
descendant (2)	avatars (12)	rancor (15)
coerced (2)	conduits (12)	flashpoints (15)
sired (3)	espoused (12)	sentries (15)

Purpose and Audience

1. To whom does Richardson seem to be writing? What assumptions does she make about her readers' values?

2. Why do you think Richardson wrote this essay? To share a painful personal experience? To express her indignation? To argue for or against something? (If so, what?) For some other purpose?

Method and Structure

1. What subclaims does Richardson make to develop her argument for moving Confederate memorials to museums? Do you find her reasons convincing? Why, or why not?

2. Consider how Richardson supports her argument. What kinds of evidence does she provide? What strategies does she use to overcome readers' potential doubts about her objectivity?

3. How does Richardson present and handle opposing arguments? Does she seem fair? Why, or why not?

4. **OTHER METHODS**   Why does Richardson **compare and contrast** Confederate leaders and Revolutionary leaders in paragraphs 10–12? How does she use **parallelism** to drive home her point?

Language

1. Richardson makes two **allusions** in this essay: "don't ask, don't tell" (paragraph 4) is a reference to the Clinton administration's controversial policy on gay service members in the military, and "we see the naked emperor" (9) is a reference to the Hans Christian Andersen story "The Emperor's New Clothes." What is the effect of these allusions?

2. How would you characterize Richardson's **tone**? Is it consistent throughout? Is it appropriate for her subject?

Writing Topics

1. **JOURNAL TO ESSAY**   Starting with the notes you drafted in your journal (p. 376), write a brief history of your family. You may need to conduct some research to expand your knowledge and provide necessary information—perhaps by interviewing a few older family members, by digging through family documents and photographs, or by looking into the historical context, as Richardson does. How does your family history align with events in American history? How have your relatives' experiences affected you and your sense of who you are?

2. How do you react to Richardson's essay? Do you agree with her assessment of Confederate monuments and the fate they deserve? Or do you find her evaluation of the issue one-sided, her examples and opinions too personal to form the basis of an argument? Write an essay that analyzes Richardson's strategies and responds to her conclusions. Be sure to cite examples from her essay to support your analysis.

3. CULTURAL CONSIDERATIONS　How do you feel about the "current uptick in neo-Nazi and white supremacist activity" (paragraph 7) that Richardson finds so troubling? Is white supremacy really more prevalent these days? more accepted? or is it simply more visible? What are the causes of racial animosity? How is the nation as a whole affected by racism on the streets? What should, or could, be done to confront the problem? Write an argumentative essay on the subject, being sure to include examples to support your opinions.

4. CONNECTIONS　Ernest B. Furgurson notes in "The End of History?" (p. 369) that he has four great-grandfathers who fought for the South in the Civil War, and Richardson describes herself as a "Daughter of the Confederacy" whose great-great-great-grandfather was a white soldier for the cause. Both authors take the issue of Confederate memorials personally, but while Richardson writes with barely suppressed anger, Furgurson calmly tries to find room for conciliation. Brent Staples, in contrast, takes a distinctly more academic perspective to the issue in "Confederate Memorials as Instruments of Racial Terror" (p. 363), trying to keep his distance even as he argues for removing what he sees as symbols of oppression. Which writer's approach to argument in general do you find most effective, and why? Drawing on the three essays in this casebook for examples, write an essay that evaluates the respective roles of *ethos*, *logos*, and *pathos* in argument.

WRITING WITH THE METHOD

▶
ARGUMENT AND PERSUASION

Choose one of the following statements, or any other statement they suggest, and support *or* refute it in an argumentative essay. The statement you select should concern a topic you care about so that argument is a means of convincing readers to accept an idea, not an end in itself.

Popular Culture

1. *YouTube* has a negative influence on society.
2. Targeted online advertising benefits individual consumers.
3. Web sites encouraging anorexia or similar pathologies should be shut down.
4. Football should be banned.
5. Sexual harassment in the entertainment industry must be stopped.

Health and Technology

6. American health care should be reformed to a single-payer system like that in Canada or Europe.
7. Terminally ill people should have the right to choose when to die.
8. Private automobiles should be restricted in cities.
9. Texting while driving should be illegal in every state.

Education

10. Students caught in any form of academic cheating should be expelled.
11. Public universities should offer free tuition for in-state students.
12. Like high school textbooks, college textbooks should be purchased by the school and loaned to students for the duration of a course.
13. College is not for everyone.

Social and Political Issues

14. Corporate executives are overpaid.
15. Feminism is dead.
16. It is time for state and federal governments to look into and implement some form(s) of gun control.
17. Public libraries should provide free, unlimited access to the Internet.
18. Transgender people should be allowed to serve in all branches of the military.
19. When adopted children turn eighteen, they should have free access to information about their birth parents.

WRITING ABOUT THE THEME

SEEKING SOCIAL JUSTICE

1. Many of the selections in this chapter focus on problems of inequality, yet the authors write from very different perspectives and with widely varied purposes. Zoe Krey (p. 345) is concerned with the consequences of social and political inequality in urban areas, while Paul Greenberg (p. 351) argues that poverty for some is not only inevitable but also desirable, and Nicholas Kristof (p. 357) considers the impacts rural underemployment can have on individuals. Martin Luther King Jr. (p. 338), Brent Staples (p. 363), and Lisa Richardson (p. 376) are all concerned with ensuring civil rights protections for African Americans. Even Jenny Price (p. 337) is dismayed at the seeming acceptance of gun violence in poor neighborhoods. In an essay, compare these writers' perspectives on the idea of equality for all. What rights, privileges, and responsibilities does US citizenship confer on individuals? What are the primary functions of a democratic society, as each author sees it? What are the primary threats to it? What assumptions, if any, do their arguments have in common? How might their differences be resolved?

2. Several of the writers in this chapter address the phenomenon of public protests over social issues. Martin Luther King Jr. was arrested for nonviolent protest during the civil rights movement of the 1960s. Zoe Krey writes in response to protests of police brutality that devolved into riots. Brent Staples describes protests of memorials erected to intimidate African Americans in the South, Ernest B. Furgurson (p. 369) notes the emergence of the Black Lives Matter movement, and Lisa Richardson mentions an "uptick in white supremacist activity." What is the purpose and function of public protests? Have you ever joined one? Why, or why not? Can gathering in the streets to argue a position make any difference? What happens when protests turn violent? And what are the risks and rewards of marching for a cause? Write an essay that defends or argues against protest for its own sake, focusing on a particular movement or cause that intrigues (or offends) you. Do we have a right — even an obligation — to speak out against injustice? Why, or why not?

3. All of the selections in this chapter address social-justice issues that have implications both for individuals and for policymakers. Jenny Price touches on the problem of widespread gun ownership, and Martin Luther King Jr. and Zoey Krey are both critical of law enforcement. Paul Greenberg and Nicholas Kristof debate the impacts of economic policies meant to help the

disadvantaged. And Brent Staples, Ernest Furgurson, and Lisa Richardson discuss issues of public history and institutional racism. Choose one of these issues, or another social-justice issue that affects you on a personal level, and argue that the government needs to take a more active (or less active) role in solving it. Describe the issue as you understand it in detail, outline the controversy surrounding it, and explain what steps should be taken to address it.

PART THREE

BRIEF NOTES ON WORKING WITH SOURCES

15

WRITING WITH
SOURCE MATERIAL

▶

Writing is a means of communicating, a conversation between writers and readers—and between writers and other writers. Finding out what others have said about a subject, or looking for information to support and develop your thesis, is a natural part of the composing process.

A **source** is any work that you draw on for ideas or evidence in the course of writing an essay or a research paper. Whether you are analyzing or responding to an essay in this book or using research to support your interpretation of a subject, the guidelines in this chapter will help you to use the work of others effectively in your own writing. The next chapter shows you how to document the sources you use with citations in MLA style.

Responding to Readings

Many of the assignments that follow the readings in this book ask you to respond directly to an essay or to write about it in relation to one or more other essays—to analyze two writers' approaches, to compare several writers' ideas about a subject, or to use the ideas in one reading to investigate the meanings of another. The same will be true of much writing you do throughout college, whether you are examining literary works, psychological theories, business case studies, historical documents, or lesson plans.

In some academic writing, you'll be able to use an idea in a selection as a springboard for an essay about your own opinions or experiences, as Nicole Lang does in "Foundations" (p. 54), her response to Edward P. Jones's "Shacks" (p. 9). Other times, when academic writing requires you to write *about* one or more readings, you will analyze the material (see Chapter 1) and synthesize, or recombine, the elements of that analysis to form an original idea of your own, as explained later in this chapter (p. 393). Your goal is to think critically about what other writers have said and to reach your own conclusions.

Whether you are writing in response to or about a reading, refer to the writer's ideas directly and cite evidence from the text to support your conclusions; the questions that follow each selection in this book can help to guide your analysis. Use summary, paraphrase, and quotation (discussed on pp. 393–95) to give readers a sense of the work, a clear picture of the elements that you are responding to, and a measured understanding of how those elements contribute to your thesis. And be sure to document the materials you cite, using the guidelines and models provided in the next chapter.

Using Research to Support a Thesis

Often when you start to draft an essay, you'll discover that you need more information to clarify part of your subject or to develop a few of your points more fully—when you need several examples to develop your draft, when you are troubled by conflicting assertions in essays you're comparing, or when you want expert opinion or facts to support your argument, perhaps. A little outside material can contribute compelling and informative support for an essay, as Nicole Lang discovered when writing "Foundations." Upon reviewing an early draft of her essay, Lang realized she wasn't sure how much the average college graduate owes in student loans, so she did a quick search online and found an authoritative source to provide the information she needed. The entire research project took all of fifteen minutes.

Sometimes, however, you'll need to do more extensive research. Several of the writing suggestions in this book, for instance, ask you to conduct focused, short-term research in service of exploring ideas for a brief essay. Other times, you may need to look up information to guide your analysis of a work or gather supporting evidence for an argument. And sometimes, you will be assigned a full-scale research paper that involves finding and using multiple sources to develop and support an original thesis.

No matter the scale of a writing project, research takes time and requires careful thought. The next sections explain the basics of researching sources and using what you find responsibly and effectively.

▶ Asking Questions

Researching a topic provides an opportunity for you to build knowledge and to think critically about what you learn. The effort will be more productive if you start your search with a specific question (or questions) in mind. Such questions might be provided for you—as is the case with the research questions that follow many of the readings in this book—or you may need to ask them on your own. In that case, think about what interests or puzzles you about a subject. What do you know about it? What don't you know? What bothers you, confuses you, or intrigues you? Do you sense a problem in need of a solution, a source of disagreement among some writers, a desire for more information?

The techniques for generating ideas and for narrowing a topic discussed in Part One (see pp. 19–27) can help you develop fruitful research questions. Whatever questions occur to you, focus on those you care about most, because you will spend significant time and effort exploring them.

▶ Finding Sources

Once you have a question in mind, you have two basic options for locating material that can help you answer it: the library and the Internet. Although both can be good resources, usually you will find that sources and information located through a library's research portals (such as catalogs and databases) are more trustworthy. Materials in the library are more likely to have gone through an editorial review process to ensure the information is accurate, reliable, and accepted by experts in the field.

When you're looking for sources, never be shy about asking librarians for help, but make a point of familiarizing yourself with the most useful research tools.

- *Library catalogs* offer a comprehensive listing of the printed and electronic materials (books, magazines, newspapers, reference works, and the like) housed in a library. Most catalogs are online, which means you can plug in a search term—subject keyword, author, or title, for instance—and pull up a list of what the library has, even from home or a coffee shop. Many colleges also let you search the holdings of related libraries and arrange for interlibrary loans (allow plenty of time to arrange for transfers).

- *Periodical databases* provide listings of the articles in thousands of magazines, scholarly journals, and newspapers. Electronic subscription services, such as EBSCO and JSTOR, often provide full-text copies of articles located in a search; other times, you will need to use the information listed in the citation to track down the relevant issue on the library shelves.

■ *Online search engines*, such as *Google* and *Dogpile*, can help to locate information unavailable in print—some government reports, for instance, many Web-only publications, current data from research groups. Navigating the Internet effectively, however, takes effort. A single word plugged into a search box can easily bring up millions of results, with no indication of which ones are worthy of your time. To get the most out of a Web search, experiment with multiple keywords and use advanced search features to focus your hunt, narrowing results by kind of document (images, news, and so on), by type of site (government, educational, or commercial, for instance), by date, and by other parameters offered by the search engine. The more detailed the search terms, the more productive the results.

■ *Wikis*, such as *Wikipedia* and *SourceWatch*, are collaborative documents hosted online; generally they are written by anonymous users and can be edited by anyone with an Internet connection and an opinion. You should never use a wiki as a source for a research paper: a post can look very different from day to day, and even hour to hour, making the information unpredictable and unreliable. All the same, *Wikipedia* can be a useful tool. Frequently it is a good place to start if you are generating ideas and looking for topics to explore. *Wikipedia* articles also tend to list sources at the bottom; those links are generally reliable (although you should judge for yourself) and could serve as valuable starting points for more involved research.

▶ Evaluating Sources

When you read a written work for an assignment, you read it closely, considering the author's intentions and analyzing the use of evidence. The same is true when you use sources to build and support your ideas. Drawing on reliable information and balancing varied opinions strengthens your essay.

Critical thinking becomes especially important when you are doing research, and crucial if you are using the open Internet. A quick search online, for instance, might bring up quality articles from reliable publications, but it will just as likely bring up political propaganda, partisan arguments using questionable statistics, social media memes filled with unproven opinions and outright falsehoods, stealth marketing sites that skew information to promote a product, and many other types of misinformation. Being able to determine what is credible or trustworthy thus becomes much more important — and much more difficult.

The good news is that you need not read everything you find in a search closely. Instead, scan potential sources to see how well each one satisfies the following criteria:

- *Relevance.* Keep your question in mind as you research, and use it to help you focus on sources that are directly related to your subject. If you are writing about the treatment of animals in zoos, for instance, your readers are not going to find information from an article on circuses convincing. With so many sources available, you can afford to be selective.

- *Type.* Know whether you are looking at a primary or a secondary source. A *primary source* is an original document written by a creator or an eyewitness — for instance, a personal essay, a short story, a lab report, a speech delivered at an event. A *secondary source* is a writer's interpretation of a primary source or sources — a movie review, a summary of recent scientific discoveries, a historian's explanation of an event. Secondary sources can be very helpful in obtaining factual evidence and general overviews of a subject, while primary sources usually provide more valuable material for analysis.

- *Purpose and audience.* Consider whether a source is meant to do: provide information, argue a point, support a political view, sell a product, entertain viewers, or something else? Pinpointing the intended **audience** can help in assessing a source's **purpose**: a document written for general readers, for instance, would likely be less thorough in its details than one written for specialists in a subject, and a source aimed at a politically oriented readership is likely to be biased toward one side of the aisle or the other. In books, the preface and table of contents will often provide clues to the author's intentions. When you're looking at a periodical or a Web site, scanning the titles of nearby articles or checking the "About" page can give you a sense of the purpose of the material.

- *Credibility.* Be sure you can determine not only who created the source but also the writer's qualifications for writing on the subject, and look for any potential biases—especially in the case of online sources. **Bias** itself is not necessarily a problem: everybody has a preferred angle on any given issue. But be wary of writers who don't identify themselves, who use inflammatory or sensationalist language, or who present opinions as irrefutable facts.

- *Reliability.* Notice also how the author uses **evidence:** reliable writers provide detailed support for their ideas, distinguish between facts and opinions, argue reasonably, acknowledge opposing viewpoints, and cite their sources.

- *Currency.* In most cases, the more recently your source was published or updated, the better. Know when a document was created, and consider how its age affects its usefulness for your purposes.

The checklist below will help you assess potential sources and determine their value for your writing project. Once you've concluded that a source is worth using, the checklist for critical reading in Chapter 1 (see p. 8) can help you to examine it more closely.

CHECKLIST FOR EVALUATING SOURCES

- *Is the source fully relevant to your subject?*
- *Are you looking at a primary or a secondary source?*
- *What is the purpose of the source? Who is the intended audience?*
- *Who created the source? Is the author an expert? What are his or her credentials?*
- *Does the author have any strong biases that might affect the argument?*
- *Is the source reliable? Does the author offer evidence that is complete and up to date?*

Synthesizing Sources

When you bring information and ideas from outside sources into your writing, your goal is to develop and support an argument of your own making, not to report on what others have written. Always strive to maintain your voice. It can be tempting to string together facts and quotations from your sources and to think that they speak for themselves—or for you—but your own argument should always be the main event. Aim for **synthesis**, weaving the elements into a new whole: gather related information and ideas from your sources and summarize, paraphrase, and quote them to support your thesis.

▶ Summarizing

A **summary** is a condensed statement, *in your own words*, of the main meaning of a work. Summaries omit supporting details and examples to focus on the original author's thesis. Here, for example, are summaries of a few of the selections in this book:

> Langston Hughes pinpoints the moment during a church revival when he lost his faith (68–70).
>
> Perri Klass's essay grapples with why doctors use peculiar and often cruel jargon and contemplates how it affects them (125–28).
>
> In a dramatic depiction of the annual spring melts in the Pacific Northwest, Rick Bass makes a poetic plea for conservation (224–28).

Notice that each summary names the author of the work being summarized and provides page numbers; they also refrain from using any of the original authors' language.

Summarizing is one of the most effective ways to bring the ideas of others into your writing without losing your voice or bogging down your essay with unnecessary details. Depending on the length of the original work and your reasons for using it, your summary might be a single sentence or a paragraph; keep it as short as possible—generally no longer than 10 percent of the original. If you're responding to a short essay, for example, a sentence or two will usually be enough to express its meaning.

▶ Paraphrasing

A **paraphrase** is a restatement, again *in your own words*, of a short pas-sage from another writer's work. While summarizing makes it possible to explain someone else's main idea without repeating specifics, para-phrasing lets you incorporate important details that support your own main idea.

A paraphrase is about the same length as the original, but it does not use any of the other writer's unique words, phrasings, or sentence struc-tures. Simply replacing a few words with synonyms won't suffice; in fact, that shortcut counts as **plagiarism**, or wrongfully taking credit for another writer's work. If you cannot avoid using some of the writer's language, put it in quotation marks:

ORIGINAL PASSAGE   "Poverty is defined, in my system, by people not being able to cover the basic necessities in their lives. Indispensable medical care, nutrition, a place to live: all these essentials, for poor people, are often and classically beyond reach. If a poor person needs ten dollars a day to make ends meet, often he or she only makes eight and a half."

—Walter Mosley, "Show Me the Money," p. 6.

PARAPHRASE   As Walter Mosley sees it, poverty is a matter of inadequate resources. The poor have difficulty obtaining adequate health care, food, and shelter—things most of us take for granted—not because they have no income at all, but because the money they earn is not enough to cover these basic expenses (6).

ORIGINAL PASSAGE   "Wealth, in my definition, is when money is no longer an issue or a question. Wealthy people don't know how much money they have or how much they make. Their worth is gauged in property, natural resources, and power, in doors they can go through and the way the law works."

—Walter Mosley, "Show Me the Money," p. 6.

PARAPHRASE   Wealth, in contrast, is defined by freedom. The rich don't have to worry about finances; indeed, their "property, natural resources, and power" confer social and legal privileges far more significant than freely available cash (Mosley 6).

Notice here, too, that a paraphrase identifies the original source and pro-vides a page number. Even if the words are your own, the ideas are some-one else's, and so they must be credited.

▶ Quoting

Sometimes a writer's or speaker's exact words will be so well phrased or so important to your own meaning that you will want to quote them. When you are responding to or analyzing passages in a written work, such as an essay or a novel, direct **quotations** will be essential evidence as you develop your points. Even when you are borrowing ideas from other writers, however, quoting can be useful if the author's original wording makes a strong impression that you want to share with your readers.

Be sparing in your use of quotations. Limit yourself to those lines you're analyzing or responding to directly and perhaps a handful of choice passages that would lose their punch or meaning if you paraphrased them. Quoting others too often will make you vanish as a writer, leaving your readers wondering what *you* have to say and why they should care.

When you do use a quotation, be careful to copy the original words and punctuation exactly and to identify clearly the boundaries and source of the quotation:

- *Put quotation marks around all quoted material shorter than four typed lines.*

- *Use block quotations for quoted passages four typed lines or longer.* Introduce the quotation with a complete sentence followed by a colon, start the quotation on a new line, and indent the whole passage five spaces or one-half inch. Don't use quotation marks; the indention shows that the material is quoted.

- *Cite the source of the quotation, giving the page number (if available) as well as the author's name* (see pp. 399–419 in the next chapter for models). For short quotations, place a parenthetical citation after the final quotation mark and before the period. For block quotations, place a parenthetical citation after the final period.

You can make changes in quotations so that they fit the flow of your own sentences—say, by deleting a word or sentence that is not relevant to your purpose or by inserting a word or punctuation mark to clarify meaning. However, such changes must be obvious.

- Use an *ellipsis mark*, or three spaced periods (. . .), to show a deletion:

    Stewart and Elizabeth Ewen have suggested that "for hardworking, ill-housed immigrants, . . . clothing offered one of the few avenues by which people could assume a sense of belonging" (156).

■ Use *brackets* ([ ]) around any change or addition you make:

> Most fashion historians echo Thorstein Veblen's assertion that "members of each [social] stratum accept as their ideal of decency the scheme of life in vogue in the next higher stratum" (84).

For examples of the use and formatting of quotations, see the sample research paper by Jarrod Ballo at the end of the next chapter (p. 414).

▶ Integrating

When you incorporate material from outside sources, make a point to introduce every summary, paraphrase, or quotation and to specify why it's relevant to your thesis. At the same time, make it clear where your thoughts end and someone else's thoughts begin. Three techniques are especially helpful in giving your readers the necessary guidance.

■ *Use signal phrases to introduce summaries, paraphrases, and quotations.* A **signal phrase** names the author of the borrowed material and thus provides a transition between your idea and someone else's. If the information is relevant, you might also explain why the author is an authoritative source or name the article or book you're referring to. Here are some examples of signal phrases:

> As neurologist Oliver Sacks explains in *The Mind's Eye*, . . .
>
> US Census Bureau data reveal . . .
>
> Not everyone agrees. Pat Mora, for example, insists that . . .
>
> In his trial summation, Darrow argued that nobody has control over his or her fate: . . .

Note that a signal phrase ending with a colon must be a complete sentence. Be careful, as well, to craft each signal phrase to reflect your reasons for including a source. Using the same phrase over and over (such as "According to _____") will frustrate your readers.

■ *Generally, mark the end of borrowed material with a parenthetical citation identifying at least the page number of your source* (see pp. 399–419 of the next chapter for models). In most cases, the citation is required—an exception would be a source lacking page or other reference numbers—and it makes clear that you've finished with the source and are returning to your own argument.

■ *Follow up with a brief explanation of how the material supports your point.* To show that the borrowed material backs up your ideas, comment afterward on what it contributes to your essay. You might, for example, comment on the meaning of the borrowed material, dispute it, or summarize it in the context of a new idea. Such follow-ups are especially necessary after block quotations.

For examples of effective integration of source materials, see Jarrod Ballo's sample researched essay at the end of the next chapter (p. 414).

Avoiding Plagiarism

Claiming credit for writing that you didn't compose yourself is considered **plagiarism**, a form of academic dishonesty that can carry serious consequences. Buying an essay online and submitting it as your own, copying a friend's essay and submitting it as your own, or copying just a sentence from a source and including it as your own—these are the most obvious forms of plagiarism. But plagiarism is often unintentional, caused not by deliberate cheating but by misunderstanding or sloppiness. Be aware of the rules and responsibilities that come with using the work of others in your writing.

- *Take careful notes.* No matter what system you use for researching—formal note cards, dedicated notebooks, photocopies, electronic files—thorough and accurate records are essential. It's all too easy to forget, when you return to your notes, which words are your own and which ones are borrowed. If you copy down the exact words of a source, enclose them in quotation marks and make note of the source. If you paraphrase or summarize, make a note that the language is your own, and double-check that you haven't picked up any of the original phrasing. Always record full source information for any material you find, using the documentation models in the next chapter (pp. 399–419).

- *Use electronic sources with care.* Just because something appears on the Internet doesn't mean you're free to use it however you wish. Any language or idea you find, regardless of where you find it, must be credited to its source. Resist the urge to cut and paste snippets from online sources directly into your working draft: later on, you won't be able to distinguish the borrowed text from your own words. Print the documents for your records, or save them as clearly labeled individual files.

■ *Know the definition of* common knowledge. *Common knowledge* is information that is so widely known or broadly accepted that it can't be traced to a particular writer. Facts that you can find in multiple sources—the date of a historic event, the population of a major city—do not need to be credited as long as you state them in your own words. In contrast, original material that can be traced to a particular person—the lyrics to a song, an article on the Web—must be cited even if it has been distributed widely. Note that even if a piece of information is common knowledge, the wording of that information is not: put it in your own words.

■ *Never include someone else's ideas in your writing without identifying the borrowed material and acknowledging its source.* Whether you quote directly or rephrase information in your own words, you must make it clear to readers when ideas are not your own. If you use another writer's exact words, enclose them in quotation marks and identify the source. If you summarize or paraphrase, clearly distinguish your ideas from the source author's with a signal phrase and a source citation. Then, at the end of your paper, list all your sources in a works-cited list. (See the next chapter).

When in doubt, err on the side of caution. It's better to have too much documentation in your essay than not enough.

16

CITING SOURCES IN MLA STYLE

▶

In most English classes, and in some other humanities as well, you will be expected to cite your sources with the system outlined by the Modern Language Association in the *MLA Handbook* (8th ed., 2016) and explained in this chapter with documentation models and a sample research paper. The purpose of citing your sources is twofold: you acknowledge the sources that helped you and thus avoid charges of plagiarism, and you enable curious readers to verify your information by looking it up themselves.

Documentation Models

MLA style calls for a parenthetical citation for each use of a source within the body of the essay combined with a comprehensive list of works cited at the end. The two elements work together: the citation in the text names the source as briefly and unobtrusively as possible, referring readers to the works-cited entry for complete publication information.

PARENTHETICAL CITATION IN TEXT

In the essay "The Box Man," Barbara Lazear Ascher says that a homeless man who has chosen solitude can show the rest of us how to "find . . . a friend in our own voice" (259).

ENTRY IN LIST OF WORKS CITED

Ascher, Barbara Lazear. "The Box Man." *The Compact Reader: Short Essays by Method and Theme*, edited by Jane E. Aaron and Ellen Kuhl Repetto, 11th ed., Bedford/St. Martin's, 2019, pp. 255–59.

▶ In-Text Citations

Citations within the body of your essay include just enough information for readers to recognize the boundaries of borrowed material and to locate the full citation in the list of works cited. Generally, they name the author of a source and the page number on which you found the information or idea cited.

Keep in-text citations unobtrusive by making them as brief as possible without sacrificing necessary information. The best way to do this is to name the author of the source in a **signal phrase**, limiting the parenthetical information to the page number. Otherwise, include the author's name in the parenthetical citation.

AUTHOR NAMED IN THE TEXT

Historian Thomas French notes that Mount Auburn Cemetery was a popular leisure destination for city residents (37).

AUTHOR NOT NAMED IN THE TEXT

Mount Auburn Cemetery was a popular leisure destination for city residents (French 37).

DIRECTORY TO MLA IN-TEXT CITATION MODELS

A work with one author   398
A work by multiple authors   399
A work by a group author   399
Two or more works by the same
   author(s)   399

No author listed   400
An indirect source   400
A literary work   400
A source without page numbers   401

A work with one author

Provide the author's name in a signal phrase or in the parentheses.

Zadie Smith worries that her neighbors seem to have accepted the absence of winter weather in England as "the new normal" (14).

London "was never as wet as . . . its famous novels suggest," nor was it as warm in December as it is now (Smith 15).

A work by multiple authors

If a source has two authors, list both of their names.

> Some of the most successful organized tours in New York bring visitors
> on guided walks or bus rides to locations featured in television shows
> (Espinosa and Herbst 228).

In the case of three or more authors, shorten the reference by naming the first author and following with et al. (This is short for *et alii*, Latin for "and others.")

> As early as 1988, scholars cautioned against educators' dependence on
> computers, warning that technology is "accompanied by rapid change, insta-
> bility, and general feelings of insecurity and isolation" (Ferrante et al. 1).

A work by a group author

For works written in the name of an organization, company, or government that doesn't list individual authors, treat the name of the group as the author.

> Progressive neurological disorders damage the body in repeated but
> unpredictable intervals, forcing patients to adapt to new losses several
> times over (National Multiple Sclerosis Society 2).

If the group author is also the publisher of the work, you will need to alphabetize the entry by title in your works-cited list (see p. 406), so provide the title in the parenthetical citation in addition to page numbers (if there are any).

> According to the Corporation for Public Broadcasting, in 2016 the
> federal government provided $15 million to fund reporting and national
> news coverage through public media outlets such as *Frontline* and NPR
> ("Journalism").

Two or more works by the same author(s)

If your essay cites more than one work by the same author(s), include the title of the specific source within each citation. In the following examples, both works are by Maura Fredey, who is named in the text.

> Maura Fredey notes that most of the nurses at the Boston Home have
> been on staff for more than five years, and at least seven boast a quarter
> century or more of service ("21st Century" 26).

> The home's high level of care includes not only medical, dental, and vision treatments, says Fredey, but also round-the-clock nursing attention and extensive social and rehabilitative services ("Bridges" 13).

If the title is long, you may shorten it. (The complete titles for the articles cited above are "The 21st Century Home: How Technology Is Helping to Improve the Lives of Patients at the Boston Home" and "Bridges to Care: The Boston Home Reaches Out.")

No author listed

If the author of a work is not named, include the title within the parentheses. You may shorten the title if it is long.

> The population of Pass Christian, Mississippi, is less than a third of what it was before Hurricane Katrina ("New Town Crier" 22).

An indirect source

Use the abbreviation qtd. in (for "quoted in") to indicate that you did not consult the source directly but found it quoted in another source.

> As psychologist Robert Sternberg has pointed out, a high IQ does not guarantee success. Just as important is "knowing what to say to whom, knowing when to say it, and knowing how to say it for maximum effect" (qtd. in Gladwell 101).

A literary work

For a novel, list the part or chapter cited in addition to the page number; this helps readers locate the quotation in an edition different from the one you consulted.

> The newspaper reporters investigating the death of Mary Dalton in Richard Wright's *Native Son* are quick to recognize the similarities between her murder and that of Bobby Franks fifteen years earlier: "This is better than Loeb and Leopold," one of them remarks enthusiastically (214; bk. 2).

If a verse play (such as a work by William Shakespeare) is divided into parts, cite any part, act, scene, and line numbers, leaving out page numbers. For a prose play (such as Henrik Ibsen's *A Doll's House*), include the page number or numbers and a semicolon before the rest of the citation.

In Shakespeare's *The Tragedy of Macbeth*, a trio of witches famously chants, "Double, double toil and trouble; / Fire burn, and caldron bubble" (4.1.12-13).

A fight over money in the opening scene of Ibsen's *A Doll's House* reveals immediately that Nora and Torvald Helmer struggle for power in their marriage (7-12; act 1).

Cite the line numbers of a poem instead of pages. Include the word line or lines in the first citation; omit it in later references.

Robert Frost's "Design" contrasts the deadliness of "a dimpled spider, fat and white" (line 1) with the curative powers of a "flower like froth" (7).

A source without page numbers

Cite an unpaginated source, such as a Web site, a video, or a game, as you would any printed source: cite the author's name if it is available, or cite the title if no author is named. For digital sources that number paragraphs instead of pages, insert a comma between the author's name and the abbreviation par. (for "paragraph"). If a source's numbering system is unstable, as is often the case with e-books, refer to section or chapter numbers with the abbreviations sec., secs., ch., or chs. If the source has no numbering system at all, include the author's name only.

At the time *Dr. Strangelove* was released, filmmakers had begun to believe that fictional portrayals of nuclear war were actually "contributing to the nuclear threat" by frightening audiences (Abbot, par. 35).

Sociologist Robert Putnam believes that most people underestimate the impact that unequal access to resources is having on children in the United States (ch. 1).

One teacher who successfully brought computers into his classroom argues that to use new technologies effectively, teachers need to become "side-by-side learners" with their students (Rogers).

▶ List of Works Cited

The works-cited list provides complete publication information for every source you refer to within your essay. Format the list as follows:

- Start the list on a new page following the conclusion to your essay.
- Center the title Works Cited at the top of the page.

- Double-space everything in the list.

- Alphabetize the entries by the authors' last names. If a work doesn't have a listed author, alphabetize by title, ignoring the initial words *A*, *An*, and *The*.

- For each entry, align the first line with the left margin and indent subsequent lines five spaces or one-half inch.

The elements of individual entries will vary somewhat, as shown in the models in this section. The basic content and formatting rules, however, can be summarized in a few general guidelines:

- Start with the author's last name, followed by a comma and the author's first name.

- Provide the full title of the work, with all major words capitalized. Put quotation marks around the titles of book chapters, periodical articles, pages on Web sites, and short creative works such as stories, poems, and songs; italicize the titles of books, periodicals, whole Web sites, and longer creative works such as plays or TV series.

- Include complete publication information. At a minimum this includes publisher, date, and location specifics (typically page numbers or a URL). More broadly, MLA style follows a system of nested "containers" for these details (for example, a scholarly article's first container would be the journal in which it was published; if you found it in a periodicals database, the database would be a second container). For each container in a citation, provide as many of the following details that apply, in the order listed here: title of the container, names and roles of additional contributors, version, sequence numbers, publisher or sponsor, date of publication, and location information.

- Separate the elements of an entry (author, title, container) with periods. Separate the details within each container with commas.

The models that follow show how these guidelines might be applied in a variety of common situations. Note that when an entry includes a URL, you should copy it from your browser and omit any http:// or https://; you may break long addresses for fit before or after internal punctuation marks such as periods, slashes, or hyphens, but do not add hyphens of your own. MLA does not require a date of access for online materials, but your instructor might. If so, place it at the end of the entry after the word Accessed and followed with a period (see pp. 412–13 for examples).

DIRECTORY TO MLA WORKS-CITED MODELS

Authors

One author

Smith, Zadie. "Elegy for a Country's Seasons." *Feel Free: Essays*, Penguin Random
House, 2018, pp. 14–19.

Two authors

List the names as they appear in the work, reversing only the first name.

Lukianoff, Greg, and Jonathan Haight. "The Coddling of the American Mind." *The
Atlantic*, Sept. 2015, www.theatlantic.com/magazine/archive/2015/09
/the-coddling-of-the-american-mind/399356/.

Three or more authors

Provide the first author's name followed by et al. (This is the Latin abbreviation for *et alii*, "and others.")

Ferrante, Reynolds, et al. *Planning for Microcomputers in Higher Education: Strategies
for the Next Generation*. Association for the Study of Higher Education, 1988.

A group author

For works written in the name of an organization, company, or government that doesn't list individual authors, treat the name of the group as
the author. If the group is also the publisher of the work, as in the first
example below, omit the author name and start with the title of the work.

"Journalism." *CPB*, Corporation for Public Broadcasting, 2016, www.cpb.org/
journalism.

United States, Department of Commerce. *Statistical Abstract of the United States:
The National Data Book*. Bernan Press / ProQuest, 2017.

More than one work by the same author(s)

Roach, Mary. *Grunt: The Curious Science of Humans at War*. W. W. Norton, 2016.
---. *Gulp: Adventures on the Alimentary Canal*. W. W. Norton, 2013.

No author listed

"The Dreamers Deferred." *The Wall Street Journal*, 27 Feb. 2018, p. A16.
"Teenagers' Argot: Purists May Disapprove, but Multi-Ethnic Dialects Are Spreading." *The
Economist*, 11 Feb. 2012, www.economist.com/node/21547298.

Articles in Periodicals: Journals, Magazines, and Newspapers

The formats for articles in journals, magazines, and newspapers are similar whether the publication appears only in print, appears in print with additional online content, or appears only online. The key differences are (1) the full page numbers for print articles and paginated online articles; (2) the volume and issue numbers for journal articles, both print and online; and (3) the DOI (digital object identifier) or URL for articles accessed online.

An article in a scholarly journal

Include the author's name, the article title, the journal title, the volume and any issue number, the date of publication, and the page numbers, if available. For journals published online, provide the DOI (digital object identifier) if one has been assigned to the article; otherwise conclude the entry with the complete URL.

Carstarphen, Meta G., et al. "Rhetoric, Race, and Resentment: Whiteness and the
    New Days of Rage." *Rhetoric Review*, vol. 36, no. 4, 23 Aug. 2017, doi:10.1080/
    07350198.2017.1355191.

Mizzi, Shannon. "*Star Trek*'s Underappreciated Feminist History." *Wilson Quarterly*,
    vol. 38, no. 1, 17 Oct. 2014, www.wilsonquarterly.com/stories/star-treks-
    underappreciated-feminist-history/.

Sewald, Ronda L. "Forced Listening: The Contested Use of Loudspeakers for
    Commercial and Political Messages in the Public Soundscape." *American
    Quarterly*, vol. 63, no. 3, Sept. 2011, pp. 761-80.

An article in a magazine

Finnegan, William. "Dignity: Fast-Food Workers and a New Labor Movement." *The
    New Yorker*, 15 Sept. 2014, pp. 70-79. *Magazine Archive*, archives.newyorker
    .com/?i=2014-09-15#folio=0C2.

Johnson, Fenton. "The Future of Queer." *Harper's Magazine*, Jan. 2018,
    pp. 27–34.

Kolbert, Elizabeth. "There's No Scientific Basis for Race—It's a Made-Up
    Label." *National Geographic*, Apr. 2018, www.nationalgeographic.com/
    magazine/2018/04/race-genetics-science-africa/.

Lamott, Anne. "A Slow Walk into the Amazing Now." *Salon*, 11 Nov. 2014, www.salon
    .com/2014/11/12/a_slow_walk_into_the_amazing_now/.

An article in a newspaper

Many newspapers appear in more than one edition, so you need to specify which edition you used (greater Boston ed. in the model below). Give the section label as part of the page number when the newspaper does the same (A1 in the model). Cite an article that runs on nonconsecutive pages with the starting page number followed by a plus sign (+). For an article online, omit page numbers and provide the full URL.

Levensen, Michael. "Youths Bring Call for Change." *The Boston Globe*, greater Boston
    ed., 15 Mar. 2018, pp. A1+.

Press, Joy. "The Creator of 'Jessica Jones' Serves Up a Dark Mirror for Our Moment."
    The New York Times, 2 Mar. 2018, www.nytimes.com/2018/03/02/arts/television/
    jessica-jones-netflix-melissa-rosenberg.html.

A letter to the editor

Dunleavy, Rob. Letter. *The American Scholar*, Aug. 2017, p. 3.

An article from a database

Cite a full-text source that you obtain through a database in the same way as a print article, followed by the database information as a second container, with the database's name and the URL—or the DOI if one is provided.

Porco, Carolyn. "Adventures in Wonderland." *The New Statesman*, 19 Dec. 2011,
    pp. 34–37. *Academic Search Premier*, web.b.ebscohost.com.ezproxy.bpl.org/.

Smithers, Gregory D. "'This Is the Nation's Heart-String': Formal Education and the
    Cherokee Diaspora during the Late Nineteenth and Early Twentieth Centuries."
    Wicazo Sa Review, vol. 30, no. 2, Fall 2015, pp. 28–55. *JSTOR*, doi:10.5749/
    wicazosareview.30.2.0028.

Books

A book with an author

Gay, Roxane. *Hunger: A Memoir of (My) Body*. HarperCollins, 2017.

A book with an editor

Freeman, John, editor. *Tales of Two Americas: Stories of Inequality in a Divided Nation*.
    Penguin Random House, 2017.

A book with an author and an editor

James, William. *The Varieties of Religious Experience*. Edited by Robert H. Abzug,
    Bedford/St. Martin's, 2013.

A book with a translator

Murakami, Haruki. *Colorless Tsukuru Tazaki and His Years of Pilgrimage*. Translated by
    Philip Gabriel, Vintage Books, 2014.

Edition other than the first

Gonzales, Manuel G. *Mexicanos: A History of Mexicans in the United States*. 2nd ed.,
    Indiana UP, 2009.

An e-book

Identify the reader platform before the name of the publisher.

LeDuff, Charlie. *Work and Other Sins*. iBook ed., Penguin Books, 2002.

A graphic narrative or illustrated book

Treat a graphic narrative written and illustrated by the same person as you
would a book with one author. For a book with text and illustrations created by different people, begin the entry with the name of the contributor
whose work you are emphasizing (author, editor, or illustrator) and identify the contributors' functions in the work.

Chast, Roz. *Going into Town: A Love Letter to New York*. Bloomsbury, 2017.
Moser, Barry, illustrator. *Mark Twain's Book of Animals*. Edited by Shelley Fisher
    Fishkin, U of California P, 2010.

An anthology

Cite an entire anthology only when you are referring to the editor's materials or cross-referencing multiple selections that appear within it.

Burns, Catherine, editor. *The Moth: Fifty True Stories*. Hyperion Books, 2013.

The next models show how to combine a citation for an entire anthology
with cross-references.

A selection from an anthology

List the work under the selection author's name. Include the page numbers for the entire selection after the publication date.

Alvarez, Julia. "The Practice of Gracias." *The Compact Reader: Short Essays by Method and Theme*, edited by Jane E. Aaron and Ellen Kuhl Repetto, 11th ed., Bedford/St. Martin's, 2019, pp. 285–88.

If you are citing two or more selections from the same anthology, you can avoid unnecessary repetition by listing the anthology in its own entry and cross-referencing it in the selection entries. Put each entry in its proper alphabetical place in the list of works cited.

Aaron, Jane E., and Ellen Kuhl Repetto, editors. *The Compact Reader: Short Essays by Method and Theme*. 11th ed., Bedford/St. Martin's, 2019.

Doyle, Brian. "How to Read a Nature Essay." Aaron and Repetto, pp. 212–14.

Tan, Amy. "The Darkest Moment of My Life." Aaron and Repetto, pp. 100–04.

A section of a book

When referring to only part of a book (such as an introduction, a foreword, or a specific chapter), name the author and indicate the part of the book you are citing, with page numbers for print books. Do not include page numbers for sections of e-books.

Kaling, Mindy. "Karaoke Etiquette." *Is Everyone Hanging Out without Me? (And Other Concerns)*, Crown Publishing Group, 2011, pp. 64-65.

King, Stephen. Introduction. *Lord of the Flies*, by William Golding, Kindle ed., Penguin Random House, 2011.

A reference work

"Social Security." *Encyclopedia Britannica*, 2018, www.britannica.com/topic/social-security-government-program.

Audio, Visual, and Multimedia Sources

A sound recording

Haydn, Franz Joseph. *Symphony No. 94*. Performance by Orchestra Camerata Cassovia, conducted by Johannes Wildner, Lydian, 1990.

Sheeran, Ed. "Castle on the Hill." *Divide*, Atlantic, 2017.

A photograph or other work of art

For original works viewed in person, provide the museum's or collection's name and location. For reproductions, provide complete publication information for the source, including a page number or URL.

Kandinsky, Wassily. *Improvisation No. 30 (Cannons)*. 1913, Art Institute of Chicago.

Magritte, René. *The Human Condition II*. 1935. *Surrealists and Surrealism*, edited by Gaëton Picon, Rizzoli, 1983, p. 145.

Riis, Jacob. *Nine Boys Waist Deep in Country Stream*. Library of Congress, Prints and Photographs Division, www.loc.gov/pictures/item/2003678185/. Accessed 12 Mar. 2018.

A television or radio program

What information you provide, and in what order, depends on your focus in using the source. If your emphasis is on a particular contributor, start with that person's name and function.

Chace, Zoe, performer. "That's One Way to Do It." *This American Life*, hosted by Ira Glass, episode 580, Chicago Public Media, 19 Feb. 2016.

If your focus is an episode or the series as a whole, start with the title and list significant contributors.

"That's One Way to Do It." *This American Life*, hosted by Ira Glass, performances by Zoe Chace and Sigrid Frye-Revere, episode 580, Chicago Public Media, 19 Feb. 2016.

This American Life, hosted by Ira Glass, Chicago Public Media, 1995-2018.

If you accessed the programming online or through a podcast, provide the additional publication information as a second container.

This American Life, hosted by Ira Glass, Chicago Public Media, 1995-2018. *Archive*, www.thisamericanlife.org/archive?keyword=that%27s%20one%20way%20to%20 do%20it. Accessed 6 Mar. 2018.

A film, video, or DVD

To decide whether and where to include the names and functions of significant contributors, follow the above guidelines for a television or radio program.

Get Out. Written and directed by Jordan Peele, performances by Daniel Kaluuya, Allison Williams, and Bradley Whitford, Universal Pictures, 2017.

International Forum on Globalization. "Greensumption." *YouTube*, 24 May 2007, www.youtube.com/watch?v=Ft5SSIfmeKU. Accessed 4 Apr. 2018.

Kelly, Richard, director. *Donnie Darko*. Newmarket Films, 2001. *Donnie Darko: The Director's Cut*, 20th Century Fox Home Entertainment, 2004.

An advertisement

In most cases, use the descriptive label Advertisement in place of a title. If the ad does have a title, put the descriptive label at the end of the entry.

Maxwell House. Advertisement. *Rolling Stone*, 18 Jun. 2015, p. 35.

National Football League. "Touchdown Celebrations to Come." *Super Bowl LII*, NBC,
4 Feb. 2018. *YouTube*, uploaded by NFL, 4 Feb. 2018, www.youtube.com/
watch?v=KUoD-gPDahw. Advertisement.

A lecture or public address

Cain, Susan. "The Power of Introverts." *TED: Ideas Worth Spreading*, TED Conferences,
28 Feb. 2012, www.ted.com/talks/susan_cain_the_power_of_introverts. Lecture.

Sedaris, David. *An Evening with David Sedaris*. Capitol Center for the Arts, 12 Apr.
2016, Concord. Address.

Other Online Sources

An entire Web site

Start with the author(s) or editor(s) of the site, followed by the site title in italics, the name of the publisher or sponsoring organization, the date of publication or most recent update, and the URL. If the site is not dated or has not been updated in a while, you may wish to include the date you accessed the material at the end of the citation.

Carson, Clayborne, director. *The King Papers Project*. The Martin Luther King, Jr.,
Research and Education Institute, Stanford U., kinginstitute.stanford.edu/.
Accessed 19 Jan. 2018.

A work from a Web site

Include a title for the work and as much information for the entire Web site as you can find (see above).

Dryden-Edwards, Roxanne. "Obsessive-Compulsive Disorder." *MedicineNet*, WebMD,
www.medicinenet.com/obsessive_compulsive_disorder_ocd/article.htm.
Accessed 16 Apr. 2018.

Enzinna, Wes. "Syria's Unknown Revolution." *Pulitzer Center on Crisis Reporting*,
24 Nov. 2015, pulitzercenter.org/projects/middle-east-syria-enzinna-war-
rojava.

A blog post or comment

Follow the above guidelines for a short work from a Web site. If an entry is not titled, use a descriptive label such as Blog post or Comment on.

Allan, Patrick. "Opinions Are Optional." *Life Hacker,* Gawker Media, 20 Dec. 2017,
    lifehacker.com/opinions-are-optional-1821468158.

Bluesnow. Comment on "Opinions Are Optional." *Life Hacker,* Gawker Media, 21 Dec.
    2017, lifehacker.com/opinions-are-optional-1821468158.

Stanton, Brandon. Blog post. *Humans of New York,* www.humansofnewyork.com/.
    Accessed 6 Mar. 2018.

Social media

Start with the user name for the author's name, followed with the writer's real name (if known) in parentheses. If the post has a title, use it. Otherwise, quote a tweet or short message in its entirety, and use Post for anything else. Provide the date and time of the posting and the URL.

@Emma4Change (Emma González). "You know what matters here? People Keep Dying.
    Until Politicians care more about People than they do about Money, random
    and innocent People are going to Keep Dying." *Twitter,* 2 Mar. 2018, 7:47 a.m.,
    twitter.com/Emma4Change/status/969600051118006272.

griffdogdesign. Post. *Instagram,* 22 Feb. 2018, www.instagram.com/p/BfgnaNqlHLY/.

Salem NH Police Department. "Taxes, Internal Revenue Service, and your Police."
    Facebook, 6 Mar. 2018, 3:22 p.m., www.facebook.com/SalemNHPolice/.

Personal Communications

E-mail

Jones, Liza. "Re: Question about Group." Received by Claude Ferrell, 9 May 2018.

Interview

Conti, Regina. Personal interview. 3 Mar. 2018.

Sample Research Paper

The research paper presented here was written by Jarrod Ballo, a part-time student at Northern Essex Community College in Haverhill, Massachusetts. After reading Barbara Lazear Ascher's "The Box Man" (p. 257), he considered the writing topic labeled "Research" that follows it:

> If you live in or have visited an urban area, you have probably seen people sleeping in doorways or scavenging for food. And you have almost certainly seen homelessness and extreme poverty discussed in the news and depicted in the media. Research the problem of homelessness and any solutions that have been proposed or attempted, whether locally or on a national level. Then, considering the information you find, your own experiences, and the observations in Ascher's essay, write an essay proposing a solution to the problem.

On reflection, Ballo found himself thinking about a friend who had been forced to sleep in a car for a few weeks. His initial research question was a practical one: "Where can a newly homeless person turn for help?" In the course of looking for answers, he discovered a fact that not only surprised him but also made him angry. The resulting research paper, which took Ballo four weeks to complete, outlines the problem he found and proposes a solution.

As you read, notice that Ballo goes beyond reporting facts and uses what he learned to develop an argument of his own. Notice also how he synthesizes information and ideas from his sources to develop his thesis without relying on those sources to speak for him. His essay isn't perfect, but Ballo does an exemplary job of combining reasoning and evidence to support an argument while also addressing opposing points of view convincingly and fairly.

Jarrod Ballo

7 March 2018

Women and Children First

When most people think of homelessness, they imagine
someone like the character Barbara Lazear Ascher describes in
"The Box Man"—an unemployed, mentally ill man who has been
living on the streets for years. That old stereotype, however, is
no longer true. In fact, working families now make up the largest
segment of the homeless population in America, and their
numbers are rising. Given the shift in the nature of homelessness,
it is time to shift focus in looking for solutions. Public service
agencies should concentrate on preventing family homelessness
by helping people get back on their feet if they fall on hard times.

When Ascher wrote her essay, most people without a place
to live were "chronically" homeless, defined by the United States
government as adult "individual[s] with disabilities who [have]
been continuously homeless for one year or more" (2). Only a
tiny fraction of homeless people were in families (Schweid xiii).
Today, however, the National Center on Family Homelessness
(NCFH) reports that families represent thirty-seven percent of
the homeless overall, more than double the number of those
categorized as chronic (9). Families also represent the fastest-
growing portion of the homeless population: while individual
homelessness has dropped by approximately ten percent over
the last decade, family homelessness has increased by a
similar ratio (United States 22, 43). Typically, a homeless family
consists of a single mother with two children in tow, and many of
those children are younger than six (NCFH 9). Innocent kids, it
turns out, are the real face of homelessness.

A lot of people assume that when children wind up homeless it must be the parents' fault—they were too irresponsible
to hold down a job, or too lazy to look for one in the first place.
Most homeless parents, however, do have jobs, sometimes two
or three, but their incomes still fall below the poverty line

---

Surprising fact grabs
readers' attention
and clearly
introduces topic

Thesis statement
makes an arguable
claim

Analysis of trends in
homelessness

Brackets indicate
changes in direct
quotation

Quotation,
paraphrase, and
summary integrate
evidence from three
sources

Follow-up comment
explains significance
of data

Causes of family
homelessness

(NCFH 74). Others believe that the parents are alcoholics or drug addicts, but homeless mothers rarely show signs of substance abuse (Culhane and Metraux 117). The real cause of homelessness for families comes down to financial emergencies: unexpected lay-offs, uninsured medical expenses, missed rent payments, disasters such as fires (NCFH 74-77). Usually such emergencies are temporary, but poor families have few resources for dealing with them.

Besides bunking with relatives or friends or staying on the street, what can a homeless family do? Traditionally, a patchwork assistance system has provided three basic options: emergency shelters, transitional housing units, and hotel vouchers. Each comes with limitations and obstacles, especially for families with children.

The first place a homeless family normally goes is an emergency shelter. As one homeless mother describes them, shelters provide meals and a place to sleep, but that's about it. Residents must leave during the day and return in time to check in for the next night—impossible for those who work late shifts—and they have to "worry about their belongings being tossed out or getting a bed" (Bell). Another advocate, Alana Semuels, points out that emergency shelters can also be dangerous for women and children: shared sleeping areas and bathrooms leave them vulnerable to theft and assault, and expose them to prostitution and drugs. At the same time, residents are deliberately treated poorly, on the theory that making shelters unpleasant will stop people from staying long (Culhane and Metraux 112).

Transitional housing programs are slightly better. They offer private rooms, let people stay for up to two years, and usually provide social services to help families regroup (United States 73). They have one big drawback, though: men and teenage boys are almost always excluded, so families may be forced to split up (Schweid 2). Transitional housing also involves interventions, such as job training and mental counseling, that are not only disruptive but also unnecessary for most residents (Culhane and Metraux 117). Families get hassled and treated like losers, when all they need is a place to stay.

Two opposing claims acknowledged and disputed

Citation for summary identifies all pages summarized

Classification of shelter options

No page numbers in citations of direct quotation and paraphrase because online articles don't have them

Concrete details support example

Authors not named in signal phrases listed in parenthetical citations

Summaries and paraphrases integrate evidence from three sources

Some cities provide hotel vouchers, paying market rates for families to stay in double rooms. While it might sound glamorous, hotel life is tough. As *New York Times* reporter Nikita Stewart reveals, participating hotels tend to be located in suburbs, forcing long commutes to work and to school. They offer no space for children to play, no room for privacy, and no kitchens; homeless "guests" are forced to live on fast food and cold cuts (A23). Families may find themselves stuck in these conditions for months, even years, before they manage to find a better place to live (Semuels). And the instability of temporary housing makes it difficult for them to transition out of homelessness, creating a vicious cycle that adds to public expense while solving nothing.

Solutions do exist, though. In 2009 Congress passed the Homeless Emergency Assistance and Rapid Transition to Housing, or HEARTH, act, which put a new emphasis on "permanent supportive housing" (NCFH 11). As Malcolm Gladwell explains in an influential essay, chronically homeless people consume the majority of assistance funds even though they represent the smallest portion of the homeless population; the idea behind HEARTH is to put them in stable homes *before* addressing issues such as addiction, improving the chances for recovery and saving millions of dollars in the long run (183–86). Although it may seem unfair to give addicted "homeless people . . . a free place to live" (Semuels), studies show that permanent supportive housing *works*. Most states have seen promising results, with chronic homelessness dropping by as much as sixty percent in some areas (United States 65)—and public expenses dropping along with it.

As successful as HEARTH has been for individuals, it has left families in the cold. Permanent supportive housing, limited to people with disabilities, now accounts for more beds than any other shelter option (United States 72). If homeless families do manage to find a spot in a shelter, many will find themselves stuck for a year or more, simply because they can't find affordable housing or scrape together the costs of moving (NCFH 74-75). Yet public service agencies spend close to $60,000

Signal phrase names author and gives credentials

Summary of newspaper article

Page numbers only because author (Stewart) is named in signal phrase

Example of solution for chronically homeless people

Definition outlines solution

Paraphrase integrates direct quotation (ellipses indicate omission)

annually for each family housed in a shelter (Semuels)—more than enough to cover the rent for a decent apartment or a down payment on a modest house.

Rather than waste so much money on temporary shelter, agencies should apply the logic behind permanent supportive housing to families: get them into real homes first. In arguing this solution, sociologists Dennis Culhane and Stephen Metraux make an important point:

> Most homeless households need temporary, low-cost assistance with resolving a recent housing loss or other displacement, or with transitioning out of an institutional living environment. They do not necessarily need a shelter stay or a shelter stay of long duration. (112)

Block format for long quotation

The HEARTH act allows for this kind of help, providing rental subsidies and moving costs, but eligibility is very restricted and few families qualify (NCFH 75). Harsh limitations put parents in a difficult situation, mostly because opponents worry that offering handouts "encourages them to behave irresponsibly" (Gladwell 190). Such concerns, however, have been proven false. Most recipients of cash assistance need help for less than three months, and almost all of them find independent housing and self-sufficiency within a year (United States 66).

Opposing claim acknowledged and disputed

Treating women and children in need as potential frauds only makes it more difficult for families to get their lives in order. Because most family homelessness is caused by short-term financial emergencies, most homeless families would be better off with short-term cash assistance. Shelters create obstacles to recovery, and they cost much more than putting people into stable homes. The success of permanent supportive housing for chronically homeless individuals has reduced costs and opened up more resources for homeless families, and that's where the money should go. By increasing access to rental assistance, we might even help families avoid homelessness in the first place.

Conclusion summarizes reasons, restates thesis, and offers solution

Works Cited

Ascher, Barbara Lazear. "The Box Man." *The Compact Reader: Short Essays by Method and Theme*, edited by Jane E. Aaron and Ellen Kuhl Repetto, 11th ed., Bedford/St. Martin's, 2019, pp. 255–59.

Bell, Beatrix. "Christmas in the Shelters." *Spare Change News*, Homeless Empowerment Project, 8 Jan. 2016, sparechangenews.net/2016/01/christmas-in-the-shelters/.

Culhane, Dennis P., and Stephen Metraux. "Rearranging the Deck Chairs or Reallocating the Lifeboats? Homelessness Assistance and Its Alternatives." *Journal of the American Planning Association*, vol. 74, no. 1, Jan. 2008, pp. 111–21. *Academic Search Premier*, doi:10.1080/01944360701821618.

Gladwell, Malcolm. "Million-Dollar Murray: Why Problems Like Homelessness May Be Easier to Solve than to Manage." *What the Dog Saw: And Other Adventures,* Little, Brown, 2009, pp. 177–98.

National Center on Family Homelessness. *America's Youngest Outcasts: A Report Card on Child Homelessness.* American Institute for Research, 2014, www.air.org/sites/default/files/downloads/report/Americas-Youngest-Outcasts-Child-Homelessness-Nov2014.pdf.

Schweid, Richard. *Invisible Nation: Homeless Families in America*. U of California P, 2016.

Semuels, Alana. "How Can the US End Homelessness?" *The Atlantic*, 25 Apr. 2016, www.theatlantic.com/business/archive/2016/04/end-homelessness-us/479115/.

Stewart, Nikita. "Hotels Used to Shelter City's Homeless Are Often Crime-Ridden, Review Says." *The New York Times*, national ed., 5 Jan. 2018, p. A23.

United States, Department of Housing and Urban Development. *The 2017 Annual Homeless Assessment Report (AHAR) to Congress.* Office of Community Planning and Development, Dec. 2017, www.hudexchange.info/resources/documents/2017-AHAR-Part-1.pdf.

List of works cited starts on a new page

Selection from an anthology

Article in an online newspaper

Scholarly article from a database

Section of a book

Online book by a group author

Book by one author

Article in a magazine published online

Article in a print newspaper

Online report by a government author

GLOSSARY

▶

abstract words See *concrete and abstract words*.

active reading Direct interaction with a work to discover its meaning, the author's intentions, and your own responses. Active reading involves taking notes and annotating passages to reach a deeper understanding. See also pp. 6–7; *critical thinking and reading*.

ad hominem argument See *fallacies*.

allusion A brief reference to a real or fictitious person, place, object, or event. An allusion can convey considerable meaning with few words, as when a writer describes a movie as "potentially this generation's *Star Wars*" to imply both that the movie is a space adventure and that it may be a blockbuster. But to be effective, the allusion must refer to something readers know well.

analogy Closely related to metaphor, a comparison of two essentially unlike subjects that uses some similarities as the basis for establishing other similarities. A medical writer, for instance, might explain the workings of neurons in the human brain by comparing them to a computer network. A favorite technique of scientists and of philosophers who wish to clarify a subject that is unobservable, complex, or abstract, an analogy may have an explanatory or persuasive purpose. See also *comparison and contrast; metaphor*.

analysis (also called **division**) The method of development in which a subject is separated into its elements or parts and then reassembled into a new whole. See Chapter 8, p. 148.

anecdote A brief narrative that recounts an episode from a person's experience. See, for instance, Adams, paragraphs 1–4, pp. 156–57. See also Chapter 5 on narration, p. 59.

annotation The practice of reading actively by taking notes on a piece of writing. Notes typically include circles and underlines within a passage, markings such as brackets and checkmarks, and marginal comments and questions regarding the author's meaning and the reader's reactions. See also pp. 6–7 and *active reading*.

antecedent The noun to which a pronoun refers: *Six days after Martin Luther King Jr. picked up the Nobel Peace Prize in Norway, he was jailed in*

Alabama. Antecedents should be clearly identified, and they should match their related pronouns in number and gender. See p. 46.

argument   The form of writing that appeals to readers' reason and emotions in order to win agreement with a claim or to compel some action. This definition encompasses both argument in a narrower sense—the appeal to reason to win agreement—and **persuasion**—the appeal to emotion to compel action. See Chapter 14, p. 330.

assertion   A debatable claim about a subject; the central idea of an argument.

audience   A writer's audience is the group of readers for whom a particular work is intended. To communicate effectively, the writer should estimate readers' knowledge of the subject, their interest in it, and their biases toward it and should then consider these needs and expectations in choosing what to say and how to say it. See pp. 4, 12, and 19.

begging the question   See *fallacies.*

bias   A writer's preference for a particular point of view on an issue. A petroleum engineer, for instance, is likely to be biased in favor of expanding fossil fuel extraction through new methods like fracking. Bias itself is not a problem: everyone has a unique outlook created by experience, training, and techniques. What does matter is whether a writer deals frankly with his or her bias and argues reasonably despite it. See p. 392.

binary classification   See *classification.*

body   The part of an essay that develops the main idea. See pp. 27–28 and 35–38.

brainstorming   A method for generating ideas that involves listing thoughts without judgment. See pp. 22–23.

cause-and-effect analysis   The method of development in which occurrences are divided into their elements to find what made an event happen (its causes) and what the consequences were (its effects). See Chapter 13, p. 295.

chronological order   A pattern of organization in which events are arranged as they occurred over time, earliest to latest. Narratives and process analyses usually follow a chronological order; see Chapter 5, p. 60, and Chapter 10, p. 207.

classification   The method of development in which the members of a group are sorted into classes or subgroups according to shared characteristics. See Chapter 9, p. 177.

cliché   An expression that has become tired from overuse and that therefore deadens rather than enlivens writing. Examples: *in over their heads, turn over a new leaf, as clear as a bell.* See also p. 53.

climactic order   A pattern of organization in which elements—words, sentences, examples, ideas—are arranged in order of increasing importance or drama. See p. 39.

coherence   The quality of effective writing that comes from clear, logical connections among all the parts, so that the reader can follow the writer's thought process without difficulty. See pp. 37–38 and 155.

colloquial language   The language of conversation, including contractions (*don't*, *can't*) and informal words and expressions (*hot* for new or popular, *boss* for employer, *ad* for advertisement, *get away with it*, *flunk the exam*). Most dictionaries label such words and expressions *colloquial* or *informal*. Colloquial language is inappropriate when the writing situation demands precision and formality, as a college term paper or a business report usually does. But in other situations it can be used selectively to relax a piece of writing and reduce the distance between writer and reader (see, for instance, Hughes, p. 68). See also *diction*.

comma splice   A sentence error in which two or more independent clauses run together with only a comma between them. See p. 45.

comparison and contrast   The method of development in which the similarities and differences between subjects are examined. **Comparison** examines similarities and **contrast** examines differences, but the two are generally used together. See Chapter 11, p. 235.

conclusions   The endings of written works—the sentences that bring the writing to a close. A conclusion provides readers with a sense of completion, that the writer has finished. Sometimes the final point in the body of an essay may accomplish this purpose, especially if it is very important or dramatic (for instance, see Doyle, p. 214). But usually a separate conclusion is needed to achieve completion. It may be a single sentence or several paragraphs, depending on the length and complexity of the piece of writing. And it may include one of the following, or a combination, depending on your subject and purpose:

- A summary of the main points of the essay (see Jamison, p. 162; Burroughs, p. 275; Kristof, p. 357; and Ballo, p. 414)

- A statement of the main idea of the essay, if it has not been stated before (see Jones, p. 9; Boylan, p. 73; Tan, p. 100; Klass, p. 125; and Kim, p. 250), or a restatement of the main idea incorporating information from the body of the essay (see Lang, p. 54; Melendez, p. 139; and Staples, p. 363)

- A comment on the significance or implications of the subject (see Fulmore, p. 79; Ojha, p. 168; Haskie, p. 320; and Boissy, p. 281)

- A call for reflection, support, or action (see Alvarez, p. 287; Kakalios, p. 306; Greenberg, p. 351; and Richardson, p. 376)

- A prediction for the future (see Krey, p. 345; and Furgurson, p. 369)

- An example, anecdote, question, or quotation that reinforces the point of the essay (see Chen, p. 107; Sedaris, p. 131; Adams, p. 156; Brooks, p. 189; and Thompson, p. 312)

Excluded from this list are several endings that should be avoided because they tend to weaken the overall effect of an essay: (1) an example, fact, or quotation that pertains to only part of the essay; (2) an apology for your ideas, for the quality of the writing, or for omissions; (3) an attempt to enhance the significance of the essay by overgeneralizing from its ideas and evidence; and (4) a new idea that requires the support of an entirely different essay.

concrete and abstract words   A concrete word refers to an object, person, place, or state that we can perceive with our senses: *lawnmower, teacher, Chicago, moaning.* An abstract word, in contrast, refers to an idea, quality, attitude, or state that we cannot perceive with our senses: *democracy, generosity, love, grief.* Abstract words convey general concepts or impressions. Concrete words make writing specific and vivid. See also pp. 52 and 95; *specific and general.*

connotation and denotation   A word's **denotation** is its literal meaning: *famous* denotes the quality of being well known. A word's **connotations** are the associations or suggestions that go beyond its literal meaning: *notorious* denotes fame but also connotes sensational, even unfavorable, recognition. See pp. 51–52.

contrast   See *comparison and contrast.*

critical thinking and reading   The practice of examining the meanings and implications of things, images, events, ideas, and written works; uncovering and testing assumptions; seeing the importance of context; and drawing and supporting independent conclusions. Critical reading applies critical thinking to look beneath the surface of a work, seeking to uncover both its substance and the writer's interpretation of the substance. See Chapter 1, especially pp. 5–8.

deductive reasoning   The method of reasoning that moves from the general to the specific. See Chapter 14 on argument and persuasion, especially pp. 334–35. See also *syllogism.*

definition   An explanation of the meaning of a word. A **formal**, or dictionary, definition identifies the class of things to which the word belongs and then distinguishes it from other members of the class; a **stipulative** definition clarifies how a word or phrase is being used in a particular context; an **extended** definition may serve as the primary method of developing an essay. See Chapter 12, p. 266.

denotation   See *connotation and denotation.*

description   The form of writing that conveys the perceptions of the senses—sight, hearing, smell, taste, touch—to make a person, place, object, or state of mind vivid and concrete. See Chapter 6, p. 89.

development   The accumulation of details, examples, facts, opinions, and other evidence to support a writer's ideas. Development begins in sentences, with concrete and specific words to explain meaning. At the level of the paragraph, the sentences develop the paragraph's topic.

Then, at the level of the whole essay, the paragraphs develop the governing thesis. See pp. 27–28 and 35–36.

dialogue   A narrative technique that quotes the speech of participants in the story. See pp. 65–66.

diction   The choice of words a writer makes to achieve a purpose and make meaning clear. Effective diction conveys meaning exactly, emphatically, and concisely, and it is appropriate to the writer's intentions and audience. **Standard English**, the language of formal written expression, is expected in all writing for college, business and the professions, and publication. The vocabulary of standard English is large and varied, encompassing, for instance, both *comestibles* and *food* for edible things, and both *paroxysm* and *fit* for a sudden seizure. In some writing situations, standard English may also include words and expressions typical of conversation (see *colloquial language*). But it excludes other levels of diction that only certain groups understand or find acceptable. Most dictionaries label expressions at these levels as follows:

- **Nonstandard:** words spoken among particular social groups, such as *ain't, them guys, hisself,* and *nowheres*

- **Obsolete:** words that have passed out of use, such as *cleam* for smear

- **Regional or dialect:** words spoken in a particular region but not in the country as a whole, such as *poke* for a sack or bag, *holler* for a hollow or small valley, *wicked* for excellent

- **Slang:** words that are usually short-lived and that may not be understood by all readers, such as *tanked* for drunk, *bling* for jewelry, and *honcho* for one in charge

See also *connotation and denotation; style.*

division or analysis   See *analysis.*

documentation   A system of identifying sources so that readers know which ideas are borrowed and can locate the original material themselves. Papers written for English and other humanities courses typically follow the MLA (Modern Language Association) documentation system, which requires brief parenthetical citations within the body of the essay and a comprehensive list of works cited at the end. See Chapter 16, especially pp. 399–413.

dominant impression   The central idea or feeling conveyed by a description of a person, place, object, or state of mind. See Chapter 6 on description, especially pp. 90–91.

drafting   The stage of the writing process in which ideas are tentatively written out in sentences and paragraphs. Drafts may be messy, incomplete, disorganized, and filled with misspellings and grammatical errors; such problems can be repaired during *revision* and *editing.* See pp. 29–30.

editing   The final stage of the writing process, in which sentences and words are polished and corrected for accuracy, clarity, and effectiveness. See Chapter 4, p. 44.

effect   See *cause-and-effect analysis.*

either-or   See *fallacies.*

emotional appeal (also called ***pathos***)   In argumentative and persuasive writing, the appeal to readers' values, beliefs, or feelings in order to win agreement or compel action. See pp. 331–33.

essay   A prose composition on a single nonfictional topic or idea. An essay usually reflects the personal experiences and opinions of the writer.

ethical appeal (also called ***ethos***)   In argumentative and persuasive writing, the sense of the writer's expertise and character projected by the reasonableness of the argument, the use and quality of evidence, and the tone. See p. 331.

etymology   The history of a word, from its origins and uses to changes in its meaning over time. See p. 268.

evidence   The details, examples, facts, statistics, or expert opinions that support any general statement or claim. See pp. 330–37 and 338–45 on the use of evidence in argumentative writing, pp. 388–92 on finding evidence in sources, and pp. 399–413 on documenting researched evidence.

example   An instance or representative of a general group or an abstract concept or quality. One or more examples may serve as the primary method of developing an essay. See Chapter 7, p. 117.

exposition   The form of writing that explains or informs. Most of the essays in this book are primarily expository, and some essays whose primary purpose is self-expression or persuasion employ exposition to clarify ideas.

extended definition   See *definition.*

fallacies   Flaws in reasoning that weaken or invalidate an argument. Some of the most common fallacies follow (the page numbers refer to further discussion in the text).

■ **Ad hominem** ("to the man") argument, attacking an opponent instead of the opponent's argument: *She is just a student, so we need not listen to her criticisms of foreign policy* (p. 336).

■ **Begging the question**, assuming the truth of a conclusion that has not been proved: *Acid rain does not do serious damage, so it is not a serious problem* (p. 336).

■ **Either-or**, presenting only two alternatives when the choices are more numerous: *If you want to do well in college, you have to cheat a little* (p. 336).

- **Hasty generalization**, leaping to a conclusion on the basis of inadequate or unrepresentative evidence: *Every one of the twelve students polled supports the change in the grading system, so the administration should implement it* (p. 336).

- **Ignoring the question**, shifting the argument away from the real issue: *A fine, churchgoing man like Charles Harold would make an excellent mayor* (p. 336).

- **Non sequitur** ("It does not follow"), deriving a wrong or illogical conclusion from stated premises: *Because students are actually in school, they should be the ones to determine our educational policies* (p. 337).

- **Oversimplification**, overlooking or ignoring inconsistencies or complexities in evidence: *If the United States banned immigration, our unemployment problems would be solved* (pp. 298, 336).

- **Post hoc** (from *post hoc, ergo propter hoc*, "after this, therefore because of this"), assuming that one thing caused another simply because it preceded the other: *Two students left school in the week after the new policies were announced, proving that the policies will eventually cause a reduction in enrollments* (pp. 297–98, 337).

figures of speech   Expressions that imply meanings beyond or different from their literal meanings in order to achieve vividness or force. See *hyperbole, metaphor, paradox, personification, simile,* and pp. 52–53 for discussion and examples of common figures of speech.

flashback   In narration, an interruption of chronological sequence that shifts backward in time to recall or explore the significance of an earlier event. See p. 60.

formal definition   See *definition.*

formal style   See *style.*

fragment   See *sentence fragment.*

freewriting   A technique for discovering ideas for writing that involves writing for a fixed amount of time without stopping to reread or edit. See p. 22.

general words   See *specific and general words.*

generalization   A statement about a group or a class derived from knowledge of some or all of its members: for instance, *Dolphins can be trained to count* or *Network news rarely penetrates beneath the headlines.* The more examples the generalization is based on, the more accurate it is likely to be. A generalization is the result of *inductive reasoning.* See also pp. 118–19 and 333.

hasty generalization   See *fallacies.*

hyperbole   Deliberate overstatement or exaggeration: *The desk provided an acre of work surface.* See also p. 52.

ignoring the question   See *fallacies.*

image   A verbal representation of sensory experience—that is, of something seen, heard, felt, tasted, or smelled. Images may be literal: *Snow stuck to her eyelashes*; *The red car sped past us*. Or they may be figures of speech: *Her eyelashes were snowy feathers*; *The car rocketed past us like a red missile* (see pp. 52–53). Through images, a writer touches the readers' experiences, thus sharpening meaning and adding immediacy. See also *concrete and abstract words*.

inductive reasoning   The method of reasoning that moves from the particular to the general. See Chapter 14 on argument and persuasion, especially p. 333.

informal style   See *style*.

introductions   The openings of written works, the sentences that set the stage for what follows. An introduction to an essay identifies and restricts the subject while establishing the writer's attitude toward it. Accomplishing these purposes may require anything from a single sentence to several paragraphs, depending on the writer's purpose and how much readers need to know before they can begin to grasp the ideas in the essay. The introduction often includes a *thesis sentence* stating the main idea of the essay (see pp. 25–27 and 34–35). To set up the thesis sentence, or as a substitute for it, any of the following openings, or a combination, may be effective:

- An anecdote or other reference to the writer's experience that forecasts or illustrates the main idea or that explains what prompted the essay (see Tan, p. 100; Adams, p. 156; Kim, p. 250; Kristof, p. 357; and Richardson, p. 376)

- Background on the subject that establishes a time or place or that provides essential information (see Jones, p. 9; Boylan, p. 73; Fulmore, p. 79; Chen, p. 107; Sedaris, p. 131; and Alvarez, p. 287)

- An example, quotation, or question that sets up the main idea (see Klass, p. 125; Burroughs, p. 275; Thompson, p. 312; and Greenberg, p. 351)

- An explanation of the significance of the subject (see Melendez, p. 139; Boissy, p. 281; Haskie, p. 320; and Staples, p. 363)

- An overview of the situation or problem that the essay will address, perhaps using interesting facts or statistics (see Jamison, p. 162; Kakalios, p. 306; Krey, p. 345; and Ballo, p. 414)

- A statement or quotation of an opinion that the writer will modify or disagree with (see Lang, p. 54; Ojha, p. 168; Brooks, p. 189; and Furgurson, p. 369)

A good introduction does not mislead readers by exaggerating the significance of the subject or the essay, and it does not bore readers by saying more than is necessary. In addition, a good introduction avoids three openings that are always clumsy: (1) beginning with *The purpose of this essay is . . .* or something similar; (2) referring to the title of the essay in the first sentence, as in _____ *is not as hard as it looks* or . . . *This is a serious problem* or . . . *We've all asked that question*; and (3) starting too broadly or vaguely, as in *Ever since humans walked upright . . .* or *In today's world . . .*

irony In writing, irony is the use of words to suggest a meaning different from their literal meaning. An ironic statement might rely on reversal: saying the opposite of what the writer really means. But irony can also derive from **understatement** (saying less than is meant) or **hyperbole** (exaggeration). Irony can be witty, teasing, biting, or cruel. At its most humorless and heavily contemptuous, it becomes **sarcasm**: *Thanks a lot for telling Dad we stayed out all night; that was really bright of you.*

journal A tool for discovering ideas for writing: an informal record of ideas, observations, questions, and thoughts kept in a notebook or electronic file for the writer's personal use. See pp. 20–21.

logos See *rational appeal.*

metaphor A figure of speech that compares two unlike things by saying that one is the other: *Bright circles of ebony, her eyes smiled back at me.* See also p. 52.

modifier A word, phrase, or clause that describes another word (or words) in a sentence. Modifiers can add emphasis and variety to sentences, but they must be placed carefully to avoid confusing readers. See p. 47.

narration The form of writing that tells a story, relating a sequence of events. See Chapter 5, p. 59.

negation A technique for clarifying the definition of a word or phrase by explaining what it does *not* mean. See p. 268.

non sequitur See *fallacies.*

nonstandard English See *diction.*

objective writing Writing that focuses on the subject itself and strives to be direct and impartial, without dwelling on the writer's perspective or feelings. Newspaper accounts, scientific reports, process analyses, and rational arguments are typical examples. See also p. 90; *subjective writing.*

organization The arrangement of ideas and supporting points in a piece of writing. See pp. 27–29 and 38–39; *chronological order; climactic order; spatial organization.*

oversimplification See *fallacies.*

paradox A seemingly self-contradictory statement that, on reflection, makes sense: *Children are the poor person's wealth* (wealth can be monetary, or it can be spiritual). *Paradox* may also refer to a situation that is inexplicable or contradictory, such as the restriction of one group's rights to secure the rights of another group.

paragraph A group of related sentences, set off by an initial indentation, that develops an idea. By breaking continuous text into units, paragraphing helps the writer manage ideas and helps the reader follow those ideas. Each paragraph makes a distinct contribution to the main idea governing the entire piece of writing. The idea of the paragraph itself is often stated in a *topic sentence*, and it is supported with sentences containing specific details, examples, and reasons. Like the larger piece of writing to which it contributes, the paragraph should be unified, coherent, and well developed. For examples of successful paragraphs, see the annotated paragraphs in the introduction to each method of development (Chapters 5–14). See also pp. 36–37 and 273–74 (unity), pp. 37–38 and 155 (coherence), and pp. 27–28, 35–36, and 183 (development).

parallelism   The use of similar grammatical forms for ideas of equal importance. Parallelism occurs within sentences: *The doctor recommends swimming, bicycling, or walking.* It also occurs among sentences: *Strumming her guitar, she made listeners feel her anger. Singing lyrics, she made listeners believe her pain.* See p. 50 and 243.

paraphrase   A restatement—in your own words—of another writer's ideas. A paraphrase is about the same length as the original passage, but it does not repeat words, phrases, or sentence patterns. See pp. 394.

pathos   See *emotional appeal*.

personification   A figure of speech that gives human qualities to things or abstractions: *The bright day smirked at my bad mood.* See also p. 52.

persuasion   See *argument*.

plagiarism   The failure to identify and acknowledge the sources of words, information, or ideas that are not your own. Whether intentional or accidental, plagiarism is a serious offense and should always be avoided. See pp. 397–98.

point of view   The position of the writer in relation to the subject. In *narration*, point of view depends on the writer's place in the story and on his or her relation to it in time (see p. 61). In *description*, point of view depends on the writer's physical and psychological relation to the subject (see pp. 90–91). Grammatically, point of view refers to a writer's choice of *pronouns*: first person (*I, we, our*), second person (*you, yours*), or third person (*he and she, it, they, theirs*). More broadly, point of view can also mean the writer's particular mental stance or attitude. For instance, an employee and an employer might have different points of view toward the employee's absenteeism or the employer's sick-leave policies.

points of comparison   The set of attributes used to distinguish and organize the elements of two or more subjects being compared to each other. See Chapter 11 on comparison and contrast, especially pp. 236–37.

post hoc   See *fallacies*.

premise   The generalization or assumption on which an argument is based. See pp. 334–35; see also *syllogism*.

principle of analysis   The interpretive framework or set of guidelines used to divide a subject into components. The choice of a principle depends on the writer's interest and will determine the focus and out-come of an analysis. One writer analyzing a contemporary television show set in the 1960s, for instance, might focus on historical context and implications, while another might emphasize production values, and yet another might focus on literary qualities such as plot and character. See Chapter 8 on division or analysis, especially p. 149.

principle of classification The distinctive characteristics used to sort things into categories or general classes. A writer's focus determines the principle, which in turn shapes and limits the contours of a classification. An essay about apartment dwellers, for example, might group them by noise (too loud, too quiet, just right), by income (poor, working class, middle class, wealthy), or by relationship status (bachelors, couples, widows); it should not, however, mix them into unrelated categories (too loud, middle class, widows). See Chapter 9 on classification, especially pp. 179–80.

process analysis The method of development in which a sequence of actions with a specified result is divided into its component steps. See Chapter 10, p. 206.

pronoun A word that refers to a noun or other pronoun: *Six days after Martin Luther King Jr. picked up his Nobel Peace Prize in Norway, he was jailed in Alabama.* The most common personal pronouns are *I, you, he, she, it, we,* and *they.* See pp. 46–47; *point of view.*

proposition A debatable claim about a subject; the central idea of an argument.

purpose The reason for writing, the goal the writer wants to achieve. The purpose may be primarily to explain the subject so that readers understand it or see it in a new light; to convince readers to accept or reject an opinion or to take a certain action; to entertain readers with a humorous or exciting story; or to express the thoughts and emotions triggered by a revealing or instructive experience. The writer's purpose overlaps the main idea—the particular point being made about the subject. In effective writing, the two together direct and control every choice the writer makes. See also pp. 12, 18–19, and 33–34; *thesis; unity.*

quotation The exact words of another writer or speaker, copied word for word, clearly identified, and attributed to their source. Short quotations are enclosed in quotation marks; longer quotations are set off from the text by indenting. See pp. 395–96.

rational appeal (also called *logos*) In argumentative and persuasive writing, the appeal to readers' rational faculties—to their ability to reason logically—in order to win agreement or compel action. See pp. 333–35.

repetition and restatement The careful use of the same words or close parallels to clarify meaning and tie sentences together. See pp. 37–38 and 155.

revision The stage of the writing process devoted to "re-seeing" a draft, focused on fundamental changes in content and structure. See Chapter 3, p. 32; see also *editing*.

rhetoric The art of using words effectively to communicate with an audience, or the study of that art. To the ancient Greeks, rhetoric was the art of the *rhetor*—orator, or public speaker—and included the art of persuasion. Later the word shifted to mean elegant language, and a version of that meaning persists in today's occasional use of *rhetoric* to mean pretentious or hollow language, as in *Their argument was mere rhetoric*.

run-on sentence A sentence error in which two or more independent clauses run together without punctuation between them. See p. 45.

sarcasm See *irony*.

satire The combination of wit and criticism to mock or condemn human foolishness or evil. The intent of satire is to arouse readers to contempt or action, and thus it differs from comedy, which seeks simply to amuse. Much satire relies on *irony*—saying one thing but meaning another.

sentence See *independent clause*.

sentence fragment A word group that is punctuated like a sentence but is not a complete sentence because it lacks a subject, lacks a verb, or is just part of a thought. See p. 45.

shift An inconsistency in *person*, *point of view*, or *tense*, in which a writer might inexplicably switch from *I* to *you*, for example, or from past tense to present. Such shifts distract readers and should be attended to in *editing*. See pp. 47–48.

signal phrase Words used to introduce a quotation, paraphrase, or summary, often including the source author's name and generally telling readers how the source material should be interpreted: <u>Nelson argues</u> that the legislation will backfire *(42)*. See p. 396.

simile A figure of speech that equates two unlike things using *like* or *as*: *The crowd was restless, like bees in a hive*. See also pp. 52–53.

slang See *diction*.

source Any outside or researched material that helps to develop a writer's ideas. A source may be the subject of an essay, such as when you are writing about a reading in this book, or it may provide evidence to support a particular point. However a source is used, it must always be documented. See Chapters 15 and 16 on working with sources.

spatial organization A pattern of organization that views an object, scene, or person by paralleling the way we normally scan things—for instance, top to bottom or near to far. See also pp. 39 and 93–94.

specific and general words A **general** word refers to a group or class: *car*, *mood*, *book*. A **specific** word refers to a particular member of a group or class: *Toyota*, *irritation*, *dictionary*. Usually, the more specific a word is, the more interesting and informative it will be for readers. See pp. 52 and 95; see also *concrete and abstract words*.

standard English   See *diction*.

stipulative definition   See *definition*.

style   The *way* something is said, as opposed to *what* is said. Style results primarily from a writer's characteristic word choices and sentence structures. A person's writing style, like his or her voice or manner of speaking, is distinctive. Style can also be viewed more broadly as ranging from formal to informal. A very **formal style** adheres strictly to the conventions of standard English (see *diction*); tends toward long sentences with sophisticated structures; and relies on learned words, such as *malodorous* and *psychopathic*. A very **informal style**, in contrast, is more conversational; tends toward short, uncomplicated sentences; and relies on words typical of casual speech, such as *smelly* or *crazy* (see *colloquial language*). Among the writers represented in this book, Ascher (p. 257) writes quite formally, Burroughs (p. 275) quite informally. The formality of style may often be modified to suit a particular audience or occasion: a college term paper, for instance, demands a more formal style than an essay narrating a personal experience. See also *tone* and Chapter 3 on revising, especially pp. 39–40.

subject   What a piece of writing is about. The subject of an essay is its general topic, such as college (Jones, p. 9; Lang, p. 54), language (Tannen, p. 119; Lutz, p. 120; Klass, p. 125, Sedaris, p. 131, Melendez, p. 139), or nature (Smith, p. 208; Genoways, p. 208; Doyle, p. 214; Keegan, p. 219; Bass, p. 226). Because writers narrow a subject until they have a specific point to make about it, multiple essays on the same subject will typically be very different from one another. See also pp. 18–19; *purpose*; *thesis*.

subjective writing   Writing that focuses on the writer's own perspective, feelings, and opinions. Memoirs, personal reflections, and emotional arguments, for example, tend to be subjective. See also pp. 89–90; *objective writing*.

summary   A condensed version—in your own words—of the main idea of a longer work. A summary is much shorter than the original and leaves out most of the supporting details. See p. 393.

syllogism   The basic form of deductive reasoning, in which a conclusion derives necessarily from proven or accepted premises. For example: *The roof always leaks when it rains* (the major premise). *It is raining* (the minor premise). *Therefore, the roof will leak* (the conclusion). See Chapter 14 on argument and persuasion, especially pp. 334–35.

symbol   A person, place, or thing that represents an abstract quality or concept. A red heart symbolizes love; the Golden Gate Bridge symbolizes San Francisco's dramatic beauty; a cross symbolizes Christianity.

synonym   A word that has nearly but not exactly the same meaning as another word. For example: *angry* and *furious*, *happy* and *ecstatic*, *skinny* and *thin*.

synthesis The practice of combining elements into a new whole. In writing, synthesis usually involves connecting related ideas from multiple sources to form an original idea of your own. See pp. 393–97.

thesis The main idea of a piece of writing to which all other ideas and details relate. The main idea is often stated in a **thesis sentence** (or sentences), which asserts something about the subject and conveys the writer's purpose. The thesis sentence is often included near the beginning of an essay. Even when the writer does not state the main idea and purpose, however, they govern all the ideas and details in the essay. See pp. 24–27 and 34–35; see also *unity*.

tense The form of a verb that indicates when an action occurs: past, present, or future. Writers must be careful to avoid unnecessary *shifts* in tense, from past to the present, for instance, so as not to confuse readers.

tone The attitude toward the subject, and sometimes toward the audience and the writer's own self, expressed in choice of words and sentence structures as well as in what is said. Tone in writing is similar to tone of voice in speaking, from warm to serious, amused to angry, joyful to sorrowful, sympathetic to contemptuous. For examples of strong tone in writing, see Tan (p. 100); Adams (p. 156), Jamison (p. 162), Doyle, (p. 214), Keegan (p. 219), Burroughs (p. 275), and Greenberg (p. 351). See also pp. 39–40 and 343–44.

topic sentence A statement of the main idea of a paragraph, to which all other sentences in the paragraph relate. See pp. 36–37.

transitions Links between sentences and paragraphs that relate ideas and thus contribute to clarity and smoothness. Transitions may be sentences beginning paragraphs or brief paragraphs that shift the focus or introduce new ideas. They may also be words and phrases that signal and specify relationships. Some of these words and phrases—but by no means all—are listed here:

- **Addition or repetition:** again, also, finally, furthermore, in addition, moreover, next, that is

- **Cause or effect:** as a result, consequently, equally important, hence, then, therefore, thus

- **Comparison:** also, in the same way, likewise, similarly

- **Contrast:** but, even so, however, in contrast, on the contrary, still, yet

- **Illustration:** for example, for instance, specifically, that is

- **Intensification:** indeed, in fact, of course, truly

- **Space:** above, below, beyond, farther away, here, nearby, opposite, there, to the right

- **Summary or conclusion:** all in all, in brief, in conclusion, in short, in summary, therefore, thus

- **Time:** afterward, at last, earlier, later, meanwhile, simultaneously, soon, then

understatement   See *irony*.

unity   The quality of effective writing that occurs when all the parts relate to the main idea and contribute to the writer's purpose. See pp. 36–37 and 273.

writing process   The series of activities involved in creating a finished piece of writing. Rather than produce a polished essay in one sitting, most writers work back and forth in a series of overlapping stages: analyzing the writing situation, discovering ideas, forming a thesis, organizing, drafting, revising, and editing. See pp. 17–18.

INDEX OF AUTHORS AND TITLES